MARC ANTONY

Vatican

THE LIFE AND TIMES
OF
MARC ANTONY

BY

ARTHUR WEIGALL
Late Inspector-General of Antiquities, Egyptian Government

ILLUSTRATED

GARDEN CITY PUBLISHING COMPANY, INC.

GARDEN CITY   NEW YORK

THE LIFE AND TIMES OF MARC ANTONY

Copyright, 1931
by
Arthur Weigall

Made in the United States of America

CONTENTS

v

CONTENTS

Chapter XIX

Chapter XX

Chapter XXI

CHAPTER XIX

CHAPTER XX

CHAPTER XXI

CHAPTER I

Tiberius and Caius Gracchus, and the Beginning of Political Violence
in Rome.

134–121 B.C.

THE outstanding achievement of modern civilization in any
country is the creation of that attitude of mind towards human
life which rejects the weapon of war as an instrument of domestic
politics. The most truly civilized states today are those in which
the home government can be carried on, or changes of government
effected, without bloodshed; and, emphatically, the mark now
of a backward people is the impatient political use of armed force
and the firing-squad.

Ancient Rome at about the date of the birth of Antony, viewed
from this angle, was astonishingly uncivilized; and its political
life can find no comparison in modern times save with that of some
tragi-comic East European or South American state where bluster-
ing revolutions are of frequent occurrence, and fights, murders, executions, and hair-raising adventures are the commonplaces of administration. Yet, even so, the comparison is not exact; for Rome
conducted its political battles with an indifference to human suffering which is now more or less extinct, and the horror, moreover,
is accentuated by the fact that the butchers and the butchered
were usually educated men, accustomed to the amenities of a cultured life far more fastidious than that which is associated with
political savagery today. The barbarous cruelty of these highly
civilized Roman party-leaders provides a paradox which has no
parallel in the modern world.

Antony was born at a time when no Roman except the very obscure could feel sure that he would survive the next change of gov-

ernment: there was always the danger of finding himself upon the defeated side, and in that case the chance of his being put to death was by no means negligible. Active politics, and even the mere holding of an official post, brought that chance to a man's elbow; and the familiar presence of the menace was followed at length, by an indifference to it which was less than heroic only because it was no more than normal. Every man who meddled in public affairs staked his head in so doing; and at a crisis he was quick to take his opponent's life in order to safeguard his own.

Matters had not always been so. The Romans in the past had managed their internal affairs with surprising restraint; but during the fifty years previous to Antony's birth in 83 B.C. political violence had become less and less able to be checked.[1] Thus, to understand the conditions amidst which Antony was brought up, and which reached their crisis in the world-war at the end of his life, it is necessary to go back to the days of the Gracchi; for it was then that the two great political parties, hopelessly confused in the final struggle, first arrayed themselves against one another to decide by force how Rome and her growing empire should be governed.

In theory the government was in the hands of the *Senatus Populusque Romanus*, the "Senate and People of Rome." According to the constitution a mixed assembly of Patricians, or men descended from the original chieftains of primitive Rome, and Plebeians, or men whose lineage, though often long and illustrious, was not in early history noble, annually elected two chief magistrates, the Consuls, who held joint office for the one year; and these Consuls nominated the men to fill the vacancies in the Senate. There were at this time three hundred members in the Roman Senate, all appointed for life, and most of them were Patricians, though a few were of Plebeian birth, which does not mean to say, of course, that their sympathies were democratic. Besides the Senate there was the Comitia, the People's Assembly, held in the open air; and technically this Assembly had equal power with the Senate, the two institutions corresponding in certain ways to the Upper and Lower Houses in modern governments. Gradually, however, the Senate had come to represent the aristocracy and upper classes;

[1] See particularly Sallust: *Bellum Jugurthinum,* xli, xlii.

and the People, overawed, had allowed the rôle of the Comitia to become a very secondary matter. It was the Gracchi who, in the latter part of the Second Century B.C., aroused the masses to a new consciousness of their strength.

At that time [2] the most pressing trouble was the condition of the agricultural population belonging to the country around Rome which had once been the backbone of the State. Foreign conquests, and particularly the annexation of Greece, had brought cheap corn into the metropolis from abroad in such quantities that there was no longer any profit in growing it at home; and in consequence most of the peasants had migrated to the city, selling their farms to the great landowners, who turned their fields into pasture and raised cattle instead of crops. A single slave could look after a herd of cattle; and the land which had once given employment to the members of several families now provided work for but a man or two. Cato the Elder, being once questioned as to what was the most profitable use to which an estate could be put, replied "Successful cattle-raising." "And, next to that, what?" he was asked. "Moderately successful cattle-raising," he replied. "And after that?" said the questioner. "Unsuccessful cattle-raising," he answered. [3]

Ruined farmers and unemployed farm-labourers streamed into Rome, where they earned a precarious livelihood or lived on doles officially or privately supplied, while the countryside was almost depopulated. Here in the city, too, there was industrial depression, for foreign goods of all kinds were being dumped in Rome; and in many industries only the wealthy, who could employ slave-labour, were able to compete at home with the manufacturers abroad. The peasant and the urban working-man were both impoverished; and amongst the lower classes the feeling prevailed that, somehow or other, they were the victims of the rich, and that the Senate was merely the instrument of a heartless capitalist tyranny. It is true that the Plebs, the People, had the right of appointing certain representatives of Plebeian race, known as *Tribunes*, to protect their interests, and that these men, who were

[2] The chief authorities for the events recorded in these early chapters are Appian, Cicero, Diodorus, Florus, Plutarch, Sallust, Valerius Maximus, and Velleius Paterculus.
[3] Cicero: *De Officiis*, ii, 25.

elected every year, and whose persons were sacrosanct during their term of office, could put their veto upon oppressive measures; but of late they had degenerated into agents of the Senate, and the disgruntled working classes had little hope of redress.

Then, in the year 134 B.C., Tiberius Gracchus, a man of some thirty years of age, of Plebeian family but of illustrious blood, came forward with a scheme for the relief of the agricultural depression. In view of the fact that the land in question had anciently been the Roman Republic's property, and that its later ownership by private individuals had never been really absolute, he proposed that no single landowner should be allowed to retain more than 500 acres, and that all the rest of the great Roman estates should be surrendered, and should be divided up into small holdings. By ousting the rich landlords, and sending the free peasantry back to the fields under government protection, he hoped to enable the latter to sell their produce profitably in the city at a price less than that asked by the foreign traders.

Popular support for this revolutionary programme was immediately forthcoming, and Tiberius was enthusiastically elected as one of the Tribunes of the People for the year 133 B.C. He was a quiet, usually restrained, and somewhat pedantic young man, very emotional when excited, always transparently honest, but not richly endowed with brains, his deficiency in that respect, however, being concealed by his eloquence and the earnest, appealing tone of his voice. From his childhood he had been brought up to believe that he ought to render some great service to his country, for not only had his father been a Consul who had conducted two very successful wars, but his mother, Cornelia, was the daughter of Scipio Africanus, the conqueror of Hannibal, and was one of those ambitious widows whose ceaseless dream it is to be the mother of mighty men. In her efforts to rear a brood of heroes she had lost nine of her twelve children; and her two surviving sons, Tiberius and Caius, were constantly being upbraided by her for not doing anything spectacular. "How long," she kept exclaiming angrily to them, "am I to be called the daughter of Africanus and not the mother of the Gracchi?" It could hardly have been her wish, however, that they should make their contribution to history on the side of the People as the leaders of the struggle against the aristocracy, for not only was she herself an aristocrat by birth but she had married her one remaining daughter, Sempronia, to Scipio Africanus the younger, the adopted son of her brother, and this man was an ardent supporter of the nobility and a bitter enemy of the aspirations of the Proletariat.

The speech with which Tiberius made his dramatic entrance into political life has been lost except for a few sentences; but these reveal its dangerous nature. The wild animals, he said, had their lairs and their dens, but the common people very often had no more from their country than its open air and its sunlight. Yet these were the men who were conscribed for the army, and had to risk their lives for the safety of the fatherland, though they themselves had no homes and no possessions to defend. Military commanders, he declared, were talking nonsense when they made speeches to the soldiers exhorting them to fight for hearth and home, for the men had neither hearths nor homes to call their own. They fought and were killed simply to maintain the capitalists in luxury. The People were termed the masters of the State, he said, but actually there was not a foot of ground of which they could claim possession: all the land belonged to the idle rich.

The Comitia was almost unanimous in its clamorous vote for the measures which Tiberius proposed, but one of the other Tribunes of the People, a certain Marcus Octavius, [4] was persuaded by the landowners to impose his veto, an action which, according to Roman law, could hold up the passage of any bill. Octavius, like his colleague and former friend, Tiberius, was an honest man, and during the following days he argued with passionate sincerity against the proposal; but when Tiberius coldly accused him of desiring to obstruct the bill because he himself was a landowner, his attitude stiffened into one of sullen and inflexible opposition.

Tiberius responded by redrafting the proposed law in a severer form, and this again having been vetoed, he begged Octavius to resign his office, quietly saying that if he did not do so, steps would be taken to depose him, since a Tribune of the People who opposed the will of the People, was an anomaly which could not be tolerated. Octavius, however, interpreted his duties as those of

[4] Second cousin of the grandfather of the Emperor Augustus.

a referee maintaining fair play between the political parties; and he refused either to remove his veto or to resign.

Very well, said Tiberius, suddenly becoming excited: if Octavius could use his veto, so could *he;* and he proceeded to do so with preposterous indiscrimination. He vetoed all the decisions of the Senate; he vetoed the judgments in the Law Courts; he vetoed the payment of salaries to Government officials; he vetoed the actions of the magistrates; he vetoed the entire business of the exchequer. Constitutionally he was entitled to do this, and the fact that a Tribune's person was sacred enabled him to go about his work without inconvenience, although he professed to be in fear of his life. Many of the landlords, on the other hand, pretending to believe that they were about to be reduced to starvation, refused, as a token of grief, to wash themselves or to shave, and appeared in the streets in the dress of mourners, smiting their heads and bemoaning their impending fate.

On the day when, in defiance of the veto of Octavius, the final voting on the redrafted bill was to take place in the Comitia, two men of consular rank pushed their way through the throng to the place where Tiberius was standing, and, grasping his hands, implored him with tears in their eyes to abandon his reckless project. The more hot-headed of the landowners, however, did not stoop to plead with him: they and their servants charged down on the polling-booth, seized the ballot-boxes, [5] and made off with them, leaving a scene of wild rioting behind them.

When order had been restored, Tiberius mounted the rostra, or platform, on which Octavius was standing, and in the sight of all men, put his arm around him and begged him to resign like a good fellow; but his colleague was adamant, and the meeting was adjourned until the next day, when the same scene was repeated. This time, however, Tiberius flung his arms around Octavius and kissed him, whereupon the distracted man burst into tears, and might, indeed, have consented to resign had he not suddenly observed a group of landowners winking and shaking their heads at him as though urging him not to weaken. He therefore told Tiberius that he was sorry, but that he must decline to oblige him; and at this his deposition was put to the vote and carried.

[5] Or, rather, ballot-*urns.*

Instantly the mob rushed the platform, but Octavius clung with both hands to the balustrade, and it was only after a violent struggle that he was dislodged and pitched into the arms of the crowd, where he would have been torn to pieces had he not been rescued by the above-mentioned band of sympathisers who fought their way to him and somehow effected his escape, though not before his personal servant had been so battered that he was permanently blinded. The confiscation of the great estates was then successfully put to the vote; and Tiberius placed himself at the head of the Land Commission which was to make the necessary survey of the properties to be seized. It was a triumph of the People; and even the most aristocratic Senators, bound by the Constitution, were obliged to recognize the measure as legal.

At about this time, the eccentric Attalus the Third, King of Pergamus in Asia Minor, died suddenly, leaving his vast fortune to the Roman People—an action inspired, it would seem, by hatred of his family and indifference to his subjects. Tiberius, who was now the unquestioned leader of the popular party, at once appropriated this windfall, and used the money for the purchase of agricultural implements, the erection of farm buildings, the stocking of the farms, and all the business incidental to the reinstatement of the peasants upon the land. The party of the landowners in the Senate was not strong enough to stop him; for, though the fact is generally overlooked, there can be no doubt that the nation as a whole was interested in this movement to rehabilitate the small farmers and to put an end to the dangerous discontent of the labouring classes.

During the next few weeks the Land Commission proceeded vigorously with its work, and Tiberius came to be the mob's hero, credited with far more revolutionary aims than actually were in his mind. But as one by one the landowners were evicted, and their public and pitiable lamentations caused disturbance upon disturbance in the streets, the opposition began to consolidate itself, and Tiberius was accused of attempting to establish a "tyranny," that is to say a personal and absolute rule, the story being spread, even, that he had taken possession of the regalia of Attalus, so that one day he might deck himself out as a King.

His enemies then announced that they were going to bring against him the capital charge of sacrilege as soon as his year of office as Tribune of the People was over, on the grounds that by his behaviour to Octavius he had violated the sanctity of the Tribuneship; and, in reply to this, Tiberius declared that he would obtain another year's immunity by having himself re-elected for a second term, although this had been generally regarded as illegal. He made it known, moreover, that in the following year, if he were elected, he would bring forward a great many more popular measures, such as the restriction of military service, the right of appeal from the law-courts to the Comitia, and so forth.

As time passed, and the abuse to which he was subjected became more violent, he began to feel considerable alarm. Indeed, when the election-day drew near he appeared in the streets dressed in mourning, leading his little son by the hand, and sobbing quietly to himself as he walked along; and presently, addressing the crowds, he told them in broken tones that if his sacrosanctity were not renewed by re-election he would assuredly be tried for his life, or assassinated. At this his supporters, greatly moved, formed an armed bodyguard around him, thereafter never leaving him by day, and camping around his house by night. On the eve of the polls he called a secret meeting of his partisans, at which it was arranged that they should by force prevent his opponents from coming near the ballot-boxes, and that if he had reason to think his life in danger, he would make a sign to them by raising his hand and pointing to his head, at which they were to attack the opposition and drive them from the Comitia.

Next morning, to his great dismay, he found that the omens were shockingly unfavourable. For a long time he had been troubled by the memory of a certain dark portent which had manifested itself one day in his house: two snakes had been found to have made their nest and to have brought forth their young in his old military helmet which had been stored away in an out-house. The sinister occurrence worried him, because it seemed to indicate that secret dangers were lurking in the very thing which was intended to protect him from his enemies; and now, just as he was coming out of his room on this great day of his life, he tripped up, and struck his toe so violently against a stone step that blood was drawn. Hobbling painfully down to the chicken-house to see whether his hens would give him the recognized and almost invariably forthcoming sign of good luck by freely eating the grain thrown to them, he was disappointed to find them unwilling to leave their coop. One hen at last ventured out, but its behaviour was most suspicious, for it fluttered its left, or unlucky, wing, stretched out its left leg, and then went back into the coop. Just then, over his left shoulder, he observed two ravens fighting upon a roof, and a stone dislodged by them fell at his foot.

At this, brave man though he was, he was so dismayed that he very nearly decided to remain at home; but his friends at length persuaded him to attend the polls, and, in deep depression, he limped forth. He was received with a tremendous outburst of cheering by his followers, but when he began to address them his voice was drowned by the uproar around the outskirts of the crowd, where the partisans of the landlords had gathered in force and were endeavouring to break in on the assembly. Presently a certain senator, named Fulvius Flaccus, who was one of his supporters, burst his way through the throng, and excitedly told Tiberius that the landowners themselves were coming down with an army of slaves and paid agents to attack the meeting. At this Tiberius at once raised his hand and pointed sensationally to his head, thus giving the battle-sign to his followers, who immediately tucked up their gowns and prepared to use the sticks and bludgeons which they had brought with them or were now improvising out of broken benches and the like.

Some of the members of the opposition on the fringe of the crowd, seeing the strange gesture which Tiberius was making, rushed off to the Senate with the news that he was evidently asking the People to crown him King; and thereupon the horrified Senators, united by this danger to the Republic, rose almost as one man, and, likewise tucking up their gowns, charged down upon the meeting, followed by their attendants armed with the legs and rungs of the senatorial chairs.

A most desperate fight ensued, in which no less than three hundred persons lost their lives, clubbed to death by these wooden weapons, or felled by brickbats, not a single sword or dagger being used. Tiberius himself took to his heels when his followers broke and fled. Somebody seized him by the gown, but he slipped out of it, and ran on in his shirt. A few moments later, however, he fell flat on his face, and, as he was picking himself up, his brains were knocked out by one of his fellow Tribunes, who, seeing how the fight was going, had allied himself with the victors and had armed himself with a broken wooden stool.

Caius Gracchus, the younger brother of Tiberius, came upon the scene after the battle was over, and, in the name of his mother, Cornelia, daughter of the national hero, Africanus, begged the senatorial authorities to allow him to bury the body; but this was refused by the angry aristocrats, and the corpses of Tiberius and his unfortunate followers were dragged through the streets and flung pell-mell into the river. Several of his chief supporters, who had escaped, were hounded down and murdered at the instigation of a magistrate named Opimius, one man being thrown headlong into a large, disused wine-cask which was crawling with poisonous snakes.

The senators justified themselves by declaring that their action had not been directed against the People, but that they had tried to save the Republic from a madman who would have made himself King. In their anxiety they expressed no hostility to his projects in regard to the land, and, much to the disappointment of the landowners, allowed the Commission to continue its work of expropriation. The battle, however, went down to history as the first occasion on which extensive bloodshed resulting from political differences had occurred in Rome since the abolition of the monarchy four centuries earlier; and it ushered in the new age of internal strife which was raging at the time when Antony was born.

For a few years the work of restoring the peasants to the land progressed, one of the Commissioners being Caius Gracchus, whose industry was notorious; but in 126 B.C. he was persuaded to accept a high official position in Sardinia, where he remained until 124 B.C. His character was very different from that of his murdered brother, Tiberius, whose junior he had been by nine years. He was a headstrong, aggressive, loud-voiced young man, clever, ambitious, and eager to avenge his brother's death. When he was speaking in public he used to become so excited that he would pace up and down the platform, wave his arms about, pull his gown off, and thump the balustrade or smack his leg. In the vehemence of his oratory, his voice was wont to rise to an unpleasant falsetto; and, being aware of this fault, he used to employ a man to stand near him, whose business it was to sound a sustained and dispassionate note upon a pitch-pipe to recall his tones to their normal range.

On his return to Rome he was elected Tribune of the People for the year 123 B.C., and he began at once to introduce a series of popular measures which soon made him the idol of the crowd and the terror of the aristocracy. Since his brother's death the Comitia had managed to pass a law making it legal for a Tribune to hold office for as many successive years as his supporters chose to grant him by annual re-election; and Caius now made it known that it was his aim so to serve his party that they would keep him in office perpetually. With the optimism of youth he felt, indeed, that there was no reason why he should not be the life-long leader of the People, enabled by the sacrosanctity of the Tribunate and by its right of veto, to control the actions of the Senate and to establish the Comitia, under his guidance, as the supreme power in the State. In speaking from the rostra the Tribunes had formerly turned towards that part of the assembly-ground which by ancient custom was allotted to the Senators and patricians; but Caius, ignoring this section of his audience, addressed himself always to the People, an innovation which, as Plutarch points out, was tantamount to a definite recognition that the government was shifted from the aristocracy to the democracy.

The first new law which Caius formulated was put forward from motives no higher than those of sweet revenge. He proposed that any magistrate who had banished or put to death a Roman citizen without trial should be called to account before the Comitia; and its immediate effect was the flight of Opimius and those directly concerned in the murder of Tiberius and the subsequent punishment of his supporters. He then proposed a law that any person who had been removed from office might not put himself forward for re-election, his object in this case being to check the attempt of the deposed Octavius to regain a Tribuneship so that he might veto the acts of Caius as he had vetoed those of Tiberius. This bill, however, was dropped by its author on the advice of his mother, Cornelia, who saw, perhaps, that Caius himself might one day be deposed.

He then successfully passed a law placing a tax on all imported objects of luxury, for he believed that without some sort of protection many of the home industries would go into bankruptcy. He lightened the conditions of military service, and attempted to put an end to the death-penalty in the army: at least, he proposed that a condemned soldier should have the right of appeal to the civil authorities. To relieve unemployment he inaugurated a vast scheme of road-making; and for the same purpose he established Roman colonies on the site of the destroyed Carthage and elsewhere, and encouraged emigration thereto. He also speeded up the eviction of the great landowners, and the creation of small-holdings; but he appears to have discouraged the growing of corn for the Roman market, the farmers being recommended, it would seem, to seek new markets in the other cities of Italy where prices were better because cheap foreign grain did not penetrate to them. At the same time he delighted the populace in Rome by lowering by one half the price of the government corn received as tribute from the subject nations, and issuing it in quantities sufficient for one month to every citizen who came himself to pay for it and take it away—this stipulation being intended, I suppose, to prevent its reaching the markets outside Rome supplied by the rehabilitated farmers.

By these and similar laws, and in various other ways, he endeavoured to serve the People and to increase his popularity, the result being that he was elected for a second year of office. He then gave up his house on the Palatine Hill, and went to live in the slums. Once, when a gladiatorial show was to be given in the market-place, and seats for the well-to-do had been erected around the arena, he ordered them to be pulled down so that the common people might have free access to the ring-side; and on this order being disobeyed, he and his men broke up and removed the structures during the night before the contest, with the result that the ticket-holders arriving next day found that they had paid their money for nothing, and that an impenetrable crowd of poor townspeople and peasants occupied all the available space. The mob applauded his action; but his fellow-Tribunes were furious at it, and thereafter worked against him to such purpose that his popularity began to be seriously affected.

One of his new bills also told against him. At this time Rome, in spite of its foreign conquests, was still a city-state; and while a great part of Italy was incorporated in the Latin League, of which Rome was the head, there were other parts of the peninsula which were inhabited by peoples who were not yet regarded as compatriots. Caius proposed that the franchise should be conferred on all the Latins, which meant that the jealously guarded privileges of Roman citizenship, including the right to vote in the Comitia, would be enjoyed by the inhabitants of all the little towns and villages throughout Latin Italy. By allowing such a bill to pass, his opponents said, the Romans would soon find themselves out-voted in the Comitia by their country-cousins, crowded out of the theatres, baths, and public places of resort, forced to share the money from time to time distributed amongst the poor, and so forth.

But what most injured his reputation was the failure of his African emigration-scheme. He had gone over to Carthage personally to inaugurate the new colony there; but the omens were disastrously unfavourable. A sudden storm of wind flung the Roman standard to the ground with its pole broken, and blew the sacrifices clean off the altars; while the boundary-marks of the new city were scratched up in the night by jackals, owing, I suppose, to the customary burial of sacrificial-meat beneath them. It was pointed out, too, that the site had been formally cursed at the time of the destruction of Carthage by the Romans in 146 B.C., and that therefore nothing could prosper in the new colony, the result being that few people could be persuaded to go there.

Towards the close of his second year of office Caius suffered a further diminution of his popularity owing to the fact that one of his fellow-Tribunes, Marcus Livius Drusus, put forward various democratic measures calculated to please the People even more than those proposed by Caius. At the same time, however, this

Drusus definitely opposed the two unpopular schemes of his rival
—the extension of the franchise, and the encouragement of emigration; and he greatly strengthened his position by carrying the
Senate with him in all that he did, thereby relieving the anxieties
of the masses, who had always felt, in following Caius, that they
were perilously close to open warfare with their political opponents. Drusus showed them that the Comitia and the Senate were
not necessarily opposed, and that the People could obtain all that
Caius was trying to get for them, and more, without any risk to
their lives. It is usually supposed that Drusus was merely the tool of
the Senate, cunningly stealing Caius's thunder for the Conservatives' sinister ends; but it may well be that he was a genuine tac-
tician, bent on preventing civil war.

The upshot was that Caius, to his amazement, failed to be
elected for a third term, and no sooner was he out of office—
in 121 B.C.—than Drusus in the Comitia and Opimius, who was
now Consul, in the Senate began to rescind the laws he had passed.
But when Caius heard that the disestablishment of the colony
at Carthage was going to be put to the vote his exasperation was
so great that he made up his mind to oppose the passage of the
bill by force. Although no longer a Tribune he still had a great
following, and when the time came for the vote to be taken
he arrived at the meeting at the head of an armed body of supporters. Everybody expected a clash and was prepared for it; but
when a servant of the Consul insolently ordered some of the supporters of Caius out of his way, and was instantly stabbed to death
by one of the latter, both sides were too startled to do anything.
They all stared excitedly at the dead man; but a sudden torrent of
rain sent everybody flying for shelter. Both sides were spoiling for
a fight, but few were willing to be drenched to the skin.

Next day the Senate invested Opimius with special powers
"to protect the state" against Caius and his supporters, and all
senators loyal to the Republic were asked to come with armed attendants to a great meeting on the following morning. The People,
on hearing this, for the most part abandoned the pacific counsels
of Drusus and threw in their lot with their former leader, Caius,
likewise arming themselves for the morrow's fray: they had no
sympathy with the colonization-scheme, but they were not going

to allow the rights of the Proletariat to be trampled upon by the upper classes. No, indeed!—the Gracchi brothers had taught them to realize their power, and "the sovereign will of the People" was a phrase which had recently come to have real meaning. They had much for which to be grateful to Caius; and when somebody said that he had been seen that day standing in front of his father's statue in the Forum, gazing up at it while the tears ran down his cheeks, a great many declared that they would not allow the poor fellow's cherished projects thus to be quashed. In the evening many of them went to his residence and stood guard over it during the night; but Caius could not sleep, and, indeed, spent many hours in bitter tears.

Early next morning he set out from his house in deep melancholy, but just as he stepped into the street his wife, Licinia, ran after him, seized his hand, and cried out hysterically that he was going to his death and that she would not even have the satisfaction of burying his body, since it would doubtless be flung into the river as that of Tiberius had been. Caius tore himself away from her depressing embraces with difficulty, whereupon she fell full length upon the ground, and lay there in a dead faint until the servants carried her away.

He had arranged a rendezvous with his followers on the Aventine Hill, whence he intended to lead his men across the valley to the Capitoline, where the opposing party was gathered; but when he arrived at his headquarters he found his friends cowed by the reports of the strength of their opponents, and anxious to negotiate a settlement of the trouble. Fulvius Flaccus, one of his chief lieutenants, in fact, had been drunk all night, and now, in his befuddled condition, could suggest nothing but that his son, a boy still in his 'teens, should be sent over to the enemy to open negotiations with them, for it was not likely that the good-looking and obviously innocent youth would come to any harm at their hands. Accordingly, he was despatched under the equivalent of the white flag to Opimius, who, however, sent him back with orders not to return unless he were to bring an offer of unconditional surrender; but, in spite of this, Fulvius sent him over a second time to plead the People's cause, whereupon Opimius very cruelly ordered him to be executed. As the wretched boy, trembling and weeping, was being taken into the prison, a certain astrologer who had accompanied him on his mission, and now expected death for himself also, suddenly turned to him, and saying "Why don't you do what *I* am going to do?" dashed his head against the stone doorpost and fell, unconscious, with a fractured skull from which he shortly died. [6]

Opimius then brought a body of archers across the valley, and ordered them to shoot down the so-called rebels. The first volley wrought havoc amongst the democrats, most of whom fled, and Caius, cursing their cowardice and seeing that all was lost, rushed into the temple of Diana, where, in a passion of despair, he prayed the goddess that the Roman People, who had thus deserted him, should for ever remain the slaves of the aristocracy. He then drew his dagger to kill himself, but he was restrained by two friends, Pomponius and Laetorius, who persuaded him to try to escape by way of the old Sublician Bridge which crossed the Tiber at the western side of the Aventine.

He was running down towards the river when he stumbled and twisted his ankle; and before he was able to continue his way some soldiers under the orders of the Consul appeared in hot pursuit. Thereupon Pomponius very gallantly stayed behind to bar the way, and though it was not long before he was overwhelmed and killed, his action enabled Caius to reach the bridge. Here Laetorius performed a similar deed of devotion, holding the pursuers at bay until he, too, was cut down. By this time, however, Caius had reached the opposite bank of the river; and as he dashed along, accompanied by a single slave, the people in the streets excitedly cheered him on and called after him to run his hardest, as though the affair were a sporting event. Not one offered to help him, however, nor responded to his incessant and agonized shouts for a horse.

At last he reached the slopes of the Janiculum, and, too exhausted to go further, ran into a garden which enclosed a certain sacred shrine; but somebody told the pursuing soldiers where he was, and they were quickly upon the scene. They found him lying on the ground, clasped in the arms of his slave. An officer ran the man through the back with his sword, and, pulling the

[6] Velleius, ii, vii.

body away, discovered that Caius had a moment before been stabbed to the heart by this faithful servant who had buried the weapon in his own breast at the instant when he was struck from behind. Caius's head was then cut off and taken to Opimius, and the decapitated body was afterwards thrown into the river. Meanwhile, his followers, flying from the Aventine, were pursued in all directions; and it is said that no less than three thousand persons lost their lives on that day, Fulvius and another son of his being amongst the slain.

Caius, of course, came to be venerated at length as a popular hero and martyr, as also did his brother, Tiberius. To the impotent disgust of the aristocratic party, their statues were set up, and the places where they were killed were consecrated, offerings to their spirits being regularly made there. They were the founders, indeed, of the democratic party whose fight with the conservatives or republicans is the "thunder off" which accompanies the whole drama of Antony's life. Their mother, Cornelia, who long outlived them, became the recipient of the deepest veneration; and her house at Misenum, near Naples, was visited by the greatest men in the land, to whom she used to talk freely about her sons, showing no emotion whatsoever, but telling tales of their exploits and their misfortunes as though they had been legendary heroes of old. In fact, so devoid of natural feelings did she appear to be, that people were obliged to find excuses for her, saying that age, or the greatness of her sorrows, had deprived her of her sensibilities. She used to relate long stories, too, about her revered father, Africanus; but when she was told that the Roman People had erected a bronze statue of her, and had inscribed it with the words "The Mother of the Gracchi," the light of proud satisfaction in her eyes disclosed the fact that the undying ambition of her heart had been fulfilled.

CHAPTER II

Caius Marius, and the Growth of the Political Troubles amidst which
Antony was Born.

121–83 B.C.

ALTHOUGH the Gracchi were not of aristocratic lineage on their
father's side, their paternal descent was, at any rate, distinguished,
and their mother was of the bluest blood. The two brothers were
both men of culture and refinement, who supported the Comitia
rather than the Senate because they believed the latter to be a
corrupt and self-seeking body far less fit than the People's Assembly to promote the true interests of the nation. But in 119 B.C.,
two years after the death of Caius Gracchus, another famous Tribune of the People, this time a genuine working man, made his bow
to the restless Roman audience. His name was Caius Marius.

He was born in 157 B.C. in a village near the little town of
Arpinum (Arpino) in the rugged Volscian Mountains, his parents
being people of small means and no importance;[1] but after a
hard-working youth he had the good fortune to come under the
notice of Cæcilius Metellus, a man of ancient and illustrious
plebeian family, but of aristocratic sympathies and high standing in the Senatorial party, who, in 133 B.C., persuaded him to
join the army, and sent him with a letter of introduction to Scipio
Africanus the Younger, the brother-in-law of the Gracchi, then
commanding the Roman forces fighting in Spain. Scipio took a
fancy to, and rapidly promoted, the young man, whose bravery,
abstemiousness, and devotion to duty caused him to be generally
respected in spite of his rough manners and his habit of speaking his mind; and once, so the story goes, when a staff-officer flat-

---

[1] Velleius (ii, 11) calls him *natus equestri loco*, but the usual correction of *equestri*
to *agresti*, to meet the strong tradition that he was a peasant, is very probable.

teringly asked where Rome would ever find another Scipio, that general put his hand on Marius's shoulder, and said "Possibly here."

When the war was over and Marius had come back home with a considerable reputation for efficiency, and an unbounded belief in himself, both Scipio and Metellus helped him to fulfil his ambition to enter political life as a Tribune of the People, although the fact that he was a poor speech-maker, halting and tactless, was likely to tell against him. In 129 B.C. Scipio was murdered, perhaps, as many people thought, by his wife Sempronia, the sister of the Gracchi, because of his violently aristocratic prejudices which led him too often to make rude remarks about the late Tiberius Gracchus; but Metellus continued to keep a guiding hand upon Marius, and it seems evident that he hoped to train him to be a useful member of the conservative or republican party—the party, that is to say, which upheld the rigid constitution of the old Republic against the restless pressure of the new democracy.

To his disgust, however, Marius conceived an overwhelming dislike for the nobility, whom he regarded as nincompoops and voluptuaries; and as soon as he became Tribune, he proposed in the Comitia a law in regard to the suffrage which had as its object the curtailing of the powers of the aristocrats' vehicle, the Senate. The Consul Cotta [2] led the senators in their opposition to this bill, and arrogantly sent for Marius to explain his conduct before the House; but to everybody's astonishment the Tribune marched into the Senate, followed by some officers of the Comitia, and told Cotta that unless he allowed the bill to pass, he, Marius, would have him thrown into prison for obstructing the People's wishes. The Senators gasped; and when Marius then turned to his former patron Metellus and angrily asked him what *he* was going to do about it, Metellus, greatly shocked at such insolence in his protégé, declared that he, too, would oppose the bill, whereupon Marius called up his officers and said "Arrest that man!" At this the nervous senators, supposing that another revolution was upon them, hastily expressed their willingness to reconsider the matter; and Marius marched out of the House again in triumph.

[2] A near relation of the mother of the as yet unborn Julius Cæsar.

A few days later, however, his delighted supporters proposed another law in the Comitia, this time in regard to the distribution of corn; and when the senators opposed it, Marius risked his popularity with the masses by upholding the objection, for the simple reason that he did not regard the measure as serving the public good. Both parties realized then that that current phenomenon, an honest patriot, had once more appeared in the democratic ranks.

From Tribune Marius rose at length to the high magisterial office of Prætor; and so influential did he become that Caius Julius Cæsar, who later was the father of the great Dictator, and who was one of the heads of the proudly aristocratic Julian family, willingly gave him his sister, Julia, in marriage.

At about this time the Romans found themselves involved in a war against King Jugurtha of Numidia in North Africa, an attractive young man who, as a prince, had served under Scipio in Spain, and was well-known to Marius. He had been a great favourite with the general, both as a dashing officer and as a sportsman, and had gone back to Numidia with such high recommendations that his royal father had made him his heir over the heads of his two other sons, with the result that a family quarrel had ensued, and Jugurtha had been obliged to kill off one of his rivals and make war against the other.

Jugurtha at length came himself to Rome to try to obtain the patronage of the Republic; and, being both rich and charming, he soon managed to win the support of the patrician senators, and did not hesitate to cement his friendship by the lavish distribution of bribes. The discovery of these payments, however, caused a tremendous scandal in the city; and the Comitia, apparently at the instigation of Marius, took sides against him, and ordered him to leave the country, which he did with a sneering remark implying that everything was a question of money in Rome, and that if only he had been richer he could have bought the whole Republic. So greatly were the People incensed with him that, in 109 B.C., they decided to drive him from his throne by force; and Metellus, who was Consul for that year, and was one of the few nobles who had not accepted Jugurtha's money, was ordered to lead an expedition against him, with Marius, whom the Comitia could trust, as his second-in-command.

During the many months of indeterminate fighting which ensued, Marius won great military renown at the expense of his somewhat incompetent superior officer, and became extremely popular with the troops, whose every hardship he shared. Metellus, on the contrary, was a man who believed only in strict discipline, and inflicted punishments which were too inhuman even for Roman taste. For example, his treatment of certain Greek and Italian deserters who had been surrendered to him by the enemy was savage almost to the degree of lunacy: he buried them up to their armpits, used them as targets for his arrows, and then, alive or dead, made little bonfires over them. [3] At last Marius decided by hook or by crook to go back to Rome, get himself elected Consul for the year 107 B.C., and ignoring in the public interest the probable charge of ingratitude, make an attempt to supersede Metellus in the supreme command. Metellus, very naturally, was not willing at first to give him leave of absence, and, quite apart from other and obvious considerations, could not stomach the idea of a common and uneducated man becoming Consul; but at last, twelve days before the date of the consular elections, he magnanimously released him, whereupon Marius made a dash for home, and arrived just in time to secure election by bluntly telling the Roman People that this war was a man's job which could never be brought to a successful conclusion by an elegant personage such as Metellus, backed by a lot of emasculated senatorial nonentities.

"My fellow citizens," said Marius to the Comitia, [4] "compare me, a self-made man, with these arrogant nobles. What they have but heard or read, I have seen or done. What they have learnt from books, I have acquired in the field. They despise my humble birth: I despise their imbecility, for I consider that all men are equal by birth and that only he who works hard is noble. But if these patrician gentlemen justly despise me, then let them also despise their own ancestors whose nobility, like mine, had its origin in merit. And if they envy me the honours I have received, let them also envy me my hard work, my abstinences, and the perils by which I obtained these honours. It is true that I cannot boast of ancestral portraits nor of the deeds of my forefathers; but if it be necessary I can show you my

[3] Appian: *Roman History*, viii, pt. ii, 3. [4] Sallust: *Bellum Jugurthinum*, lxxxv.

military rewards and the scars of my wounds. These are my family heirlooms, these my nobility—honours not inherited, like theirs, but acquired amidst innumerable toils and dangers."

"My speech, they say, is inelegant," he went on; "but I have never thought that of much importance. Nor can I speak Greek; for I have never had a wish to learn a language which adds nothing to the valour of those who know it. They jeer at me as being unpolished, because I have but little skill in getting up an entertainment, and do not give my cook higher wages than my steward. I admit it, for I learnt from my father that vain indulgences belong to women, and work to men. Let the nobility, if they wish, pursue the pleasures which are so dear to them; let them devote themselves to licentiousness and luxury; let them pass their lives in revelry and feasting, the slaves of gluttony and debauchery. But let them leave the toil and dust of the field to us, to whom such things are better than banquets."

Here, indeed, was the spirit of the Gracchi again, and the People cheered the familiar sentiments to the echo; nor was it long before Marius was given his heart's desire—the supreme command against Jugurtha. He then took a step which was so revolutionary that even his supporters must have been startled by it. Regular Roman troops could not be spared from their many duties to act as reinforcements for the African campaign, and Marius therefore enlisted the Latins from all over Italy, who had never before been allowed to serve in the proud and exclusive legions of Rome, and with them he enrolled as many suitable men from the rabble of the city as he could find, although, until then, the lowest classes had, likewise, been contemptuously debarred from regular military service. This was the beginning of the vast and heterogeneous Roman army of the future, in which the legions were recruited from all over the world; but the innovation must have been regarded with horror by the conservatives who doubtless thought that it would lower the whole tone of the forces. Marius, however, soon licked his recruits into shape, and his experiment was fully justified by their subsequent behaviour in battle.

By the time that he arrived back in Africa with authority to take over the supreme command, the enemy's resistance was broken, and it was not long before Jugurtha was in flight. Metellus, of course, was cut to the quick at being deprived of the final glory, and, refusing to meet Marius, went home to Rome, where the Senate saw to it that he received the honours which were his due, whether the People liked it or not. Marius, meanwhile, was left to catch the elusive Numidian monarch, a task which was well nigh impossible. Jugurtha, however, sealed his own fate in the following year, 106 B.C., by placing himself under the protection of his father-in-law, King Bocchus of Mauretania, who secretly opened negotiations with the Romans for his surrender.

At this point a new character makes a dramatic appearance in the pages of Roman history, in the person of Lucius Cornelius Sulla, the most extraordinary figure of that age. He was at this time a yellow-haired young man of thirty who had been taken up by Marius, and had been given the position of his quæstor, or lieutenant. The choice was curious, for he was an aristocrat by birth and a scholar by nature, whereas his chief was a man of little education; but Marius was no doubt attracted by Sulla's strong character, and his notorious ability to make himself pleasant and polite when it served his dark purpose. He was remarkably daring, and both his bravery and his cunning were displayed in the incident which introduces him to history.

King Bocchus did not wish to incur the odium of handing Jugurtha over as a prisoner, and Sulla therefore obtained the permission of Marius to go with a small force to the Mauretanian capital and personally make the arrest, in doing which, however, he had to place his life in the hands of a man even more treacherous than he was himself. Bocchus proved to be undecided as to what to do, and it was only after protracted conversations that Sulla's exceptional diplomatic ability obtained him his host's permission to kidnap Jugurtha and make off with him in such a way that the honour of Bocchus would not be too deeply stained. Thus the Numidian King was captured, and sent in chains to Rome. But just as Marius had taken from Metellus the victor's crown, so now Sulla arrogated to himself the honour of thus ending the war; and it was on this account that that deadly enmity between the two men developed which ultimately caused the wholesale slaughter whereat Rome was trembling at the time of Antony's birth.

The year 105 B.C. was spent by Marius in Africa, winding up Numidian affairs; but meanwhile the fatherland was threatened by a menace from the north more terrible than any yet experienced by the Republic. A vast horde of barbarians of mixed Celtic and Teutonic stock, migrating from Germany, had marched southwards with their women and children in search of new lands, and had carried all before them. In October, 105 B.C., an army sent to check their incursion into Roman territory was cut to pieces; and thereafter all eyes were turned to Marius and to the army which he was bringing back from Africa. While he was still on his way he was elected Consul again for the year 104 B.C., and on his arrival in Rome he was accorded a Triumph, the chief feature in the procession being the captive King Jugurtha who had been dressed up for the occasion in all his finery, but whose deportment was spectacular in an unexpected sense, owing to the fact that his brutal treatment in prison had sent him off his head.

At the end of the day's festivities the wretched man's royal robes were dragged from his back, and in the struggle to get possession of the single gold ring which, in African style, he wore in the tip of one ear, his gaolers tore off a piece of the flesh. He was then lowered, naked and bleeding, into the Tullian dungeon-pit, beneath the Capitol, and as he fell into the damp slime at the bottom he was heard to utter a blood-curdling laugh and to exclaim "O God, how cold your bath is!" He was left there to shiver and starve to death, but it was six days before his demented sufferings were ended by a gaoler who went down into the pit and strangled him. [5] The case is typical of the savagery of Rome's traditional treatment of foreign enemies.

To everybody's immense relief the victorious hordes from the north did not march on Italy, but wandered off towards Spain; yet so great was Rome's dread of them that Marius was elected Consul again for the third time in 103 B.C., and for the fourth time in 102 B.C. In the latter year, however, the invaders began to move once more towards Italy in two bodies; and thereat Marius marched out against them at the head of an army which he had trained into a perfect machine. The first battle was fought near Aix: the tall, blonde Teutons, wearing heavy metal helmets, came

[5] Eutropius, iv, 11.

on, linked hand in hand, in dense masses; but Marius out-maneuvered them, and annihilated them and afterwards their women and children. In the following year, being made Consul for the fifth time, he attacked the other body of the invaders in northern Italy with a like result, but when the men had been slaughtered the women took up the fight amongst the baggage-wagons, and those who did not fall before the Roman swords brained their children and hanged themselves with their own plaited yellow hair.

When Marius came back to Rome he was hailed almost as a god, and the adoration of the lower classes for him was all the more extreme because, in spite of his aristocratic marriage, he was one of themselves, a true son of the People. The nobility, however, attempted to counteract this popularity by paying high honours to Sulla, who had greatly distinguished himself in these campaigns, and who, being a patrician by birth and inclination, had thrown in his lot with the Senate in its rivalry with the Comitia. Sulla, fastidious, intellectual, and licentious, detested the rough and ignorant mob from which Marius derived his chief support, and gradually, with deep cunning, he undermined his rival's prestige, the process being aided by the fact that Marius, who was really a very simple man, allowed himself to become a tool in the hands of the most selfish elements in his party. Once more Rome was divided into two hostile camps—that of the nobles or conservatives, acting through the Senate, and that of the People or democrats, acting through the Comitia.

Marius managed, not without difficulty, to be elected Consul for the sixth time for the year 100 B.C.; but his age, and the fact that in these days he was drinking somewhat heavily, had caused him to lose his grip, and he was unable to control the actions of his two chief supporters, Saturninus, a violent and sinister ruffian who nursed a personal grievance against the Senate, and Glaucia, a tub-thumping demagogue, famous for his vulgar wit. These two men induced Marius to push forward a programme of popular reforms much like that for which the Gracchi had stood; and when Metellus, since the days of the war against Jugurtha the bitter enemy of Marius, had refused to be a party to the Senate's enforced approval of the measures, he was driven into exile. Riots and murders, the outcome of class-hatred, now began to occur in

Rome with startling frequency; senatorial politicians were beaten
or stoned to death in the streets by angry mobs who would no longer listen to their former hero's orders; and at last the younger members of the patrician party banded themselves together to defend
their class by force against the unruly Proletariat.

Marius, who had now grown corpulent and unwieldy, was bewildered by these events; and from under his shaggy eyebrows he
stared about him like an angry bull perplexed by its tormentors.
At length in 99 B.C. Saturninus passed completely out of control,
and, at the head of an excited mob, seized the Capitol, it being
his intention, so it was said, to overthrow the Republic and make
himself sole ruler of the state. Too late Marius realized his intentions, and repudiated him: the leadership was taken out of his
hands, and "a mob of gentlemen," quietly instigated by Sulla,
pelted Saturninus and his men to death with tiles snatched from the
roofs of the out-buildings, after which they caught and killed
Glaucia also.

The reputation of Marius was ruined by the incident, and
therewith he passed into a temporary obscurity which was only
lightened for him by a superstitious conviction that the stars
had promised him a seventh Consulate before he died. Unable
to bear his present humiliation, and exasperated to hear that the
Senate had exercised its recovered authority by ordering Metellus
back from exile, he set out on a tour of Greece and Asia Minor,
ostensibly to fulfil a vow he had made to Cybele, the great
Asiatic mother-goddess, but actually to study the lie of the land
in anticipation of an expected rising there against Rome. Plutarch,
indeed, thinks that he was prepared to foment trouble and bring
the incipient insurrection to a head, in the hope that the danger
would lead to his destined seventh Consulship, and that he would
regain his lost popularity by commanding the Roman army which
would be sent out against the rebels; but this, perhaps, is to credit
the fallen hero with a cunning of which his artless nature seems to
me to have been incapable.

In Rome during the next few years the aristocratic party
was in control of the situation, and when Marius returned from
his tour he found himself almost ignored, and retired to his villa
on the Bay of Naples, that same house which had formerly be-

POMPEY (?)

Capitol Museum, Rome

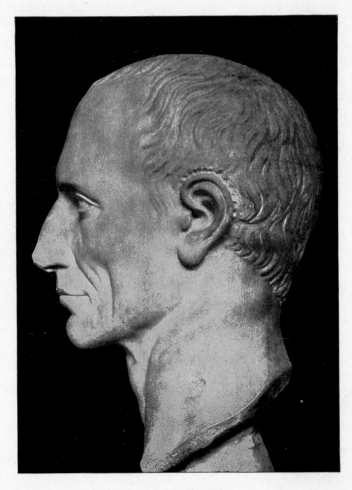

JULIUS CÆSAR

British Museum

longed to Cornelia, the mother of the Gracchi, and which his patrician wife had enlarged and beautified. There he mooned about in surroundings too sumptuous for his simple mind to appreciate, and became gouty and heavy through too much drinking and too little exercise. But suddenly in 90 B.C. the outbreak of an insurrection in Italy itself called him back into public notice. The various peoples of the Italian peninsula, not being Roman citizens, and knowing no way of protecting themselves from the arrogance of those who were, leagued themselves together to destroy Rome and establish a new republic. The menace to the city was so great that party-differences were set aside, and Marius and Sulla both found themselves in command of Roman armies during the two years of subsequent war, and both shared in the final victory, though the greater honour went to the dashing Sulla, Marius being regarded as somewhat too slow. But it was a terrible blow to Marius when Sulla was elected Consul for 88 B.C.

No sooner was the war over than the expected rebellion in Asia Minor took place, but on a scale and with a ferocity which was wholly unlooked for. The Roman governor, Aquillius, was taken prisoner by the rebels, and, in revenge for the greed for money which he had shown, was horribly put to death by the pouring of molten gold into his mouth; and on the same day no less than eighty thousand Roman residents in the country were massacred.

When the news reached Italy in 88 B.C., Marius hastened to Rome, feeling that at last his great chance had come. He had studied the lands through which the Romans would have to march; his plan of campaign was already settled in his mind; and he saw himself once more elected Consul and Commander-in-Chief. He was nearly seventy years of age; but in order to create an impression of energy he went each day to the Campus Martius, and there exercised himself with the young men on the public athletic grounds and riding-track. Puffing and panting, and once or twice nearly fainting from his exertions, he bravely struggled to overcome the weight of his years, so that the Comitia should give him the longed-for command; and at last, to his great joy, he succeeded in bribing Sulpicius, a Tribune of the People for that year, to secure his appointment.

Sulla at that time was still with the legions which he had commanded during the Italian war, encamped at Nola in Campania; and, coming to Rome to try to have the appointment of Marius rescinded in his own favour by the Senate, he was set upon by Sulpicius and driven again from the city. Marius then sent him a peremptory order to hand over his troops; but this he refused to do, and boldly marched on Rome at their head. The aristocratic party gave him their support; and after scenes of dreadful violence, Sulpicius was killed, and Marius, almost brokenhearted at the shattering of his dreams, was forced to fly for his life with a price upon his head.

With the help of friends he was able to charter a ship at Ostia, the port of Rome, and put to sea; but a storm so nearly wrecked the vessel and caused the fugitive such miseries of seasickness that the dangers to be feared on land were forgotten, and the ship was beached near Circeium (Circello), about half way between Rome and Naples. Going ashore, Marius hid himself in a wood, where he passed a night of great discomfort, and next day he and his friends wandered along the beach without hope or plan. After a while, however, they saw, to their dismay, a troop of cavalry coming towards them, and thereat they plunged into the sea and swam towards two ships which happened to be passing by. Marius was too fat and too exhausted to make much progress through the water, but he was helped by his companions, and at last, half-drowned, was taken aboard one of the vessels, and was conveyed to the mouth of the river Liris (the Garigliano), a day's sail to the south, where the crew set him ashore and went their way.

For some time he sat disconsolately on the sand, but at length he made his way inland, floundering through marshland and splashing across ditches full of water, until he came to the hut of a peasant, who good-naturedly hid him in a pit and covered its mouth with reeds. A little later, however, some soldiers who were scouring the country in search of him arrived at the hut, whereat Marius, thinking the man would reveal his hiding place, crawled out of the pit, and divesting himself of his clothes, ran down to a neighbouring pond, where he attempted to conceal himself in the cold and muddy water, only his head remaining above the surface. The soldiers, however, found him, and dragged him out, shivering, naked, and covered with mud, and took him to the nearest village, where the inhabitants, not knowing what to do with him, decided to lock him up for the night. As he was being taken into the building where he was to be lodged, a donkey ran towards him, brayed loudly, and, kicking up its heels in apparent pleasure, ran off to drink at a trough nearby. Marius took this to be a sign from heaven that he should escape by water; and, somewhat comforted, he lay down and soon fell into an exhausted sleep.

He was awakened by the opening of the door, and, starting up, saw a soldier, sword in hand, coming towards him. The man, who was a German—one of the prisoners captured by Marius a dozen years before, and subsequently released[6]—had been sent by the village council to put him to death, that course of action having been decided upon at their meeting; but when he saw the eyes of the old general glaring at him out of the semi-darkness, and heard his slow and awe-inspiring voice cry out, "Fellow, do you dare to kill Caius Marius," he flung down his sword and rushed from the house. At this the villagers, standing outside, once more changed their minds, and decided to help him to escape. They therefore entered the room in a body, and, taking the panting old man by the hands, ran him down to the sea, and bundled him aboard a ship.

Landing by chance on the island of Ænaria (Ischia) he there came upon the rest of his company who had escaped in the second of the two vessels to which they had swum out, as recorded above; and all together they sailed for Sicily. Here, however, on landing near Eryx (S. Guiliano), on the north-west coast, they were attacked by a Roman officer and his men, who killed most of them; but Marius made good his escape to the ship, and got away. Thence they steered their course to the colony founded by Caius Gracchus on the site of Carthage, where they went ashore in the hope that the colonists, who owed the existence of their settlement to the party of the People, might take pity on them; but they were met by an officer of the governor, who ordered them, whoever they might be, to leave his shores immediately. At this Marius, seat-

[6] Velleius, ii, xix.

ing himself upon a block of stone which had once been part of a busy wharf in the city that was no more, said to the officer, "Go and tell the governor that you have seen Caius Marius sitting in exile amidst the ruins of Carthage."

As chance would have it, news had just arrived from Rome which changed the whole fortune of the fugitives. Sulla had gone to Asia Minor at the head of the Roman army to suppress the rebellion there; but on his departure the fight between the aristocracy and the People had once more broken out, and Cinna, one of the Consuls for that year, who belonged to the popular party, had been driven from the city by his aristocratic colleague, but had collected a large fighting force in Italy and was preparing to march back on Rome, giving out openly that if Marius were still alive and would come to him, he would gladly receive him.

The arrival of Marius at Carthage was therefore hailed with enthusiasm by the many refugees and outlaws from Rome who had fled to the African coast at the time of Sulla's triumph; and a few weeks later he sailed for Italy at the head of a rabble of no less than a thousand persons, to join Cinna. They found him already victoriously approaching the city, and soon Marius and the Consul were encamped with their army on the Janiculum hill, close to the spot where Caius Gracchus had met his death. The Senate sent messengers to them to beg them to enter the city in peace and to spare the citizens; but the stern and wild aspect of Marius, who, as a token of mourning, had not cut or combed his hair nor shaved his face since his exile, gave little promise that he would forego his revenge.

Cinna then marched into the city with his troops, but Marius remained at the gates, proudly refusing to enter until the death-sentence upon him had been rescinded by public vote. A meeting of the Comitia was therefore called to pass this motion; but it seems that the voting was not unanimous, for, in a blaze of anger, Marius impatiently entered the city surrounded by his armed guard, to whom he gave a savage order that they should kill at sight any man whom he should point out to them as one of his enemies. As a result of this order the streets along which he made his way were soon dotted with little groups of horrified townspeople clustered around the bodies of the unfortunate persons who had been cut down by the passing soldiers; and presently the frightened senators and men of importance began here and there to hasten forward to kiss his hand so that they might save their skins by pretending to be rejoiced at his return. A certain senator named Ancharius, however, on running up to him with unctuous smiles and exclamations of pleasure was received with a stony stare, whereupon the guards immediately killed him; and after this every personage of the kind who was not greeted in return by Marius was immediately butchered, with the result that his real well-wishers were terrified of the consequences either of coming forward or of holding back.

During the next few days his old enemies were hunted down in all directions, and slaughtered. One man, a certain Cornutus, was saved by his slaves who secured the body of one of the slain and passed it off as that of their master. Cnæus Octavius, and Cornelius Merula, both of whom had been Consuls, were amongst those who met their deaths, the former being murdered, and the latter cheating his pursuers by cutting the veins of his wrists and dying with curses against the democrats upon his lips. But the fury of Marius was not often balked; and never before had political strife brought such bloodshed or such terror into the heart of Rome.

This horrible massacre introduces into our pages for the first time the great plebeian family of the Antonii, of which Antony, the subject of this biography, born four years later, was the most famous member. His grandfather, Marcus Antonius, who was born in 143 B.C., had been Consul for the year 99 B.C., that year so disastrous for Marius, when, owing to the uncontrolled behaviour of Saturninus, the hopes of the People's party were wrecked. This Marcus Antonius was one of the most distinguished orators of his time, and was famous both for his successful pleadings at the Bar and for the political speeches which had helped him to attain the highest honours in the State. Although of plebeian rank, his ancestry was illustrious, [7] and his many aristocratic connections had induced him to take the side of the Senate against that of the Comitia, for which reason he had incurred the enmity of Marius. He had two sons, Marcus and Caius. The elder son,

[7] Cicero: *Philippic iii, vi.*

Marcus, afterwards the father of the famous Antony had married Julia, the daughter of a celebrated patrician, Lucius Julius Cæsar, and the distant cousin of that other Julia who had married Marius. Lucius Julius Cæsar had been one of the important generals in the war against the Italian confederacy, and, being a friend of Sulla's, was as obnoxious to Marius as was Marcus Antonius, the orator.

Both men were therefore condemned to death, and Lucius was quickly found and killed, together with his brother Caius Julius Cæsar, another celebrated orator. Marcus Antonius, however, was successfully hidden for a few days by a certain poor man, but the secret of his whereabouts was discovered at length by a wine-merchant, who went with the news to Marius. Marius was at supper at the time, and on receiving this information gave a ferocious shout of pleasure and clapped his fat hands together, thereafter sending an officer named Annius and some soldiers to put him to death. The soldiers, however, were so touched by the voice of the orator as he pleaded for his life that they refused to despatch him, and stood weeping around him in the little upper room where they had found him, until their officer was obliged to do the deed with his own hand. His severed head was exhibited on Marius's dinner-table, [8] and then with that of Lucius Julius Cæsar, and those of some of the other more important victims, was stuck up on the Rostra in the Forum—the curious custom of placing the heads of political enemies on the platform from which other politicians made their speeches having been introduced by Sulla at the time of the disturbances which resulted in the exile of Marius.

Towards the end of the year news, which later proved to be untrue, was brought to Rome that Sulla was marching home at the head of his victorious army; and since his coming would mean that the aristocracy would take its revenge upon the People, the latter party decided to elect Marius as Consul for the new year, 86 B.C., and to give him power to defend the Proletariat. Marius, however, knew that the pitiless Sulla and his troops would make short work of him, and he fell into the deepest despondency, protesting in tones of anguish that he was too old to bear these new anxieties, and that he could never again face the horrors

[8] Florus, iii, xxi.

of exile. Sleep forsook him, or, if he did sleep, he was terrified by frightful dreams; yet he was afraid to lie awake at nights, and therefore drank himself into a dazed condition every evening.

In the second week in January, after the seventh Consulship promised to him by the astrologers had been his for but ten days, he caught a chill which rapidly turned to pneumonia. In his delirium he fancied that his dearest wish had been attained, and that he was in command of the Roman forces in Asia Minor. Leaping from his bed, he shouted orders to the soldiers of his fevered imagination, and hurled defiance at the phantom army of the enemy, throwing his heavy body into heroic postures, and glaring about the room, brandishing a sword which none but himself could see. On the seventh day of his illness he died. [9]

But Sulla, detained by the war, did not yet come back, and for three years Cinna was the ruler of Rome, the People's party having complete control of the situation. Then in 84 B.C. came a ferocious letter from Sulla saying that he was returning, victorious, to the capital, and that he would punish all those who had not been loyal to him. At this Cinna gathered an army and went out to do battle with him; but his soldiers refused to fight their own countrymen, and in the mutiny Cinna was murdered.

The reins of government were then taken up by two other leaders of the People, Carbo and Marius the Younger, the son of the old general. Sulla landed in Italy in 83 B.C.; and at just about the time that he did so, [10] when the fate of the Republic was hanging in the balance, and the two parties—the republicans or conservatives and the democrats—were at daggers drawn, the young Julia, daughter of the murdered Lucius Julius Cæsar, and wife of Marcus Antonius, the son of the murdered orator, gave birth to a male child, who received the family name of Marcus Antonius, and is known to us more familiarly as Marc Antony.

[9] January 17th; but another account says January 13th.
[10] Gardthausen: *Augustus und seine Zeit,* ii, p. 5.

CHAPTER III

The Infancy of Antony, during the Rule of Sulla.

83–78 B.C.

LUCIUS CORNELIUS SULLA was about fifty-five years of age when he came back to Italy, for he was born in 138 B.C. Although of patrician family and the great-grandson of a man who had twice been Consul, he had found himself in his youth so impoverished by the extravagances of a dissolute father that he was obliged to live in some cheap lodgings in Rome until a good-natured and extremely successful prostitute, named Nicopolis, who had ruined her business by falling in love with him, conveniently died and left him all that remained to her of the money she had received from his friends. His rise to fame and fortune has been recorded in the previous chapter; but since he held the centre of the Roman stage for the next few years it will be as well for us now to look more closely at him.

He was a man of startling appearance, having a thick crop of faded hair which had once been yellow, staring eyes of blue, and a dead white complexion so disfigured by pimples and red blotches, due to drink, that somebody described his face as being like "a mulberry sprinkled with flour." [1] His character has, for us who are not at his mercy, the charm of inconsistency, and he at once attracts and repels us. When sober he was polite and urbane to his friends, and even diplomatically deferential to those whose good offices he needed; but while his heart was tender, and he easily shed tears of compassion, his brain was cold and pitiless, and he had the mental equipment of a murderer. When drunk, which was his frequent condition, he was good-natured, generous,

[1] Plutarch: *Sulla*.

and anxious to oblige; and since it seems to be true that a man in his cups reveals his real nature, one may say that there was a wealth of natural good in him held in check by his monstrous and passionless intellect.

He was a very fine scholar, deeply read in Roman and Greek literature; and, combining wide knowledge with a love of beautiful things and the fastidious taste of a connoisseur, he derived keen enjoyment both from artistic and intellectual pursuits. He sought the company of painters, sculptors, actors, philosophers, men of letters, and, indeed, anybody on whose wits, like steel upon steel, he could sharpen his own; and nothing gave him greater pleasure than the kind of conversation which obliged him to exercise his brain. It amused him to outwit people, and Sallust says that "his depth of thought in disguising his intentions was incredible"; [2] yet nobody found more relief than he did in talking elegant nonsense and giving himself up to laughter. His reason did not permit him much belief in the religious systems of his age, yet he was preposterously superstitious, and was firmly convinced of the omnipotence of his lucky star.

He was flagrantly vicious, and some lack in his spontaneous emotions obliged him to exert a remarkable ingenuity in his pursuit of sensual pleasure, in which respect he was as entirely devoid of shame as he was of decency; yet he could be a normal lover, and, when he was not seeking perverted adventure, was so incorrigibly domestic that he entered the bonds of matrimony no less than five times.

He did not often permit his pleasures, however, to interfere with his duties; and if he was too frequently drunk, he was never idle when he was sober. He was a man of iron will, courageous but impatient, and neither fear of the consequences nor any instinct of mercy—nothing, in fact, except boredom—ever turned him from his purpose. The nature of that purpose is the redeeming feature in a character terrifying to contemporary Rome because of its pitilessness; for Sulla undoubtedly acted in what he believed to be the best interests of the Republic, and showed so little personal ambition that he resigned office as soon as he deemed his work done.

The war in Greece and Asia Minor from which he was now

[2] Sallust: *Bellum Jugurthinum,* xcv.

returning had proved him to be a brilliant general. His small army which marched out to suppress the Greek rebellion was soon left to its fate by distracted Rome, and received no support from the government of Cinna; but by his skilful leadership it succeeded in reconquering the lost provinces and in humbling the arch-enemy, King Mithradates[3] of Pontus, who from his headquarters at Ephesus had organized the insurrection. Sulla took Athens by storm in March, 86 b.c., but called his soldiers off before its sack was complete, announcing that he had decided to spare that fallen generation of Athenians as a mark of his respect for their great countrymen of long ago—Plato, Pericles, Socrates, Thucydides, and the many others. As his personal share of the loot he appropriated the library of the philosopher Apellicon of Teos, who had recently died, which contained the original manuscripts of Aristotle's works, and other literary treasures more pleasing to him than gold or silver. He then marched against Archelaus, the general of Mithradates, and having twice defeated him, crossed the Hellespont, and early in 84 b.c. concluded peace. Thence he returned to the port of Dyrrhachium (Durazzo) on the Greek coast opposite Italy, where he gathered a fleet of twelve hundred vessels in which to transport his victorious army across to Brundusium (Brindisi).

Just before he sailed a curious incident occurred which may be mentioned here because of the light it throws upon the mental outlook of the age. [4] Not far from Dyrrhachium stood the town of Apollonia, near which was the Nymphæum, or Abode of the Nymphs, a tract of mountainous and wooded country wherein there were hot springs and other volcanic peculiarities. Here, one day, some of his soldiers, carelessly trespassing upon this uncanny preserve of the half-gods, came upon a little bearded man like a satyr, asleep under a tree; and, having caught him, they brought him to Sulla. He was earnestly questioned by interpreters as to who he was, whether mortal or elfin; but he only uttered strange, frightened cries, "something between the neighing of a horse and the bleating of a goat," and this so dismayed Sulla that he hastily

---

[3] The usual spelling of this name, Mithridates, is shown to be incorrect by the coins, as is evident, also, from the name of the god Mithra which it incorporates.

[4] Plutarch: *Sulla.*

told the soldiers to take him away, and for some time was greatly troubled as to what the bringing in of so primeval a prisoner might portend. We are not told, unfortunately, whether the little creature was set free to return to his woodland glades and mountain streams; nor would it be true to the spirit of the old world to seek a natural explanation of the phenomenon.

The arrival of Sulla and his army in Italy, expressly sworn to the restoration of the aristocracy, caused the greatest consternation in Rome; and Marius the Younger and Carbo led out the forces which were loyal to the party of the People to do battle with him. Many of the patricians, however, went over to him, and amongst these mention must be made particularly of Crassus and Pompey, who afterwards figured conspicuously in the affairs of the Republic.

Marcus Crassus, born about 107 B.C., was the son of an ex-Consul who, because he belonged to the aristocratic party, had been forced by Marius to commit suicide, but he himself had fled with some others to Spain, where for eight months he and his friends lived in hiding in a spacious cavern beside the sea. The owner of the land in which the cave was situated was a friend of his, and used daily to dispatch a servant thither who, without ever seeing the noble fugitive or knowing his identity, left food for him and his companions upon the rocks. The historian Fenestella, who lived a generation later, but whose works are lost, used to tell, moreover, how he met an old woman who in her youth had been sent by this considerate host to the cave to distribute her charms amongst the little band of outlaws, a mission upon which she looked back with the greatest pleasure as the most agreeable of her life. [5] But when both Marius and Cinna were dead, Crassus, now about twenty-four years of age, was able to come out of hiding; after which he joined forces with another exile of aristocratic sympathies, Metellus, the son of that Metellus of whom we have read in the previous chapter, and together they offered their services to Sulla.

Cnæus Pompeius, whom we now call Pompey, was no more than twenty-three years of age when he, too, threw in his lot with Sulla; but already he was an outstanding figure in Rome and

[5] Plutarch: *Crassus.*

was greatly beloved by the rank and file of the patrician party, in spite of the intense unpopularity of his father, a former Consul, who, in the end was struck dead by lightning—a fate which most people believed to be a divine punishment for his cruelty and avarice. He was an extremely good-looking young man, whose features were often compared to those of Alexander the Great, and whose eyes were so "languishing," as Plutarch relates, that women were always falling in love with him. Indeed, a famous and beautiful courtesan, named Flora, declared that she could never resist biting him; and when he refused to have anything more to do with her out of consideration for a friend of his who had lost his heart to her, she very nearly died of grief. He was a happy-go-lucky youth, so charming that he could do whatever he liked without giving offence, and so easy and simple in his manners that his vast opinion of himself and his youthful assurance were tolerated with the greatest good-nature by his elders.

Nowhere was he more beloved than in Picenum, the country on the east side of the Italian peninsula opposite Rome, for that was his ancestral home; and now at his audacious bidding thousands of his countrymen flocked to his standard, and soon the amazing young man had organized and drilled them into three first-rate legions, complete with arms, munitions, and baggage-wagons. It troubled him not at all that the country between him and Sulla was held by the forces of the People; and in the first battle he rode out alone in advance of his men, met the fire-eating leader and champion of the opposing cavalry in a hand to hand duel, and killed him with such unruffled ease that the others thought him to be superhuman and fled. Shortly after this his little army came face to face with a large force under the command of the People's Consul for that year, Scipio Asiaticus;[6] but these troops at once came over to his side, and Scipio was obliged to fly for his life. He then outmaneuvered another army sent against him by Carbo, and, having obliged them to surrender, made them hand over their fine arms, armour, and horses, and then let them go.

The road to Sulla's headquarters was now open, and when Pompey had come in sight of the camp he drew up his troops in parade-order—glittering rank upon rank of them, infantry and

[6] Great-grandson of Scipio Africanus, the grandfather of the Gracchi.

cavalry, and riding forward to meet the astonished Sulla, politely dismounted and hailed him as *Imperator*, the title given to a victorious Commander-in-Chief. At this Sulla also dismounted, and addressed the young man with the same most exalted title, *Imperator*, an unprecedented honour for a youth of that age. Pompey accepted the generous compliment with a happy smile: his head was not in the least turned by it, nor did he show any signs of modest embarrassment when the pimpled but dignified Sulla, at all future meetings, gravely stood up and saluted him with exaggerated deference.

Meanwhile, in Rome, the father and mother of the baby Marc Antony must have been living in fear of their lives; for the successes of Sulla, who had sworn to reinstate the aristocratic or republican party, had exasperated the leaders of the People, and they were quite capable of exterminating this little family which, if Rome fell to Sulla, would doubtless seek its revenge for the murder of the old orator who had been the head of the house. Already several nobles and men of aristocratic sympathies had been arrested, and some of them executed on trumped-up charges; and the younger Marius was showing himself to be as bloodthirsty as his father. It was a period of terror for the senatorial party, and, with beating heart, Antony's mother must have clutched her baby to her bosom at every unusual sound. On all sides it was felt that Rome had reached a crisis in its affairs which marked the end of an epoch, and none could say whether the approach of Sulla would precipitate the destruction of the city or bring it a new lease of life; but when in July, 83 B.C., the Capitol was accidentally burnt to the ground, and the best copy of the Sibylline Books destroyed, no doubt remained in the minds of the citizens that, for better or for worse, Rome's violent hour of change had arrived.

To the anxious parents of the baby it seemed that the birth of this son of theirs was not unconnected with the turmoil which ushered him into the world. Perhaps, they said to themselves in the nepotism of their parental pride, he was the nation's hoped-for deliverer; perhaps he had been born to avenge the murders not only of his two grandfathers, but of all the other victims of the People's rule; perhaps it would fall to his lot to sweep away the ruins of the old Rome and to build a fairer city in its place. An outstanding career at any rate was surely to be expected of a male child, born to an important family at such a time as this, when portents and omens were everywhere being discussed, and fearful occurrences were almost daily shocking their minds. But for the present their eyes were turned to the approaching Sulla, the champion of their cause, whose coming was the one hope they had of safety for themselves and their child of destiny.

During the following months Sulla defeated the enemy several times, and gradually broke their resistance, Marius the Younger finally shutting himself up in the town of Præneste (Palestrina), some twenty miles from Rome, where he was closely besieged. In the early spring of 82 B.C. Sulla was thus able to march on Rome; but when his approach was reported the leaders of the People began a last, savage massacre of their political opponents, in which so many patricians and their sympathisers were killed that the escape of the baby Antony and his parents seems to have been almost miraculous. The war, however, was not yet at an end; and Sulla was soon obliged to take the field again against Carbo and a formidable army concentrated in Etruria, north of Rome. But while he was thus engaged, the Samnites from central Italy, who were tired of Rome's quarrels and, under the pretence of helping the People's cause, wished to take this opportunity to destroy the city entirely and massacre its inhabitants, made a sudden rush on the capital; and Sulla returned only just in time to prevent their entry.

The two armies met at sunset just outside the Colline Gate, on the northern side of the city, and Sulla was very nearly defeated, for his men were exhausted by their rapid march. The young Crassus, it is true, who commanded one wing, was victorious, but the main body was pressed back against the walls of the city. Sulla himself, mounted on a white charger, his pimpled and blotchy face terrible in his anguish, his voice hoarse from shouting, was within an ace of being killed. Two javelins at the same moment flew through the air towards him while he was looking the other way; but his groom saw them coming and struck the horse a sudden blow, at which it bounded forward, and the javelins missed their mark by inches. At this Sulla pulled from his bosom a little golden image of Apollo which he had bought at Delphi, and fervently kissed it, praying aloud to that god to come to his aid;

but it was the falling darkness which saved him and Rome, for
the battle was suddenly discontinued by the enemy in order that
they might gather their scattered forces in preparation for the
final onslaught upon the gates.

Just then the news was received by both sides that young
Crassus had driven back the Samnites opposed to him, and was in
a position to outflank the remainder, whereupon the latter retired
in dismay; and by break of day Sulla and Crassus effected a
juncture, as a result of which eight thousand of the enemy surrendered and were marched, disarmed, to the western side of the
city, where they were penned into a small area of the Circus
Flaminius between the Capitoline Hill and the river.

Close to this spot was the temple of Bellona in which the
Senate was accustomed occasionally to meet; and here Sulla called
the senators together, after their night of terror, to receive their
thanks for the saving of the city, and to give his orders in regard to the future government. But while he was addressing them,
the most terrible screams and cries penetrated the building, at
which the senators rose to their feet in alarm, thinking that a new
attack upon the city was being made. Sulla, however, without
raising his voice or changing the expression of his face, told them
to be seated and kindly to give their attention to him, not to the
disturbance outside. "What you hear," he said, "is merely due to
my having given orders for the punishment of some criminals."
Actually, Sulla had instructed his men to kill all the eight thousand prisoners, his justification for this slaughter being that they
had, on their side, intended to massacre the citizens.

During the day four of the enemy's generals were brought in
and summarily executed, after which their heads were carried to
Præneste, where Marius was besieged, and, having been fixed on
long poles, were bobbed about in front of the walls. On seeing them
Marius killed himself, [7] and the city surrendered. His head was
sent to Rome, and was stuck up on the Rostra, where Sulla went
to see it, and addressing it in scholarly criticism, quoted a line from
Aristophanes: "You should have worked at the oar before trying
to handle the helm." He then hastened to Præneste where, next
day, he gathered the civil and military prisoners in an open space,

[7] Or was killed: Velleius, ii, xxvii.

to the number of twelve thousand, and callously told his soldiers to kill the lot, the women and children, however, being spared. He had the politeness to exempt also the owner of the house in which he had spent the night; but the unhappy man could not bear the cries of the dying, and, rushing in amongst them, eagerly submitted himself to the soldiers' swords.

Having come back to Rome, Sulla began at once to reestablish the power of the republican aristocracy and the Senate and to reduce that of the People and the Comitia to a minimum, with which end in view he decided, in the interests of the Republic, to kill all the democrats of any note or standing, that being the surest way of preventing political arguments. He therefore issued a list or *proscriptum* of eighty names of persons who were to be killed at sight, a reward being given for their heads and the penalty of death being decreed against any who should aid their escape. The property of the proscribed was to be confiscated, and their sons and grandsons were to be prohibited from holding any public office.

Few of the unfortunates got away: most of them were killed during the same day by soldiers or even by their own slaves, and their pallid, blood-drained heads were arranged in rows on the Rostra from which Sulla made his pithy speeches. Two days later he issued a second list of two hundred and twenty names, and on the following morning another list of the same number appeared. In addressing the people after this third proscription had been posted up, he told them casually that these were all the names he could think of at the moment, but that if he found that any had escaped his memory he would issue supplementary lists, which, in fact, he continued to do for some weeks. Altogether more than four thousand persons, [8] including fifty senators of democratic sympathies, lost their lives as a result of these proscriptions; and there can be no doubt that there were many who were the victims of personal envy or spite, their names being sent in to Sulla even because somebody coveted their property.

Quintus Aurelius, for example, the owner of a desirable farm in Alba, near Rome—a perfectly harmless man whose only crime

[8] The much larger numbers given by Appian (i, 103) and Eutropius (v, 9) seem to include those who fell in the previous fighting, as Mommsen has observed.

was that he had offered his condolences to a family thus bereaved
—went into the Forum to read the list, and, to his horror, found
his own name in it, whereupon he exclaimed, "O my God!—
my Alban farm has convicted me," and a few minutes later was
murdered and his head added to the horrifying collection on the
Rostra.

These fearful proscriptions bring into our pages two more
persons who played leading parts in the subsequent drama, namely, the great Julius Cæsar and Cicero. Caius Julius Cæsar was born
in July, 102 B.C., and was therefore about twenty years of age
at the time. He was the scion of a particularly proud patrician
family, but his own branch of it had not of recent years performed
any striking public service. His father, of whom practically nothing is known, had been Prætor and had died in 84 B.C.; but his
mother, Aurelia, who belonged to the Cotta family, was living,
and, indeed, survived to see her son the greatest man of his time.
Little is recorded of her in history, which is an indication, perhaps,
that her character was not outstanding; and Plutarch has un-
intentionally pilloried her for ever by describing her in later
life as "a discreet woman who was continually around her son's
wife." His father's sister, Julia, had married the great Marius, who
was thus his uncle and Marius the Younger his cousin; and this
was enough in itself to damn him in Sulla's eyes. Again, he had
recently been married to Cornelia, the daughter of the late Cinna,
who, it will be recalled, had been one of the chief leaders of the
People and had been one of Sulla's arch-enemies. Moreover, for the
last three years or so he had been notoriously the lover of Servilia, the wife of Marcus Junius Brutus, a man whose whole family
was closely connected with the party of Marius; and it was even
rumoured that he was the father of her child, the little Brutus (who
ultimately was one of his murderers), although he was not more
than seventeen when the boy was born. Servilia was the sister of
that curious fanatic, Cato the Younger, who was later the mainstay
of the aristocratic party; but he, too, was opposed to Sulla.

Cæsar, however, was such a curled and scented young fop,
so overdressed and effeminate in appearance, [9] that nobody could
then accuse him of being a supporter of the rough Proletariat,

[9] Suetonius: *Cæsar*, xlv, xlix, lii; Dion Cassius, xliii, 20.

or a menace to the aristocratic party whose most exaggerated manners he emulated. Sulla therefore decided to deal leniently with
him, and merely ordered him to divorce the offending Cornelia;
but, to his great surprise, the pink-and-white young Cæsar absolutely refused to do this, and fled from Rome, his property being
thereupon confiscated and his name, apparently, proscribed. His
aristocratic relations, however, including, no doubt, the mother of
the little Antony, who was a member of the family of the Cæsars,
pleaded with Sulla to forgive him; and, after some hair-raising
adventures as a fugitive, he was pardoned, whereupon he went
away soldiering, which was the wisest thing he could do, even
though some lady's boudoir seemed to be a more natural place for
him than the camp.

Marcus Tullius Cicero, afterwards Antony's most deadly enemy,
was at this time a rising young barrister of twenty-five, having
been born in January, 106 B.C., the same year in which Pompey
first saw the light. His ancestral home was that same Arpinum, in
the Volscian Mountains, from which Marius had come. He was not
of patrician blood, but he belonged to the local bourgeoisie, and no
doubt he would from the first have sided with the aristocratic party
in Rome had not Sulla, the enemy of his great fellow-townsman,
been its leader. He was afraid, of course, to say anything against
so powerful and so dreaded a man; but he now dared to plead the
cause of one who had suffered indirectly by Sulla's actions, [10] and
thereby he must have endangered his life. A certain wealthy citizen
of Ameria (Amelia) in Umbria, named Sextus Roscius, was murdered by some distant kinsmen, who, in order to escape punishment, persuaded Chrysogonus, a man in Sulla's employ, to get the
name of their victim inserted in one of the proscription-lists; and
when this had been done, Chrysogonus bought the dead man's
confiscated property for a song and divided it with the murderers.
Roscius, however, had left a son of the same name, and, in order to
remove him, these scoundrels now accused him of having himself
killed his father for private motives before his proscription had
been published.

Cicero defended the younger Roscius before the senatorial
court, and boldly laid bare the wickedness of Chrysogonus, al-

---

[10] Cicero: *Pro Roscio Amerino.*

though he knew well enough that the man was high in Sulla's favour. With diplomatic flattery, he declared that Sulla himself was no more to blame for the occurrence than God was for man's frequent misfortunes, for Sulla, like God, was far too busy to know always what his servants were up to; but he asked whether the aristocratic party had won back its control of the State only that rascally menials and lackeys should thus be able to rob innocent men of their goods under pretence of obeying their busy masters' orders. He demanded the punishment of Chrysogonus and the rehabilitation of Roscius, and he won his case so brilliantly that he established himself at once both as a great advocate and as a man of some courage. Sulla, however, seems to have been greatly annoyed by the affair, for his was not the type of mind to overlook the reproach behind Cicero's likening him to God; and the young barrister decided to get out of danger's way by going to Greece, for the ostensible purpose of improving his health and studying rhetoric. Neither he nor Julius Cæsar returned to Rome until after Sulla's death.

Meanwhile Sulla, who had caused himself to be made Dictator, with absolute power for as long as he deemed necessary, energetically set about the reorganization of the government. In order to deprive the Comitia of its power, he decreed that no proposed law should be put to the vote in that assembly until it had already received the sanction of the Senate; but he did not interfere with the technical right of the Comitia to reject measures sent down to them by the Senate, for now that the People's party had not a single man of any standing left alive, this right, he knew, would not be used. At the same time, however, he enfrancised ten thousand of the slaves of the men killed in his proscriptions, and thus created a solid body of voters who looked to him as their patron and were capable of swamping any meeting of the Comitia to which they were called. He also destroyed the powers of the People's Tribunes by the simple device of decreeing that no Tribune could hold office for more than one year, and that the holding of that office debarred him from occupying any other magisterial post. Thus, only men of no importance and without political ambition would be likely to accept the Tribuneship, and dangerous persons like Marius or the Gracchi would not again be found in the

position to exercise the tribunitial veto or to shield themselves behind the sacrosanctity of the office. Moreover, the Senate was empowered to impose a crushing fine upon any Tribune whose conduct
was deemed unbecoming.

It was further decreed that the great offices in the State were
to be held annually, in strict rotation, and at fixed ages, so that
a man in rising from Quæstor to Prætor and from Prætor to Consul
would have to be out of office for long periods between, nor was
he to be allowed to hold the Consulship twice unless an interval of
ten years had elapsed before his second election. Thus he guarded
the State against continuous goverance by one outstanding politician, and placed the real power in the hands of the senators, whose
influence as a body he increased in numerous ways, and whose election he limited, in actuality, to candidates drawn from his own
party. His measures, in fact, insured the absolute control of affairs by the aristocracy, and the People were reduced to complete
impotence. Everything that the Gracchi and Marius had stood for
went by the board; and, at the moment, the great fight between
the Senate and the Comitia, the republicans and the democrats,
was ended by the utter rout of the latter. For the time being Sulla
was like a king, and more than a king, in Rome; but it is certainly
to be said in his favour that he used his unlimited authority in
what he sincerely believed to be the best interests of the Republic.

He was not altogether to blame for some of the atrocities committed in his name. For example, the circumstances of the murder
of Marcus Marius Gratidianus, one of the remaining members of
the family of Marius, were probably beyond his control. This
man was taken to the grave of Catulus, a victim of the great
Marius, and, after being kept there for some time, was tortured to
death as a kind of human sacrifice to the spirit of the dead. He was
first flogged, then his eyes were put out, next his nose, hands, and
feet were cut off, "that he might die as it were piecemeal," [11] and
finally he was decapitated, the severed head being carried away
by Catiline, of whom we shall presently hear more. Another democrat, Bæbius by name, was literally torn limb from limb by a mob
of the opposite faction.

Sulla's attempt to force the youthful Julius Cæsar to divorce

[11] Florus, iii, xxi.

his wife has already been mentioned; and he now interfered like-wise in the matrimonial life of the brilliant young Pompey. Sulla's wife at this time was Cæcilia Metella, niece of that uncompromising supporter of the aristocrats, Metellus, whom Marius had ousted from his command in the war against King Jugurtha. She had previously been married to Aemilius Scaurus, a former Consul, by whom she had had a daughter, Aemilia, who was now Sulla's step-child; and this Aemilia had been married to Manius Glabrio, and was about to have a child by him. But in spite of this fact, her mother, Cæcilia, and Sulla both decided to marry her to Pompey, so that this rising young man might be brought into the family. Unfortunately, Pompey was already married to a girl named Antistia, daughter of the distinguished orator Antistius, who had been killed by the younger Marius because of his aristocratic sympathies; but a trifle such as that was brushed aside by Sulla, who obliged Pompey to divorce her, whereat her mother, deeply feeling the disgrace of it, committed suicide. Aemilia was then divorced from Glabrio and married to Pompey; but she spoilt Sulla's plans by dying a few weeks later when giving birth to her first husband's child in her second husband's house.

Sulla's stern and despotic rule is well exemplified in an incident which occurred at the close of 82 B.C. A certain Lucretius Ofella, who had once belonged to the party of Marius but had deserted to that of Sulla, offered himself as a candidate for the Consulship of the following year, although he had not yet been either Quæstor or Prætor, and was thus acting in defiance of the new law made in that regard by the Dictator. Sulla, therefore, forbade him to stand for election; but Ofella nevertheless went down into the Forum, surrounded by his friends, to canvass votes. Sulla saw him, and, without a moment's hesitation, ordered an officer to go and kill him; and a few minutes later Ofella lay dead.

At the beginning of the year 81 B.C. Sulla celebrated his Triumph, in honour, particularly, of his victories in Greece and Asia Minor. The procession was one of the most splendid ever seen in Rome, but its most striking feature was the group of returned exiles of the aristocratic party, banished under Marius and Cinna, and brought back by Sulla. They were crowned with garlands, and marched joyfully along the streets shouting the praises of their saviour until they were hoarse. Sulla then asked, and of course received, permission to call himself by the name Felix, "the Happy," or, rather, "the Lucky"; for he declared that he was obviously the child of good fortune, the favoured of the gods.

For many days after this he feasted the citizens so lavishly that the surplus meat had to be thrown in quantities into the river, while valuable wine, forty and more years old, was drunk as though it were water. During the festivities, however, his wife, Cæcilia, who had recently given birth to twins, became fatally ill; and Sulla was so upset at thought of anything so unlucky as a death taking place in his home circle that he hastily divorced the dying lady and had her removed from his house, refusing to visit her in her last hours, but giving her a very fine funeral to show his respect for her.

Meanwhile the young Pompey was covering himself with glory in Sicily and Africa, where he had been sent in pursuit of the remnants of the People's army. Having hunted down and killed Carbo and other democratic leaders, he returned to Rome, and went smiling to Sulla, mightily pleased with himself and quite at his ease in the Dictator's awe-inspiring presence. Sulla at once conferred on him the name Magnus, "the Great"; but he was staggered when Pompey then asked for a Triumph, although he was hardly twenty-five years of age and was not old enough even to be a senator. Sulla told him that it was quite impossible to grant his request, but Pompey, nothing daunted, reminded him that the rising sun was more generally worshipped than the setting, thereby indicating that his glory was only beginning whereas Sulla's was on the wane. At this bold remark those who were present held their breath in amazement and fear, while Sulla, who could not believe his ears, asked him to repeat what he had said. Pompey blandly did so, and Sulla was so astounded at his audacity that he seemed for some moments to be quite stupified. But at length he turned with a laugh to the others, and said: "O, very well, then; let the boy triumph, let him triumph!" The irrepressible Pompey thereupon crowned the incident by asking that his triumphal chariot might be drawn by four elephants instead of horses, so that the spectacle might be really unique.

Thus, in September, 81 B.C., Pompey "the Great" celebrated

his Triumph, and thenceforth was second only to the Dictator in the estimation of his party. Meanwhile, Crassus, who had allied himself with Sulla, it will be recalled, at the same time that Pompey had done so, had made a great name for himself as a military leader, but had incurred Sulla's grave displeasure by ordering the execution of certain persons in the provinces without first asking permission, and by seizing their money and also the pay-box of the defeated forces, and enriching himself thereby. For this reason Sulla gave him no further military command, and thereupon Crassus turned his attention to money-making, and soon earned for himself the names *Dives*, "the Rich." He seems to have been bitterly jealous of Pompey, and since he was now debarred from rivalling that dazzling young man's military career, he did his best to establish a commanding position for himself in the city's financial life, and his success in that respect will presently bring him before us as one of the big men of Rome.

It has been pointed out that Sulla, in spite of the hard work of which he was capable, was fond of good living, and was, in fact, a very heavy drinker, as his "mulberry" face testified; and now that he had destroyed the power of the People and the Comitia and had established that of the aristocratic and senatorial party, he began to indulge his inclinations with increasing frequency. In spite of the fact that he was nearly sixty years of age, pretty women and handsome young men continued to attract him as much as they had always done, for, like so many Romans, he was strangely indifferent to the sex of those who caught his roving eye. For years he had expressed a passionate devotion to a romantic actor named Metrobius, and though this personage was now long past his beautiful prime, Sulla still delighted in his very intelligent society. Roscius, a comedian, and Sorex, a mime-dancer, were also his constant companions at dinner, not, however, by any means to the exclusion of several well-known actresses and ladies of easy virtue.

His fourth wife, Cæcilia Metella, it will be recalled, had died at the time of his Triumph; but now, notwithstanding his years and his catholic interests, his erratic fancy was taken by a young society-lady, Valeria, the daughter of Valerius Messala, one of Sulla's noble supporters, and sister-in-law of Hortensius, the famous orator. [12] The story of their meeting is told by Plutarch, and may best be related in his own words. "At a gladiatorial exhibition, this Valeria, who was a beautiful woman of noble birth but had lately been divorced from her husband, had a seat near Sulla; and passing along to it behind him she leaned on him with her hand, and, plucking a little bit of wool from his cloak, carried it to her seat. Sulla looked round, wondering what was the meaning of her action, whereupon she whispered: 'What harm is there, sir, in my wanting to share a little in your good luck?' It was apparent at once that Sulla was not displeased, but was, in fact, intrigued; for he immediately took steps to find out her name, her parentage, and her past. During the performance many side glances passed between them, each of them continually turning to look at the other, and frequently exchanging smiles; and afterwards an introduction was effected, and, in the end, a marriage was arranged." [13]

At the beginning of the year 79 B.C., Sulla nonchalantly resigned his stern and pitiless Dictatorship, and retired with his charming young wife to his villa near Puteoli, close to Baiae, the fashionable resort on the Bay of Naples, where he hoped to enjoy himself in his own way for the remainder of his life. He had always been impatient of the restraints imposed upon him by his office, and he could not be bothered any longer with the worries of autocratic rule. He had created new machinery of government, which, in any case, he wished to test, but which could not be tested so long as he kept the command in his hands. *His* method had always been to kill off his political opponents, or to scare them into obedience; but he was well aware that permanent government could not be carried on by such rough and ready means, and he wanted the senatorial party to learn to stand upon its own feet without that aid from him, the giving of which was becoming more and more tedious now that the pleasure of actual construction was gone.

He wanted leisure in which to write his memoirs; he wanted time for his various intellectual and artistic pursuits; but, above all, he wanted to be left alone to enjoy himself in his own way, to

---

[12] The sister of Hortensius had married Valeria's brother, Valerius Messala Niger.
[13] Plutarch: *Sulla.*

make love, to be merry, and to get drunk to his heart's content, without the critical eyes of the world being fixed upon him. He had become enormously wealthy during his career, and his house and gardens beside the Neapolitan sea were luxurious and beautiful. The charming estates of his friends were dotted all over this part of the country. Hortensius, for instance, lived near by, and had so vast a wine-cellar that he left ten thousand casks of Chian [14] to his heir; while his parks were celebrated for their beautiful trees, for the rare animals which they contained, and for the ponds beside the sea which were stocked with fish. The best society of Rome congregated at Baiæ and other watering-places round about; and thus Sulla could expect to be far more happy here than ever he could be in his office in the capital.

But a year later, in 78 B.C., an early death cut short his hopes of earthly happiness. It is said that he contracted the horrible disease of phthiriasis, that is to say his body became the breeding-ground of lice; but a similar misfortune is attributed to many well-known persons in ancient history, and the story is not readily to be credited. He certainly became very ill, however; and his death was not unexpected. One day he was told that a magistrate named Granius was deferring the payment of a public debt because he believed that Sulla, who was the only man who could force him to pay up, was about to die; and thereupon Sulla sent for him and, after an exchange of hot recriminations, ordered him to be strangled in his presence. The excitement of this violent scene, however, caused him to break a blood-vessel, and he died next day.

On hearing the news the mob went wild with excitement, thinking that the rule of the aristocracy would soon be at an end, and that the party of the People would come back to power. They surrounded the house, shouting that they would not allow the dead man a public funeral; but the young Pompey, who happened to be in the neighbourhood, took matters in hand, and caused the arrangements for the funeral to be made. Meanwhile the reading of the will was proceeded with, and it was found that Sulla had left legacies to every one of his friends and prominent supporters with the one exception of Pompey, whose popularity he had evidently come to resent. But the light-hearted young man pretended

[14] The wine of Chios, the island in the Ægean Sea, was famous in antiquity.

to take no offence at this slight, and himself escorted the body to Rome, where, after a funeral of unprecedented magnificence, it was cremated on the Campus Martius, while senators, nobles, officials, and soldiers marched in procession around the pyre, and countless flute-players poured forth a wild and tender lament.

The little Antony, who now had two younger brothers, Lucius and Caius, was five years of age at this time, and it is hardly likely that in after life he remembered any of these events; yet the fact that his father was one of the Quæstors at about this period, and was a man of social importance, suggests that the child and his brothers may have come under Sulla's polite notice from time to time. The family, however, was not well off, and was generally in debt, on which account it is not to be supposed that their shabby house in Rome was a rendezvous of statesmen and politicians. Nevertheless, Antony's subsequent actions cannot be understood clearly unless we follow further the movement of public affairs which accompanied his growth to manhood.

CHAPTER IV

Antony's Growth to Manhood Amidst the Political Struggles which Culminated in the Catilinarian Conspiracy.

78–62 B.C.

THE Consuls for the year 78 B.C. were Quintus Lutatius Catulus, son of one of the noblest of the victims of Marius and an ardent supporter of Sulla's party, and Marcus Aemilius Lepidus, a wealthy and rather unscrupulous nobleman, who, partly owing to a quarrel with Sulla, was inclining toward the leaderless People's party at the time of the ex-Dictator's death. Lepidus had obtained his Consulship by the aid of Pompey, who, for some unknown reason, had canvassed votes for him in spite of Sulla's warning that the man was not to be trusted and would ultimately turn upon him; and now the prediction proved correct, for Lepidus at once placed himself at the head of the awakening democrats and gathered around him all those discontented sons of Sulla's victims who had attained manhood but were forbidden by the terms of the proscriptions ever to hold office.

Amongst these was Cinna, whose sister, Cornelia, the young Julius Cæsar had married, and who was the son of the famous democratic Consul, Cinna, the colleague of Marius; and immediately upon the death of Sulla this Cinna sent a private message to Cæsar, his brother-in-law, urging him to come home and to throw in his lot with the People's party which, under the leadership of the Consul Lepidus, was going to make short work of the late Sulla's republican government.

The elegant young Cæsar was both ambitious and adventurous, and came back post haste to Rome to see for himself how matters stood, bringing with him a curiously paradoxical reputation. On the one hand, he had unexpectedly distinguished himself by his soldierly qualities while serving at the siege of Mitylene, the chief city of the island of Lesbos, which had been in revolt against Roman rule; and for gallantly saving a soldier's life he had been given the coveted oak-leaf chaplet, the wearing of which on state occasions entitled its possessor to a public salute, the entire audience at a theatre, for instance, rising to its feet on his entry. But, at the same time, his behaviour at the court of the King of Bithynia, [1] whom he had visited more than once on official business, was such that people put the worst construction upon his relationship to this potentate. King Nicomedes the Third, the monarch in question, was then no longer a young man; [2] but his well-known peculiarities, considered in conjunction with Cæsar's notorious effeminacy at this time, give color to a story which one would like to discredit. At any rate, the youthful hero of Mitylene had to submit in Rome to the jests of the ribald, who nicknamed him "The Queen of Bithynia," and declared that his official duties at the court of Nicomedes had been confined to the royal bedchamber. [3]

Yet, at the same time, he was still the recognised lover of Servilia, and people smilingly pointed to that lady's little son, Brutus, and said that Cæsar was certainly the father of the child, if not also the mother. He was, moreover, a fine athlete, a strong swimmer, a perfect horseman, and a brilliant swordsman; and these accomplishments, combined with his courage, his brains, and his self-assurance, already suggested that he was no ordinary young man, and that his phase of effeminacy would presently pass.

He was very good-looking. He was somewhat taller than the average, and had a fresh, fair complexion and skin, a graceful figure, a fine forehead, and dark, thoughtful eyes. The hair on his head always displayed the art of the barber, but on other parts of his body it was carefully removed by tweezers—a practice which afterwards became pretty general in Rome, but which was considered then, as it would be now, an unnecessary and slightly per-

---

[1] The northern corner of the modern Turkey, east of Constantinople.
[2] His father was grown up when he came to the throne in 149 B.C., and he himself seems to have been the eldest son and to have been more than a youth when he succeeded in 91 B.C.
[3] Suetonius: *Cæsar*, xlix; Dion Cassius, xliii, 20.

verted onslaught upon the peculiar and primeval heritage of the male. He had various little mannerisms imitated from those of the fashionable youths of Rome and Greece, and, in particular, he used to adjust his hair by running his fingers lightly and gracefully over it with a feminine movement which in our own day is still char-acteristic of subnormal man. "When I see his hair so carefully ar-ranged," said Cicero at a later date, "and observe him adjusting it with his finger, I cannot imagine that it should enter into such a man's thoughts to subvert the Roman state." [4]

He was what may be described as artistic in his dress, and wore his rather showy garments loosely draped about him with a carefully studied carelessness which had once caused Sulla to speak of him as "that ill-girt young man." Yet he was always well-washed and groomed; and if he was a little too heavily scented, he at any rate never reeked of wine as did so many Romans, for he was extremely temperate. His manners were perfect, he was usually affable to all, and was scrupulously polite, although sometimes his remarks could be very caustic.

He was about twenty-four years of age when he returned to Rome, and, in spite of his love of adventure, was remarkably astute. He saw at once that the revolt of the democrats which was being engineered by the Consul Lepidus, assisted by Marcus Junius Brutus, Servilia's husband, was premature, and he would have nothing to do with it, although his aunt Julia, the widow of Marius, probably joined her appeals to those of his brother-in-law, Cinna, in the attempt to persuade him to take up the People's cause. Lepidus raised an army outside Rome and recklessly marched on the city, declaring that he was coming to bring liberty to the citizens. The capital, however, was successfully defended by his colleague in the Consulship, Catulus; and Pompey, having been given the command of the other senatorial forces, attacked and de-feated Brutus whom he put to death, and thereupon Lepidus fled to Sardinia, where his misfortunes, which included the infidelity of his wife, so preyed upon his mind that he fell sick and died, leav-ing behind him, however, a son who will appear later in these pages as one of Antony's colleagues. The hopes of the People's party were thus speedily crushed, and the young Cæsar must have

[4] Plutarch: *Cæsar.*

thanked his lucky stars that he had not followed the advice of his brother-in-law, who was now a fugitive in Spain.

For a short time Cæsar remained in Rome, puzzling his friends as to whether he was to be regarded as a person of promising character, or a fashionable man about town whose brilliance and charm would prove to be his undoing; but after a while he revealed a daring spirit by taking an active part in the prosecution of the ex-Consul, Dolabella, an important figure in the aristocratic party, on the charge of bribery. His speech against him, though delivered in rather a high, shrill voice, proved him to be a natural orator, with a fine sense of language, a little cold and pedantic, perhaps, but unquestionably eloquent. Dolabella was acquitted, however, and thereupon Cæsar made a second attempt at oratorical honours by conducting the prosecution of Caius Antonius, Antony's aristocratic but rather disreputable uncle, on a similar charge, again without winning the case. It was seen, of course, that the young man had the democratic leanings to be expected of a nephew of the great Marius; but since these views were out of season just now in Rome, and many angry looks were turned upon him, he wisely went off to study oratory in Rhodes for a while, with the object of making for himself a career later at the Roman Bar. Servilia, meanwhile, married a second husband, Decimus Junius Silanus, a rising politician, but retained, nevertheless, a romantic affection for the charming young dandy, the angle of whose approach to the wide subject of sex evidently appealed to the peculiarities of her own nature.

On his way to Rhodes, Cæsar had the misfortune to be captured by Cilician pirates near the little island of Pharmacusa (Fermaco) off the coast of Asia Minor. These men at once demanded a ransom of twenty talents, but with great bravado their elegant young captive laughed at their ignorance of his social importance, and, telling them that he was worth at least fifty, despatched his attendants to raise the larger sum at Miletus and other not distant cities where his family was known. For five or six weeks he lived in the pirates' camp, treating his bloodthirsty captors with such a mixture of insolence and patronizing banter that it is a marvel his throat was not cut. He insisted upon joining in their sports and exercises, running races with them and jeering at them for not being able to beat him. Around the camp-fire at night he used to read them his own poetry, and when they did not applaud he smacked their heads and called them illiterate savages; or, when he wished to sleep, he sent them peremptory orders to make less noise.

At length his messengers returned bringing the ransom-money; and thereupon Cæsar bade the pirates goodbye, cheerily promising them that he would come back one day and have them all crucified, at which they laughed heartily, having conceived quite a liking for the audacious fellow. But he meant what he said, and having raised a small force at the port of Miletus, sailed back to the island, took the pirates by surprise, brought them in chains to Pergamus, and there, not waiting for authorization from the Roman governor, had them all crucified. But having gone to jeer at them as they hung on their forest of crosses on the hillside outside the city, he was unexpectedly touched by their sufferings which, in the ordinary course of events, would have lasted for several days until hunger, thirst, and exposure had slowly killed them; and he therefore very kindly ordered his men to get up on ladders and cut all their throats. He then went his way to Rhodes, where he entered the school of Apollonius the orator, an institute which Cicero had just left.

Cicero arrived back in Rome in 77 b.c., at the age of twenty-nine—a tall, thin young man, with a high and thoughtful forehead, a sallow skin due to indigestion, and a voice pitched so far up the scale that when he spoke with any excitement people feared lest he should injure his vocal chords; [5] and soon he began to make a name for himself in public life, being sent as Quæstor to Sicily in 75 b.c. Meanwhile, Pompey had been ordered to Spain to deal with a rebellion there, and was therefore not available when the government was looking for a capable officer to command the military and naval forces which it had decided to despatch against the pirates, whose widespread activities had become intolerable. Marcus Antonius, the father of the now eight-year-old Antony, was Prætor at this time; and at last it was agreed that he should be given the command, although he probably had as little taste for it as he had ability. He was the son of the great orator,

[5] Plutarch: *Cicero.*

who had been an artistic, eccentric personage of improvident habits, notorious for throwing his money in showers to the people when he happened to be in funds; and he himself was a careless, good-natured, generous man, generally more or less bankrupt;[6] and much afraid of his patrician wife Julia, the kinswoman of the young Julius Cæsar, for she was a stern upholder of the honour of the Cæsars and the Antonii, about which her easy-going husband does not appear to have cared very greatly.

An illuminating story is told of him by Plutarch. A friend came to see him one day to borrow some money, but as usual, there was very little in the house, and, even if there had been sufficient for the purpose, it would have been in the charge of Julia. Marcus Antonius therefore hit upon the novel expedient of sending for a basin of water, saying that he wished to shave himself; and when the servant, having regard to the presence of a guest, had brought the water in the best silver basin the family possessed, Antonius pretended to begin to shave, then sent the servant away, and gave the basin to his friend to convert into money. Unfortunately, however, Julia quickly missed it, and stormed about the house, accusing everybody in the place of having stolen it; and at last her husband was obliged to confess what he had done and to ask her pardon.

The campaign against the pirates obliged him to make his headquarters in the area of hostilities, and it seems that the little Antony and his two brothers were left in their mother's care in Rome. She was a proud woman, and she appears to have impressed upon the boys the glory of their lineage, explaining to them that they were the direct descendants, both through her and their father, of the immortal gods, for the Julian family, that is to say the Cæsars, claimed descent from the goddess Venus, while the Antonii, although remotely of plebeian stock, traced their pedigree back to Hercules. But her pride must have received many cruel blows when from time to time during the next two years news was brought to Rome that her husband was hopelessly bungling the war, that he had been completely outmanuevred by the pirates, and that he had become little better than a pirate himself, by reason of the endless demands he was making for food and money for his men from the towns

[6] Cicero: *Philippic ii,* xviii; iii, vi.

within the range of his activities. People in Rome began sarcasti-
cally to call him *Creticus*, because of his ineffectual actions against
Crete, the pirates' base; and at last, in about 73 B.C., came the
tidings that he had died. The little Antony, then ten years of age,
was old enough to feel the loss of his kindly and indulgent father;
and for some time he and his brothers were, no doubt, the object of
the commiserations of all the ladies and gentlemen of Rome's fashionable world who came to the house to offer their sympathy.

Julia, the widow, however, was not broken-hearted: she was
glad, perhaps, to be rid of one who had so signally failed to add
any lustre to his line; and very soon afterwards she married another man, Publius Cornelius Lentulus, a member of one of the
proudest patrician families, who had already been Prætor and
was expecting soon to be Consul. Lentulus was a rather shameless personage, often mixed up in society scandals, and notorious
for a kind of lazy impertinence at which people were pleased to
smile because he carried it off with such a charmingly aristocratic air.

When he had been Quæstor in 81 B.C. he had been called before the terrible Sulla to answer charges of corruption brought
against him; but he had merely shrugged his shoulders and, making a half turn away from the Dictator, had extended the back of
his leg towards him, in a gesture which Plutarch explains as that
of a boy who has made a blunder in playing at ball and expects
a smack for it. The cheeky movement was called *Sura*, the presenting of one's *leg;* and thenceforth Sura was his nickname. His
manners and appearance were so elegant that Cicero [7] coined the
word *lentulitas* to denote the outward qualities of the blue-blooded;
but he had more charm than wisdom, and was too bored and lan-
guid [8] to be taken very seriously, although, ever since a certain
soothsayer had told him that he was destined to rule Rome, he
had shown an unexpected interest in political movements which
offered any promise of an easy attainment of this half-hearted
ambition. As a stepfather to the young Antony he does not appear to have been a conspicuous success, and since he was neither
rich nor economical, the same struggle against debt [9] which had

---

[7] Cicero: *Ad Familiares,* iii, 7.
[8] Cicero: *In Catilinam,* iii, 7, 16; Dion Cassius, xxxvii, 32.
[9] Sallust: *Catilina,* xvii.

troubled the household in the boy's infancy continued to form the
dark background of his growth to adolescence; but Antony seems
to have been fond of him, and in later life showed much respect
for his memory.

In this same year, 73 B.C., Julius Cæsar returned to Rome
from Rhodes, having daringly crossed the Adriatic in a little,
four-oared boat so as to escape the attentions of the pirates, [10] and
he was, no doubt, a frequent visitor at the house of Lentulus, over
which Julia, his kinswoman, presided; for the political discussions
in her salon may well have been to the young man's liking, since
they were inspired by a spirit of mild revolt from the hidebound
aristocratic party and a leaning towards democracy, wherein Lentulus saw a better chance of personal advancement. There was
now a widespread feeling that the government bequeathed by Sulla had not been at all successful, and that the massacre of the
leaders of the People's party had removed an opposition which was
necessary to the health of the State; and in this house Cæsar was
able to criticise the men in power without arousing any animosity
in his host, whose loyalty to his fellow-aristocrats was not conspicuous.

In the house of Servilia, which he also frequented, he was
able to speak even more openly of the future of the People's party; for in spite of the fact that that lady had presented her
husband, Silanus, with three children since Cæsar last saw her,
she was still very much in love with the clever young man, and
shared with him his keen interest in the reviving activities of
the democracy, although her brother, Cato, was becoming a strong
supporter of the aristocracy. Cæsar, in fact, was beginning to feel
that his relationship to the late Marius, and to his surviving widow,
Julia, was no longer a drawback; and in several houses which he
visited there was a decided movement away from the government
instituted by Sulla, and a consequent attitude of respect to Cæsar
as the nephew of Marius.

One of the most powerful of the younger men in Rome at this
time was Crassus, now thirty-four years of age. Ever since Sulla
had checked his military career he had given his attention, as has
been said above, to the making of his fortune. One of his ingen-

[10] Velleius, ii, xliii.

ious methods of acquiring property is worthy of notice. He organized a highly-trained, private fire-brigade, some five-hundred strong; and whenever a fire was reported he went to the spot with his men, and offered to buy the burning house and the endangered buildings around, these generally being sold to him, in view of their peril, at absurdly low figures. He then set his highly skilled men to work to put out the fire. If, however, his offer was refused, he called the firemen off and left the place to burn. In this manner, says Plutarch, a very large part of Rome passed into his possession.

He also made a great commercial business of the supplying of highly skilled slaves. He bought likely young men cheaply in the open market, and trained them, in schools which he had instituted, to be manuscript-copyists, letter-writers, secretaries, accountants, household servants, waiters, cooks, gardeners, carpenters, silversmiths, and so forth. He himself supervised their education, and often personally lectured to them; and in the end he sold at very high prices those whom his own houses and vast business concerns could not absorb.

Now, in this year 73 B.C., a very remarkable insurrection broke out which at one time seriously menaced the security of the state. A certain Lentulus Batiates, following somewhat the methods of Crassus, had organized a super-school for slaves in Capua, north of Naples, where he trained a large number of Gauls and Thracians as gladiators, and sold them at good prices to fight at the public shows which were contantly taking place in Rome and other cities. These men were no better than prisoners condemned to death, for they were kept in captivity until ordered out to fight, and one by one they were then killed for the entertainment of the thoughtless crowds which watched their enforced and pitiful duels. Gladiators usually had a great respect for their calling and were notoriously obedient to their masters and trainers. "Even when sinking under his wounds," says Cicero, "a gladiator will send a message to his master to know whether he has any further orders, since, if the master thinks he has done enough, he would be glad to be allowed to lie down and die." [11]

But Batiates was a particularly heartless man, and his pupils at length revolted. Under the leadership of a heroic Thracian

[11] Cicero: *Tusculanarum Disputationum,* ii, 17, 41.

named Spartacus, a number of them escaped to the hills, where they were joined by all the outlaws and run-away slaves who could reach them. In battle after battle they defeated the forces sent against them, and took possession of their arms; and at length Spartacus is said to have been able to place no less than forty thousand well-armed men in the field, though how he collected so great a force is a mystery which has never been solved.

Pompey was still away in Spain at the time, and Lucullus, the only other military officer of distinction, was in the East, trying to suppress a renewed insurrection of Mithradates. When both the Consuls for the year 72 B.C. had been badly defeated by Spartacus, the distracted government called upon Crassus to take command, for his brilliant work under Sulla had not been forgotten; and after a protracted campaign he succeeded in 71 B.C., in cornering the rebels in southern Italy, and inflicting a complete defeat upon them, the brave Spartacus being cut to pieces with the best of his men. A certain number, however, escaped northwards, and, after many adventures, were approaching the Alps, when Pompey, who was returning with his victorious army from Spain, chanced upon them and overwhelmed them. Six thousand prisoners were taken, and these were crucified at intervals along the whole length of the highroad between Rome and Capua, so that for days afterwards those who travelled along that road were obliged to witness, every two hundred yards or so, the agony of a delirious or fainting man, fastened to a cross, slowly dying of thirst and exposure.

Both Pompey and Crassus reached Rome with their armies at about the same time; but the former, in view of his victories in Spain, which were painted by him in most glowing colours, received the greater honours, and was at once elected Consul for the coming year, 70 B.C. Crassus then, swallowing his pride, asked his help in obtaining the other Consulship for himself, and, with this generously-given aid, was forthwith elected.

These two men, it will be remembered, had been strong supporters of the aristocratic party, but Sulla had insulted them both—Pompey, by leaving him out of his will, and Crassus, by obstructing his military career; and now each followed his own inclination and also the trend of public opinion by coming out on the side of the democrats and by undoing Sulla's work. It is true that Crassus was not so whole-hearted as his colleague in this change of front; but if he acted every now and then as a break upon the wheels of Pompey's popular progress, it was chiefly from motives of personal jealousy that he did so. At any rate they together rescinded the law which obliged the measures placed before the Comitia to be approved first by the Senate; and they raised again to its former level the power of the Tribunes of the People, who were now allowed once more to hold other magisterial offices after that of the Tribuneship. They also restored the office of Censor which Sulla had abolished; and they approved of the first measure proposed by him, namely that of turning out of the Senate all those aristocrats whose private lives were not above reproach.

This drastic action, which involved no less than sixty-four senators, fell particularly heavily upon the family of young Antony, who was now a boy of thirteen, already old enough to understand the disgrace of it; for both his stepfather, Lentulus, who had been one of the Consuls of the previous year, 71 B.C. and his uncle, Caius Antonius, the younger brother of his late father, were expelled from the Senate in this political clean-up, on the grounds of "luxury" and ill-living. As a consequence of this disaster, Lentulus found himself cold-shouldered by the aristocracy, and scorned by the party of the People towards which, as has been said, he had been inclining slightly; and for the next few years Antony must have heard nothing that was good of either side.

Meanwhile the famous trial of Caius Verres, in which the ambitious Cicero made his name, became the central point of the struggle between the conservatives and the People. Verres had been one of Sulla's trusted officers, and later, from 73 to 71 B.C., had been governor of Sicily, where he had behaved with such arrogant despotism that, immediately on his departure, the Sicilians had brought an action against him. The prosecution was placed in the hands of Cicero, who, gauging the trend of public opinion, had found it expedient to become a supporter of the democrats; and the defence was entrusted to the aristocratic Hortensius who, it will be recalled, was related by marriage to the late Sulla. On the one side, the People were determined that Verres should suffer for his tyranny; on the other, the nobles were equally determined that he should be acquitted.

The charges against him were manifold. He had amassed such wealth from the unfortunate Sicilians that he himself declared he would still be a rich man even if he were forced to disgorge two-thirds of it. He had accepted money from everybody in the form of bribes, or had taken it from them by sheer robbery. He had appropriated public funds to his own use, and had so continuously cheated the farmers and vine-growers of the sums due to them that he had reduced the agricultural population to beggary. He had seduced the daughters of respectable citizens by the score; he had unjustly caused people to be put to death or imprisoned; and, worst of all, he had refused to listen to the appeal of a certain condemned prisoner who, as a Roman citizen, had claimed his right to be sent back to Italy for trial, and had crucified him on the seashore in sight of the Italian coast, so that in his last agonies the wretched man might see before him his unattainable land of refuge.

Like many Roman noblemen of this period, Verres was a keen collector of works of art and antiques; and since Sicily had been full of works of art and antiques and *objets d'art*, he had carried away with him a priceless collection of masterpieces which he had acquired either by purchase at absurdly low prices dictated by himself, or by actual extortion. Glorious pieces of sculpture by the famous Greek masters Praxiteles, Myron, Silanion, and Polycletus, had passed into his hands; he had made off with the magnificent gold and silver plate from the tables of rich men with whom he had dined; he had filched the gold and ivory ornaments from the gates of the temple of Pallas at Syracuse; from the walls of the same temple he had taken the historic paintings; he had stolen the statue of Ceres from her own holy shrine at Enna (Castro Giovanni); and even the statues standing in public places in the various cities had been taken down from their pedestals and added to his collection.

The rich aristocrats of Rome smiled at these latter transgressions, for most of them were themselves enthusiastic collectors, not above a little villainy in the acquisition of artistic treasures; but the democrats, who knew nothing of the connoisseur's delight in competitive possession, appraised this man at his true worth and called him a common thief. So greatly did they despise all artistic pretensions that Cicero, in denouncing these robberies, was obliged to pretend that he himself did not know anything about art, and had merely learnt the names of the famous Greek sculptors during the preparation of his brief. "One of these statues," he said with a smile, [12] "was by Praxiteles—you see that in getting up my case I have learnt the names of the artists. Another was a work by Myron—yes, Myron was the name, I think. A third was by . . . Now what was the name of the artist? Let me see. O, yes, thank you for reminding me; he was called Polycletus."

For thirteen days the trial of Verres proceeded amidst intense excitement, and gradually it became apparent that the opinion of plain men—mere proletarians—was going to prevail against that of the aristocrats. On the fourteenth day Verres fled from Rome.

There was now no doubt that the People's party was once more to be reckoned with; but it was the impetuous Julius Cæsar, who, at the age of thirty-four, first put public opinion openly to the test. In the year 68 B.C. his aunt Julia, the widow of the great Marius, died; and at her funeral Cæsar had the boldness to display publicly the statues of Marius which nobody had dared to exhibit since the days when Sulla had declared him an enemy of the State. Their appearance caused a certain amount of booing on the part of the opposing faction, but the crowd in general clapped their hands and shouted their applause. Yet Cæsar was not satisfied that the tide had really turned, and he preferred to avoid committing himself. He was, moreover, immensely proud of his aristocratic ancestry, and if the People were beginning to see in him a future leader of their party, he gave them no reason to regard him as one of themselves. He was no plebeian, like Marius, and he let them know it.

"My aunt Julia," he declared in his funeral oration, "derived her descent, on her mother's (my grandmother's) side, from a race of kings, and, on her father's (my grandfather's) side, from the immortal gods. For the Marcii Reges, her mother's family, trace their genealogy back to Ancus Marcius, the fourth King of Rome; and the Julii, our family, derive their descent from the goddess Venus. We therefore unite in our lineage the sacred majesty of kings, the

---

[12] Cicero: *In Verrem*, iv, 2, 4.

chiefest of men, and the divine majesty of gods, to whom kings themselves are subject." [13] Such words, spoken by an elaborately dressed and scented personage with peculiar and effeminate gestures, were the reverse of democratic; and yet there were these figures of Marius to remind the crowd that the speaker was no other than his nephew.

In this same year, 68 B.C., Cæsar's wife, Cornelia, the daughter of Cinna, the colleague of Marius, also died; whereupon he married Pompeia, daughter of Quintus Pompeius Rufus, and grand-daughter of Sulla. Pompeia's father was one of the men murdered by Marius; and both on this account and because her mother was Sulla's daughter, she must have been by every instinct an enemy of the People's party. The marriage, therefore, suggested that Cæsar desired to belong neither to one political camp nor to the other, but wished to hold an individual position as a man with equally balanced aristocratic and democratic connections. He was already a prominent figure in Rome; and he had now definitely begun his political career by obtaining the post of Quæstor.

He had a great deal to live down. When people talked about the exploits of the popular Pompey and said that he was a very King of Rome, there were those who laughingly declared that Cæsar, then, was *Queen* of Rome; [14] and once when he was asking the Senate to make a grant to the Princess Nysa, daughter of King Nicomedes of Bithynia, and had spoken of that king's great kindness to him, the highly respectable Cicero sharply replied "Please say no more of that; we all know what he gave you and what you gave him!" [15]

Moreover, his love-affairs with fashionable women in Rome which, as he grew older, were crowding out the episodes of the Bithynian kind, were causing a new crop of scandals. Everybody knew that Servilia, the wife of Junius Silanus, and sister of Cato, was his mistress, and most people guessed that her son, Brutus, was his child; and now it was being rumoured, with apparent truth, that he was in love with Mucia, the wife of Pompey, while, at the same time, his name was linked with those of Tertulla, the

[13] Suetonius: *Julius Cæsar,* vi.
[14] *Ibid.,* xlix.
[15] *Ibid.,* xlix.

wife of Crassus, Posthumia, the wife of a rising statesman named Servius Sulpicius, and Lollia, the wife of Aulus Gabinius, a man who was afterwards to be the friend and patron of the young Antony.[16]

At about this time the government decided to make another attempt to exterminate the pirates whose activities had been increased by the failure of Antony's father to check them. The above-mentioned Gabinius, therefore, proposed that Pompey should be placed in command of the operations; and Cæsar seconded the motion so eagerly that people were unkind enough to say that he evidently wanted the handsome husband of Mucia out of the way. At any rate Pompey was duly appointed, being given such extraordinary powers that a good deal of fear was felt in Rome that he might take advantage of them to the detriment of republican institutions. In a very few weeks he utterly destroyed the power of the pirates, captured ninety of their battleships and innumerable smaller vessels, took prisoner no less than twenty thousand men, and received the surrender of all their strongholds; but, being now a good democrat, he dealt very leniently with his conquered foes, and turned most of them into honest colonists, a proceeding which greatly outraged the republicans in Rome whose militaristic and aristocratic tradition was one of blood and iron, and who expected him to crucify every man who fell into his hands, as he crucified the followers of Spartacus.

Meanwhile, the aristocrat, Lucullus, who was in command of the Roman armies in the east, in spite of many victories was having great difficulty in bringing the war against Mithradates to a successful conclusion; and now the Comitia proposed that Pompey, their own beloved democrat, should be created generalissimo with the powers of Dictator in the East, a measure almost tantamount to making him "absolute monarch of all the Roman Empire."[17] The aristocratic party opposed the bill with vehemence, and Crassus lent this opposition his support; but Cicero, who still belonged to the People's party which later he deserted, was strongly in favour of it, as also was Julius Cæsar, and, indeed, the public in

---

[16] Suetonius (*Julius Cæsar*, *l*) says that his relations with these ladies "are admitted by all."

[17] Plutarch: *Pompey.*

general was so confident that Pompey was the right man for the job that when somebody suggested at a meeting that the command should be divided, the shout of "No!" was loud and sharp enough—so the story went—to cause a bird which happened to be flying overhead to drop stunned from the sky. In the spring of 66 B.C., therefore, Pompey was given the supreme command, whereupon he set out upon a career of conquest which raised his already tremendous reputation to sublime heights.

But during the next three years or so, while he was marching from victory to victory, very serious events took place in Rome which, in the end, involved the young Antony's immediate domestic circle in ruin. The trouble was caused in the first place by the fact that as soon as Pompey had gone, the aristocratic party began to conduct a ruthless campaign against the democrats, with the object of crushing their attempts to reorganize themselves. But the democratic spirit had already infected once more the minds of people of all ranks; and the nobles themselves were now sharply divided into those who supported the existing government and the strictly conservative institutions of their class, and those who, like Antony's stepfather, Lentulus, were leaning towards the popular party.

A great many young patricians were breaking away from the rigid traditions of aristocracy; and fashionable society now regarded it as rather smart to sympathise with the aspirations of the People. But the reins of government were in the grip of an oligarchy of elderly senators of noble birth and hereditary wealth who looked with disfavour upon this unconventional attitude of the younger set, and were determined to keep out of office all those who were tainted with democratic sympathies, and also all who were leading the rather fast life which was at this time the fashion. Thus the many young men whose extravagances had landed them in financial difficulties saw no hope of recovering their fortunes by the time-honoured expedient of obtaining lucrative government posts; and these men all looked to the day when the power should pass from the hands of what may be described as the Old Brigade.

A new leader of the democracy, however, was rising into promi-

nence. Lucius Sergius Catilina [18]—Catiline, as he is now called—
was a middle-aged man of noble birth, who, in spite of a somewhat tarnished reputation, moved in the highest society, [19] was
looked up to by most of the younger aristocrats, both those who
were in financial straits and those who were blessed with plenty, [20]
and, at the same time, had an immense following amongst the
People. [21] He was an arresting figure: a man of powerful and compelling character, violent, unscrupulous, and lacking in morals, but
a born leader of men. History, however, has heaped such abuse upon him, and has so established him as a sort of fiend—in fact, the
Guy Fawkes of Rome—that it is almost useless for me to defend
him as the facts impel me to do; but there is no doubt, at any
rate, that some of the most eminent Roman patricians of his time
courted him and were his enthusiastic supporters, [22] and the point
is not to be overlooked that what we have against him can all be
traced back to the envenomed tongue and pen of his bitterest enemy,
Cicero. [23]

In the Consular elections of 66 B.C., the two Consuls chosen
for the following year were Publius Autronius and Publius Sulla,
both of whom were democrats, and their victory over the aristocratic candidates threw the government into a state of panic, for,
since the death of the Dictator Sulla, the Consuls had always belonged to the conservative party. A trumped-up charge of bribery
was therefore brought against these two men by the nobles, their
election was quashed, and the government announced that its own
two candidates, Aurelius Cotta and Manlius Torquatus, had been
chosen in their stead.

At this, Catiline, burning with indignation, conspired with his
democratic friends to prevent these two taking office at the new
year. It was whispered that he was prepared to have them killed if

[18] The chief authorities for the famous Catilinarian conspiracy are Cicero's Orations against Catiline, which were the main source of Sallust's monograph on the
subject; the *Julius Cæsar* of Suetonius; Plutarch's *Cicero;* Appian's *Civil Wars,* book
ii; Dion Cassius; and Florus.

[19] Cicero: *Pro Cælio,* 6.

[20] Sallust: *Catilina,* xvii; Cicero: *Ad Atticum,* i, 14, 5.

[21] Sallust: *Catilina,* xxxvii.

[22] Florus, iv, i; Appian: *Civil Wars,* ii, 2.

[23] In 1865 Prof. E. S. Beesly put forward a solitary defence of him in the *Fort-
nightly Review,* with which I find myself in agreement; but it had little effect.

necessary, and there were rumours that Julius Cæsar, the budding democrat, was in secret agreement with him—a report which was the more readily believed because Cæsar had already been accused of complicity in other plots of this kind, [24] and was regarded as a very dangerous man. Be this as it may, the two aristocrats entered upon their Consulship at the beginning of 65 B.C. without disturbance, and gossip had to be content to say that Catiline's dark plans had miscarried.

Catiline now determined to stand, himself, for the next Consulship—that of the coming year, 64 B.C.; but just before the elections in the summer of 65 B.C., the aristocratic party, repeating its successful policy, brought a charge of corruption against him—a brazen piece of trickery intended solely to interfere with his candidature. At this, Cicero, who intended to stand for a Consulship himself in the following year, made the proposal that he should defend Catiline, and obtained the consent of the prosecution thereto, his purpose being to place Catiline under an obligation to him, so that they might the more amicably work together if they were both candidates at the next year's elections. [25] Catiline apparently declined his aid; but he was obliged to resign his candidature pending the trial; and Lucius Cæsar, Antony's uncle, who was a conservative, was elected, with another aristocrat, Marcius Figulus, as his colleague. Catiline cleared himself of the charge, of course, but this fact only added to his bitterness and to the rage of his supporters, who now saw clearly that the government would not stick at anything to keep its opponents out of office.

Matters rapidly approached a crisis; and in the next year, 64 B.C., the young Antony must have found himself in the very centre of the disturbance, and the disaster which was to come upon him must already have been scented in the air. It was the irony of fate that the dark clouds began to gather just when things were going so very well for the family of the Antonii, and when, in spite of their chronic insolvency, they were being received everywhere as people of the highest social distinction. Fashionable Rome had agreed to forget that Lentulus, Antony's stepfather, and Caius Antonius, his uncle, had been expelled from the Senate a few years ago; and, in fact, society now regarded that occurrence as a politi-

[24] Suetonius: *Cæsar*, ix.   [25] Cicero: *Ad Atticum*, 1, 2.

cal contretemps which might have happened to anybody. In this
year, Lucius Cæsar, Antony's mother's brother, was Consul; Caius
Antonius was a candidate for the Consulship of the following year;
and Lentulus was a candidate for the Prætorship, a post which
would serve as a stepping-stone to his candidature for a second
term of office as Consul. Antony, therefore, who was now nine-
teen, must have been cutting quite a figure in society, being so
well-connected; and there can be little doubt that he was one of
that ever increasing host of young men who regarded Catiline as
their hero. [26]

Catiline, who was a close friend of Antony's family, put himself forward once more as a candidate for the Consulship for the
year 63 B.C.; and he and Caius Antonius were already planning
what they would do if they were elected together. The lazy and
elegant Lentulus was an interested party to these discussions;
and amongst the men of note who talked matters over were Julius
Cæsar and the multi-millionaire, Crassus. In various ways, Catiline
attempted to win support for his candidature. To those who were
in the hands of money-lenders he said that it would be his first
business to relieve them of their burdens; and the fact that Crassus
was connected with the project indicates, I think, that the great
financier had some scheme of relief which would be profitable to
himself in the end, such as the paying off of the usurers and the
taking over of the debts on terms easier to the debtors. To the vast
numbers of small landowners, many of them old soldiers, who had
mortgaged their properties, [27] Catiline offered a bill which would
remove the immediate menace of ruin from them, though in the
end, I dare say, it would commit them to the mercy of Crassus.
And to the impoverished working classes in general he promised
that share in the pillage of the rich which every demagogue dan-
gles before the eyes of the electorate.

"Ever since the government has fallen into the power of a
few," he said, [28] "all the rest of us, whether patricians or plebeians, have been regarded as a mere mob. All influence, power,
honour, and wealth, are in their hands; and to us they have left

[26] Sallust: *Catilina*, xiv, xvi, xvii.
[27] Cicero: *In Catilinam*, ii; Sallust: *Catilina*, xvi.
[28] Sallust: *Catilina*, xx, xxi.

only rebuffs, difficulties, prosecutions, and poverty." He spoke with all the more bitterness because he himself was deeply in debt, and knew that before the year was out he would have to meet his obligations. [29]

The man he most feared was Cicero, who had lately abandoned the democratic party—as was inevitable in a personage of his profoundly conventional outlook—and now was also a candidate for the Consulship, in the interests of the oligarchy. Being a provincial of modest family, and having thus espoused the cause of the old-fashioned and exclusive aristocracy, he was far more concerned about being a gentleman of the old school than any born gentleman of that school could ever trouble to be. He practised high-principles not unconsciously, as a natural code dictated by the heart, but consciously, as something to be proud of and to boast about. "I never experience so much pleasure," he once wrote with disarming candor,[30] "as I do in the contemplation of my own incorruptibility. It is not so much the credit I get for it, though that is immense, as the thing itself which delights me."

He was not so thin now as he used to be; his digestion was better, and he was putting on flesh. He was, in fact, becoming a pompous and imposing personage, very correct and ceremonious, and astonishingly vain and self-important;[31] and with all his heart he detested these gentlemen-adventurers—Catiline, Lentulus, Julius Cæsar, and the like—who were always being involved in unsavoury scandals, who were reckless and dissolute, not caring a bit what people thought of them, and yet whose misdeeds were strangely insufficient to obscure the fact that they were something which Cicero was not. Unprincipled though they were, and playing at being democrats largely for their own ends, they obviously belonged by a kind of natural right to Rome's most fashionable society, whereas Cicero, with all his acquired dignity, was aware that he had no such birthright, and, indeed, smarted under the consciousness of the fact. It was only by a paradoxical transference of allegiance which is not infrequently to be observed in the political field, that he was the exponent of the

[29] Cicero: *In Catilinam,* i.
[30] Cicero: *Ad Atticum,* v, 20, 6.
[31] The ancient authorities are agreed as to this. Sir Charles Oman (*Seven Roman Statesmen,* p. 189) describes him as a man of "idiotic vanity."

ideals of the conventional Roman nobility, and that Catiline and his friends were the representatives of the People; and he was touched on the raw when Catiline disdainfully called him a mere immigrant,[32] from the provinces.

As the consular elections drew near it became clear that Caius Antonius was fairly sure of being chosen as one of the two Consuls, but the rivalry of Catiline and Cicero as candidates for the other Consulship was intense. Cicero ostentatiously stood for honour, integrity, and the highest traditions of Roman political life; and he advocated a strong rule by a republican oligarchy which would keep the frivolous young nobles under control, and the masses in their place. Catiline, on the other hand, stood for a more even distribution of wealth, easier treatment of the people, the humanizing of the government, the widening of its sympathies, and the wresting of the power from the hands of those obstinate and old-fashioned nobles who had turned so large a part of the nation into potential rebels. The People's party was being steadily deprived of all the hopes which had lately begun to be revived, and the Comitia seemed to be unable to make any headway against the hidebound Senate; for even the Tribunes of the People were forced upon them by the government. In the year 63 B.C., for instance, Cato was Tribune, and he was an aristocrat of the old school, whose hatred of democracy was intensified by the galling fact that his sister, Servilia, was the mistress of Julius Cæsar.

Catiline was a man of restless, highly-strung temperament, recklessly brave, clever, versatile, and eloquent. He was a romantic figure, having a pale, haggard face, and haunted eyes; and he is described as being always in pursuit of the unattainable,[33] and perhaps a little mad.[34] When he was in luck he was prodigal of his money, being at all times surrounded by hosts of friends, particularly young noblemen of adventurous spirit—"young fops with youthful little beards," Cicero calls them;[35] and when hard times were upon him he endured hunger and cold, and even want of sleep, without complaint. But he had a bad

---

[32] Sallust: *Catilina*, xxxi. The word is *inquilinus*, "lodger."
[33] Sallust: *Catilina*, v.   [34] Appian: *Civil Wars*, ii, 2.
[35] Cicero: *Ad Atticum*, i, 14, 5.

reputation; and had he not been of noble birth—the last, indeed, of an ancient race,[36] he would hardly have escaped punishment for some of his escapades.

In his early life he had fallen in love with a young society girl; and, in consequence, she had become the mother of a daughter, who in turn, scandal said that he had seduced.[37] His rival for the Consulship had particular reason to dislike him, for Fabia, a Vestal Virgin, or nun as we should now say, who was the sister of Cicero's wife, Terentia, was one of the women whom he had led astray, though she had been acquitted of the charge[38] and had escaped the punishment of being buried alive, which was the Vestal's penalty for allowing natural instinct to get the better of her. He was now married to an exquisite creature named Aurelia Orestilla, "in whom," as Sallust says, "no decent man at any time of her life commended anything but her beauty"; and his enemies said that he had committed murder to get her, "from which cause distraction was plainly apparent in his every feature and look."[39]

Cicero, whose voice had wonderfully responded to a severe training in oratory, was an extremely eloquent and persuasive speaker, and he made so forceful an attack upon the character of his rival that Catiline was rejected. His tirades against Caius Antonius, however, were not so successful; and although Cicero had described him as a mere gladiator and charioteer, in reference to sports which he enjoyed, and had said that he and Catiline were two daggers drawn against Rome,[40] the great orator could not prevent his election. Thus Cicero and Caius Antonius found themselves the two chosen Consuls; but when they came into office at the beginning of 63 B.C. Cicero managed to persuade his colleague to abandon his association with Catiline. Lentulus, Antony's step-father, however, maintained his friendship with the unsuccessful candidate; and this fact must thus have brought bitter dissension into Antony's home. Catiline then put himself forward as a candidate for the Consulship of the next year; but Crassus this time gave his support to somebody else; while Julius

[36] Ammianus Marcellinus, xxv.
[37] Cicero: In Toga Candida, xvi.
[38] Orosius, vi, 3.
[39] Sallust: Catiline, xv.
[40] Cicero: In Toga Candida.

Cæsar favoured a third candidate, Silanus, the husband of his now middle-aged mistress, Servilia.

The new elections were characterised by the utmost bitterness, for Cicero was furiously attacking Catiline in speech after speech, and was constantly warning the electorate that the man was a scoundrel who would not stop at murder to get the power into his own hands. Catiline, deeply chagrined and hopeless of gaining his ends by constitutional means, then began to plan a revolution; and wild stories were soon in circulation that he was going to assassinate Cicero, destroy Rome, and massacre all his enemies in the Senate. There can be no doubt that he was soon at the head of a widespread secret society,[41] the members of which were sworn to the regeneration of Rome; but it is extremely unlikely that their leader ever intended to perpetuate the atrocities with which he was credited. True, he was deeply in debt and was yearning for the power to enrich himself, and he was certainly enraged at the treatment he had received at the hands of the government; but the unquestionable fact of his great popularity with large numbers of well-to-do people is a proof that his plans were not so very demoniacal.

One of the conspirators, however, had a mistress, Fulvia, whose suspicions were aroused by the fact that her lover had lately begun to talk very grandly about the wealth which would soon be his, and about the wonderful jewels he would presently be able to give her; and at last she confided her fears to Cicero, with the result that, just before the elections, he was able to expose the existence of a plot.

Then, on the day of the elections itself, Cicero appeared in public wearing a military breast-plate concealed under his clothes, and surrounded by troops; and when all eyes were upon him he contrived to let his toga fall open, revealing this armour, at sight of which the crowd realized that his life was in danger, and, being thus made aware of what was to be feared, rejected Catiline at the polls. Thereupon, the defeated candidate, mad with anger and disappointment, sent one of his supporters, Caius Manlius, a disgruntled veteran of the late Sulla's army, into the country around Fæsulæ (Fiesole) to raise a fighting force, there being in

---

[41] Sallust: *Catilina*, xxxvi.

that region a great many old soldiers who had lately looked to Catiline to relieve them of their debts. He himself, meanwhile, boldly remained in Rome, and rumour said that he intended to take the first opportunity to murder Cicero. A considerable sum of money had been collected by the conspirators, much of which, as Appian caustically remarks,[42] had been given by women who hoped that their husbands would get killed in the rising; and Catiline was thus able to buy the support of many waverers.

At length Crassus, whom Catiline had again approached, went to Cicero's house by night, and revealed what he knew of the conspiracy, and at this Cicero convened the Senate. Catiline, always audacious, went himself to the meeting, but everybody cut him, and when he had taken his seat, all the Senators around him moved over to other parts of the assembly, leaving him alone. Cicero then delivered that impassioned speech which he afterwards published, and which is now known as the *First Catilinarian Oration;* and Catiline, seated there in dramatic solitude, with clenched teeth and defiant, unabashed eyes,[43] listened while the great orator told all the secrets of the plot, knowledge of which, even to the minutes of the conspirators' council of the previous night, had been brought to him by Fulvia and his other spies.

"I will have you put to death, Catiline," he said, pointing his finger at his haggard victim, "but it shall be later on, when it will be impossible to find anyone so vile, anyone so abandoned, anyone so like yourself, as to deny that I am justified. So long as there is anybody left to plead for you, you shall live; but you shall live, as you live now, hemmed in by my agents, so that you cannot stir a finger against the State. The eyes and ears of many shall, in the future as in the past, spy out your doings when you least expect it, and keep watch on your actions."

He then ordered him to leave Rome, and scathingly bade him join his doomed army of reprobates who were gathered under the standard of Manlius. At this Catiline rose to his feet, and replied that surely the senators could not believe all that Cicero had said against him, nor suppose that he, a patrician of ancient lineage, should want to ruin the State. But his words were drowned

[42] Appian: *Civil Wars*, ii, 2.   [43] Cicero: *In Catilinam*, i.

by shouts of "Traitor!", and, muttering a threat, he walked out
of the assembly. That evening he took his departure from the
city, accompanied by many of his friends, leaving Antony's stepfather, Lentulus, in charge of his affairs in Rome. Cicero then
went to the Forum and addressed the people, delivering his *Second
Catilinarian Oration*, in which he advised Lentulus and Catiline's
other agents to go and join their leader at Fiesole. "There is no
guard set upon the gates, no ambush upon the road," he sneered.
"If anyone wishes to depart, he may do so. But if anyone dares
to stir a finger in the city, then I say that I will make him feel
that here in Rome there are Consuls who will not sleep, there
are magistrates who will do their duty, there is a Senate which
will stand firm, there are troops under arms, and there is a prison
which our forefathers built to be the place of vengeance for
wicked and bloody crime."

For nearly a month Catiline remained in camp with Manlius,
where an army of between ten and twenty thousand revolution-
aries was gathered; and here he assumed the dress and insignia
of a Consul, protesting that since Cicero had prevented his proper
election to this office, he was justified in seizing it. To a friend
in Rome he wrote a letter [44] in which he said: "Provoked by in-
juries and insults, I have taken up the public cause of the dis-
tressed; and because I have seen unworthy men enriched with
honours, and myself rejected on groundless suspicions, I have
adopted the only course for preserving what honour is left me."
And he added: "I now commend and entrust my wife Orestilla
to your protection, imploring you, as you love your own children, to shield her from harm."

Meanwhile in Rome, Lentulus, Antony's stepfather, was leisurely preparing a *coup* which should be carried out at the moment when Catiline should begin his expected march on the
capital. It is said, though the story is probably exaggerated, that
he intended to set fire to the city so as to distract the attention
of the authorities, and then to kill Cicero, massacre the Senate,
and seize the government with the aid of some Gallic mercenaries
whom he had arranged to call in. Although lazy by nature, he
had been galvanised into some sort of action by the great per-

---

[44] Sallust: *Catilina*, xxxv.

sonal danger in which he was situated, and by his hatred of Cicero who, in these days, was immensely proud of himself and was behaving with an overweening vanity which ultimately brought great ridicule upon him.

He, Lentulus, though wasting precious time and showing signs of nervousness,[45] seems to have been hopeful of the success of the revolution, for the Senate had trustingly placed the forces upon which it relied under the command of Caius Antonius, Cicero's colleague in the Consulship, and there was some reason to believe that that personage would return to his former allegiance and would join, rather than fight, his old friend Catiline. There was a rumour, too, that Pompey was returning from the East; and in the hope that, as a democrat, he would take sides against Cicero and the aristocratic party, Lentulus had planned the seizure of Pompey's children, so that he might appear to be their guardian and protector, and might hand them over to their father, on his arrival, as an earnest of the political bargain to be made with him, or, alternatively, might hold them as hostages for Pompey's friendly behaviour.

It is not known whether Antony, who was now twenty years of age, approved of his stepfather's plans; but it seems, as has already been said, that he was one of those who regarded Catiline as a hero, and, at any rate, it is more likely that his sympathies were with Lentulus than that they were with his turncoat uncle, Caius Antonius,[46] while there is reason to suppose that he detested the pompous and impressive Cicero, the perfect correctness and prudence of whose behaviour, and the high-sounding nobility of whose words, were so completely out of harmony with the adventurous and unconventional spirit of Antony's home circle. In any case, however, the young man's position must have been most awkward; for he was at once the stepson of this widely suspected conspirator and the nephew of the Consul who was in command of the forces now moving against Catiline.

At last, at the beginning of December, Cicero caught some of the agents of the conspiracy red-handed, with incriminating documents in their keeping, and, having convened the Senate, ordered Lentulus and four of his confederates to be brought before them.

---

[45] Sallust: *Catilina*, lviii.   [46] Cicero: *Philippic ii*, xxiii.

Lentulus, under examination, pretended innocence, but his agents turned against him to save their own skins, and confessed that one of the seized letters, which was unsigned, had been written by him to Catiline. In it the writer had said that all was in readiness in Rome for the *coup*, and had advised Catiline to hasten his advance on the city; and as soon as the document was read Lentulus and his four friends were placed in custody. A sixth conspirator was arrested next morning as he was leaving the city; and, to the amazement of the Senators, confessed that he had been on his way to Catiline with a message from the great financier, Crassus, urging him not to lose heart, but to march with all the more speed to Rome.

This piece of information appeared to be incredible, for a great many of the senators, whom Catiline was supposed to wish to massacre, owed Crassus large sums of money; and, in any case, it seemed to be very unlikely that Crassus, considering his financial interests, would have desired a destructive revolution. The whole assembly, therefore, began to shout "False witness!" as the prisoner was repeating his testimony, and in the end the man was sent away, Crassus being declared innocent of the charge; and it may be added that in after years Crassus gave it as his opinion that Cicero had concocted the whole story out of enmity against him.[47]

The name of Julius Cæsar was inevitably dragged in during these enquiries, for so many persons involved in the affair were his friends, and in character and associations he was readily to be classed with the Catiline group, several of whom were aristocratic libertines and spendthrifts like himself, in need of money, worried, and politically restless. As a result of these suspicions about him he was greeted with catcalls by the republicans, and his life was threatened by Cicero's bodyguard of young gentlemen, who came towards him as he sat in the Senate, and made spectacular thrusts at him with their swords. Thereupon his own youthful friends—for, like Catiline, he always had a following of admiring young exquisites—clustered around him to protect him, led by a certain Scribonius Curio, an undersized and effeminate personage who was evidently far more courageous than his

[47] Sallust: *Catilina,* xlviii.

appearance would suggest, and now, with his sword in one hand and his cloak in the other, was prepared to give his rotten little life for his hero. Cicero, however, called his retainers off, and Curio then led the unruffled and ever dignified Cæsar out of the assembly, holding up the cloak behind him as a sort of shield.

It may be mentioned, by the way, that Curio, who was an admirer of Catiline, was at this time the young Antony's inseparable companion, and it is therefore not unlikely that Antony was present on this occasion. Curio's father, I may add, who was a senator, and probably witnessed the scene, would have been happy enough to see Cæsar killed, for he deemed him a menace to the morals of his son and all the younger generation, and, had once publicly denounced him as "every woman's man and every man's woman"; [48] and, indeed, in later years he and others often told Cicero that he had made a terrible mistake in ordering his bodyguard to sheath their swords. There were people who said that Cæsar's complicity in the plot could be proved by letters he had written, and his butchery there and then might have been justified; but he was able to call upon Cicero to affirm that he, Cæsar, was one of those who had actually warned him of the existence of the danger,[49] and thus the Consul did not feel able to allow him to be harmed.

On December 5th Cicero called the senators together once more, and asked them what should be done with Lentulus and the other prisoners. The first person to reply was Silanus, the Consul-elect, who voted that they should be put to death; but at this Cæsar, undaunted by his recent experience, made a masterly speech, urging that they should only be exiled and should suffer the confiscation of their property. This speech is history's first revelation to us of the future Dictator's great mental equipment; and, after the unpleasing start of his career, it comes as a very satisfying surprise.

"I am indeed of opinion," he said, "that the utmost degree of torture is inadequate to punish their crime; but mankind in general dwells on that which happens last, and, in the case of criminals, forgets their guilt and talks only of their punishment, should that punishment have been unusually severe. The proposal

⁴⁸ Suetonius: *Cæsar*, lii. ⁴⁹ *Ibid.*, xvii.

of Silanus to put these men to death appears to me, I will not say cruel—for what can be cruel that is directed against such characters?—but foreign to our policy. True, in trouble and distress, death is a relief from suffering, and not a torment: it puts an end to all human miseries, and beyond it there is no place either for sorrow or joy; and who, it may be asked, will blame any such sentence against these traitors? I answer that time, the course of events, and fortune whose caprice governs nations, may blame it." The danger was, he declared, that in after years these men should be regarded as martyrs by their supporters, and that the present government, by unnecessarily taking their lives, would reintroduce the bloodthirsty methods which had caused so much misery in the time of Sulla.

Cato, however, whose narrow patriotism and ever hardening support of the stern old conservative tradition had made him a curiously callous partisan, ruthlessly demanded the death-penalty; and his opposition to Cæsar's proposal was stiffened by an incident which then occurred. A note was privately handed to Cæsar, which he read with some embarrassment and then concealed; whereupon Cato accused him of receiving a communication from the conspirators, and demanded to see the letter. Cæsar handed it to him. It was a love-letter from Servilia, Cato's sister; and Cato, having read it, furiously flung it back, saying "Take it, you sot!" [50] He then proceeded to make a bitter speech, in which he took the opportunity also to castigate his fellow-senators for their love of their pleasures and their comforts.

"In the name of heaven," he cried, "I call upon you, who have always set a value upon your houses and villas, your statues and pictures, higher than that of the welfare of your country— if you wish to preserve these possessions to which you are so attached, if you wish to secure quiet for the enjoyment of your pleasures, arouse yourself, and do something for once in defence of your country. Does anyone talk to me of gentleness and compassion? For some time past, it is true, we have ceased to call things by their proper names; for to be lavish with the property of others is called generosity, and audacity in evil-doing is called heroism. But let those who thus misname things have a

[50] Plutarch: *Brutus*.

care before they play with our lives, and, whilst they spare a few criminals, bring destruction on all the guiltless." Thus, in the end the House was induced to decide that the prisoners had merited death.

Thereupon, Cicero, surrounded by senators, officials, and soldiers, went in majestic and funereal state to fetch Lentulus from his prison on the Palatine hill, and thence conducted him through the Forum to the Tullian dungeon beneath the Capitol, where, some forty years earlier, King Jugurtha had been done to death. Here Antony's unfortunate stepfather was solemnly let down by ropes into the black and evil-smelling pit, in which three or four soldiers were awaiting in silence to receive him; and, as his feet touched the ground these men pounced upon him in the semi-darkness, slipped a cord about his neck, and strangled him. When Cicero, looking down from above,[51] was notified that life was extinct, he went off to fetch the other four prisoners, and in like manner supervised their lowering into the dungeon and their strangulation. It was the great moment of his life. Usually hesitant and not quite sure of himself, to-day he was a mighty man dealing out death to the enemies of his country; and he was quite carried away by this sudden consciousness of his ability to be terrible.

In the late afternoon he returned to his house through streets crowded with citizens who, having had their fill of rumours of massacre, acclaimed him as their preserver and the saviour of the city, to which salutations he graciously bowed his acknowledgements to right and left.

Shortly afterwards, however, public opinion turned against him, it being stated that he had acted illegally in executing these men without allowing them the usual appeal to the People;[52] and before the year was out he was shouted down when he tried to defend his action at a public meeting.[53] But the troops under the command of Caius Antonius pursued the desperate Catiline to his doom, and early in the new year the fatal battle took place. Antonius, refusing to lead his men against his former friend,

[51] Appian: *Civil Wars,* ii, 6.

[52] Mommsen, in his *Roman History,* has called Cicero's action a "brutal judicial murder."

[53] Dion Cassius, xxxvii, 38.

pretended to be ill, and handed over the direction of the fight to his second-in-command; but Catiline took his place at the head of his troops, and at the end of the day his body was found far in advance of those of his own soldiers—who were killed almost to a man—and surrounded by a ring of the corpses of his enemies.

The death of Lentulus, of course, had brought sorrow and ruin into Antony's home; but though history tells us nothing of the young man's life at this tragic time, we may conjecture that his devotion to his kinsman, Cæsar, who had tried at any rate to save the prisoners' lives, and his dislike of Cicero, were greatly increased by this calamity. The Catilinarian Conspiracy has so generally been regarded by historians as a dastardly and insane attempt to destroy Rome, that the association of Antony's family with it, and particularly Julius Cæsar's conduct in this connection, have been blushingly glossed over; but the above interpretation, I think, supplies the explanation of an affair which so long has remained inexplicable because of the discrepancy between the extensive popularity of the movement and its leader on the one hand and the supposed absence of any but criminally destructive motives on the other. It was an understandable revolt against an aristocratic tyranny; and in after years Antony had no reason to be ashamed of his stepfather or of the cause for which he died.

CHAPTER V

Antony's Entrance into Politics on the Side of the Democrats.

62–58 B.C.

THE crushing of the Catilinarian revolution by no means reduced the democratic party to impotence. Most of the extremists, it is true, had been killed around their leader, Catiline; but other suspected men, such as Cæsar, were still alive, and the whole party eagerly awaited news of Pompey, whose expected return in glory, like a second Alexander the Great, at the head of a glittering, irresistible army, was the subject of excited speculation. After his military triumphs, after nearly four years of absolute power in the East, was he still an unspoilt democrat, or would he give some support to the aristocratic oligarchy? The latter party, under its chief spokesmen, Cicero and Cato, was now more powerful than it had ever been since the death of the Dictator Sulla; but this very fact had given the People's cause the impetus of resentment, and had lent them the boldness to show openly their hostility to the astonished Cicero, who felt himself just now to be a very king amongst men and was amazed to find that there were those who did not agree with him upon this point.

During his Consulship, a certain Metellus Nepos, one of Pompey's most trusted officers, had returned to Rome to stand for a Tribuneship of the People for the year 62 B.C. His father had been a first-cousin of that Metellus who was the patron of Marius and afterwards his rival in the war against Jugurtha; and though his family was of plebeian origin, it had had such a long and illustrious history that, as in the case of Antony, Metellus was accepted as one of Rome's socially elect. He was, however, an ardent democrat, and the conservatives therefore attempted to oppose his election, their own candidate being the austere and fanatical Cato, who was an uncompromising and slightly absurd aristocrat. There were other candidates, of course, but in the end both these men were elected, and at the beginning of 62 B.C., when they assumed office, everybody wondered how long it would be before they came to blows.

Metellus was the first to start the fight. He had the hardihood openly to attack Cicero on the grounds that his execution of Antony's stepfather had been illegal; and he put forward a proposal that Pompey should be asked to come back to Rome at once "to restore order," that is to say to defend the People's party against the tyrannical behaviour of the conservatives. Cæsar, whose efforts to save the Catilinarian prisoners had endeared him to the mob, strongly supported the motion; but Cato attacked it with vehemence, and he and Metellus so thoroughly lost their tempers that people began to think that they were both a little crazy.[1] When the day arrived for the bill to be put to the vote in the Comitia, Metellus, anticipating trouble, drafted a strong force of armed men into the assembly, and took his seat upon the rostra, with Cæsar beside him, surrounded by a powerful bodyguard. As they sat talking, however, Cato charged through the crowd, sprang onto the platform, and sat himself down with a thud between them, suddenly interrupting their conversation and causing them the profoundest astonishment.

The clerk then rose to read Metellus's motion; but Cato at once jumped to his feet and forbade him to do so. Metellus grabbed hold of the document and was about to read it when Cato snatched it from him and tore it up. Metellus, however, knew the words by heart and began to recite them; but Cato pushed him back onto his seat, and, with the assistance of a friend who had come to his support, held his colleague's mouth shut with his hand, so that only a stifled mumble passed his lips. Thereat, his armed followers scrambled onto the platform to protect him, and, after a free fight, Cato was dragged away to safety by some of his friends. Metellus then began to recite the motion again; but suddenly the battered Cato, who had collected some armed men of his own, burst into the meeting once more, and Metellus

[1] Plutarch: *Cato.*

and Cæsar were obliged to take to their heels. The upshot was that the government stupidly asserted its despotic power by commending Cato, and deposing both Metellus from his Tribuneship and Cæsar from the Prætorship which this year was his. Metellus thereupon fled from Rome, and with difficulty made his way to Pompey; but Cæsar, always daring, remained where he was, and when an angry rabble marched to his house to offer him their protection and support, he handled them so diplomatically and dispersed them with such obvious regard for law and order, that the startled Senate highly commended his conduct and used the pretext to reinstate him in his office, his unexpected popularity with the masses having brought them to their senses.

But Pompey was not yet ready to come home. He had just crowned his career of conquest by capturing Jerusalem, where, at the fall of the city, it may be mentioned, he had entered the temple and had boldly walked into Jehovah's Holy of Holies to have a look at the Ark of the Lord, the seven-branched candlestick, the golden table of the Law, and all the other mysterious objects of that interesting faith, for which, however, he showed his gentlemanly regard by looting none of these things nor touching the temple's treasury.[2] From Palestine he sent a report to the Senate recounting his victories, and he also wrote a private letter to Cicero wherein he said nothing complimentary about the orator's behaviour in the Catilinarian affair, of which he had just heard; and this omission greatly offended that personage, who, in view of the hostile behaviour of the mob towards him, was painfully eager for commendation.

There are many features of Cicero's character which must always arouse derision in the minds of those whose reverence for the outward proprieties is not over-developed. He was so precisely what is now called a pillar of the church and state that had he been living some ninety years later in the country from which Pompey wrote to him he would assuredly have come under the castigation of that Teacher who could not abide a parade of virtue. Yet there was one quality at least in him which endears

---

[2] Josephus: *Antiquities of the Jews,* xiv, 4; Cicero: *Pro Flacco,* xxviii, 67. Dion Cassius (xxxvii, 16) is therefore wrong in saying that he took the money in the treasury.

him to us, notwithstanding his self-importance, his vanity and his cant, namely his frank admission of his love of applause, and his ability sometimes to laugh at himself on this account. In a letter to his friend Atticus [3] he asks if there were ever a human action in history so glorious as his handling of the Catilinarian conspirators; but he says with a smile "I hope you don't object to my blowing my own trumpet." As soon as his Consulship was over he began to write a history of it both in Latin and in Greek; and he told Atticus [4] that he was going to compose a poem about it "so that I may not omit any form of self-laudation." He wrote, too, to the historian Lucceius, begging that he would praise his Consulship unstintingly, and if possible, write a special treatise about it.[5]

He was frankly hurt, therefore, at Pompey's casual letter, and he replied [6] saying how sorry he was to observe that it contained such scant expressions of regard. "My achievements have been such," he complains, "that I did expect some recognition of them in your letter, for I assure you that my action for the preservation of our country has met with a chorus of approval." The chorus to which he referred, however, was only that of the aristocratic party, who, indeed, at Cato's suggestion had conferred on him the title of "Father of his Country"; but he did not mention the fact that the mob was now in the habit of booing him. In regard to this title, by the way, he wrote in the above-mentioned poem of self-praise the famous line *"O fortunatam natam me consule Romam,"* [7] of which a good paraphrase is "O happy fate of Rome to date her birthday from my consulate" [8]— words which, in their vanity, are almost without parallel.

His unbounded conceit—a conceit so ridiculously human as almost to win our smiling indulgence—now led him into financial transactions which were not at all in keeping with his professed ideals. During his Consulship he had made a compact with his colleague Caius Antonius, Antony's uncle, that at the close of their year of office Antonius should be given the governorship of the province of Macedonia, and it seems to have been agreed between

[3] Cicero: *Ad Atticum,* i, 19, 10.   [4] Idem.
[5] Cicero: *Ad Familiares,* v, 12.   [6] Cicero: *Ad Familiares,* v, 7.
[7] Juvenal, x, 122.   [8] Tyrrell.

them that they should share whatever money could be wrung from the Macedonians,[9] for every Roman provincial governor expected to make a fortune out of his province. But before this money arrived Cicero's sense of his own importance induced him to buy from the millionaire Crassus a magnificent house on the Palatine hill. The price was colossal, and to raise the amount he had to borrow large sums from all those who wanted his services in the law-courts, where his eloquence always commanded high fees.

It is not possible to suppose that he could have expected to pay back these debts, or even to live in a style commensurate with this mansion, without setting about the making of his fortune by more or less corrupt means; and there can be no question that from now onwards his professions of high principle in financial matters were somewhat hypocritical. The common people knew this, and henceforth they regarded him as one of the thieving rich. It is true that Cæsar was also deeply in debt at this time; but the difference was that Cæsar had spent his money on the People in pursuit of their votes and support, whereas Cicero, who did not need to do this so long as the wealthy aristocracy was behind him, was incurring his financial obligations entirely for his own social aggrandisement. The unfortunate Antony, meanwhile, and his mother and brothers, were more or less impoverished, and, if we are to take literally a later sneer of Cicero's,[10] had not even a home they could call their own.

Antony, however, was a light-hearted young man, and having been brought up from childhood in an atmosphere electric with the demands of creditors, gave little attention to the dark menace of his ever-growing debts. He could not pay for the good time to which he was accustomed to treat himself; but neither his father nor his stepfather had ever allowed an actual or a partial bankruptcy to interfere with their social life,[11] and Antony did not know what it was to deny himself. Indeed, he may well have asked why on earth he should do so, for most of his young friends were

---

[9] This is the interpretation generally placed upon the references to *Teucris* in *Ad Atticum*, i, 12, 13, and 14, and *Ad Familiares*, v, 5 and 6, that being apparently Cicero's code-name for Caius Antonius.

[10] Cicero: *Philippic ii.* xix.   [11] *Ibid.*, xviii.

in debt, and yet were sowing their wild oats with the utmost prodigality; [12] and, in his own case, his relationship to Caius Antonius and to the Cæsars indicated that one day he would find means to make a fortune—an expectation which was usually sufficient for the money-lenders.

Moreover, Antony happened to be a very attractive stripling, and for the last few years various men older than himself had attached themselves to him and had seen that he did not want; [13] for fashionable society at that time was even more prone to curious, romantic attachments of this sort than it is at the present day, and a youth without such a companion was almost a phenomenon. In spite of the fact that Antony in after years was only abnormal in the excessive masculinity of his behaviour, there is no doubt that in early life he was all too similar to his friend Julius Cæsar at the same age.

Scribonius Curio was to Antony what the King of Bithynia had been to Cæsar. Curio was some years older than Antony, but was described by Cicero as "a slip of a girl," [14] which indicates that he was an effeminate little man, although, as we have already seen, he had been prepared to defend Cæsar that day in the Senate even at the cost of his life. He had been a friend of Catiline and was a keen democrat, having by his very nature a hearty distaste for the habits of the conservative. His father, still living, was a man of wealth who had been Consul in 76 B.C., and was the son of a famous orator, who, like Antony's grandfather, the orator Marcus Antonius, was of illustrious plebeian family. "No boy," says Cicero, "was ever so wholly in the power of an elder man as Antony was in the power of Curio, who, burning with devotion, was unable to bear the misery of being separated from him." [15] They went about together everywhere, and into such wild extravagances did Curio lead him, or he Curio, that soon his debts amounted to a considerable fortune, and he was obliged to borrow a large sum from money-lenders, Curio standing as surety for the loan. On hearing of this, however, the elder Curio refused to invite Antony into his house, and told the serv-

---

[12] Sallust: *Catilina*, xiii, xiv.
[13] For this phase of his life see Cicero: *Philippic ii*, xviii; and Plutarch: *Antony*.
[14] Cicero: *Ad Atticum*, i, 14, 5.   [15] Cicero: *Philippic ii*, xviii.

ants not to let him in, after which his friend, always ready for adventure, was obliged to smuggle him into his own quarters by way of a ladder and the roof.

In due course the money-lenders demanded repayment, and Curio was faced with the prospect of having to pay up, whereupon his angry father threatened to bring an action against Antony in this event for the recovery of as much of the money as possible. At this Curio went to Cicero, who was an old acquaintance of his father's, and begged him with tears in his eyes to try to set the matter to rights, for, he declared, if Antony were to be condemned as a debtor and expelled from Rome he himself would go into banishment with him, having been the real cause of the trouble, and being unable, anyway, to tolerate the thought of existence without his friend. Such, at least, is Cicero's account of the interview; but it is not unlikely that Curio's object was to ask Cicero to help Antony and his family to recover some of the money lost, if not actually confiscated, at the time of his stepfather's conviction, or, alternatively, to induce Caius Antonius to help the young man. Cicero, however, if he is to be believed, persuaded the elder Curio to pay the debt himself, but advised him to forbid his son ever to meet Antony again. It is unknown whether or not this advice was put into execution; but it may be supposed that the intimacy, in any case, came to an embarrassing end as Antony began to grow a beard and to develop that prize-fighter's physique and those robust manners which presently earned for him the name of Hercules.

Towards the close of the year 62 B.C. while all Rome was anxiously awaiting the return of Pompey and his victorious army, and while Cæsar, who was engaged in a violent love-affair with Mucia, Pompey's wife, was gradually becoming the acknowledged leader of the democrats in their struggle against a tyrannical aristocracy led by the plausible Cicero and the fanatical Cato, a very curious incident occurred which developed into a first-class political scandal. One of the outstanding figures amongst the younger politicians at this time was Publius Clodius, nicknamed Pulchellus, "The Beauty," who although he must have been some thirty years of age, had a face like a girl—a fact which often led him, for the entertainment of his friends, to dress up as, and to imitate the manners of, a woman.[16] It is generally thought that he was, indeed, an effeminate creature whose undoubtedly licentious and immoral habits were of the emasculated kind so common in Rome at that time, but I believe this to be a mistake: he was, as our authorities really make quite clear, so masculine in his behaviour that his feminine appearance must have been a matter for laughter rather than disgust.

Of extremely aristocratic ancestry, he was the son of one of Sulla's patrician officers who had died at the Colline Gate in 82 B.C., and in 70 B.C. he had served in Asia under Lucullus to whom his sister, Clodia, was married. A few years later, being a born fighter, he had joined the Syrian army in their war against the Arabs, and, after many breathless adventures, had returned to Rome in 65 B.C., where he came into prominence as one of the aristocrats who brought the charge of extortion against Catiline for the purpose of preventing his candidature for the Consulship; but in 63 B.C., after a year of service in Gaul, he gave his support to the conspirators,[17] and, in spite of some further changes of face, came out at last on the democratic side for good. Plutarch describes him as a man of brave and resolute character,[18] eminent, too, both for his wealth and his eloquence;[19] but although there were some who considered him a very decent, and even religious, member of society,[20] it seems to be widely agreed that when he was not gallantly fighting or violently engaging in politics, his life was really outrageous in its profligacy.

Now it so happened that in this year 62 B.C. his latest mistress was none other than Cæsar's wife, Pompeia, the great Sulla's granddaughter, who, having been married for some six years to a man incapable of being faithful to her for as many weeks, had at last retaliated by responding to the overtures of this wealthy and dashing young nobleman with the girlish face and the lion's heart. The fact that Cæsar's mother, Aurelia, lived in the house with Pompeia, and kept an annoyingly watchful eye upon her, only added to the ardour of Clodius; and at length, in December,

---

[16] Cicero: *De Haruspicum Responsis*, xxi, 44.
[17] Asconius: *In Ciceronis Milonianam*, 55.
[18] Plutarch: *Cicero*.　　　　　[19] Plutarch: *Cæsar*.
[20] Cicero: *Philippic viii*, v.

he planned a daring escapade by which he hoped to find himself alone with his lady-love in her own house, in the middle of the night, and under very exciting conditions.

One of the great goddesses of Rome, whose worship under various names was almost world-wide, was Bona Dea, the patroness of women, particularly in their character of actual or potential mothers; and twice in the year—in May and December—there was an important festival in her honour, the former being, I fancy, the date of its original celebration in Rome, and the latter that adapted from foreign usage.[21] At the December festival the women were wont to gather at the house of one of the Consuls or Prætors, where the Vestal Virgins performed certain very secret rites relative to the propagation of the race, and the whole company kept a night-long vigil, playing games and listening to music to pass the time, nobody of the other sex being allowed in the house from nightfall until the following morning. This year the ceremonies were to be performed at the house of Cæsar, who was Prætor; and since he would have to sleep elsewhere that night, the daring idea of attending the secret rites, disguised as a woman, presented itself to Clodius, who supposed that he would thus be able to enjoy a little time alone with Pompeia.

By arrangement with her maid he was admitted into the house, when the time came, disguised as an Egyptian singing-woman, wearing an Egyptian headdress and veil, a sleeved gown, and a sash around his middle, his feet being bandaged to make them look smaller;[22] but while he was awaiting the return of this maid, who had gone to see whether her mistress were ready to receive him, the glances directed at him by passing women made him feel so uneasy that he decided to find his own way to Pompeia's room. He had not gone far, however, when one of Aurelia's own maids encountered him and asked him whom he was looking for, whereupon his stammered reply, uttered in a very masculine

[21] May is the date attested by Ovid (*Fasti*, v, 147), but the festival to which reference is here being made was, I think, evidently in December, as shown by Cicero, *Ad Atticum*, i, 12, etc., and, I suppose, corresponded to the "Mothers' Night" celebrated with an all-night vigil on December 24th–25th in various countries, which was one reason why that date was chosen for our Christmas (See my *Paganism in Our Christianity,* chap. xxiii).

[22] So Cicero says in his speech against him, of which a few fragments alone remain.

voice, revealed his sex, and soon the place was in an uproar.
Aurelia rushed into the hall wherein the rites were to be performed and covered up the sacred images and symbols; the doors
of the house were shut; and at last Clodius was discovered hiding in a dark room into which he had been dragged by Pompeia's
maid. His clothes were half torn from him by the furious women;
his identity was revealed; and he was driven into the street again
with a chorus of screams and imprecations following him as he
ran painfully through the darkness in his tight shoes.

Next morning everybody was talking about his impious prank,
and a few days later the very serious charge of sacrilege was
brought against him, to which was added that of adultery with
Pompeia. Thereupon Cæsar let it be understood that he did not
think she was guilty, but divorced her nevertheless on the afterwards famous grounds that Cæsar's wife ought to be above suspicion. The aristocratic party were glad to discredit Clodius, who
had recently been making himself obnoxious to them; and, raking
amidst the refuse of his past, they produced the further charge
that he had had incestuous relations with his three sisters, one of
whom, at any rate, was so notorious for her immoralities that
anything might be believed of her—she was, in fact, nicknamed
Quadrantia, which may be translated "Pennyworth," because of
the low price at which her favours had been valued by a certain
disillusioned lover of hers, and she had lately caused a scandal
by buying a villa from which she could obtain a good view of the
place where the young men bathed.

The trial which ensued, early in the new year, 61 B.C., became a *cause célèbre*, like that of Verres eight years before. The
aristocratic party, headed in this case by Cato, was determined
that he should be punished; the People were determined that he
should be acquitted, and were very pleased with Cæsar when he
refused to make any charge against him. Cicero was all for hush-
ing up the whole affair, but his wife Terentia, who at this time
dominated him, urged him to support the prosecution; and when
Clodius audaciously put forward an alibi, saying that he had
been at Interamna (Terni), fifty miles from the capital, at the
time in question, Cicero gave evidence that, on the contrary, the
accused had visited him at his house in Rome on that day. Crassus,

on the other hand, not only gave his support to Clodius, but so heavily bribed everybody who would take his money that most of the large body of jurors voted for his acquittal, and those whose consciences would not permit them to do so scrawled their written verdicts so illegibly that nobody could read them. Clodius thus escaped punishment, and the democratic party was able to congratulate itself upon an important victory over the republicans or conservatives.

While this affair was engaging the attention of the public, Pompey arrived back in Italy; but to the blank astonishment of both parties he immediately disbanded his army instead of marching it to the gates of Rome, as everybody had breathlessly expected, to support either one side or the other in the political troubles with which the city was seething. The conservatives were delighted, and Cicero prepared himself to take advantage of Pompey's pacific gesture by attempting to win him over to the side of the aristocracy; but these plans were thwarted by Cato, who, mistrusting the great general, abused him so openly that Pompey was thrown back upon the democrats. He was in something of a dilemma because, on the one hand, he did not like the rigid conventionality and despotic tendencies of the aristocratic party, and, on the other, he detested the unruly habits of the mob which formed an important part of the democratic party. Moreover, although he was at heart a true democrat, the situation was a little complicated for him by the fact that Cæsar, who was now the real leader of the People, had been making love to his, Pompey's, wife Mucia during his absence, as has already been said. That matter, however, was amicably settled. Pompey divorced Mucia because of her adultery with Cæsar, and shortly afterwards arranged to marry Cæsar's girl Julia instead, to show that there was no ill-feeling. Julia was the daughter of Cæsar's first wife, Cornelia, daughter of the famous democratic leader, Cinna: she was a beautiful young woman in the early twenties, and Pompey was twice her age; but, fortunately, she found him so attractive as a lover that she was able to respond with genuine warmth to his equally genuine ardour, and was evidently delighted to make amends in person to him for her father's theft of Mucia.

Cæsar, however, very wisely did not remain in Rome to attempt the impossible task of sharing the leadership of the People with Pompey. Now that his term of office as Prætor was over, he was anxious, too, to go abroad to try to make some money by means fair or foul, for at the moment he required about twenty-five million *sesterces*[23] to make him worth precisely nothing, as he put it. He therefore accepted a governorship in Spain, and although he had great difficulty in pacifying his creditors, and had in the end to ask Crassus to stand surety for him for a huge sum of money to keep the most dangerous of them quiet, he was enabled in the end to make a successful escape from the others, although, to do so, he had to slip away before his baggage and a military escort were ready.[24]

In the autumn of 61 b.c. Pompey celebrated his Triumph, and for two days the Roman populace gazed in wonder at a seemingly endless procession of soldiers, booty, and captive kings and princes. It was the barbarous Roman custom to kill the important prisoners after they had been led in chains through the streets; but Pompey again revealed his humanity by putting to death only two such persons out of the three hundred and more who had been brought to Rome, and by sending almost all the others back to their own countries at the public expense. He also displayed an exalted sense of citizenship by divesting himself of his military apparel and marks of rank at the end of the Triumph, and going quietly to his house, dressed as an ordinary civilian. His behaviour at this time, in fact, was like the abdication of a monarch at the height of his glory; but it was far too altruistic for the taste of Rome, and his popularity was doffed with his raiment.[25] The democrats did not altogether trust him, and the conservatives, unable to win him over, did their best to crush him.

Matters, however, now hung fire for a while in Rome, though in Spain Cæsar proved himself to be a very energetic military commander, and conducted some minor campaigns with distinction; but in the middle of the next year, 60 b.c., Cæsar, aching

---

[23] About $1,250,000, but with a greater purchasing value then than now.
[24] Plutarch: *Cæsar;* Suetonius: *Cæsar,* xviii; Appian: *Civil Wars,* ii, 8.
[25] Cicero: *Ad Atticum,* ii, 19, 2–3.

with ambition, returned home in order to become a candidate for one of the Consulships of 59 B.C. The aristocratic party did its best to oppose his election, but the most it could do was to put forward its own candidate for the other Consulship, a man named Calpurnius Bibulus; and the result of the elections was that Cæsar and Bibulus, representing the two political extremes, became Consuls together, entering into office at the beginning of 59 B.C. to the accompaniment of the rival acclamations of the two parties. They were like opposing fighting-cocks rather than colleagues, the one being backed most prominently by Pompey and Crassus, and the other by Cicero and Cato. The democrats, however, obviously had the better champion; and they felt sufficiently confident of their strength to try to pay off their old scores against the opposing faction in regard to the treatment of the late Catiline and his friends.

If there be any lingering doubt in the mind of the reader as to the correctness of the assertion which I made in the previous chapter that Catiline, with all his faults, was the beloved leader of the People, and not merely the irresponsible monster which official history has deemed him, it must surely be dissipated by the fact that the bulk of the democratic party behind Cæsar now began to devote its energy to the punishment of those who had brought about the destruction of the so-called Catilinarian conspirators, and Cæsar, himself more moderate in this matter, had difficulty in keeping his followers in control. One of the first moves was the impeachment of Caius Antonius, Antony's uncle, for the second time, on the nominal charge of having extorted money from his province of Macedonia, but for the real reason that he had turned against Catiline and had commanded the forces sent to overthrow him. Cicero, of course defended him; but he was condemned nevertheless, and was exiled to the island of Cephallenia, in the Ionian Sea, off the coast of Greece, where he remained, it may be added, for the next fifteen years. The young Antony, now twenty-four years of age, seems to have sided with those who condemned his uncle, for he had already attached himself enthusiastically to the democratic party and had struck up a great friendship with Clodius,[26] who, in spite of his affair

[26] Cicero: *Philippic ii*, xix.

with Cæsar's wife, was now his most active supporter. Antony's mother, Julia, widow of that Lentulus whom Cicero had caused to be put to death as Catiline's chief agent, was also glad enough, no doubt, to witness the punishment of her former brother-in-law. She was herself of the family of the Cæsars, and her sympathies would naturally have been with her kinsman, Julius Cæsar, and his party, even if his political opponent, Cicero, had not been her personal enemy. As soon as Caius Antonius was condemned a crowd of people hurried off to the tomb of Catiline, and triumphantly decked it with flowers; [27] and it may well be that in that crowd Antony and his mother were to have been seen.

The various measures which Cæsar, as Consul, brought forward were of a popular character, and were designed to benefit the masses; but they were all opposed by his colleague Bibulus, and at length a serious riot took place. One day, while Cæsar was speaking in the Forum, Bibulus, who had just had a basketful of dung emptied over his head, burst into the meeting to stop him, whereupon a free fight ensued. Bibulus leapt upon the platform, and thrusting his head forward and pointing to his throat, shouted out to Cæsar's supporters to kill him if they dared. "If I cannot persuade Cæsar to do right," he cried, "I can at least affix upon him the stigma of my death!" His friends, however, dragged him away; and thereupon the irrepressible Cato mounted the platform and began to denounce Cæsar and all his works. The democrats at once pounced upon him, and carried him off kicking, depositing him outside the circle of the crowd. Cato, however, made his way by side streets around to the back of the rostra, and suddenly climbed up onto it again, and there stood shouting his denunciations until once more he was lifted off his feet and thrown down at a safe distance, while the meeting, after further uproar, ended in a victory for the democrats.

One of Cæsar's measures was that of approving all the dis-

[27] Cicero: *Pro Flacco*, xxxviii. Dion Cassius (xxxviii, 10) states that a second charge against Caius Antonius was that of conspiring *with* Catiline; but if this had been so the verdict would not have been a triumph for Catiline, nor would Cicero have defended him, since it was Cicero who, a little earlier, had accused him of being a party to the conspiracy in an oration of which only fragments have survived (*In Toga Candida*).

positions made by Pompey in the countries he had conquered, these having been refused ratification by the aristocratic party on the disgruntled advice of Lucullus, their own deposed general whom Pompey had replaced in the East. Cæsar and Pompey, in fact, were now working together on terms of apparent friendship, although Pompey, who had now completely lost his heart to his new wife, Julia, Cæsar's daughter, was far more interested just now in her than in politics, and could with difficulty be dragged from her side[28]—a condition of mind which Cæsar at once turned to his own advantage by borrowing a handsome sum of money from the ardent lover.[29] Cæsar himself had just married Calpurnia, daughter of Lucius Calpurnius Piso, the democratic Consul-elect for the following year; but this was a political union and in no way interfered with business—the marriage, in fact, had led Cato to make the caustic remark that the State nowadays seemed to be nothing more than a matrimonial agency.

During the second half of the year Cæsar's behaviour became very autocratic, and at last Bibulus, finding himself deprived of all power and not a little in danger of his life, shut himself up in his house and could not be induced to show his nose at any public meetings or functions. The Senate, which, almost to a man, belonged to the aristocratic party, was powerless to act; and, indeed, so entirely was the control of affairs in Cæsar's hands, and so blindly did the Comitia, the People's assembly, follow him, that the democrats jestingly referred to this Consulship of Cæsar and Bibulus as that of Julius and Cæsar.

Presently he caused a law to be passed that any senator who obstructed the passage of one of his popular measures should be put to death, after which he had little further trouble with any member of that body, except, of course, with Cato, who did not cease to challenge everything he did, until at last he was carried off struggling, and pitched into prison for a while. The Comitia having now more or less taken over the functions of the Senate, Cæsar thought it would be as well for his chief lieutenant, Clodius, "The Beauty," to serve as a Tribune of the People; but since this office could only be held by a man of plebeian family, and the family of Clodius was patrician, Cæsar caused him to be

[28] Plutarch: *Pompey*.   [29] Cicero: *Ad Atticum*, vi, 1, 25.

adopted by a certain plebeian gentleman as his son, and thus, by a stroke of the pen, made him eligible.

It is a very remarkable fact that at this time the leaders of the now dominant democratic party, with its rough, working-class following, were men of elegant, effeminate appearance. Curio, that "slip of a girl," as Cicero called him was one of Cæsar's chief supporters. Clodius looked like a woman, and had passed himself off as one at the Bona Dea rites in Cæsar's house. The debonair Pompey, although a normal man in his habits, is described by Plutarch as having "languishing eyes," and a gentle, graceful bearing. Cæsar himself, in spite of his vital energy, his commanding character, and his reckless bravery, was still laughed at as an effeminate fop. In the Senate, at about this time, when he had declared that in spite of his enemies he would obtain what he desired and would make that assembly submissive to his pleasure, one of the senators sneeringly retorted: "That will not be an easy task for a *woman!*" [30] And Antony, who, as the close friend now of Clodius, was beginning to play an active rôle in the party, had only lately begun to reveal those manly qualities which later were his particular characteristic, but which in his youth had been concealed behind the soft manners and appearance typical in all ages of the male of the intermediate sex. In his case, obviously, this was to a great extent a fashionable pose; but it is not without a sense of surprise that one observes how the rude proletariat had allied itself with these charming exquisites, and how the aristocratic party, on the other hand, was identified with the more severe and manly tradition of ancient Rome.

The highly respectable Cicero was all at sea in this paradoxical situation. Shocked and frightened at the bitter criticisms levelled against him by the democrats, he bored his friends almost to distraction [31] by repeating to them at great length the story of the Catilinarian conspiracy and of his behaviour at that time, stating over and over again that he had saved the fatherland on that occasion. He tried hard to fortify his failing courage by telling himself what a very noble person he was, and by writing to his friends describing his successful speeches and the approval they evoked in the minds of all virtuous men.

---

[30] Suetonius: *Cæsar*, **xxii.** [31] Plutarch: *Cicero.*

"I am maintaining my position with dignity," he declared. [32]
"I am supported by everybody's good will." "You know how I
can deliver my thunders," he wrote to his friend Atticus in reference to his defence against his enemies. "Well, this time I brought
the house down! Great heavens!—how I battled and spread deso-
lation around me! What onslaughts I made on my opponents! I
wish you could have seen how grandly I was fighting." [33] Herein
he was deliberately refusing in his vanity to face the fact that he
was now hated by the masses; but when his letter-writing was
finished, and ugly reality returned to brush aside this pathetic
pretence, his depression was deep, and, as in the case of most boastful men, his bombast collapsed like a pricked balloon. As Appian
says, he was "utterly unnerved." [34]

It has already been pointed out that Cæsar was closely co-
operating with Pompey at this time, and presently these two drew
the enormously wealthy Crassus into their mutual league, as a
result of which the three of them became the absolute rulers of
Rome. The coalition was nicknamed the *Tricaranus*, the "Three-
headed Monster"; and for their chief agent they used Antony's
great friend, Clodius, who, as soon as he entered, in December,
59 B.C., upon his duties as Tribune of the People, launched a
violent attack upon the fallen Cicero, having for its object nothing
less than the ex-Consul's banishment from the city. In this onslaught Antony played a very prominent part, and was, indeed,
described as the brand which fired every conflagration. [35] Daily
Clodius pressed more vigorously the charge against Cicero of having acted illegally in putting Lentulus to death; and Antony, excited by the thought of avenging his stepfather, helped him in every
way to arouse the anger of the people.

Time after time Cicero came to verbal blows with his antagon-
ists, and not all the scurrilous invective for which he was famous [36]
saved him from frequent humiliation. Once when it had been mentioned that Cicero had paid a recent visit to Baiæ, the fashionable
and exclusive watering-place on the Bay of Naples, the elegant

[32] Cicero: *Ad Atticum*, ii, 24, 4.
[33] *Ibid.*, i, 14, 4; i, 16, 1.
[34] Appian: *Civil Wars*, ii, 15.   [35] Cicero: *Philippic ii*, xix.
[36] Plutarch: *Cicero*.

Clodius cut him to the quick by asking with a sneer what on earth a mere person from Arpinum could find to do at a place patronised by society. And when Cicero talked of laying his case before a jury, Clodius replied with the remark—all the more scathing because it was rather true—that no jury would believe a word he said even when he was speaking on oath. [37]

At the close of the year 59 B.C. Cæsar's somewhat uninspired Consulship came to an end, and by arrangement with Pompey and Crassus he obtained for himself the governorship of Cisalpine Gaul, that is to say the part of northern Italy corresponding more or less to Lombardy, to which was added an indefinite region beyond the Alps; and at his special request a law was passed giving him the military command of these regions for five years. Just as he was about to leave Rome a law was proposed in the Comitia by Clodius that any man who had condemned a Roman citizen to death without allowing him the right of appeal to the People should be exiled; and at this the unfortunate Cicero abandoned all attempts to maintain his dignity or self-respect, and, with the dread of exile hanging over him, dressed himself as a suppliant and visited his friends or accosted them in the street, pouring out his woes to them and weeping over his lot until his unseemly behaviour aroused general disgust and ridicule.[38] The mob booed and hissed him whenever they saw him, calling him the murderer of Lentulus and his comrades; and sometimes they flung mud and garbage at him as, blinded by tears, he groped his importunate way from door to door under cover of night. The old conservative or republican party, however, lay powerless beneath the weight of the Three-headed Monster, and could not save him from the wrath of Antony and Clodius; while Cæsar, Pompey, and Crassus, although rather sorry for him, could not now check the storm of popular hatred against him which at first they had allowed Clodius to raise. Cæsar, in particular, tried to find him a loophole of escape by offering to give him a job on his staff in Gaul, a kindly action inspired, one may suppose, by a genuine admiration for Cicero's oratory and mastery of elegant language —an admiration which was reciprocated by Cicero, who, in later years, admitted that Caesar was in command of "a splendid, noble,

---

[37] Cicero: *Ad Atticum,* i, 16, 10.   [38] Appian: *Civil Wars,* ii, 15.

and magnificent vein of eloquence." [39] Cicero, however could not bring himself to accept a minor post of this kind, and the matter dropped.

At last, in the first days of March, 58 B.C., Cicero ignominiously fled from Rome; and as soon as Cæsar had gone to his new post in Gaul, and Pompey and Crassus to their country seats, Clodius and Antony led a mob to the orator's gorgeous mansion on the Palatine, and, turning his wife Terentia and her children out of it, set the house-wreckers to work to raze it to the ground. When the destruction was complete, builders were called in to erect a temple to the goddess of Liberty upon the site; and at its dedication one may suppose that Antony and his widowed mother, Julia, were the guests of honour.

The two Consuls for this year were Piso, whose daughter Cæsar had married, and Aulus Gabinius, the man who in 65 B.C. had proposed Pompey as commander-in-chief against the pirates: both of them were democrats. It was arranged that at the end of their term of office Gabinius should be given the governorship of the province of Syria; and now this personage invited Antony to join his staff there when the time came. Antony, however, did not like the idea of a staff appointment, but said that he would willingly accept a cavalry command, so that there might be some chance of active service for him; and eventually this was arranged.

Meanwhile, however, he was feeling somewhat uncomfortable in Rome; for not only were his creditors pressing him, but he had involved himself so deeply with the more violent elements of the democratic party that he could see a good deal of trouble brewing for him in the future. His friend Clodius was altogether out of hand; and, although Antony had enjoyed the overthrowing of Cicero, now that he had avenged his stepfather he was not happy in the situation which had developed. Cæsar, Pompey, and Crassus were all moderate democrats, who might at any moment repudiate the reckless Clodius; and a change in public opinion might bring Cicero back from exile.

He therefore decided that the best thing for him to do would be to go over to Greece for the purpose of taking lessons in ora-

[39] Suetonius: *Cæsar,* lv.

tory at Rhodes or somewhere, just as Cæsar had done; and then, when Gabinius should pass through Greece on his way to Syria at the beginning of the next year, he would meet him and go with him to take up his cavalry command. He was now twenty-five years of age, and he must have been conscious that so far his career had not been at all reputable. He had in recent years involved himself in a serious love affair with a girl named Fadia, whose social standing was deplorable [40]; and the fact that he made quite a boast of his being the father of her two or three babies seems to have been thought a little more unconventional than was necessary. The phase of his effeminacy, at any rate, was over, but it had been followed by a period of violent tub-thumping and mob-leading which had culminated in the recent scenes of destruction on Cicero's Palatine property; and perhaps Cæsar, who was his hero, had warned him to mend his ways, and had advised him to learn that self-control which a school of oratory best could teach. At any rate it is to the young man's credit that he set forth from Rome, in this year 58 B.C., with the intention not only of returning thus to tutelage for a while, but of passing on thence to the discipline and the hardships of military service in far lands. As Plutarch puts it, he was weary of madness.

[40] Cicero: *Philippic xiii, x.*

CHAPTER VI

Antony's Military Service in Syria and Egypt, and his Appointment to the
Staff of Cæsar in Gaul.

58–54 B.C.

HISTORY has little to say as to how Antony passed his time
in Greece during the remainder of the year 58 B.C. and the early
part of 57, while waiting for the coming of Gabinius; but Plutarch
tells us that he made some use of this opportunity to study the art
of oratory at one of the celebrated Greek schools. He had a natural
talent in that direction, inherited from his grandfather, the famous orator, which, no doubt, he was anxious to develop; and,
in fact, in later years, according to the same author, he proved to
be unequalled in the art of addressing a crowd and carrying them
with him by the power of his words. The style of speaking which
he cultivated was that known as the Asiatic, then very popular—a
rather poetic, careless, flowery style, full of heroics, but greatly
differing from the sonorous, pompous, carefully worded bombast
of Cicero. Cicero always spoke from the head, Antony from the
heart. Cicero prepared what he called his "thunders" and studied
the form in which they were delivered, using pure and beautiful
Latin and giving close attention to "period" and "turn," "antithe-
sis" and "trope"; [1] but Antony, on the other hand, seems to have
poured out his words with native eloquence, relying upon that and
the few tricks which he was now learning to create the effects so
diligently rehearsed by Cicero.

Plutarch says that he also occupied himself in Greece with
military exercises, that is to say swordcraft, horsemanship, and
so forth; but one may guess that the bulk of his time was spent
in enjoying himself as thoroughly as his small means would per-

[1] Cicero: *Ad Atticum,* i, 14, 4.

mit. He had grown into a fine-looking, muscular, young man of strikingly noble carriage, moderately tall, exceptionally well-developed, and having the shoulders and arms of a pugilist. It was the Roman custom at this time to allow the youthful hair upon the chin and jaws to grow untouched by a razor until somewhere about the twenty-fifth year of a man's age; and Antony, who had not yet decided upon his first shave, was now possessed of quite a handsome beard, [2] which, with the thick, curly hair of his head, his powerful frame, and what Plutarch calls his "bold, masculine look," made people say that he reminded them of a young Hercules.

As has already been mentioned, the Antonii traced their genealogy back to Hercules, Anton, the founder of the family, having been the reputed son of that fabulous hero; and Antony, being ingenuously proud of the fact, and glorying now as much in his brawn as once he had gloried in his lack of it, began to dress for the part, often wearing his tunic girt low about his hips, a heavy sword hanging at his side, and a cloak of coarse material tossed magnificently over his great shoulders. His expression, however, was boyish, kindly and slightly humorous, his eyes were thoughtful and frank, his forehead was broad and intelligent, and his mouth a good deal more sensitive than his rather heavy chin would have led one to expect. [3] His nose was somewhat hooked, [4] and his upper lip short; and these features, considered together with his thick eyebrows, added a certain aquiline strength to his otherwise jovial and good-natured face.

His nature was very loveable. "His generous ways," writes Plutarch, "his open and lavish hand in gifts and kindnesses to his friends, did a great deal for him in his first advance to power, and, after he had become great, long maintained his fortunes when a thousand follies were hastening their overthrow. In love affairs, also, he was very agreeable, gaining many friends by the assistance he gave them in theirs, and taking other people's jokes about his own with good-humour. What might seem to some very insupport-

[2] Plutarch: *Antony*.
[3] See the Vatican bust, said to have been found at Tor Sapienza, Rome, about 1830.
[4] As shown on coins and medals.

able—his showing off, his fun, his drinking in public, his sitting down with common soldiers while they were having their meals, or eating, as he stood, off their tables—made him, later, the delight and pleasure of the army." There was no snobbishness about him, and he was as much at his ease with people of no social standing as with the high and mighty. He enjoyed the luxuries and refinements of life, but, like Catiline and Cæsar, could endure hardships and privations without complaint; and, as Plutarch says, "in necessity and adversity he came nearest to perfection." He was a tender-hearted, sentimental, and sometimes chivalrous young man; and, as the following pages will reveal, he stands out as one of the few notable vehicles of occasional humane dealing in a savage and intensely cruel age.

His simplicity, however, is the feature of his character which most fully wins him our sympathy; for, from this time onwards, he is never unintelligible, nor ever functions in a mental atmosphere which is not transparent to the critical eye. To his biographer, indeed, the only phase of his life difficult to understand is that which links his effeminate adolescence to his masculine maturity; and, for my own part, I find it hard to visualise the transformation of the beautiful youth whom Curio loved into the giant who was adored by women. But perhaps the explanation is to be found in a certain aptitude for play-acting which was undoubtedly a marked feature of his character. As a boy, he played at being an elegant young fop because it was the fashion to do so; and as an adult he played at being a cave-man because it was a part for which nature had outwardly built him. Actually, however, he was at heart unsuited to either rôle; for he was too rough for the one and too gentle for the other. In after years he became famous for his hard-living and his clumsy disregard of other people's feelings; yet apart from one or two notable falls from grace, he was the type of burly ruffian of whom one says that he would not hurt a fly.

Some time in 57 B.C. he took up his commission as the commanding officer of a troop of rough Gallic cavalry, and went with Gabinius to Judea, where affairs were in an uproar. On the death of Alexander Jannæus in 78 B.C., the Jewish royal authority had passed to his widow, Alexandra, who gave the office of High-Priest of Jehovah to their son, Hyrcanus; and this personage re-

ceived also the Jewish sovereignty at his mother's death in 70 or
69 B.C. But in 68 B.C. his younger brother, Aristobulus, drove him
from the throne, and forced him into exile. In 63 B.C., however,
Pompey captured Jerusalem, as has already been mentioned, rein-
stated Hyrcanus, and carried Aristobulus and his son to Rome as his
captives. But shortly before Gabinius entered upon his governorship
of Syria, the two prisoners escaped, and, returning to Judæa, headed
a revolt against Hyrcanus, this civil war being at its height when
the new governor arrived.

Gabinius sent Antony ahead with his picturesque Gallic cavalry
to attack Aristobulus, who shut himself up in the fortress of Alex-
andrium in Samaria, not far from the north end of the Dead Sea.
The Romans assaulted this place, and Antony covered himself
with glory by being the first man to scale the walls. [5] The Jewish
leaders, however, escaped, and made for Machærus, a day's march
to the south; but Antony followed them, fought a pitched battle
with the reserves they had there mustered, annihilated them, and
captured Aristobulus and his son, who, at the beginning of 56 B.C.,
found themselves back in their prison in Rome, while Hyrcanus
ruled once more in Judæa.

Antony's dashing leadership and reckless bravery in this his
first campaign won him the devotion of his men and the warm
regard of his commanding officer, Gabinius, who in future thought
that whatever the young man did was right. [6] The army, too—
Romans as well as Gauls—made a hero of him, and were ready
to follow him upon whatever adventure he should wish to take
them. Nor was such an adventure long in presenting itself.

South of Judæa lay the Idumæan desert, the Biblical land
of Edom, which separated Palestine from the wealthy and powerful kingdom of Egypt, which was one of the few remaining countries of the civilized world still independent of Rome. A dynasty of
Greek sovereigns, or Pharaohs as they were called by their native
Egyptian subjects, had now ruled the land of the Nile for nearly
three centuries, each being named Ptolemy after the founder of
the line, who had been one of the generals of Alexander the Great;
but upon the death of King Ptolemy Alexander in 80 B.C., it was
found in his will that he had bequeathed his kingdom to the Ro-

[5] Plutarch: *Antony;* Josephus: Antiquities, xiv, 5, 3.   [6] Cicero: *Philippic ii,* xix.

man Republic, just as King Attalus of Pergamus had done in the time of the Gracchi. His nephew, Ptolemy Neos Dionysos, nick-named Auletes, "the Flute-player," seized the throne notwith-standing, and very soon began to negotiate with Rome for his recognition by that paramount Power, having heard that the Sen-ate was not at all inclined to accept the inheritance owing to the disturbances which were certain to ensue if they did. For twenty years and more Auletes reigned on sufferance in Alexandria, the Egyptian capital, always expecting to be deposed by Rome; but in 59 B.C., during the Consulship of Cæsar, who was ever in need of money, he managed at last to buy at enormous cost his right to the throne, the will of his uncle being declared invalid.

In the following year, 58 B.C., however, his own subjects de-posed him, mainly because he was so seldom sober; whereupon he went to Rome to attempt to effect his restoration, while his daughter, Berenice, his deadly enemy, reigned in his stead. The negotiations were protracted throughout 57 and part of 56 B.C.; but at last, having uselessly spent a vast fortune on bribes to the senators, Auletes left Rome in disgust, and retired to Ephesus, in Asia Minor, while, at just about the same time, Queen Berenice married Archelaus, [7] the High Priest of Komana in Cappadocia, who thus became King of Egypt.

Auletes then decided to make a last, desperate bid for his crown. Having obtained letters of recommendation from Pompey, he approached Gabinius, and offered to pay him ten thousand tal-ents [8] if he would lead his Roman legions and Gallic cavalry across the Idumæan desert to Egypt and replace him upon the throne, the suggested pretext for the campaign being that Arche-laus and Berenice were encouraging piracy along the North African coast, and, moreover, were building a fleet which was likely to be a menace to Rome. Gabinius, deeply in debt like so many others, was greatly tempted by the money, but was afraid of the dangers of the desert march, and, in spite of the support which Pompey had given to the undertaking, was pretty sure that it would not have the full approval of the Roman public owing to the curious fact that any meddling with Egyptian affairs was regarded as ill-omened. While Auletes was in Rome trying to obtain military aid,

[7] Son of the General of Mithradates whom Sulla defeated.   [8] About $12,500,000.

the statue of Jupiter on the Alban Hill had been struck by lightning, and when the Sibylline Books were consulted as to the meaning of this sign from heaven, attention was called by the meddle-
some Cato to a passage which read thus: "If the King of Egypt
come requesting aid, neither deny him friendship nor assist him
with any great force." [9] Gabinius did not regard the small army at
his disposal as constituting a "great force"; but, at the same time,
he was not easy in his mind as to the project.

Antony, however, was all for the campaign; and the exceptional trust imposed in his judgment at headquarters enabled him
to carry the day. Perhaps he had met Auletes in Rome and had
taken a fancy to the drunken little man, for Plutarch says that he
was anxious to do him a service; and, at any rate, Cæsar had once
befriended him, which was enough for Antony, who was prepared
to follow wherever Cæsar led. Moreover, there was his share of the
ten thousand talents to be considered; and, above all, there was
the excitement of the adventure, and, when the job was done, the
possibility of some pleasant weeks or months in Alexandria, a
purely Greek city, reputed to be the gayest and most luxurious in
the world.

Thus, [10] to the unbounded delight of Auletes, Gabinius agreed
to help him; and in the autumn of 56 B.C., when the heat of summer was over, the legions were concentrated at Gaza or some such
point in the south of Judæa, while Antony was sent ahead with
his cavalry to cross the desert and to capture the fortress of Pelusium (the *Sin* of the Bible) at the Egyptian end of the caravan-
road, so as to make safe the route which the legions would have
to traverse. Antony performed this task with great credit. Passing through Rhaphia on the sea-coast, the last outpost of Palestine,
he probably accomplished in one day the ride to Rhinokolura,
the modern El Arîsh, where water was to be obtained from a well
which is still in use. Thence, two days hard riding across the most
dangerous and waterless part of the route brought him, probably
at nightfall, to Pelusium. Fortunately for him this fortress surrendered after a brief resistance—fortunately, because, had it held

[9] Dion Cassius, xxxix, 15.
[10] The authorities for the Egyptian campaign are Plutarch (*Antony*), Dion Cassius,
Appian, and Josephus; but none supply detailed accounts.

out for long, his men would have soon become the prey of thirst. By his orders the garrison was treated honourably as prisoners-of-war; and here he settled down to await the coming of the main army.

But when Gabinius, accompanied by Auletes, had arrived with the legions, Antony was hard put to it to prevent the dethroned monarch from regarding the Egyptian prisoners as traitors for not having opened their gates at once. Auletes wanted Gabinius to put them all to death; but Antony, with great kindness of heart, pleaded for their pardon and finally obtained it. The whole army then advanced into Egypt, Antony's cavalry leading the way; and in various skirmishes he revealed his personal contempt for danger. In the first pitched battle with the Egyptians the Romans could make no headway until Antony outflanked the enemy with his cavalry, attacked them in the rear, and thus brought about their complete defeat. The advance was then continued towards Alexandria; and on the banks of one of the branches of the Nile, not far from the sea, the main Egyptian army was encountered and routed, Archelaus himself being killed. Here again Antony displayed his humanity; for, after the fight, he sought out the body of Archelaus, and, in spite of the protests of the revengeful Auletes, gave it a funeral with royal honours.

Having entered Alexandria in triumph, Gabinius replaced Auletes upon the throne, whereupon the Egyptian monarch at once put his daughter, Queen Berenice, and her chief supporters to death. By a second marriage, however, Auletes had four other children, two sons and two daughters, of whom the eldest was the famous Cleopatra, at this time a girl of some fourteen years of age; and, according to the matriarchal system of the Egyptians, this young lady now became the all-important heiress of the kingdom. As such, there can be little doubt that Antony made her acquaintance during his stay in Alexandria; but no importance is to be attached to the meeting. It is probable that she was then quite a plain little girl with rather a large nose; and her celebrated charms—of which her actual beauty was never a conspicuous feature—had probably not yet begun to reveal themselves in any very noticeable degree. Antony, however, was such an exceptionally fine-looking young man, and, though only twenty-seven

years of age, held such an important position in the estimation of
Gabinius and the army, that one may imagine him coming, at any
rate, under the interested scrutiny of this child of destiny. Girls in
her family, after all, were often married at fourteen, with children
of their own to remind them of their already fading romances.

The outbreak of another revolt in Palestine early in 55 B.C.
called Gabinius back to his Syrian province, and with him Antony,
who is said by Plutarch to have left behind him a very great
name amongst the Alexandrians. In Rome, however, both he and
his chief came in for considerable adverse comment on the part of
the conservatives, who regarded the Egyptian adventure almost
as a sacrilege in view of the Sibylline oracle, and who were egged
on by Cato to record their at present impotent protest against it.
But Pompey was still powerful, and for the moment Gabinius
escaped official censure for his hardihood in accepting Auletes'
money and risking a Roman army in the perilous march to and
from Egypt across the desert.

The situation in Rome had undergone considerable change
since Antony left the capital in 58 B.C.; and it is necessary now
to go back a while to see what had happened. In the spring of that
year Cicero, it will be recalled, had gone into a voluntary exile
which, so soon as he had departed, was extended into an official
banishment. It was his wish to retire to Athens, and, in his great
despair, he tried to console himself with the baseless thought that
his wide reading in philosophy had made a philosopher of him,
and that in Athens he would find his heart's comfort in the
society of the famous Greek thinkers. But, as Plutarch remarks,
the love of glory has great power in washing the tinctures of philosophy out of the souls of men; and the memory of all he had lost
rendered him incapable of deriving consolation from this source.
He had sunned himself too long in the warmth of Rome's flattery
to be able to endure the coldness of exile: he could not forget the
days of his glory.

His vanity, "always clinging to him like a disease," [11] caused
him to think of his case as history's prime example of man's ingratitude. Never since the world began had there been such a
fall as his, he declared; [12] and the tears ran down his cheeks as he

---

[11] Plutarch: *Cicero*.   [12] Cicero: *Ad Atticum*, iii, 15, 2.

pictured to himself the sorrow of his family and his friends at the misfortunes of so great, so good a man as himself. Even so, however, his letters to his wife, Terentia, at this time cannot fail to arouse our pity for the exile, whose collapse into the Slough of Despond was as astonishing as had been his flights into the clouds of self-glorification. "Night and day you are always before my eyes," he wrote to her;[13] "but, as you love me, do not let your anxiety injure your health, which is so delicate." As a matter of fact, Terentia was as strong as a horse, and lived to be a centenarian; but Cicero could hardly have been speaking in sarcasm. "I cannot write to you without shedding many tears," he told her, "when I picture you to myself as plunged in the deepest affliction—you whom my dearest wish has been to see perfectly happy. Alas, my light, my love!—that you should be in such misery, and all through my fault!"

He abandoned the thought of going to Athens, at length, because he had heard that some of the men whose banishment he had caused on account of their sympathy with Catiline and Antony's stepfather, were living there, and he did not dare to face them; and in the end he took up his residence at Thessalonica (Salonika) in Macedonia, where the chief Roman official was a conservative and was likely to treat him with respect. For the best part of a year he lived there, pouring out his lamentations in letters to his friends; but in the spring of 57 B.C. hope dawned again in his heart as the answering letters from Rome began to tell him of the development of the political situation at home.

It will be remembered that Antony's friend Clodius, who was Cicero's bitterest enemy, was the protégé of Cæsar, the little affair with Cæsar's wife having been forgiven and forgotten; but now that his patron was away in Gaul, Clodius had come to blows with Pompey, who, as a very gentlemanly and moderate democrat, had aroused his impatience, and matters reached such a pass that Pompey believed himself to be in danger of his life, and even went so far as to shut himself up in his house for some time, while gangs of men in the employ of Clodius paraded the streets. As a result of this split in the democratic ranks, which left Clodius with no more than the rabble behind him, Pompey was not

[13] Cicero: *Ad Familiares*, xiv, 2.

unwilling to consider the recall of Cicero, whose exile had been brought about by this reckless mob-leader.

One of the Consuls for the year 57 B.C. was that same Metellus Nepos, Pompey's former agent, who had led the first attack on Cicero five years previously; and this man, at his patron's instigation, now declared that he was ready to forget his feud with the fallen orator and to allow him to come back. The Tribunes of the People for this year, and in particular, one named Titus Annius Milo, also signalized their disapproval of Clodius by stating that they would not stand in the way of Cicero's recall; and at last Cæsar himself was induced to turn upon his former agent and to send from Gaul his written approval of the exile's pardon. All the more sober leaders of the democracy, in fact, were dissociating themselves from Clodius, and could think of no better way of demonstrating their attitude than by allowing the decree of banishment to be rescinded, even though to do so were to play into the hands of the conservatives.

The news of these events, it may be mentioned in passing, must have been received at the time by Antony in Syria with very mixed feelings. Clodius had been his friend: Cicero was his enemy. But when Cæsar, his hero, also broke with Clodius, he, too, repudiated him, and swallowed the bitter pill of Cicero's coming pardon with as good a grace as possible.

When the bill for the exile's recall was at last brought forward, Clodius filled the streets with his roughs, and so fierce a battle was fought in the Forum that the ground was soaked with blood and many lives were lost, Cicero's own brother, Quintus, being amongst the wounded. The Tribune Milo, whose sympathies were with the conservatives, then organised a private fighting-force of his own to counter that of Clodius, and soon the whole city was in a state of daily uproar, the question of Cicero's recall thus receiving a prominence which it would not otherwise have obtained. Cicero, of course, attributed the intensity of the struggle to his own importance; but this was by no means the case. Like his colleague in the Consulship, Antony's uncle, he might have remained for many a year a more or less forgotten exile, had not the resentment against Clodius raised him, as that man's victim, to the status of a martyr.

At length, in August, 57 B.C., after somewhat less than seven‹
teen months of exile, Cicero was recalled; and when he set foot
once more on his native shores he declared, with tears of pride in
his eyes, that Italy herself had brought him on her shoulders home.
On all sides he was warmly congratulated, [14] and Pompey made a
nice little speech in his praise, while even Crassus, the financier,
who used to quarrel with him continuously, patted him on the
back. Crassus had once made the remark that no member of his
family lived beyond sixty, and to this Cicero had replied that in
saying so Crassus was evidently trying to gain popularity, knowing
how pleased people would be to hear it—a jest which, with other
rude remarks, had led to the complete estrangement now happily
ended.

One of the returned exile's first acts was that of inducing the
Tribunes to expunge the records of the tribunate of Clodius in
the previous year, on the grounds that his adoption into a plebeian
family, by which stratagem he had satisfied the public that he
was eligible for the office, had not legally qualified him for the
post; but here that Jack-in-the-box, Cato, jumped up to protest
that this deletion of a whole year's doings in the Comitia was
much too high-handed. Cicero next attempted to revenge himself upon Clodius in another way: he pleaded that his beautiful
house on the Palatine, which Clodius, with Antony's aid, had
razed to the ground, should be rebuilt at public expense; and so
bitter was the feeling against Clodius that this measure was agreed
to. The temple of Liberty, which had been erected on the site, was
pulled down; and the figure of the presiding goddess, which, as a
matter of fact, was a Tanagran sculptor's portrait of a certain
well-known prostitute, [15] was removed elsewhere, the wrath of
Clodius notwithstanding. But the re-erection of the former mansion
was not carried out without interruption, for Clodius and his mob
attacked the workers on one occasion, and destroyed the walls they
were building. They also pelted Cicero himself more than once with
brick bats, but, as luck would have it, without hurting him; and
they set fire to the house of his unfortunate brother, Quintus, who
but lately had been knocked senseless in the Forum.

---

[14] Beesly (*Catiline, Clodius, and Tiberius*), however, thinks that his reception was
only half-hearted.   [15] Cicero: *Pro Domo,* xliii, 111.

After the first excitement of the return of Cicero had died down, public opinion began to be more divided about him. He was so ludicrously pompous and vain. "He offended so many people," writes Plutarch, "by continually praising and magnifying himself; for neither Senate, nor Comitia, nor court of law could meet without him being heard to boast of his action against Catiline and Lentulus; and he filled his speeches and writings with his own praise to such an extent as to render a style, in itself most pleasant and delightful, tiresome and sickening." Many of the democrats who had been sorry for him now found him rather impossible; and, as a consequence, Clodius began to receive more sympathy, even Crassus giving him some support. [16] The relationship between Cicero and Pompey at this time was very friendly, and it looked as though Pompey were inclining towards the aristocratic party, particularly since he was known to be on rather bad terms just now both with Crassus and the absent Cæsar.

Cæsar's position had undergone a complete change since he had been away. He had left Rome for Cisalpine Gaul, after his Consulship, with no very nice reputation: his effeminate youth, his later affairs with other men's wives, his immense debts, his implication in various plots and intrigues, his patronage of the fire-eating Clodius, his fights with his consular colleague, Bibulus, and so forth, had caused a good deal of adverse comment. He had set out under a decided cloud; and people had smiled, too, to think of him as the commander of the Roman armies in Gaul—this elegant, unscrupulous spendthrift, who knew nothing about Gaul and hardly anything about military tactics except what he had learnt in Spain, and was, moreover, a man of delicate health, subject to occasional fits of some sort. Within a few months news had come that he had recklessly attacked a huge horde of Swiss barbarians—the Helvetii—who were peacefully migrating towards the Rhine, and, after being very nearly defeated by them, had concluded a by no means triumphant peace with them. People shook their heads, and wondered what disasters were in store for him.

Then came the change. The German King, Ariovistus, who had crossed the Rhine and was moving into Gaul, was attacked

[16] Cicero: *Ad Q. Fratrem*, ii, 3, 4.

and completely defeated by Cæsar, who killed eighty thousand of his men and drove him back into his own country from which he never dared again to venture. Next he dispersed a general gathering of the Belgæ, and then the Nervii were routed, with a loss of fifty thousand men and nearly four hundred chieftains. For centuries the so-called barbarians who lived in the almost unknown lands north and north-west of Italy had been a menace to the safety of the Republic; and stories of their gigantic stature and their appalling bravery were still told in Rome by old soldiers who had fought against them under Cæsar's uncle, the great Marius, forty-five years ago. But now the exploits of Marius were being excelled by those of his nephew; and Rome was amazed to hear that he was showing not only entirely unexpected skill as a military commander but also the most wonderful energy and endurance. "There was no peril," says Plutarch, "to which he did not willingly expose himself, no labour from which he pleaded exemption. His contempt of danger was not so much wondered at, but his enduring so much hardship very much surprised his soldiers, for he was a slightly-built man, with a skin which was soft and white."

Stories about him and his adventures began to circulate in Rome. It was said that he made incredibly long and rapid journeys on horseback or in his four-wheeled carriage, slept in the open, and ate the roughest food. One story related how, during a storm, he had given the only available shelter to an officer of his who was in bad health, and had himself spent the night outside in the rain; another anecdote told how, from motives of politeness, he had eaten without complaint some asparagus which the man on whom he had billeted himself had, in his excitement, dipped in scented ointment [17] instead of olive-oil; and yet another tale affirmed that he had covered a distance of some seven hundred miles in eight days, sleeping by night in his carriage, and spending part of the day in dictating correspondence, as they trundled along, to two secretaries at once. It was said that he went bare-headed in sunshine or storm; galloped his horse along the roads, sometimes, with his hands clasped behind his back; [18] dived into the rivers which impeded his progress and swam across them; had arrested with his

[17] So Plutarch (*Cæsar*); but Suetonius (*Cæsar*) says it was merely rancid oil.
[18] Nor were stirrups used by the Romans.

own hands the flight of some of his men in battle, taking them by the scruff of the neck and turning them round; and had again and again performed prodigies of valour.

These tales aroused a variety of emotions in the leading men of the time. Pompey was too much of a gentleman to reveal the professional jealousy which he undoubtedly felt; but it was mortifying to him to find his own famous victories eclipsed by these exploits of a younger man, and to feel that, at the age of fifty, he was not able to free himself from the ties of home to seek adventure abroad. He knew in his heart that his former daredevilry, his initiative, his self-assurance, had left him; he could not even be sure of his own political views; and the only certainty in his life was his inability to tear himself away from his adored young wife, Julia, the daughter of this new idol of the people whose stature was daily increasing as his own diminished.

Crassus was chiefly stirred by the reports of the enormous wealth which Cæsar was collecting from the conquered nations of the north: he had looted the temples and treasuries of the barbarians, and had stripped the living and dead of their jewellery and ornaments, until his coffers were full of gold, and he was selling it in Italy by the pound at a price far below its value. The financier's mouth watered to hear of it; and he told himself that if the delicate Cæsar could accomplish these lucrative victories, so could he. His commercial interests had brought him frequently into contact with the merchants from Asia, and having thus heard tales of the fabulous wealth of Parthia, Persia, and India, he began to dream of leading a Roman army into those far-off lands and of plundering the east as Cæsar was plundering the north. After all, in his youth he had won a splendid victory at the Colline Gate, and had only been turned from a brilliant military career by the obstruction of the late Sulla: perhaps it was not too late to become the Cæsar of the Orient.

By Cicero the news of Cæsar's victories was received with a surprise which soon gave place to a determination to make a friend of him as already he had done in the case of Pompey; and presently he wrote a letter to him asking him to find an appointmen on his staff for his brother, Quintus, his pleasure being extreme when Cæsar replied that he would be delighted to do so.

Cato, too, was stirred by the tidings, and, in his own begrudging way, gave the new conqueror some meed of praise by saying that Cæsar, at any rate, "was the only man amongst all those who were engaged in ruining the State who was not addicted to drink," [19] Cæsar always being notorious for his abstemiousness.

Antony's enthusiasm over the victories seems to have been intense; and now that he had made a name for himself as a cavalry leader in the war in Palestine and Egypt his dearest wish was to serve under Cæsar in Gaul. It would appear that he wrote to him to this effect, but for the time being he was obliged to remain with Gabinius, who was by no means a brilliant general and was much more interested in making a fortune for himself than in fighting or governing.

The news of Cæsar's successes was followed by the breathtaking announcement that he had formally annexed the whole of Gaul to the Roman empire. It is true that this step was ridiculously premature, for there were several small nations in that vast country which were unconquered, and others which had made peace with him on terms not affecting their independence. But Cæsar was now confident that he could make the so-called annexation practical without much more fighting, and, even if further campaigns were called for, he could always describe them as being necessitated by subsequent revolts. He did not hesitate, therefore, to proclaim that Gaul was henceforth a Roman province; and the consequent rejoicings and celebrations in Rome included a Thanksgiving-festival of fifteen days duration—the longest ever decreed. The whole city went mad with excitement; and in that storm of popular enthusiasm the new Cæsar was born—the national leader, the master-statesman, the unwearying autocrat, in whom the dandified and rather disreputable politician was lost to sight. When he had left Italy in the spring of 58 B.C. he had declared that he would rather be the leading man anywhere in Gaul than the second man in Rome; but now, suddenly, he had forged ahead of Pompey, Crassus, Cicero, and everybody else, and was unquestionably the first citizen of the Republic.

As such, in the spring of 56 B.C., he summoned a meeting

[19] Suetonius: *Cæsar*, liii.

at Luca (Lucca), the southernmost city of Cisalpine Gaul, [20] to which not only Pompey and Crassus came, but also some two-hundred senators, these latter tumbling over one another to be the first to congratulate him, democrat though he was. In the secret talks between the three Triumvirs it was agreed that Pompey and Crassus should compose their private differences and should get themselves elected as the two Consuls for the coming year, 55 B.C., and that at the end of their term of office, Crassus should succeed Gabinius as governor of Syria, and should have his heart's desire, namely, to lead an army against Parthia and on into India if the fates were willing, while Pompey should be assigned the governorship of Spain for five years, with the right to reside in Rome and to administer his province through the agency of his lieutenants. Cæsar, meanwhile, was to retain his Gallic command also for five years, so as to consolidate his labours in the new province, this being really the piece of work which most interested him at the moment—he was enthusiastic about it and had no fears that either Pompey or Crassus would ever be able to supplant him now as the hero of Rome.

In due course these proposals were put into execution, though not without opposition from what remained of the republican party. When the consular elections were due to take place in the summer of this year 56 B.C., Cato persuaded his little party of irreconcilable conservatives to put forward his aristocratic brother-in-law, Lucius Domitius Ahenobarbus, [21] as a candidate in opposition to one or other of the Triumvirs; but the only result was that riots broke out in which this personage was nearly killed, and Cato, with a broken arm, was thrown bodily out of the election-meeting—a contretemps to which he was by now quite accustomed. Pompey and Crassus were then duly elected, but when they entered office at the beginning of 55 B.C. there could have been little hope that their Consulship would be fruitful in reforms or in any sort of administrative work, for Crassus was now obsessed with his Parthian schemes, and Pompey could think of nothing else but his wife, Julia, and her happiness. He was violently in love with her

---

[20] At a later date it was included in Etruria, the province south of Cisalpine Gaul.
[21] Great-grandfather of that Ahenobarbus whose son was the Emperor Nero.

and she with him; and as her health was delicate at this time, owing to the fact that she was going to have a baby, he was devoting himself to her more entirely than ever before. In one of these riots, however, he was splashed with the blood of a man whose head was broken close to him, and having sent his stained clothes back to his house, he was horrified to hear shortly afterwards that Julia had seen them, and, thinking he was murdered, had fainted dead away. As a result of the accident she had a miscarriage and nearly died.

In the spring of 55 B.C. Cæsar went north across the Alps again, to fight out this matter of the annexation of Gaul with those tribes which declined to be annexed; and having been thoroughly scared by the invasion of two German tribes—the Usipetes and the Tencteri—he attacked them when they were off their guard and believed themselves to be under the protection of an armistice. It was afterwards reported in Rome that he had slaughtered no less than four hundred thousand of their men, women, and children; and at this news Cato, believing that the law of nations had been broken, proposed in the Senate that Cæsar should be arrested and handed over in chains to the Germans—a not altogether improper suggestion which, however, was laughed out of court. Cæsar, indifferent to criticism, followed up this massacre by making a raid across the Rhine into the territory of other Germans, whom he thoroughly defeated once more near Bonn on the Rhine—that is to say, in their own country. In the summer of 55 B.C. he made a raid on the coast of Britain to find out what chance there was of conquering the island; and though the expedition was something of a fiasco he was able to report it to Rome as a triumph. These new successes made Crassus so impatient to be off on his own plundering adventure that he could not be prevailed upon to wait even until the end of his term of office as Consul, but set out in November 55 B.C., at the head of the army which he had collected, in spite of the desperate opposition of the conservatives, who declared that Rome had no quarrel with Parthia. This opposition was chiefly voiced by a certain Tribune of aristocratic sympathies, named Ateius Capito, who, when he could do no more, followed Crassus out of Rome, solemnly cursing him and the expedition in general, and, at the gate of the city, "took a chafing-dish with red-hot charcoal in it," as

Plutarch relates, "and, burning incense and pouring libations upon it, cursed him with dreadful imprecations, calling upon several strange and horrible deities." It was a shocking send-off for the great financier, and the subsequent disaster to the expedition was by many blamed upon the hysterical Tribune.

In the meantime Cicero was engaging himself in courting the friendship of Cæsar, who, on his part, responded with warmth to these overtures, realising that the great orator might become the link between the party of the People and the aristocracy in that coalition which was already his dream. It must be admitted that Cæsar was rather wicked in the brazen way in which he played upon Cicero's vanity, flattering him in the most audacious manner, and evidently smiling sardonically as he heard how the orator was now wont to speak of "my dear old friend Cæsar." "I have taken Cæsar to my bosom and will never let him slip," wrote Cicero [22] to his brother, Quintus, in a letter which he expected Cæsar to see. "He comes next to you and my children in my affection, and not far behind." [23] To his friend Atticus he said: "I have full evidence of Cæsar's love for me"; [24] and to another he boastfully wrote: "I have the benefit of Cæsar's influence, overwhelming as it is, and the enormous wealth he now possesses, as though they were my own." [25]

When Cicero recommended any friend to Cæsar's notice the latter would take pains to do him honour. "As for Mescinius Rufus, about whom you have written to me," said Cæsar in a letter which Cicero proudly quotes, [26] "I will make him king of Gaul, if you like." And when the orator found himself deep in debt owing to the money he was spending like water upon the beautifying of his rebuilt mansion on the Palatine, and the erection of grand houses for himself at Pompeii and elsewhere, Cæsar at once lent him a large sum. [27]

The result of all this was that Cicero began to show less anxiety to maintain his friendship with Pompey—a breach which was just what Cæsar was aiming at, for he wished all eyes to be

[22] Cicero: *Ad Q. Fratrem*, ii, 11, 1.
[23] Cicero: *Ibid.*, iii, 1, 18.
[24] Cicero: *Ad Atticum*, iv, 15, 10.
[25] Cicero: *Ad Familiares*, i, 9, 21.
[26] *Ibid.*, vii, 5, 2.
[27] Cicero: *Ad Atticum*, v, 4, 3; v, 5, 2; v, 6, 2.

turned upon himself, and did not want any sort of rapprochement between Pompey and the aristocratic party: if ever the
democrats and conservatives were to come together it must be
under *his* leadership, not Pompey's. But though Cæsar was thus
scheming to keep Pompey's position subordinate to his own, Pompey was never inclined to assert himself at the expense of Cæsar,
for he could not for one moment forget that his adored Julia
was Cæsar's daughter, and her delight in her father's pre-eminence
was something which the fond lover was not willing to jeopardise.
He was not as great a man as his father-in-law, and he knew it,
but he was very much more honourable.

In August, 54 B.C., Cæsar made a second invasion of Britain,
and penetrated as far inland as Verulam (St. Albans), north of
London; but on his return to Gaul in the middle of September,
he received letters from Rome which struck him a double blow.
In the first place he heard that his mother, Aurelia, had died; and
hard on the heels of these sad tidings came the terrible news of
the death of his daughter Julia, who had presented Pompey with
a baby girl and had died as a consequence, the child following her
to the grave shortly afterwards. Cæsar's grief was only exceeded
by that of Pompey, who, of course was distracted; but to the
Romans in general the disaster was tragic chiefly because it
severed a family tie between Pompey and Cæsar, and seemed to
presage a mutual movement away from one another which might
have the most perilous consequences for the State. Cæsar, himself, however, had little time for tears. Revolts broke out in Gaul
which required his full attention, and soon he was once more in
the thick of battle.

Crassus, meanwhile, had replaced Gabinius in Syria, and was
making his preparations for the invasion of Parthia from that
base early in the new year. Gabinius himself was making a leisurely progress towards Rome, being unwilling to hurry himself
since he had heard that the conservatives, headed by Cato, were
likely to give him a warm reception and to try to bring him to
trial for his Egyptian adventure. It was reported to him, moreover, that in consequence of a serious flood in Rome, and the
vulgar belief that it was heaven's punishment for the disregarding
of the Sibylline oracle, the mob was liable to demand his death

or to lynch him itself. He was a brave man, however, and he duly presented himself in the capital in September, though, it is true, he entered it by night, and shut himself up in his house thereafter for some days. Cæsar, meanwhile, had sent an urgent request to his friends in Rome to defend the unfortunate man, and to this end Pompey also lent his aid; and when the trial took place he was acquitted, in spite of the fact that the speech for the prosecution was delivered by Cicero who had not then realized that Cæsar was on the other side, and who was urged to heights of oratory by a yelling rabble outside the courthouse, eager for the sacrifice of Gabinius to the wrath of the gods.

Having failed to convict him on this charge the conservatives, aided for once by the superstitious mob, pressed another charge—that of bribery, corruption, and extortion—against him; but on hearing of this, Cæsar seems to have written to Cicero asking him to use his wonderful eloquence this time in the defence of Gabinius, and Pompey at the same time urged him to do so. Cicero was not the man to resist such pressure. True, Gabinius was an old political and personal enemy whose defence would be all the more difficult because Cicero had just been denouncing him on the other count; but he had no wish to offend Pompey and he was eager to do Cæsar this favour. He therefore undertook the defence; but his heart was not in his work, and Gabinius was found guilty and sentenced to exile—a not altogether unpleasant rustication from which he was recalled after a while by Cæsar.

In regard to Antony, the only fact which is known as to his movements at this time is that, having been summoned by Cæsar, he made the journey from Syria to Gaul without passing through Rome.[28] Gabinius had made a slow business of handing over his province to Crassus, and it is known that he left some of his officers there to clear up the affairs of the country before resigning their posts to the newcomers. It is to be supposed, therefore, that Antony did not leave for home until the late summer of 54 B.C., and that a timely letter from Cæsar, permitting him to join his staff, diverted his journey towards Rome and sent him northwards to the Alps with light heart and high hopes to serve under his hero.

[28] Cicero: *Philippic ii*, xix.

CHAPTER VII

Antony's Service with Cæsar in Gaul, and his Tribuneship in Rome which
was Interrupted by the Outbreak of Civil War.

54–49 B.C.

AT the time when Antony took up his new work in Gaul,
Cæsar's popularity, as has been said, was very great—greater than
Pompey's. Cato might angrily call him a blackguard and a
butcher; but these were not the sentiments of the general public,
whose feelings for him were like those of their fathers for his
uncle Marius. Pompey in Asia Minor might have overthrown
kings and princes by the score, but he had never been confronted
with such perils as Cæsar had faced, nor had he brought such
wonderful new lands and unknown peoples under Roman sway.

Cicero, basking in the apparently warm friendship of the
popular idol, voiced the opinion of the country when he said
in the Senate: "He has striven on glorious battlefields with fierce
tribes and mighty hosts, while others he has terrified, checked,
tamed, and taught to obey the command of the Roman People;
over lands and countries with which no book, no traveller, no
report had acquainted us, Cæsar has led the way for our soldiers;
and now at last he has brought us this consummation, that our
empire extends to the uttermost limits of the earth, so that beyond
those Alpine peaks which Providence has thrown up to be a ram-
part for Italy, as far as the extremest verge of the outer Ocean,
there is nothing left for us to fear." [1] This oration was one of
Cicero's most magnificent, and as the rolling sentences fell from
his lips his eyes and those of the senators were wet with tears of
patriotic pride.

[1] Cicero: *De Provinciis Consularibus,* xiii, 33. In a letter to Atticus (iv, 5) Cicero
speaks with some shame of a recantation he had recently made, and some critics suppose he is referring to this speech; but this is unlikely in view of his genuine
pride in Cæsar's friendship.

Antony's admiration for his new chief, and his eager desire to please him, are not to be wondered at; for Cæsar's quick intellect, his tireless energy, his clever administration of the new lands, his brilliant generalship, and his unexpected supremacy in so many fields, had, from a bad beginning, raised him now immeasurably above his fellow men, while, at the same time, his weaknesses, especially in regard to women, made him not unpleasantly human in the view of his young admirer. Cæsar was at this time forty-eight years of age, and was, to his great annoyance, fast becoming bald; but he was still a very handsome man, whose whimsical smile and dark, penetrating eyes few women could resist. Antony, aged twenty-nine, was also having his successes in this respect; for his handsome face, much improved by the removal of his beard, his tremendous physical strength, and the bold and rather swashbucklering manner he was now cultivating, made him very attractive to the other sex. When Cæsar marched into a city his soldiers used to sing a ribald ditty,[2] the first line of which was *Urbani, servate uxores: calvum mœchum adducimus,* "Citizens, look after your wives: we are bringing in our bald-headed old adulterer!" And though history does not tell us what they sang of their chief's lusty lieutenant, the fact is on record, as has already been said, that they made many a jest about his various affairs of the heart. A pretty couple!—and yet these two, the ruthless master and the loyal servant, were soon to shake the world to its foundations.

It must be remembered, of course, that Roman society was at this period hopelessly immoral, and that the treatment of women was callous in the extreme. An absurd incident occurred in about this year which well illustrates the indifference felt for the ties of matrimony even in old-fashioned aristocratic circles; and, strange to say, the chief actor in the comedy was none other than the austere Cato. The second wife of that odd personage was a young lady named Marcia, daughter of Marcus Philippus,[3] who had been Consul in 56 B.C.; but by his first wife, Atilia, Cato had a grown-up daughter, Porcia, who was married to the ex-

---

[2] Suetonius: *Cæsar,* li.
[3] Philippus afterwards married Atia, the widowed mother of Octavian, and thus became the stepfather of the future Emperor, as will presently be recorded.

Consul, Bibulus, Cæsar's former antagonist, whom she had already presented with two children. A great friend of Cato's family was Hortensius, the wealthy conservative orator who has already entered these pages as the defender of Verres against Cicero: he was now a man of nearly sixty, and happening at the moment to be a widower in search of a new wife, he had cast a covetous eye upon this Porcia, Cato's daughter, in spite of the fact that she was already married to Bibulus. He therefore asked Cato for her hand, giving as his reasons the fact that she was obviously likely to bring a lot of children into the world, that Bibulus, who was not a wealthy man, could ill afford them, that he, Hortensius, on the contrary, was rich and wanted children, and that, anyway, he would very much like to use Porcia "as a fair plot of land to bear fruit for him," and thus to unite his race with that of Cato. He added that if Bibulus would not part with Porcia for good and all, he might at least consent to lend her to him for a few years on the understanding that Hortensius would hand her back after she had produced two or three little Hortensii.

Cato answered gravely that, much as he loved Hortensius, he really could not ask Bibulus to hand Porcia over; and thereupon Hortensius made the alternative proposal that Cato should give him his own wife, Marcia, instead. It was true, he admitted, that the fact that Marcia was then with child by Cato made the change of husbands a little awkward; but he said that when the baby was born he would adopt it, since Cato did not really need any more children, and that he would then try to have some children of his own by Marcia, after which he would be quite willing to return her to Cato. Cato replied that Marcia's father, Philippus, ought to be consulted; and they therefore sent for him, and at once received his consent. Marcia was then divorced and married to Hortensius, Cato being the "best man" at the wedding; and I may add that when the elderly bridegroom died, six years later, Cato remarried Marcia, while, on the death of Bibulus, Porcia married her cousin Brutus, the son of Servilia and Cæsar.[4]

The customary matrimonial bargaining of which this is an

---

[4] The story is given in Putarch's *Cato,* on the authority of Thrasea, an emulator of Cato who was put to death by Nero, Thrasea having received the details from Munatius, Cato's great friend.

instance, presently led Cæsar to make a proposal to Pompey that a new alliance of this kind should be effected between them to replace that broken by the death of his daughter Julia, Pompey's wife. Cæsar's elder sister, another Julia, had been married to a certain Atius Balbus, by whom she had a daughter, Atia, who had been married first to Caius Octavius, a widower, who had died in 58 B.C., leaving a daughter, Octavia, by his first wife, and a son, Octavian, by Atia;[5] and, secondly, to Marcus Philippus, the above-mentioned father of Cato's wife, Marcia. Octavianus, now generally called Octavian, played an important part in the later drama of Antony's life, and was afterwards the Emperor Augustus, while Octavia, his half-sister, was ultimately married to Antony; but at the time with which we are now dealing, she had recently been married to Caius Marcellus, a rising politician. Cæsar now suggested that this Octavia, his niece's stepdaughter, should be divorced from Marcellus and married to Pompey in place of the late Julia; and that Pompey's daughter by an earlier marriage, who was betrothed to Faustus Sulla, son of the great Sulla, should be released from this proposed union and should be married to Cæsar, who, for this purpose, would divorce his own wife, Calpurnia. Pompey, however, did not take kindly to the suggestion, and deeply offended Cæsar by refusing to consider it, and by marrying his daughter to Sulla forthwith. To Cæsar it was as though Pompey had refused an offer of alliance, and had expressed his preference for a definite independence and rivalry.

Antony's first year with Cæsar was passed in a series of hard campaigns forced upon the Romans by the various revolts in Gaul; and although we have no details of his movements at this time, it is to be supposed that he was kept exceedingly busy by his greatly harassed chief. Then, in the summer of 53 B.C., the most appalling news from the East reached Rome and struck dismay into the whole Empire's heart. The financier Crassus had crossed the Euphrates and had advanced towards Parthia in the spring; but near Carrhæ (Haran), in northern Mesopotamia, half way between Syria and Armenia, he had been overwhelmed by the enemy, his army had been almost annihilated, his son, Publius Crassus, had been killed, and in the frenzied negotiations with

[5] Plutarch: *Antony.*

the victors which had followed, he himself had been treacherously murdered, and his severed head sent in triumph to the court of the King of Parthia.

The result of this disaster was that the public began to be troubled also about the fate of the Roman armies under Cæsar. If the barbarians of the Orient could so utterly outwit a cautious man like Crassus and destroy the magnificent troops under his quite capable command, the Gauls and Germans might do the same with Cæsar and his forces. At any rate, they said, Cæsar seemed to be barely holding his own. They were no longer delirious about his annexation of Gaul: they doubted now whether he had ever properly subdued it, and they began to wonder if he really were the superman they had supposed him to be. After all, Pompey's victories had produced pretty permanent results, and there had been no need to go on fighting and refighting over the territories *he* had conquered. It seemed that Pompey was the better man, and now that Crassus was dead the public began to turn to him as the most trustworthy leader of the nation. Pompey responded by showing a renewed interest in events and a fresh access of energy; and so as to dismiss from his mind the depression which had followed the death of Julia, he decided to marry again, the lady of his choice being Cornelia, daughter of Metellus Scipio and widow of the younger Crassus, recently killed in the Parthian disaster, who must have been enormously wealthy. Plutarch describes her as a very well-educated young woman, who played the guitar, was rather good at geometry, and regularly attended lectures on philosophy, but "had not become in the least unamiable or pretentious as sometimes young women do when they take up such studies." She was pretty, too; but people said that she was far too young for Pompey, who, they thought, looked somewhat undignified, crowned with garlands, at the wedding, and joking with his youthful bride.

The elections for the Consulships and other important offices for the coming year 52 B.C. were now at hand, and amongst the candidates for the Prætorship was Clodius, "The Beauty," who had been dropped by Cæsar, but was still the most outstanding mob-leader in Rome. From his headquarters in Gaul Cæsar was watching the movements of political events in the capital with anxious eyes, and some of the vast wealth which he had acquired was being spent by his agents in secretly maintaining his inter- ests there against those of Pompey, who, though outwardly his friend and colleague, seemed now to be his rival. During the past year Cæsar had come to place very great confidence in Antony, and at this juncture he decided to send him home to Rome to stand for the Quæstorship, so that he might begin a political career which, as it advanced, would become more and more valu- able to his patron.

Antony therefore returned to the metropolis, and very soon was in the thick of the disorders and riots incidental to the elec- tions, nor was it long before he discovered that Cæsar's most dangerous enemy was his former friend Clodius, who was thirst- ing for revenge on the leader who had repudiated him. Any enemy of Cæsar was Antony's enemy, too, and one day in the Forum, in the heat of some forgotten riot, the ardent young man drew his sword and rushed at Clodius, intending to kill him. Clodius, however, managed to escape, and that is all we know of the incident, except that Cicero, always the deadly enemy of Clodius, appears to have commended Antony for his action, calling him "a most noble and gallant young man," and Antony seems to have told Cicero that since he, Cicero, was now so friendly to Cæsar, Antony would have been glad of the opportunity to serve him at the same time that he served Cæsar, by killing their common enemy.[6] Thereafter Cicero was wont to tell people how much he liked this handsome young admirer of his dear friend Cæsar;[7] but Antony's feelings towards the orator do not seem to have carried him beyond the instructions he had received from Cæsar—namely, to avoid offending the pompous old wind-bag.[8]

Antony was duly elected Quæstor, and therewith returned to Gaul; and shortly afterwards, in January 52 B.C., Clodius met at the hands of Milo the end he had so recently escaped at those of Antony. Milo, it will be recalled, was a man of aristocratic sympathies who had organized a gang of roughs to oppose those

---

[6] The incident is referred to by Cicero, *Philippic ii,* xx, and *Pro Milone,* xv, 40, and in a quotation from Cicero by Dion Cassius, xlv, 40; but there are no details.

[7] Dion Cassius, xlvi, 3.

[8] As Prof. Beesly calls him.

under the orders of Clodius; and for a long time now these two
firebrands had each been looking for an opportunity to kill the
other, their endless fights often making the streets of Rome un-
safe for law-abiding citizens. Clodius was far and away the more
popular of the two, and had the sympathy of the rabble; but
history has taken such an unfavourable view of his character that
it is hard to find anything good to say of him. I have already
pointed out, however, that he was at any rate a brave and adventurous leader, and was certainly not the startling specimen of
the intermediate sex which his once girlish face might lead us to
suppose him to have been. Cæsar had thought very highly of him
at first, and had trusted him as he was now trusting Antony, only
dropping him when his riotous behaviour had passed all bounds;
and it must be admitted that the retaining of so shrewd a master's favour, even for a few years, says more for his character
than history can deny.

His death occurred in this wise. Milo was riding with his wife
and a large escort along the Appian Way, bound for his house in
Lanuvium (Lavigna), a day's march south of Rome, when, near
Bovillæ, about half-way, he encountered Clodius and a smaller
company riding towards the capital. As they passed each other
they exchanged no more than the customary scowls and oaths,
but one of Milo's retainers managed to slip in, unseen, amongst
the hostile party, and stabbed Clodius in the back with his dagger. The dying man was carried into a wayside inn, and for some
moments Milo hesitated as to what should be done; but presently,
realizing that in any event he would be accused of the murder,
he led his followers into the house for the purpose of finishing
his opponent off. The reckless "Beauty," however, had already
breathed his passionate last, so it seems, and Milo's own hands
were not, therefore, stained with his blood.[9]

The corpse was carried to Rome, and its arrival produced such
a wild outburst of anger on the part of the mob against the
conservative party which Milo represented that on all sides the
members of the latter were murdered: any well-dressed person, in

[9] Asconius (*In Milonianam*) says that Clodius was dragged out of the inn still
alive, and dispatched outside, but Cicero (*Pro Milone*) gives the other version. See
also Appian, *Civil Wars*, ii, 21.

fact, who chanced to be encountered was attacked and killed for an aristocrat. The body of Clodius was then placed on the rostra in the Forum, after which it was carried to the Senate-house, where the frenzied mob heaped up a great pyre of chairs and benches, and, setting fire thereto, consumed not only the corpse but the entire building and the houses around as well. Milo himself, after making a brief appearance in public, went into hiding, and for several days the rioting continued, the people demanding that Pompey, or else Cæsar, should be made Dictator and that Milo and his conservative supporters should be punished.

When some sort of order had been restored he was formally brought to trial, and Cicero was asked by the aristocratic party to undertake his defence, which he consented to do in view of the fact that both Cæsar and Pompey—whom not for anything would he offend—had long ago become tired of the lawless behaviour of Clodius, and could hardly disapprove of Milo's action. The orator, however, was not at his best, for, in spite of the presence of large bodies of soldiers, he was naturally nervous of the mob; and, in fact he seems to have found it difficult to rake up anything very culpable about Clodius except his pugnacity and quarrelsomeness.[10] Thus, although Cicero worked himself up to an emotional climax, and ended by saying that he was choked with sobs and could speak no more, Milo was found guilty and exiled to Massilia (Marseilles). Cicero afterwards wrote up his speech into a splendid oration, and sent a copy to the exile; but it so differed from the feeble defence actually delivered at the trial that Milo was constrained to remark: "It is just as well that Cicero did not succeed in delivering this harangue, or I should never have known the taste of these excellent mullets of Massilia!"

Meanwhile, Antony was sharing the fresh troubles which were crowding upon Cæsar owing to the revolt led by Vercingetorix, a Gallic prince whose father had been at one time the paramount chief of the whole country. It must have been at just about the time when Clodius was killed that the rebellion broke out; and Cæsar, who was in northern Italy was obliged to cross the Alps with his army in mid-winter in order to relieve the garrisons cut off by the rising. But having done this he took the city of Avaricum

---

[10] Cicero: *Pro Milone*, xxvii.

(Bourges) by storm, leaving less than eight hundred persons alive out of a population of forty thousand. At Gergovia however, he was repulsed, and after a period of the greatest anxiety, when his annihilation seemed imminent, he at last got the upper hand and bottled Vercingetorix up in the hill-fortress of Alesia, not far from Dijon.

But soon a Gallic army of nearly a quarter of a million men came to their leader's relief, and Cæsar was obliged to face about to meet them. A terrific battle ensued in which we catch a glimpse of Antony fighting with desperate courage, and keeping up the spirits of his men in a situation of the extremest peril; but at last the day ended in a complete Roman victory and an awful slaughter of the enemy, and thereafter the heroic Vercingetorix surrendered. He came riding out of Alesia fully armed, and having dismounted in front of Cæsar, laid his weapons down, removed his armour, and silently seated himself at the conqueror's feet, after which he was sent as a prisoner to Rome.

During the remainder of the year 52 and part of 51 B.C. further revolts had to be suppressed, and Cæsar, having been unnerved by the dangers through which he had passed, now behaved with pitilessness in ending the rebellion. He caused the captured chief of one tribe to be flogged to death in the presence of the legions; at the surrender of another city he cut off the right hands of all the prisoners; and elsewhere he acted with a severity which at last cowed the whole country into sullen submission, and so, to some extent, justified itself—that is, of course, if we care to employ the ethically questionable argument that mercilessness to the few, being sometimes productive of a terrorized quiescence which saves the lives of the many, is more humane in the end than a leniency of which foolish advantage may be taken.

The almost ceaseless fighting and slaughter in Gaul since Cæsar had first descended upon that country in 58 B.C. leaves upon the mind a picture so savage that we are inclined to forget that these campaigns had also their more civilized aspect. Cæsar was a man of great culture, and whenever his military duties permitted him to settle down for a while at one of his headquarters, the vast wealth which was now flowing into his private coffers enabled him to live in magnificent state. The men whom he gathered about him were, many of them, not merely soldiers but well-known representatives of the progressive and intellectual section of high Roman society—persons that is to say, of refinement and education, if not of strict morals, and the company assembled around his table was often brilliant. Cæsar himself was as fastidious a scholar and man of letters as he was a finicking man of fashion. He spoke a very perfect Latin, and had a most polished style of writing which, by the way, he was now employing in preparing his famous *De Bello Gallico*, a work written to vindicate himself before his critics in Rome, who had begun to think that only by luck had he escaped the fate of Crassus. He enjoyed the society of authors and men of learning, so long as they were also men of the world, and he was usually ready to find a post near him for anybody recommended to him as a person of distinction in this respect.

Among his officers there were Plancus, an eloquent and witty young man, who had made a name for himself at the Roman Bar; Trebonius, who later collected and published the witticisms of Cicero; Matius, who translated the *Iliad* into Latin verse; Hirtius, the historian, of whom we shall hear later, as Consul and military leader opposed to Antony; Quintus, Cicero's brother, who was something of a poet and playwright; Balbus, a great patron of literature and philosophy; and so on. Antony himself, too, if not intellectual, was a fine speaker, and a man of taste, who had received a particularly good education,[11] and had, from his youth up, moved in the best society in Rome, wherein at this period it was the fashion to be a connoisseur of works of art and a judge of Greek and Latin literature; and the fact that in later life he was the leader of a group of men who believed themselves to represent the last word in the material refinements of civilization, indicates that already he was not out of place in the sparkling entourage of this many-sided ruler of Gaul.

Cæsar was very particular in the choice of the men who surrounded him, and since he was primarily a statesman, an administrator, and an intellectual, and only as it were by chance a soldier, he demanded a high standard of brains and accomplishments in the members of his suite. His generals might sometimes

[11] Dion Cassius, *xlvi*, 4.

be chosen for their sterling military abilities alone, but his intimate companions, even here in Gaul, were selected in consideration of much wider qualities, of which some of the essentials were
an up-to-date education and culture, a sort of social elegance, a
knowledge of the world, a progressive and democratic vision
linked to, but unfettered by, an aristocratic ideal, and, especially,
a certain audaciousness and high courage. It is sometimes said
that he merely gathered a crew of fashionable reprobates around
him; but this was the opinion only of the old conservatives who
could not distinguish between unconventional views and criminal-
ity, nor between courage and effrontery.

Curio, for instance, was a man of fashion who was regarded
as a shocking libertine; but we have seen him with drawn sword
gallantly defending Cæsar in the Senate-house, and his stout
little heart won him a place in the great man's affections. Dolabella,
who shortly after this time married Cicero's already twice married daughter Tullia, and was now beginning to enjoy Cæsar's
particular regard, was an elegant young man whose profligacy
greatly troubled his father-in-law; but, as will be seen later, his
reckless bravery cannot be denied. Cælius, another fashionable
young intellectual, who was closely attached to Cæsar—though
this was a little later—was not only a wit, a brilliant speaker, an
inimitable dancer,[12] and one of the best-dressed men in the country:
he was also almost idiotically brave, and was never so happy as
when he was in peril of his life.

It was this courageousness in Antony, likewise, which together
with his abilities, endeared him to Cæsar. He came to Gaul with
a great reputation for bravery in the field, and in many a battle in
that country he had shown his heroism. Yet in this regard, as in what
may be called his drawing-room accomplishments, he was at this
time but one of the brilliant group of well-dressed, well-groomed,
pleasure-loving, licentious, adventurous men of culture and fashion,
who heroically followed their heroic leader over the mountains and
through the plains and forests of rebellious Gaul, enduring hardship like the toughest veterans. He differed from the others chiefly
in respect of his Herculean strength, his mighty muscles, and a
kind of studied roughness with which he concealed the sensitive-

[12] Macrobius: *Saturnaliorum,* ii, 10.

ness of his nature. He was the bull-dog amongst the poodles; but even the poodles in this unique company of adventurers knew how to fight and how to die gallantly. Antony's trouble was that he drank too much, and was inclined to become noisy; but the influence of Cæsar, who, like many men of genius, found all the stimulants he required in his own active thoughts and keen feelings, no doubt kept him in order.

In his province of Gaul, Cæsar was, of course, like a king. His power was absolute. But in Rome, as has been said already, there were doubts now about his super-eminence, and greater reliance was placed upon Pompey. The disorders in the city which had followed the death of Clodius had been so serious that the law-abiding citizens, both republicans and democrats, demanded some kind of dictatorship; and presently Pompey was invited to act in that capacity. Sulla, however, had made the very word "Dictator" objectionable, and Cato therefore proposed that Pompey should be given dictatorial powers under the name of Sole Consul; and to this everybody agreed. His appointment, naturally, was very distasteful to Cæsar, who, after his long autocracy in his province, was not prepared to play second-fiddle to any man; and it was a bitter thought to him that he himself was not regarded in Rome as the nation's one hope.

Now that he had at last completed the conquest of Gaul he had expected to come back to the capital in such a blaze of popularity that he would be able to effect the union of the republicans and democrats under his leadership. That was the chief reason why he had shown such friendship to Cicero of late, he being one of the leading representatives of the aristocratic party. But in this he had overlooked the fact that the conservatives always thought of him as a "dangerous" man, a demagogue, who had once been mixed up in the Catiline affair, and had been the former patron of the fire-eating Clodius. It was to Pompey that cautious people turned.

And now Pompey had forestalled him, and was himself playing up to the aristocrats so successfully that a real coalition under *his* leadership was almost an accomplished fact. For the first time in several years Cato, the recognized leader of the republicans, was showing marked friendliness to Pompey, and was constantly warning him to beware of Cæsar.

Cicero, of course, presented something of a difficulty to Pompey, for he had apparently fallen under the spell of Cæsar, and, in the event of an open rupture between the two great men, was more likely to back the Gallic autocrat than the Roman. Thus, Pompey, it seems to me, felt that it would be best to get him out of the way by offering him a provincial governorship, and bringing pressure to bear on him to accept it. It was with this purpose in view, I think, that he ingeniously caused a law to be passed that ex-Consuls and other high officials eligible for provincial governorships, who had passed more than five years without taking up such offices, should be obliged to do so when a vacancy had to be filled. Now Bibulus, the son-in-law of Cato, was also due for a province, but there was only the choice of Syria and Cilicia at the moment, the latter being the country which formed the south-east corner of Asia Minor, adjoining Syria; and, as luck would have it, when lots were drawn, Syria fell to Bibulus, and Cicero had to be told to take the other much less interesting province, to which the island of Cyprus was appended. He did not at all relish the thought of leaving Rome and making his residence at Tarsus, the Cilician capital, but the great inducement offered him was that he stood a very good chance of making a fortune out of the usual perquisites of a governor, and just now he was sorely in need of money. He was not sorry, more-over, to have the opportunity of separating himself for a while from his wife, Terentia, a hard, imperious, and, what was worse, pious woman to whom he had been married for some twenty-six years and who failed to make his home attractive to him now that his beloved daughter Tullia was grown up and gone. His son Marcus, though only about fourteen years of age, he took with him, however, and also his brother Quintus, who had recently been serving with Cæsar in Gaul.

During the summer of the year 51 b.c. Pompey felt himself to be strong enough to clip Cæsar's wings, and through his agency pro-posals were made in the Senate that the conqueror of Gaul should be recalled when his five years' term of office expired in March of the coming year, 50 b.c. Cæsar, on his part, hoped to prolong his command until 49 b.c., and then to get himself elected Consul for the second time for the year 48 b.c., that is to say after the ten years required by law had elapsed since his first Consulship; but

Pompey, now definitely bent on retaining his own supremacy by forcing his rival into private life, secretly took all the necessary steps to deprive Cæsar of his Gallic province in the spring, although publicly professing friendliness to him.

When he was asked in the Senate, however, what he would do if Cæsar insisted on remaining at the head of his army beyond that date, he revealed his thoughts by replying: "What should I do if my son boxed my ears?" [13]—by which he implied that such an act on the part of Cæsar, whom he regarded as a younger and less important man than himself, would seem to him to be like an impudent declaration of war. And when Cato stated that if Cæsar desired the Consulship he should be made to disband his army and come to Rome as a private citizen to canvass votes in the usual way, Pompey shrugged his shoulders, but made no reply, thus indicating that he accepted Cato's opinion as being constitutionally correct.

At this dangerous juncture the plucky little Curio made up his mind to take a hand in Cæsar's interest, and, for that purpose, managed to get himself elected as one of the Tribunes of the People for the year 50 B.C. It is usually said that he was bribed by Cæsar to espouse his cause,[14] and it is true that Cæsar, out of his great wealth, had recently discharged all Curio's debts; but this was not necessarily more than a friendly act towards the man who had once saved his life, and the accusation of direct bribery cannot be proved.[15] Curio, it will be remembered, had once been romantically attached to Antony; but all that sort of abnormality was as much a thing of the past as it was in the case of Cæsar himself.

Curio had recently married Fulvia, the widow of the murdered Clodius, a turbulent, masculine, ambitious woman, as hard as nails, the daughter of a certain Fulvius Bambalio of Tusculum (Frascati), a hill-town near Rome which was also the native home of Cato. By Clodius she had a young daughter, Clodia, who was afterwards the first wife of Octavianus, Cæsar's grand-nephew; and it seems likely that she was already anxious for her new husband to be on good terms with the great man whose friendship her late lamented Clodius had unfortunately lost, and it may have been on her

[12] Cicero: *Ad Familiares,* viii, 8.
[14] Appian: *Civil Wars,* ii, 26; Plutarch: *Pompey;* etc.
[15] Velleius, ii, 48.

advice that Curio now took the daring step on Cæsar's behalf which jeopardised his relations with Pompey.

By skilful handling of the problem of Cæsar's future, he managed to get the whole discussion postponed beyond the date in the spring of 50 B.C. when the conqueror of Gaul was supposed to lay down his command; and having succeeded thus in obtaining breathing-space, he made the alternative proposal either that Cæsar should be left for the time being at the head of his army or else that both Cæsar *and* Pompey should resign their offices and should together become private citizens once more, on an equal footing. The public had become very apprehensive of the rivalry between the two men, and, dreading the possibility of a quarrel which would lead to civil war, they welcomed Curio's suggestion with enthusiasm, congratulating him on his pluck in daring to make such a proposal. After his speech in which he had done so, they escorted him to his house in the greatest excitement, throwing flowers before him, and hailing him as a hero, which, indeed, he was, for the thought of resigning office was likely to infuriate Pompey just now when he felt that Cæsar had lost public favour and had left the road to his own lifelong supremacy easy to tread. Thereafter, with increasing audacity, he attacked Pompey in speech after speech, declaring that he, Pompey, had no right to call Cæsar's behaviour in not disbanding his army unconstitutional, when Pompey himself had broken every law by allowing himself to be made Sole Consul at the same time that he was governor of Spain, an office which he still improperly filled without residing in that province.

Pompey, indeed, had light-heartedly overridden the laws in many respects. There was a law, for example, that no public speech should be made in favour of a man awaiting his trial; and yet a certain official, who was in this situation, had been praised by him in that manner, and this was so flagrant an illegality that Cato, the invariable stickler, had ostentatiously put his fingers in his ears and had refused to listen, in spite of his desire at this time to be friendly with the speaker. On other occasions, too, Pompey had attempted to interfere with the course of justice where friends of his were concerned; for his consciousness of his power had made him impatient of restraint, and, anyhow, it was a characteristic of his nature to act on the impulse of the moment without following a preconsidered line of action. Not even Cæsar, he thought, could prevent him doing whatever he chose, and on one occasion he declared that he only had to stamp his foot and in an instant there would be an invincible army at his command.

But when Curio thus requested him to lay aside all this power which he had misused, he was staggered, and did not know what to answer. He concentrated his attention, however, on the elections at the end of the summer for the magistracies of the following year, 49 B.C.; and, hearing that Cæsar was supporting the candidature of one of his generals, Galba, for the Consulate, he put two candidates into the field to oppose this man, while for the other posts he had his nominees ready to contest the seats with Cæsar's men.

Curio's Tribuneship would end a few days before the close of 50 B.C., and Cæsar therefore decided to invite Antony to stand for that office so that he might carry on Curio's good work. For this purpose he sent him back to Rome, and soon he was once more in the thick of the political battle. The townspeople, who had not seen him for three years, and then only for a short time, were delighted with him. His eloquence, his splendid physique, his manliness, his reputation for bravery, and withal, his complete absence of conceit and his indifference to social barriers and distinctions, endeared him to the crowd; and he was without difficulty elected as one of the Tribunes of the People for 49 B.C., though Galba and Cæsar's other candidates for office were defeated, Pompey's men being triumphant all along the line. He then successfully stood for the additional office of Augur, that is to say the directorship of the board of priests who studied the official auspices; after which it is to be supposed that he went back to Cæsar in Cisalpine Gaul to take his instructions from him, returning to Rome in December to be ready to assume office.,

The close of the year 50 B.C. was a period of extreme excitement in Rome, for Pompey's success at these elections in defeating nearly all Cæsar's nominees caused him to lose his head, and to feel that his rival in the north had no chance against him. Early in December, Caius Marcellus,[16] who was one of the Consuls for that year, made a violent speech in the Senate in which he denounced Cæsar as having designs on the peace of the State, and proposed that

[16] Husband of Cæsar's niece's stepdaughter, Octavia.

Pompey should be given supreme military command at home to defend the city in case Cæsar should raise a revolution rather than give up his army; but when the measure went before the Comitia, Curio bravely used his right as Tribune of the People, and placed his veto on it. Thereupon Marcellus went off with a band of excited young aristocrats to Naples, where Pompey was staying, to offer him this command in spite of the veto. A week or two later Curio's Tribuneship expired, and he at once set out for Cæsar's headquarters, leaving Antony to face the music in the capital.

Then came the news that Pompey had accepted the command, and, though deprecating war, had set out to place himself at the head of the available troops; and at this, Antony made use of his sacrosanctity as a Tribune to denounce Pompey and all his works. He knew now that civil war could hardly be prevented, and that although the mob was on Cæsar's side, all the rest of the people in the city were for Pompey; he knew that in the event of a sudden outbreak of hostilities his Tribuneship would be annulled, and he would be arrested and probably executed; yet he could not hear his beloved Cæsar traduced by speaker after speaker in all public meetings without making some reply. Furiously he urged the crowds to stand by Cæsar and not to give their support to Pompey, who was no democrat but an aristocrat, if ever there was one; but only the rabble would listen to him.

Meanwhile Cicero had just returned to Rome, having completed his short term as governor of Cilicia. He came back bursting with self-satisfaction, as well he might, indeed, for he had not only governed his province in a most exemplary manner, but he had managed to make a little fortune out of it and yet had kept within the law. Apart from this matter of money—and in regard to money it may be said that Cicero was never intrinsically, but always speciously, honourable—the government of his province had certainly been both correct and wise; and history would have praised him for it in unqualified terms had he not himself spoilt the picture by daubing it over with the glaring colours of his own vanity. With the aid of his brother Quintus, who had learnt soldiering under Cæsar in Gaul, he had inflicted sharp punishment upon some hill-tribes notorious for brigandage; and at the close of this little punitive expedition he had allowed his soldiers to confer on him the title of *Imperator*, which was only applied to victorious generals after very great victories; and thereupon he wrote home asking that he might be decreed an official Triumph on his return to Rome. In his mind's eye he saw himself driving in state through the streets of Rome, hailed as a conqueror by the populace; and he was bitterly hurt when Cato told him that he was asking too much. "Cato has been disgustingly unfriendly to me," he complained to his friend Atticus; [17] "he bears testimony to the purity of my life, my justice, kindliness, and integrity, which are self-evident, but refuses what I asked for!"

In regard to the political situation, the development of which had been reported to him in Cilicia and on his journey home, he was extremely worried; for it seemed to him now that Cæsar was likely to be the loser in the coming struggle, and Pompey the winner. It was most unfortunate for him; for he had been expressing such unbounded admiration for Cæsar in recent years, and had accepted money from him, but had been by no means careful to flatter Pompey. The apparent mistake, however, must now be rectified; and thus we find him declaring in his letters: "My regard for Pompey increases every day of my life," [18] and "I am heart and soul for Pompey." [19] But when he arrived in Rome, and realized that he would be forced soon to make his choice of sides, he was terribly perplexed; nor were matters helped by a letter he received from Cæsar, advising him to go back to Greece and keep out of the mess altogether: he pretended to be indignant at the suggestion, but he was too afraid of Pompey even to do this. Moreover, he could not make up his mind how to treat Antony, who, as Cæsar's defender in Rome, had managed to gain the support of the mob but had incurred the bitter enmity of the Pompeians and the aristocrats. Not so long ago he, Cicero, had been telling people what a fine young man Antony was: how was he going to laugh that off?

The attitude of Pompey and Cæsar, meanwhile, is tragically clear. For years Pompey had watched his rival's movements with troubled eyes, but so long as Cæsar's daughter, Julia, had been alive there had been a tie between the two men which could not be broken.

[17] Cicero: *Ad Atticum*, vii, 2, 7.
[18] *Ibid.*, vi, 2, 10.
[19] Cicero: *Ad Familiares*, ii, 13, 2.

Since her death, however, and since Cæsar's loss of popularity in Rome owing to the troubles in Gaul, Pompey had come to feel that he himself was destined to be all his days the sole ruler of his country; and he had become so accustomed to the thought, so used to autocratic power, that now the demands of Cæsar to be allowed to retain his command of his army and his province until he could exchange them for a second Consulship, seemed an outrageous piece of impertinence. What was Cæsar, after all, but an adventurer who, as the nephew of the great Marius, would use this democratic lever to overthrow the constitution? Pompey had always thought of him as unscrupulous and not quite a gentleman, a man of brains and culture but of little honour; and he dreaded to think of the fate of his country in such hands. Was he, Pompey "the Great," to go into retirement, and to leave Rome to the mercy of such a man? Would it not be better to fight it out, now that the home forces were at his disposal, and the bulk of the citizens with him? It was inconceivable that Cæsar could be victorious in the struggle.

At this period Pompey was fifty-six years of age, but time had dealt kindly with him, and he was still a handsome man, of buoyant, light-hearted character, and of kingly manners. He was what is called "a great gentleman," the soul of honour; a man, too, whose romantic passion for Julia, and whose overwhelming sorrow after her death, had won him the sympathy of thousands of sentimental hearts. Unlike Cæsar he could count the number of his adulteries; but, like him, he was temperate in regard to food and drink. Cæsar had been guilty in Gaul of great cruelty, and had ruthlessly slaughtered his enemies; but Pompey was usually humane to a fault, and had on many occasions spared the lives of those who expected death at his hands. Nor had he appeared to seek the greatness which fate thrust upon him; and once when a new command was offered to him he had been heard to cry out: "Am I never to end my labours, nor escape from this offensive greatness, so that I can live quietly in the country with my wife?—I wish I were an unknown man!" Yet, having attained autocratic power without conscious effort, he could not brook a rival, and certainly not one who, like Cæsar, had schemed and fought and almost worn himself out, impelled by a burning ambition to be what the casual Pompey now was—the first man in Rome.

Cæsar was Pompey's junior, being now fifty-two years of age.
Like his rival, he was dignified, regal, and always courteous and
polite; but he was infinitely harder, more stern, more purposeful.
People could easily tell what Pompey was thinking, but they could
not keep abreast of Cæsar's quick intellect, nor know from the expression of his thin-lipped mouth and his dark, inscrutible eyes what
was going on in that tremendous head of his. His polished, incisive
language, his keen and sometimes cruel wit, his intellectual brilliance, were in marked contrast to Pompey's rather easy-going manner of speaking. At a later date, when a certain young politician had
opposed some of his measures, Cæsar quietly told him that he would
put him to death if any more were heard of his dissent; "and this,
you know, young man," he said, "is more disagreeable for me to
say than to do." The grim remark was characteristic. Yet he could
be very forgiving and graciously lenient, and his anger was not easily
aroused: even now, in fact, at this crisis of his career, he felt no bitterness against those who were slandering him in Rome and pretending that he was a public enemy. He did not hate Pompey: he
rather admired him.

He was staying at this time at Ravenna, in the south-east corner of Cisalpine Gaul; and from there he now dispatched Curio with
a letter to the Senate and another to the Comitia, saying in the
latter that, in order to avoid hostilities, he would be willing to resign his command and become a private citizen again if Pompey
would do likewise. Even then he did not believe that war could not
be avoided, [20] and he was prepared to make every possible conces-
sion. But when Curio, after racing to Rome at top speed, presented
these letters, there was a concerted attempt to prevent their being
read, and neither Curio nor Antony could at first make themselves
heard, though in the end Antony managed to obtain a hearing for
Cæsar's messages. A decree was then drawn up by the Pompeians
that Cæsar should be given until July the first to lay down his command, and that if he then refused to do so war should be declared
upon him; but here Antony intervened in the Comitia, and, reckless
with anger at this insult to his chief, and heedless of the consequences to himself, placed his tribunitial veto upon the bill. It was
one of the great crises of his career, and his action in obstructing

[20] Hirtius: *De Bello Gallico*, viii, 52.

this decree at the risk of his life was not forgotten by his grateful chief.

Cicero now made an attempt to effect a compromise. He proposed that Cæsar should be allowed to retain his command in his province and to stand for the Consulship without coming to Rome, and that, in the event of his being elected, Pompey should spend the year in his Spanish province; but Cato and the conservatives would not listen to these moderate counsels, and proposed that Antony should be deposed from the Tribuneship. Nevertheless, the exasperated young man boldly went to the Senate-house and repeated to the sullen senators Cæsar's offer to disarm if Pompey would do likewise; but the Consuls for that year, refusing to listen, rudely ordered him to leave the assembly, and thereat Antony lost his temper, hurled execrations at them, and stormed out of the building "like one possessed," as Appian says, [21] "predicting war, massacre, prescription, banishment, confiscation, and various other impending horrors, and invoking terrible curses." He and Curio then disguised themselves, and, procuring a carriage, fled from the city by night, galloping off on the road to Ravenna to tell Cæsar that the sacrosanctity of the Tribuneship had been violated, the tribunitial veto disregarded and all hope of peace destroyed.

"It was you, you, Marc Antony," declared Cicero in later years, [22] "who gave Cæsar the principal pretext for war; for what else did he allege except that the power of interposition by the veto had been ignored, the privileges of the Tribunes taken away, and Antony's rights denied by the Senate? The cause of the war was *you!* The fact is recorded in history, is handed down by men's memories, and our most ultimate posterity in the most distant ages will never forget it. *You* were the origin of that war. Do you, Senators, grieve for the soldiers slain?—it is Antony who slew them! Do you regret your lost comrades?—it is Antony who deprived you of them! Everything which then happened we must attribute wholly to Antony."

When Cæsar heard what had happened—it was then the middle of January, 49 B.C.—he sent orders to his legions in Gaul to come to his support immediately, and, taking with him the troops available

[21] Appian: *Civil Wars,* ii, 33.
[22] Cicero: *Philippic ii,* xxii.

at Ravenna, he set out to march upon Rome. As he crossed the little river Rubicon which separated his province of Cisalpine Gaul from Italy, he exclaimed "The die is cast!"—and, with Antony, his gallant kinsman, by his side, he set his face towards the capital.

CHAPTER VIII

The Civil War between Cæsar and Pompey, in which Antony Acted as
Cæsar's Chief Lieutenant.

49–48 B.C.

CÆSAR's advance into Italy with only a small force was a
perilous move, and was intended more to give his enemies a taste
of what he was prepared to do than to precipitate a general conflict. He still hoped to be able to negotiate a satisfactory peace; and
when, having entered Ariminum (Rimini), just over the border, he
was presently approached by two messengers from Pompey who
suggested terms of peace, he was in high hopes of a settlement satisfactory to himself. The two men were Roscius Fabatus, who had
served under him in Gaul and was now Prætor, and Lucius Cæsar,
Antony's cousin, son of his mother's brother. He received them
courteously, and sent them back with his offer to adhere to the terms
of Cicero's proposal, namely that both he and Pompey should disarm, and that Pompey should remain in Spain during the year of
Cæsar's Consulship.

While waiting for a reply he marched on down the eastern
coast of Italy, taking possession, without bloodshed, of the towns as
far south as Asculum (Ascoli), which was more or less opposite
Rome; and those Pompeian officers who fell into his hands he treated
with the utmost politeness, sending them back to their master with
his compliments. When Pompey's messengers returned, however,
with the impossible answer that terms could only be discussed after
Cæsar had disbanded his army and had recrossed the Rubicon, it was
obvious that war could not be avoided.

Cæsar therefore despatched Antony at the head of a force of
Gallic cavalry across the mountains to seize Arretium (Arezzo), a

town in Etruria on the main road to Rome; and meanwhile he himself waited to see which way Pompey would move. He was much
discouraged, however, when one of his chief officers, Labienus, who
had held high command under him in Gaul and had been his intimate friend, now deserted him and fled to Pompey; but he controlled his indignation, and contemptuously sent the renegade's baggage and money after him. It seemed that even his own officers did
not think that he had much chance of success against the supposedly
large forces at Pompey's command; and when dispatches arrived
announcing that the faithful Antony had captured Arretium without a fight and was there awaiting his chief's further instructions
Cæsar could have had no idea yet what those instructions would be.

Meanwhile, in Rome, however, an astonishing situation had
developed. At the news that Antony, the insulted Tribune, was
astride the road to the capital, at the head of his invincible Gallic
cavalry, everybody in the city thought that Cæsar was contemplating
a rapid march on Rome, and thereupon the wildest panic occurred.
Senators and officials swarmed into Pompey's house, and, brushing
aside the frightened servants, pushed their way into his presence,
imploring him to bestir himself and do something. What orders
had he given to the troops, they asked? What troops were available,
anyway? Where was the vast army which he had declared would
arise when he had need of it? Why did he not stamp his foot, as he
had boasted, and produce them? Why had he allowed matters to
come to this pass when he was wholly unprepared to defend the
capital?

Pompey was bewildered, and he needed all his gentlemanly self-
control to prevent himself being infected by the prevailing terror.
Suddenly he realized that Cæsar was a greater man than he, and
his heart must have sunk as the abuse hurled at him by these frightened men revealed to him how precarious was that position of supremacy to which he had so long accustomed himself. With all the
dignity he could command he told them not to worry, but to rely on
him to take the necessary steps for the safety of the State; but he
had no more idea what those steps would be than had Cæsar how to
oppose them. Cicero pushed his way in—a big, ponderous, grey-
haired man, haggard with anxiety—and implored him to send ambassadors to Cæsar to treat for peace: he was horrified at the turn af-

fairs had taken, just when he had hopes of being allowed to celebrate his public Triumph for his precious expedition against the Cilician brigands. Those fond dreams must now for ever be banished, [1] and in their place must remain for many a day this nightmare of fear that by backing the wrong side he should incur a second exile or even death. Cato, too, came stalking in like a spectre of doom, telling the distracted Pompey that war was the only honourable course, and that he must bravely do or die.

After a day or two of indecision, Pompey announced his plan. Rome must be evacuated, and the government removed to Capua, a few miles inland from Naples.

This decision caused a mad panic, and the horror and confusion in the city were heightened by wild stories of terrible portents which had been observed. Somebody said that it had rained blood during the night; somebody else spread the report that the statues of the gods had been seen to sweat; yet another declared that an unearthly flash of lightning had descended upon one of the temples; and, most horrible of all, a stable-hand announced a prodigy—a mule had foaled. People were praying in the streets; but the senators, frantically packing their belongings, forgot to pray or to perform the daily sacrifices to the gods. Soon the Appian Way, the highroad to Capua and the south, was blocked with important fugitives and their slaves and baggage. The women and children were left behind, and at the gates of the city there were indescribable scenes of emotion, men sobbing and women shrieking as they bade goodbye.

Cicero was one of the first to depart, leaving his unloved wife, Terentia, to mind his great mansion in Rome. Pompey, not knowing what to do with him, had told him to go down into Campania, the province in which Capua was situated, and to act as best he could as a sort of semi-official governor of that district; but before he left he received news that his son-in-law, Dolabella, the new husband of his daughter Tullia, had declared for Cæsar. The unfortunate orator was stunned at the evacuation, and at Pompey's collapse, [2] and, in private, he poured out his abuse alike upon him and upon Cæsar, the one as incompetent, the other as mad. Then, thinking that it would be best to go into retreat and try to keep out of

---

[1] Cicero: *Ad Atticum,* ix, 7, 5.   [2] *Ibid.,* vii, 10.

harm's way, he settled himself at a villa of his near Formiæ (Mola), half way between Rome and Naples, and in utter dejection awaited what fate would bring him, sending messages to Pompey saying that he was discharging his duties faithfully in Campania, but at the same time writing to Cæsar to say that he was neutral and was living quietly on his estate.

Presently, however, he received a reply from Cæsar, suggesting that he should return to the capital as a non-belligerent; and at this he wrote frantically to his friend Atticus, begging for his advice. "Would it show me a brave man," he asked, "if I were to remain in Rome where I have filled the highest office in the State, have achieved immortal deeds, and have been crowned with honours, but now would be but an empty name, and would moreover incur some danger, and the stigma of disgrace if Pompey should be victorious? Or shall I follow Pompey in his ignominious flight?—and, if so, whither? But if I do this, what a raid Cæsar, if the victor, will make on my possessions when I am out of the way—fiercer than on those of other people, because he will think perhaps that such attacks on me will be popular with the masses," [3] who had never forgotten or forgiven Cicero's action against the Catilinarian conspirators. Antony always had that grudge against him, and it was Antony who was now leading the supposed descent on Rome.

Meanwhile Cato had been sent to Sicily to keep that island quiet, and Pompey had gone to Luceria (Lucera) on the eastern side of Italy, opposite Naples, where the bulk of his forces was concentrated. Eighty miles to the north of this place was the fortress-town of Corfinium (Popoli); and here Pompey had placed a strong body of troops under the command of the aristocratic Domitius Ahenobarbus, husband of Cato's sister, Porcia, who had been selected by the Senate before the debacle to succeed Cæsar as governor of Gaul. But by the middle of February, Cæsar had decided not to march on empty Rome, had recalled Antony from Arretium, and, having made up his mind to come to grips with Pompey at once, had invested Corfinium as the first step in his new plan.

After a siege of a few days Domitius surrendered, giving his parole to Cæsar, who thereupon allowed him to go unmolested back to Pompey, while all his troops went over to the conqueror and were

[3] Cicero: *Ad Atticum*, viii, 3.

enrolled in his ever increasing army. Several senators and young
aristocrats were captured in the town, but all were allowed to depart with their baggage and their money, for, said Cæsar, [4] "I am
quite indifferent to the fact that those whom I release are said to go
away to make war on me again: my only wish is that I should act
like myself and they like what they are."

This extraordinary clemency won the gratitude of thousands,
and its effect was more valuable to Cæsar than many victories. He
published abroad the announcement that he would never imitate
the harshness of Sulla at the overthrow of his, Cæsar's, great uncle,
Marius, but was determined to be generous and merciful, since, he
declared, he was always hoping for a reconciliation with Pompey.
"What a man!" wrote Cicero [5] on hearing of this leniency. "How
keen, how careful, how well-prepared! I declare that if he puts no
one to death and robs no one of his goods, he will soon become the
idol of those who most dreaded him." "The country-towns," he
added in a later letter, [6] "are beginning to hold Cæsar for a god, and
there is no pretense about their feelings as there was when they
made their vows for Pompey."

At the fall of Corfinium Pompey retired from Luceria southwards to Brundusium (Brindisi), which city Cæsar reached in the
second week in March, giving out that he was still anxious for an
interview and a reconciliation with his rival; but in the following
week Pompey, who retained command of the seas, skilfully evacuated the town by night and shipped his army and the many senators who were with him across the Adriatic to Greece, and when day
dawned Cæsar found the enemy gone, the first phase of the Civil
War being thus brought to a bloodless but unsatisfactory end.

Pompey's flight to Greece may be described as a strategic retreat
"according to plan." He had hoped at first to be able to hold southern Italy, but, failing to do this, he was clearly wise in making his
new base in Epirus, across the sea; for his reputation in eastern Eu-
rope, Asia Minor, and Syria was enormous, and the fact that he
had with him the two Consuls and most of the senators, would make
his cause seem to the native rulers and subservient peoples of these
lands to be worthy of aid. Cicero, in fact, was greatly troubled on

[4] Cicero: *Ad Atticum,* ix, 16A.   [5] *Ibid.,* viii, 13.
[6] *Ibid.,* viii, 16.

this account, and pictured Pompey "leaving no sea or land unran-sacked, arousing the passions of barbarian kings, and bringing whole nations of armed savages into Italy in immense armies." [7] Moreover, having absolute command of the seas, Pompey assumed that he would be able freely to dispatch messengers, or make the journey himself, by way of Sicily, and North Africa to Spain, where his two generals, Afranius and Petreius, were in command of large armies.

Cæsar's position, indeed, was hardly as satisfactory; for he was bottled up in Italy without a fleet, with Greece and the east on one side and Spain on the other, both in Pompey's favour, and Gaul, to the north and west of him, ready to revolt. The first thing to do, ob-viously, was to seize Rome, after which he would have to secure Sicily and Sardinia, if he could find the ships in which to transport a few troops thither, and, then, leaving a force to guard Italy and an-other to protect the Dalmatian coast against invasion by land, he would have to march into Spain, relying on a victory there to keep Gaul quiet. It was a stupendous task; but only when it was accom-plished could he hope to be in a position to invade Greece and fight it out with Pompey.

He was worried and anxious, therefore, as he turned towards the capital; and he was not much relieved when he heard stories of the bad omens which had manifested themselves on Pompey's landing in Greece—how spiders had been found upon some of the military standards, how a snake had glided across Pompey's foot-steps, and so forth. He was too intelligent to pay much attention to such portents; but Antony was probably heartened by them, as, of course, were the troops.

On his journey to the metropolis by the Appian Way, Cæsar paid a call upon Cicero at Formiæ, and invited him once more to come to Rome so as to give tacit support to his cause; but the un-fortunate man was still in a quandary, not knowing which side would win in the end, and the interview gave him the fright of his life, because he dared neither offend Pompey by going to Rome nor Cæsar by refusing to do so. Cæsar, however, was extremely consider-ate, and, realizing Cicero's predicament, offered him time to think the matter over, which led the orator to feel that he had won a dip-

[7] Cicero: *Ad Atticum,* viii, 11, 2.

lomatic victory, and caused him to write that evening: "I fancy
Cæsar is not much in love with me, but no matter: I am in love with
myself."[8] He did not think much of Cæsar's staff, the members of
which seemed to him to be very much like a gang of desperadoes;
and the Herculean Antony, travel-stained, and clanking fearsomely
in his military armour, must have been peculiarly upsetting to his
nerves.

When Cæsar reached Rome he camped outside the gates, while
Antony rode into the city at the head of a troop of his awe-inspiring
Gallic cavalry, receiving, no doubt, a vociferous welcome from the
mob. It was now the end of March, and not much more than two
months had elapsed since the Senate had driven Antony away like a
dog; yet, today, here he was, riding through the streets as a conqueror, and the Senate was in exile. He was still Tribune of the
People, and the crowd hailed him as their rightful representative;
and when he gave orders that all senators and members of the government who had remained in Rome were to come to him, the excited
rabble dashed off in all directions to round them up. They were a
mere handful, but Antony marched them out through the gates to
Cæsar's tent with great gusto, and there Cæsar addressed them as
though he were speaking to the full Senate and government, declaring that it was his object to avoid bloodshed and that he wished to
open negotiations with Pompey and his misguided followers.

He then entered the city, which he had not seen for nine
long years, while Antony rode at his side, pointing out to him the
new buildings erected in his absence, these including the great
theatre in the Campus Martius, built six years ago by Pompey at
his own expense to hold forty thousand spectators. Some sort of
provisional government was then set up, and Marcus Aemilius Lepidus, Prætor for that year, who had remained at his post, was made
acting-Consul. Lepidus was a patrician, but had been brought up in
the democrat party, his father having been that Lepidus who in 77
B.C., just after the death of Sulla, had led the premature and unsuccessful rebellion against the conservatives, as already recorded;
and he had married the daughter of Servilia, Cæsar's mistress, thus
linking himself with the Cæsarian party. Curio, meanwhile, was
sent off to deal with Cato in Sicily; Dolabella was dispatched with

[8] Cicero: *Ad Atticum*, ix, 18, 1.

Antony's younger brother Caius to Illyria, at the top of the Adriatic, to prevent Pompey marching northwards towards Italy by that route; and another officer, Quintus Valerius, was sent to obtain the surrender of Sardinia.

To Antony, however, fell the plum of Cæsar's nominations: he was appointed Commander-in-Chief of all the forces in Italy— which appointment, together with his Tribuneship, would, during Cæsar's coming absence in Spain, place him in absolute control of Rome and the whole country. That he should have been chosen for this work shows clearly enough the high regard Cæsar entertained for his abilities; and though Antony's human weaknesses in after life, and the simplicity of his nature, tend to make us think of him as a man of no very high attainments of mind or character, we must not forget—as every historian seems to do—that at this great crisis the amazingly sagacious Cæsar chose him out of all his officers for this most responsible and dangerous position.

In accepting the post Antony must have known that he staked his life; for if Cæsar were to be defeated in Spain and his cause overthrown, all the force of the Pompeian storm would fall directly upon his, Antony's, head. But his faith in Cæsar never wavered, and it was with a light heart that he faced his difficult duties when, during the first week in April, his chief set out for Spain to attack Pompey's lieutenants, Afranius and Petreius, in that country. It was all very well for Cæsar to say, with a confident smile, that he was marching out against an army without a general and that he would soon come back to fight a general without an army: [9] the hazard was far greater than that, and well Antony must have known it.

His first business was to help Lepidus to enlarge the diminutive Senate into a sound working body, and to fill the various offices left vacant by the flight of the government. The law made by Sulla that the descendants of the men proscribed by him could not hold office, was still in force, in spite of the various attempts of the democrats to abolish it; but Antony, at Cæsar's order, now caused it to be removed from the statutes, and thereby was able to make numerous appointments from the democratic ranks. Rome, indeed, was soon entirely in the hands of the democracy, and Cæsar's cause

[9] Suetonius: *Cæsar*, xxxiv.

came to be definitely the cause of the People, while Pompey's party became as definitely a conservative or republican movement, since the old nobility and the traditionists had embraced it whole-heartedly and its members had gone with Pompey to Greece.

The political situation, in fact, was now thoroughly clarified, and the civil war had assumed the character of a straight political fight between the ideals of the People and those of the republicans, Cæsar and Antony, his right-hand man, being the two arch-demagogues, and Pompey being the leader of the coalition of old-fashioned conservatives and conservative-minded democrats. This being so, some of the senators who had vaccilated and had remained in the capital, now slipped away to Greece in spite of Antony's efforts to detain them; and soon there was hardly a man of politically aristocratic sympathies left in Rome, though the city was full of men of socially aristocratic standing who by being democrats were in the fashionable movement of the time. Pompey might claim to be the representative of the old order; but smart, up-to-date society, as personified in the younger generation of intellectual and elegant men of fashion, looked to Cæsar as its leader.

Thus, Rome retained its gaieties and its emancipated and rather loose social life, even though it was the headquarters of a democracy with the rabble in tow. Now Antony was decidedly a man about town, a leading light in the fast society of the metropolis; and though Cæsar placed his trust in him more completely than he did in any other living soul, he was not consistently a hard-worker, and was as much concerned with giving himself what he considered a good time as he was with advancing his career. Politics, as such, did not deeply interest him, but he enjoyed power, was elated by the excitement and turmoil of public life, and was always happy when he was serving Cæsar, whose trust and affection he repayed with a blind devotion. Here in Rome he was temporarily under no restraint, and after so many years of campaigning, he threw himself into all the fatalistic fun of the town in such a spirit of youth that the pride of his mother, Julia, in him must have been tempered by not a little anxiety.

His mistress, Fadia, by whom he had had two or three children when he was a young man, was now dead or in retirement, and there was talk of him making a match of it with his cousin Antonia, the daughter of his exiled uncle, Caius Antonius; but meanwhile he amused himself with various women, and, when he was not busy with his public duties, led the wild life which was then common amongst the members of Rome's fashionable set, and which now derived a new zest from the uncertainty of the future. To be bacchanalian at such a time had all the mordant thrill of a game of dice with Death.

There was a Greek actress named Cytheris [10] who was at this time Antony's mistress, and he gave some offence to respectable people by gallantly calling her Volumnia, [11] a name almost sacred to the Romans because it was that of the wife of Coriolanus, the woman who, in 489 B.C., saved Rome from her husband's vengeance. Antony took her about with him on the various political journeys he had to make to towns in the neighbourhood of the capital, and caused a good deal of outraged comment by introducing her to the local notables who received him.

He was, in fact, very proud of being her lover, for the stage and its celebrities thrilled him—newly come as he was from the camp— as greatly as it thrilled men ten years younger than himself who lived in Rome; and his was not the nature to conceal his feelings. It has often been said that Antony never grew up, but remained, as Renan puts it, "a colossal child, capable of conquering a world, in capable of resisting a pleasure"; yet at this period of his life, at any rate, that criticism does not quite meet the case: his boyish attitude towards Rome's gaieties was due, rather, to his having been out of reach of them during the years in which young men were generally having their fill of them and becoming blasé.

When he had thus to go out of Rome he used to take his mother with him, assigning her a carriage or litter and its escort not any more splendid, as Plutarch tells us, than that given to Cytheris, a circumstance which led Cicero in after years to pretend that the elder lady, utterly neglected, was forced to follow the mistress of her profligate son as though the hussy had been her daughter-in-law. [12] But the fact that he did take his mother about with him suggests, on the contrary, that he was a very affectionate son whose goings-on were indulgently smiled at by the broad-minded Julia, accustomed as she had been all

---

[10] Plutarch: *Antony.* [11] Cicero: *Philippic ii,* xxiv.
[12] *Ibid.*

her life to the lax morals of the fashionable world. It is conceivable that she was very fond of Cytheris.

Plutarch says that on these outings "he took with him golden cups and dishes fitter for the ornaments of a state procession than for wayside picnics, and had pavilions set up and sumptuous repasts laid out on the banks of rivers or in the woods," music being provided by a company "of singing-girls who, in the towns, were billeted in the houses of serious fathers and mothers of families"; while Cicero adds that in his entourage were carriages full of his jolly companions and the caterers in charge of the festive arrangements.

In Rome Antony enthusiastically patronized the theatres, and went to a great many parties; but, with characteristic indifference to social propriety, he was as often the guest of mere men on the stage as of the leaders of the social world, two of his great friends being Sergius, the actor, and Hippias, the comedian. At these entertainments he sometimes drank more than was good for him, and "spent the next day in sleeping or walking off his debauches." But at last a shocking misadventure befell him. He had been out all night at the wedding-party of Hippias, and early next morning had to address a meeting. He was feeling deadly sick when he stepped up onto the platform, and he had hardly uttered a sentence before he was overcome with nausea in the sight of his entire audience, one of his friends snatching away his gown only just in time to prevent it being ruined.

After this disgusting incident it is to be supposed that he mended his ways somewhat, for he knew that Cæsar, while having a sympathetic understanding of the libertine, could not tolerate a drunkard; and it was not long before his mother persuaded him to marry his cousin Antonia and to make some effort to settle down. If one may judge by the fact that after a while he became very jealous of her men-friends, it may be supposed that, as sometimes happens, he found himself in love with the wife chosen for him: and, at any rate, a year or so later, she had become the mother of a little Antonia, and was being angrily accused by Antony of flirting with Dolabella, who was married to Cicero's daughter, Tullia—all of which suggests that he was an exemplary husband.

But whatever was the nature of his private affairs at this

time, he was active enough in the interests of Cæsar in his public life, and incurred without flinching the personal, if distant, hostility of Pompey, Cato, and all the other prominent men residing out of Italy. He was the first man in Rome, and the Pompeian spies reported all he did, exaggerating his public deeds and his private misdeeds until the conservative senators and officials; fretting at their exile, must have writhed in their impotence.

But as spring passed into summer the news from Cæsar became increasingly bad. His route to Spain had obliged him to pass by Massilia (Marseilles), but here the scoundrelly Domitius Ahenobarbus, whom he had released on parole after his surrender at Corfinium, had established himself with a powerful army, and for weeks held up Cæsar's advance, while the Pompeian forces in Spain were able to prepare themselves for battle. It is true that in Sicily Curio had found no difficulty in driving Cato out of the island and forcing him to cross the sea in flight to Pompey; but this small success was poor compensation for the thwarting of Cæsar's plans, and such an atmosphere of gloom and apprehension descended upon Rome that even Antony's efforts to be gay were decidedly macabre.

Cicero, of course, was one of the first to sense this feeling of nervousness, and he began to congratulate himself upon having maintained his outward neutrality; yet, as Pompey's chances of ultimate victory brightened, he was filled with dread lest his continued residence in Italy might put him in bad odour with the exiles in Epirus. "The one thing which tortures me now," he had already written some weeks before this,[13] "is that I did not follow Pompey into Greece. When I saw him in January he was a panic-stricken man, and the ugly appearance of his flight without caring what happened to *me* put a stop to my affection for him; but now that affection is coming again to the surface, and I cannot endure our separation. For whole days and nights, like a caged bird, I gaze at the sea and long to fly away."

Cæsar himself had written to him sternly advising him to remain neutral, and, after the check at Marseilles, Antony also wrote the following carefully worded and diplomatically friendly letter [14] to him:—

---

[13] Cicero: *Ad Atticum,* ix, 10.   [14] Copy enclosed in Cicero's *Ad Atticum,* x, 8.

"But that I have a strong affection for you—much greater, indeed, than you suppose—I should not have been seriously alarmed at the rumour of your proposed flight which has been circulated, particularly as I took it to be a false one; but my liking for you is far too great to allow me to pretend that even the report, however false, is not to me a matter of much concern. That you will really go across seas I cannot believe when I think of the deep regard you have for Dolabella and his admirable wife, your daughter Tullia, and of the equal regard in which you yourself are held by us all, to whom, upon my word and honour, your name and position are seemingly dearer than they are to yourself. Nevertheless, I did not think myself at liberty as a friend to be indifferent to the remarks even of unscrupulous people; and I have been the more anxious to act because I hold that the part I have to play has been made more difficult by a coolness between us, originating, indeed, more in suspicion on my part than in any injury on yours. For I beg you will thoroughly assure yourself of this, that there is no one for whom my feeling of friendliness is greater than for yourself, with the exception of my dear friend Cæsar, and that among Cæsar's most honoured friends a place is reserved for you. Therefore, my dear Cicero, I entreat you to keep your future action entirely open. Reject the false honour of this man, Pompey, who did you a great wrong in allowing you to be exiled that he might afterwards lay you under an obligation. Do not, on the other hand, fly from one who, even if he shall lose his love for you—and that need never be the case—will none the less make it his study that you shall be secure and rich in honours."

By the second week in June, however, the reports of Cæsar's difficulties at Marseilles had led a few more senators to slink away to Greece, and when a false rumour was spread that Pompey was marching north and would take Cæsar in the rear, Cicero at last made up his mind to bolt. He wrote to his wife saying that he was confident of Pompey's coming victory, and that he was therefore going to him in the full expectation of "returning with kindred spirits on some future day to the defence of the Republic." [15] That night he sailed for Greece.

His departure must have been a great blow to Antony, for it

[15] Cicero: *Ad Familiares,* xiv, 7.

caused the uneasiness of the Cæsarians to be increased, and Cæsar, no doubt, had told him to do his best to prevent the orator's flight. Plutarch tells us, also, that at this time Antony was none too popular, and that although he was greatly beloved by the troops, in whose exercises and labours he personally joined, he was accused of being too lazy and impatient to listen to the complaints of civilians who petitioned him, and had got himself a bad name all round by making love to other men's wives. Yet it is admitted by the same writer that Cæsar had no fault to find with him, and that his bravery, energy, and military skill were never in question, which suggests that the attacks made upon him were malicious rather than true. Nevertheless, there seems to have been a certain amount of actual disaffection in Rome during these trying days of anxiety, and when, in July, news arrived that Cæsar had left the siege of Marseilles to his subordinates, had marched against Pompey's legions in Spain, and had been defeated by them, there was something like a panic in the city.

In August, however, the whole situation changed. Dispatches were received announcing that Cæsar, after his first reverses, had outmaneuvered and trapped the enemy in Spain, and that the entire Pompeian army there had surrendered, while at Marseilles a victory had been won which made the speedy fall of that city certain. Thereupon, in September, the acting-Consul, Lepidus, with the help of Antony, passed a law through the Senate and the Comitia investing Cæsar with the powers of Dictator; and this move was all the more popular because of the reports of Cæsar's continued leniency, for he had allowed all the conquered troops an absolutely free choice of action—they could enter his service, retire into civilian life, or even make their way to Pompey, as they wished. It all seemed too wonderful to be true: the victory was miraculous; Cæsar was god-like. Everybody was cock-a-hoop, and Antony no doubt celebrated the glad tidings by getting drunk.

News of two reverses elsewhere, however, somewhat cooled the popular enthusiasm, and to Antony brought much personal sorrow. After turning Cato out of Sicily, the dashing Curio—that "slip of a girl" as Cicero, it will be remembered, had once called him—had collected enough ships to transport two legions to North Africa where Atticus Varus was in command of a considerable Pompeian army; and having disembarked at Utica, near the ruins of Carthage, he quickly gained a victory over that general, and then proceeded to attack King Juba of Numidia, [16] who was supporting Pompey. Misled by false reports, Curio found himself with a small force outnumbered and surrounded by the enemy in desert country in the heat of summer; and there, as Appian records it, "he perished, fighting bravely, together with all his men," his head being afterwards cut off and carried to Juba. On hearing the news the officers in command of the ships at Utica weighed anchor and sailed away, whereat the remaining soldiers of Curio's army, who were in reserve there, seized upon all the shipping in the harbour in order to make their escape, and in the confusion many of them were drowned, while the others, unable to get away, surrendered and were slaughtered by Juba in cold blood.

Curio, it will be remembered, had been Antony's earliest friend, and more than friend, and in the ensuing years they had stood side by side in many a dangerous situation. His death, therefore, was a sad blow to him, from which he had hardly recovered when news arrived that Dolabella had been defeated by Pompey's general in Illyria, and that Antony's younger brother, Caius, had been taken prisoner. The return of the victorious Cæsar to Rome from Spain, however, consoled him; and in the excitement of the rush of events which ensued he had no time to mourn his friend or to worry about his brother.

In November Cæsar arrived back like a whirlwind, recklessly determined to waste no time in getting to grips with Pompey himself. He gave orders to his army to march straight down to Brindisi, where, it was understood, a great mobilisation would take place during the winter in preparation for the invasion of Greece in the spring. Actually, however, his secret intention was to undertake that invasion immediately; but had he told his soldiers, weary after their campaign in Spain and their march back to Italy, that they were now going to be shipped across the perilous seas and flung against Pompey's fortified headquarters, they would probably have mutinied. Cæsar's decision, however, was no more than was to be expected of him, for his rapidity of action was usually phenome-

[16] Son of the cousin of King Jugurtha, the Numidian monarch whose fate has been recorded in Chapter ii.

nal; and, indeed, there was a certain impetuosity about him which sometimes landed him in extremely awkward situations. Time after time, good luck rather than good generalship extricated him from positions into which audacity and not forethought had led him; and in observing the wild risks he took the historian cannot fail to ask himself on occasion if he were really a great general at all.

Pompey, however, erred as much on the side of anxious indecision as Cæsar did on that of rash confidence; and, strange to say, neither of them looked far ahead, the difference between them being that Cæsar could make up his mind in a flash and could concentrate with astonishing intensity upon his immediate object, while Pompey, as he grew older, found an increasing difficulty in forming a decision of any kind. Cæsar was a man of immense brainpower, indefatigable energy, and the highest courage; but just as, in his private amours, "the marvel is that he did not end in some dark corner with a dagger between his ribs," [17] so in his military career it is startling to see how often he thrust that wonderful cranium of his into the lion's mouth and escaped, unscathed, by sheer good fortune.

It has already been remarked that he liked to gather about him men of audacious courage, such as Clodius and Curio had been; and it was just that quality in Antony, combined with his undying loyalty, which he loved. Antony, though transparent and somewhat of an actor to boot, was in many ways a man after his own heart—cultured, up-to-date in his tendencies, democratic in principle, aristocratic in taste, heedless of conventions, a hater of hypocrisy; but it was his dash and gallantry which endeared him to his chief, and now in this desperate adventure which had been decided upon it was to Antony that Cæsar turned, confiding in him his audacious plan to transport the army piecemeal to Greece in the ships he had built and the merchantmen he had commandeered, in the teeth of Pompey's watching fleet.

Only eleven days did Cæsar remain in Rome; but during that brief space he had himself elected Consul for the coming year, 48 B.C., with one of his officers as a nominal colleague; he abdicated his Dictatorship in place of this more regular office; he set the

---

[17] Sir Charles Oman: *Seven Roman Statesmen.*

government in order; and he reorganised its finances. Incidentally he recalled from banishment Gabinius, Antony's former commander-in-chief in Syria and Egypt, and various other exiles, with the notable exceptions of Milo and Antony's uncle, Caius Antonius, both of whom were too closely allied to the aristocratic party to be pardoned with popular approval. Then, with Antony at his side, he set out for Brindisi, and, having arrived, broke the news to those troops which were already there that he was going to take them across to Greece at once. The ships he had collected could carry no more than about fifteen thousand men, that is to say five out of the twelve legions which were at his disposal, and a small body of cavalry; but he declared that this would be quite a big enough army to start with, and that the ships could then be sent back to fetch the rest, many of whom had not yet reached Brindisi.

In the first week in January 48 b.c. he set sail, and Antony, who was left behind to bring the second lot over, watched his departure, one may suppose, with feelings of the greatest anxiety, knowing that if the enemy's fleet were encountered Cæsar and his men would be lost, and that though it were eluded he would find himself isolated on the shores of Greece, and outnumbered by Pompey by at least five to one. In three or four days, however, the ships returned bringing the news that Cæsar had landed safely near Oricum (Ericho), and was pushing north to Dyrrhachium (Durazzo), Pompey's base of supplies, which there was great hope of taking by surprise, for Pompey and his main army were an equal distance from the place. It was a fifty-mile race between the two armies.

Antony's business, of course, was to embark another fifteen thousand men, and take them across to Cæsar's aid; but before he could do so, Bibulus, Cæsar's old enemy and joint-Consul ten years earlier, who was now Pompey's admiral, dispatched a powerful fleet across the sea and blockaded Antony's ships in Brindisi harbour. Then developed a situation which was trying in the extreme to the nerves of all concerned. Antony, and with him now Gabinius, were unable to put to sea, knowing that Bibulus would send them to the bottom; and they therefore kicked their heels in Brindisi, waiting for the opportunity which never seemed to come. Cæsar, on his part, just failed to reach Durazzo before Pompey, and, in bitter disappointment, was obliged to dig himself in, a few miles to the south, taking possession of a certain amount of country behind him from which he could obtain supplies, but having no ships, and being open to a combined attack by land and sea.

As the weeks went by and Antony did not come, Cæsar became more and more desperate. Food was running short, and his men were complaining: there was sickness, too, in his camp. He could not understand what was delaying Antony, and began to wonder whether he were playing him false. At last in desperation he ventured upon one of those wildly daring exploits with which his life abounds. Disguising himself in mean clothes, he boarded a small cargo-boat which, apparently, had a permit to make the crossing to Italy; for, though he risked shipwreck and capture, he felt that his only hope was to find out what was wrong at Brindisi and to bring the rest of his army over to Greece himself. But the attempt was a failure: a storm drove the vessel back to the shore in a sinking condition, Cæsar was recognized, and when, wet and cold, he at last struggled back to his headquarters, everybody was indignant with him for taking such an absurd risk.[18] His anxiety to know what had happened to Antony, however, was his excuse: for the first time he mistrusted him.

Meanwhile, in Pompey's camp all was at sixes and sevens—a fact which alone saved the little Cæsarian army from annihilation. Though he placed his reliance chiefly on his Roman legions, of which he had eleven as against Cæsar's five, together with a strong force of cavalry, he had under his command formidable bodies of the famous Cretan archers, Thracian slingers, and Pontic javelin-throwers, while auxiliaries had been sent to him from Arabia, Armenia, Athens, Bithynia, Bœotia, Cappadocia, Cilicia, Ionia, Macedonia, Palestine, Pamphylia, Sparta, Syria, and many other countries. His sea-power consisted of six hundred men-o'-war in perfect fighting trim, and swarms of armed transports and merchantmen; while a fleet of sixty warships—then awaiting orders at Corfu—had been sent to him by Cleopatra and her brother Ptolemy, who had succeeded the bibulous Auletes as joint sovereigns of Egypt.

[18] There are two or three versions of the story: Plutarch (*Cæsar*) says he disguised himself as a slave; but Appian (*Civil Wars*, ii, 57) says he impersonated an official messenger in a ship chartered for this service. See also Dion Cassius, xli, 46.

Quarrelsome foreign potentates and generals were tumbling over one another in the camp, and the place was swarming with Roman senators, government officials, military commanders, naval officers, and the like. Cato was there, urging Pompey to stake all on a big battle with Cæsar. Cicero was there, very dejected and miserable, having been snubbed by Pompey and told he was not wanted by Cato, who said he ought to have remained neutral: indeed Plutarch writes that Cicero "was sorry he had ever come, and showed it by depreciating Pompey's resources, finding fault in an underhand way with all he did, and continually indulging in jests and sarcastic remarks at the expense of his colleagues, but going about the camp with a gloomy and melancholy face himself." [19] Amongst the many other men of note who worried Pompey with their contradictory advice mention must be made of Marcus Brutus who now for the first time plays a part in the events which are being related in these pages. Everybody had expected that he would join the opposite side, for Cæsar was supposed to be his father and had certainly been his mother's lover for years; and when, instead, he arrived at the headquarters in Greece, Pompey had been so surprised and pleased that he had thrown his arms around him and had kissed him. Now, however, Brutus was suffering from the prevailing but unaccountable depression, and, being a very studious young man, spent all his days sitting in his tent, writing an epitome of Polybius, the great Greek historian, apparently to deaden the pricks of his conscience which told him that he ought to have been with Cæsar.

It is impossible to understand why Pompey did not attack the harassed Cæsar, and the only explanation is that he doubted the fidelity of his Roman legions and placed no reliance on the fighting qualities of his foreign troops. Cæsar, of course, expected a battle at any moment, and could no more comprehend than we can why his rival held his hand. It seems, however, that Pompey was no longer a great man: his genius had bloomed too soon, and from a light-hearted, brilliant, and charming heyday he had passed to a depressed and hesitant decline by gradual stages which had hardly been observed by his supporters until too late. He was a haughty, silent, melancholy man at this time: it may perhaps be said that

[19] Plutarch: *Cicero*.

he had never been the same since the death of his adored wife, Julia, Cæsar's daughter; and his present wife, Cornelia, who was awaiting events in Lesbos, was nothing to him except, as she seemed to suppose, a bringer of ill-luck.

But if Pompey was depressed, Cæsar was frantic. He knew now that Antony was blockaded in Brindisi, and somehow he managed to get a message across to him advising him to march by land around the north end of the Adriatic and down into Greece. Antony, however, was still hoping to break the blockade, yet dared not risk the total loss of his army which would mean the end of Cæsar. At last it was decided that the forces should be divided, and that Gabinius should attempt the long march by land and Antony the dash by sea, so that, in the likely event of disaster to the latter half of the army there would still be a chance of success for the former. Thereat, one morning in the spring, Gabinius marched forth, and Antony was left to choose the best moment for the perilous adventure upon which he had decided.

Just then, as luck would have it, news came through that Bibulus, the enemy admiral, had died; and a few days later, while there was a chance that the Pompeian fleet was without orders, a strong south-west wind sprang up. Seizing the opportunity, Antony embarked some ten or fifteen thousand men, and set sail at dead of night, thus staking his life and his all upon this one throw of Fate's dice. In the darkness most of his vessels passed the blockading fleet unobserved, but when at length the alarm was given a few of his small battleships attacked the enemy, thus distracting them until the transports had escaped; and when day dawned he was far out to sea. The following morning found him close to the Greek shore, thirty miles south of Cæsar's camp at Durazzo; but now the wind dropped, and the pursuing ships of war, propelled by their five and six banks of oars, bore down upon them. Antony's men could do no more than prepare to sell their lives dearly, and the first enemy vessel which approached was received with a shower of arrows.

Just then, as by a miracle, the wind revived in increased force, and soon the transports were scudding northwards under full sail, while the oared battleships plunged after them in a heavy sea which in the end drove them onto the shore, where many of them were wrecked. Antony, thus, got clean away, sailed past Cæsar's camp, and safely landed at Lissus (Alessio), some thirty miles to the north of Durazzo. Pompey at once marched upon this place to annihilate the newly landed troops, leaving, however, a sufficient garrison at his base; but Cæsar marched after him, giving Durazzo a wide berth, and by a rapid maneuver joined forces with Antony, whereupon Pompey had to retrace his steps, this time pursued by his reunited enemies.

Thus Antony's breathless adventure ended in complete success, and he could congratulate himself upon having literally saved his chief's life. It was a perilous feat after Cæsar's own heart, and it strengthened the bond between them so that nothing, it seemed, could sever it.

Cæsar now felt himself strong enough to undertake a spectacular movement designed to impress all Greece and the neighbouring provinces with his power. With a sudden rush he occupied the semicircle of hills around Pompey's camp, and so rapidly dug trenches and threw up earth-works that in a few days the Pompeians found themselves in a state of siege. They replied by making their own lines a short distance back from Cæsar's, a narrow No-man's-land being left between the two opposing armies; and in this condition of stalemate matters remained for several weeks while spring passed into summer, the deadlock being at last broken by a sharp battle in which Pompey's men were the victors, and Cæsar, who was, as usual, in the thick of the fight, very nearly lost his life. At about the same time news arrived that Gabinius had been defeated in Illyria, and was dead and his army dispersed; but these disasters only had the effect of making Cæsar all the more anxious to force a full-dress battle, and at last, in June, he abandoned his entrenchments and marched south-eastwards into Thessaly where one of Pompey's generals was still at large.

His object was to enhance his reputation by overpowering this force, and also to entice Pompey away from his base and the sea, and then to outflank him. Neither Cæsar nor Antony were happy men at this time, for their enemies still had the advantage, and the war seemed likely to be protracted; but their depression was as nothing compared with that of Pompey, who could not make up his mind whether to follow Cæsar, or to stay where he was, or to invade Italy.

At last, however, he decided to march into Thessaly also, and to give battle, leaving a small force at Durazzo under the command of Cato; but when the army was about to march, Cicero excused himself on the time-honoured plea of ill-health, and remained with Cato. Once again his nervous doubts as to which side would win had led him to keep out of the whole business; but when it was reported to Cæsar and Antony that he was not with the oncoming Pompeian army they must have laughed together and have been not a little heartened, for Cicero was the best of weather-cocks. As a matter of fact the orator was not in good health. "Mental anxiety is wearing me out," he wrote,[20] "and is causing me also extreme bodily weakness"—a condition which may well have been aggravated by a proposal made by Domitius Ahenobarbus (who had escaped from Marseilles back to Pompey) that all senators who had not immediately come to Greece at the outbreak of hostilities should now be put to death. The suggestion, of course, was not taken up; but the very thought of it must have brought the cold perspiration out on Cicero's intellectual forehead.

Early in August Pompey's army came up with Cæsar's in the plain of Pharsalia, near the city of Pharsalus (Farsa), in the heart of Thessaly; and having some fifty thousand fighting men as against Cæsar's twenty-five thousand, he decided, after much hesitation, to fight it out. On the morning of the battle he addressed his troops, telling them to make an end of this madman who had thrown the whole empire into confusion. "Fight in the consciousness of a just cause," he said, "for we are contending for liberty and country, and on our side are law and honourable tradition."[21] Cæsar, on his part, encouraged his men by reminding them that it was Pompey who had demanded that they should be disbanded without rewards after all their triumphs in Gaul. "Yet this Pompey has now become slow and hesitating in all he does," he declared, "and his star has obviously passed its zenith. As for his foreign allies, pay no attention to them whatsoever, but fight only with the Roman

---

[20] Cicero: *Ad Atticum,* xi, 4.
[21] Appian: *Civil Wars,* ii, 72.

legions. Yet after your victory, spare your countrymen, for they
are your own flesh and blood. Kill only these wretched foreigners."

Pompey then placed himself in command of his right wing,
and assigned the left to Domitius Ahenobarbus; while Cæsar, on
his side, took the right wing opposite Domitius, and gave the left
to Antony who thus faced Pompey himself.[22] The long-expected
battle, which was to be the crisis of this war between the conservatives and democrats, was neither very sanguinary, as battles go,
nor long protracted. Pompey's cavalry were officered for the most
part by young aristocrats "in the flower of their youth and the
height of their beauty," as Plutarch tells us; and with his whimsical
smile, Cæsar instructed his veterans to aim all their blows at the
faces of these elegant young men, for experience had taught him
that this type of soldier "would not be willing to risk both a present
danger and a future blemish." And so it proved; for at the first
encounter these young officers ducked their heads, put up their
left arms before their faces, lost control of their horses, and threw
the whole brigade into confusion and finally into flight.

The foreign auxiliaries, meanwhile, proved to be quite worthless, and got in the way of the legionaries, whose hearts, anyhow,
were not in the fight; and soon an indescribable muddle developed
amongst the Pompeians, which ended in a general panic and rout.
Antony, like Cæsar, was never able to remember in battle that a
general's business is to keep out of the actual fighting; and in this
case he seems to have hurled himself into the thick of the fray, and
to have fought his way through to Domitius Ahenobarbus, and to
have killed him with his own hand.[23] Cæsar lost about two hundred men all told; [24] the enemy about six thousand, [25] together with
nearly two hundred standards and the eagles of eight legions.

Pompey could not stem the flight, became bewildered, and at
last rode in a sort of stupor back to his camp, where he sat down in
his tent, speechless. "He was no longer himself," says Plutarch,
"nor remembered that he was Pompey the Great, but was like one

[22] Plutarch (*Antony*) disregards the other commands, and makes it clear that
Cæsar's entire reliance, apart from himself, was placed upon Antony, whom he
describes as Cæsar's most trusted officer.
[23] If Cicero (*Philippic ii*, xxix) is to be taken literally.
[24] Cæsar: *Civil War*, iii, 99.
[25] Asinius Pollio, quoted by Plutarch (*Cæsar*) and Appian, *Civil Wars*, ii, 82.

whom some god had deprived of his wits." When the shouts and cries warned him, however, that the Cæsarians were coming, he sprang to his feet, and moaning "What!—even into my very camp?" mounted his horse and fled northwards along the road to Larissa and the sea. And when Cæsar, bareheaded and breathless, dashed in amongst the tents, with Antony, sweating in the summer heat at his side, he found his rival gone. "He *would* have it," he groaned, as he saw the havoc around him; "he brought it upon himself!"

Curiously enough, the victor's first thought was for Brutus. Before the battle Cæsar had given strict orders that on no account was this son of Servilia and perhaps of himself to be harmed; and now, hearing that he had fled, he scribbled a note to him telling him that all was forgiven, and sent a detachment of mounted men to find him and give him the message. The young man was soon traced, and wrote a reply apparently explaining his conduct in joining Pompey as being due to his conscience; whereupon Cæsar sent for him and presently received him with every mark of affection. He then asked him whither Pompey was directing his flight; and when Brutus told him that he supposed it would be towards Syria or Egypt, Cæsar made up his mind personally to hunt him down before he could get out of Greece.

Most of Pompey's forces surrendered during the following day, and Cæsar and Antony were soon free to gallop off with a squadron of cavalry in pursuit of their fallen enemy; but when some days later, they reached the Hellespont, they heard, to their bitter vexation, that Pompey had sailed for the east, and thereupon Cæsar made perhaps the most reckless decision of his career. In spite of the fact that the home government had to be re-established, the empire pacified, Pompey's troops in various provinces rounded up, the unconquered fleet captured, Cato and the other "die-hards" arrested, and a hundred outstanding tasks performed, he announced that under the escort of such ships-of-war as he could now command he was going to take a legion or two to Syria or Egypt or whatever the country might be wherein Pompey would seek asylum. He had no idea what perils on sea and land would be encountered, or when he would be back: possibly he would be away for months, but he would not return until he had given the *coup de grâce* to Pompey. As to the cleaning up of the situation here at home, he would leave the whole business to Antony; and therewith he gave him his instructions and, with an affectionate slap on the back, sent him off on his long journey to Rome to play, at the age of thirty-five, the part of vice-autocrat of the Roman world.

When Antony arrived once more on the shores of the Adriatic he heard that, after Pharsalia, Cato, Cicero, and others had fled to Corfu, where the broken-hearted Cicero had narrowly escaped being put to death as a traitor by the distracted Pompeians, and had sought refuge at last at Patræ (Patras) at the mouth of the Gulf of Corinth; while Cato had gone at length to North Africa. Antony then crossed the sea, was met at Brindisi by his mistress, Cytheris, and so returned in triumph to Rome.

Meanwhile Pompey had played out in all its horror the rôle of a vanquished and fugitive leader. A day or two after the battle, the skipper of a Roman merchantship which was about to sail from the port of Tempe in north-eastern Thessaly, was just telling his men, as he leant idly over the stern, how he had dreamed that Pompey had appeared before him, travel-stained and dejected, when, suddenly clapping his hand to his forehead, he recognized Pompey coming in actuality towards him in a small boat. The skipper's political sympathies were republican, and he therefore took the wretched fugitive on board and agreed, at a price, to carry him whithersoever he wished to go, at which Pompey asked to be taken first to Lesbos where he might pick up his wife, Cornelia, and their young son, Sextus. On arriving there, a sailor was sent ashore to fetch Cornelia; but when the man was ushered into her presence —and she was housed, of course, like a queen, her husband's defeat being still unknown—he burst into tears, and conveyed his news rather by his sobs than by his words. Thereupon, Cornelia dropped at his feet in a dead faint.

As soon as she had revived she ran headlong down the street to the docks, and, boarding the ship, flung herself into Pompey's arms. "It is *my* fault!" she cried. "It is I who have brought you bad luck. O, why have you come back to me? You ought to have left to her evil genius one who has involved you only in her own ill-fortune. I ought to have killed myself when I brought disaster to my first husband, Publius Crassus, instead of letting myself be reserved for a worse mischief, the ruin of Pompey the Great!" To this Pompey replied that at any rate she had had a few years of happiness with him, a little longer, in fact, than was usual in the case of the great. "We are all mortals," he said, "and we have to endure these ups and downs, hoping for better luck next time. After all, it is no less possible to retrieve my position than it was to lose it." [26]

The townspeople, headed by the philosopher Cratippus, then came down to the ship, offering to take care of him, but he told them to submit to Cæsar without fear, saying that he was a man of great goodness and clemency; and he began to argue with Cratippus upon the nature of Providence, having much to say just then in dispraise of the gods, to which, however, the philosopher refused to reply, being convinced in his heart that all was for the best. He decided, however, to remain with Pompey and Cornelia to look after their spiritual welfare, and soon, taking their son Sextus with them, they set sail for Attalia (Adala) in Asia Minor, where, on their arrival, they found some sixty fugitive senators and a certain number of troops and ships, and heard that Cato had gone to Africa, and that a great part of the fleet had not yet surrendered to Cæsar. Thereupon Pompey made some show of renewing the war, and, transferring himself to a battleship, set out for Egypt with a considerable escort, his object being to recoup his forces in that country, over which the young Cleopatra and her brother Ptolemy, who were friendly to him, were supposed to be ruling jointly. Actually, Cleopatra had just been driven out of her kingdom by this brother of hers; and when Pompey arrived off the Egyptian shore in the last days of September, it was the latter to whom the news was conveyed. Tales of the battle of Pharsalia and its consequences, however, had already been brought to Egypt; and Ptolemy's councillors decided that the best thing to do would be to put the fugitive to death.

A boat was therefore sent out to the battleship with an invitation to Pompey to land, and, in spite of Cornelia's frantic protests that he was going to his doom, he stepped into it and was rowed towards the shore, passing the time by reading over the speech which he proposed to make to the Egyptian monarch. Only a short distance

[26] Plutarch: *Pompey*.

had been covered, however, when one of the men in the boat stabbed him in the back, at which the others also set upon him. Pompey, in the old aristocratic manner, pulled his gown over his face, and sank to the bottom of the boat; and a moment later his head was severed from his body. Cornelia witnessed the murder, and her shriek of horror was heard by those on shore. The Roman ships at once weighed anchor, and escaped to sea.

Three days later, Cæsar arrived in hot pursuit; and thereupon an Egyptian deputation brought him Pompey's head as a token of good will. Cæsar, however, turned in abhorrence from them, and, moving aside, bent down his face and wept.

CHAPTER IX

Antony as Vice-Dictator in Rome, and his Temporary Estrangement from Cæsar.

48–45 B.C.

WHEN the news of the death of Pompey had run its breathless course through the crowded streets of Rome one day in November, 48 B.C., it was generally understood by the Cæsarians that the war was over, and that a Utopian age of democratic liberty had dawned; for, though Cato might hold out for some time in Africa, and other conservative leaders might try their luck again elsewhere, their ultimate suppression did not seem to be in doubt. The Roman world had passed into the hands of the People; the aristocratic or republican party was practically wiped out; and as a token of the changed outlook, the statues not only of Pompey but of Sulla, the last great aristocrat, were removed from the Forum. The absent Cæsar was given the Dictatorship until the end of the coming year, 47 B.C.; he was authorized to hold the Consulship for five consecutive years; and his person was made sacrosanct by his being elected a perpetual Tribune of the People, in spite of his patrician rank.

Meanwhile, however, the astonishing man had disappeared into the unknown. The tidings were that he and his troops had gone ashore at Alexandria, the Egyptian capital, and that he had apparently involved himself in the war then being waged there between King Ptolemy and his sister Cleopatra. Nobody knew when he would come back; but Antony was his deputy, his Master of the Horse as it was called,[1] and to him the western world now looked. The first thing Antony did was to issue a proclamation forbidding

[1] Dion Cassius (xlii, 21) says that Cæsar personally appointed him to this office; but Cicero (*Philippic ii*, xxv) implies that Cæsar's friends rather than Cæsar himself nominated him. There cannot be much doubt, however, that the appointment came direct from the fountain-head.

any partisan of the late Pompey to return to, or to reside in, Italy pending further orders from the Dictator, with the exception of two or three persons, amongst whom was Cicero, his case receiving particular consideration through the good offices of Dolabella, his son-in-law, a young man much liked by Cæsar.

Cicero had already crossed over from Greece to Italy, and had taken up his residence at Brindisi, where, it may be said in anticipation, he spent the next nine or ten months until Cæsar's return. He was a miserable man, broken-hearted at the loss of all the money—the bulk of his fortune—which he had lent to Pompey, and bitterly vexed at the collapse of his worldly hopes. His brother Quintus, in attempting to make his peace with Cæsar, had put all the blame for his deflection to the Pompeians upon Cicero, with whom he was now on terms of open hostility; his son, Marcus, now nearly eighteen years of age, was turning out to be a dissolute young rascal; his daughter, Tullia, was leading a very unhappy life with her youthful husband Dolabella; and his wife, Terentia, was showing him neither love nor respect.

He hated living at Brindisi, and yet his vanity refused to permit him to proceed further into Italy until the new government should authorize him to travel in state with lictors marching before him and with the correct equipage of an ex-Consul. "How is it possible for me to come nearer to Rome," he petulantly asked,[2] "without the official retinue given me by the nation, which cannot be taken away from me without a robbery of my rights?" At the same time he was very glad to have severed his connection with the remnant of the Pompeian party. "There was such ferocity in those men," he complained, "such intimate alliance with barbarous foreigners; and a proscription had already been sketched out by them, not of isolated individuals but of whole classes." Wars, proscriptions, bloodshed, always frightened him; and his only connection with armed force had been on those occasions when he had believed that any other course of action might have endangered his own skin. He was a man of peace, and his fears often made of him a turncoat [3] and a toady; but his frank admission of the fact

---

[2] Cicero: *Ad Atticum*, xi, 6.

[3] In the *Declamation against Cicero*, anciently attributed to Sallust, Cicero is called "The most fickle of renegades, trusted by none."

adds just that touch of the ludicrous to his behaviour which wins him our sympathy.

Antony's character was precisely the reverse. He was so indifferent to personal danger that he stuck to his friends in all the vicissitudes of their fortune with a heart so light that he did not always receive the praise for his fidelity which should have been his. He, too, is often ludicrous, but it is not because of any floundering attempts, such as Cicero's, to keep out of danger, but because of a blind indifference to public opinion. He goes his own rollicking way, following his heart's fidelities, loyal to his friendships, and sometimes butting his head against the stone wall of tradition with such force that one laughs to see him stagger back.

In these days when the maintenance of Cæsar's interests depended entirely upon him, he faced the difficult situation in the spirit, and, indeed, in the guise, of a soldier. Having once commanded the Gallic cavalry, he now dressed himself—a little theatrically, perhaps—in the very becoming uniform of that force, wearing the Gallic cloak fastened at the shoulder by a jewelled brooch, and having Gallic shoes upon his feet.[4] His sword hung by his side wherever he went, nor did he unbuckle it even at parties or public entertainments.[5] A body of soldiers accompanied him everywhere; and although the lictors and other civil officials who were in his train gave some hint of the vitality of the institutions he was supposed to be supporting, he deemed it better for Rome to understand that he was holding the empire for his master by means of the mailed fist. He was quite aware that he cut a very fine figure thus armed and arrayed; and if some of the fashionable young cavaliers of his own social circle smiled at his heroic pose, and impotently marvelled at his ability to drink and carouse with his burly veterans when the day's work was done, there was none who doubted his courage or regarded his sword as a mere ornament.

He needed all his courage just now; for Rome was in a very abnormal condition, and the dread of what might occur filled the air with rumours and portents. The doors of the Temple of Fortune were said to have burst open of their own accord; blood had issued from a baker's shop and had streamed towards another

---

[4] Cicero: *Philippic ii*, xxx.   [5] Dion Cassius, xlii, 27.

temple; babies were born holding their left, or unlucky, hands to
their heads; bees swarmed on the statue of Hercules on the Capitol;
and owls were seen in the city. There was an earthquake, too; and
in a series of severe thunderstorms the Capitol was struck by lightning, and a valuable horse was killed in Cæsar's own stables. It was
all very trying to the nerves, and the tonic of Cæsar's presence was
sorely needed.

The situation required the most careful handling, and yet
Antony did not allow his strenuous work to interfere with his
pleasures. At this time he was living in a house which had once
belonged to Marcus Piso, who had been Consul in 61 B.C.; and
here he entertained lavishly, although he was always pressed for
money and must have been deeply in debt. His domestic life, however, was not a very happy one just now, for, as has been said, he
was sufficiently fond of his wife, Antonia,—who, as already mentioned, had presented him with a daughter,—to be jealous of her;
and he was very suspicious in particular of her friendship with
Dolabella, Cicero's son-in-law, who was constantly at the house.

Dolabella was a heavily-built, handsome young man of about
twenty-two years of age, an aristocrat of the bluest blood by birth,
who, having strong democratic views, had followed the precedent
set by Clodius and had allowed himself to be adopted into a plebeian family in order to become a Tribune of the People for the
new year, 47 B.C.[6] His private life was thoroughly disreputable.
As a boy of sixteen or seventeen he had been married to a girl
named Fabia, but a year later she had left him because of his infidelity, and he had divorced her.

In 51 B.C., when he was eighteen, he had married Cicero's
daughter, Tullia, a union which had at first pleased the orator because it had linked him with the aristocracy he so dearly loved; but
Dolabella had proved an entirely unfaithful husband and had made
Tullia thoroughly miserable. Cæsar had taken him up because he
displayed that audacious courage which he always liked. He had
fought under Antony at Pharsalia; and now, at the beginning of
47 B.C., he was behaving himself, in his political work, as a budding
Clodius, exciting the rabble with fiery, socialistic speeches which
Antony thought were extremely indiscreet, and, at the same time,

[6] Dion Cassius, xlii, 29.

in his private capacity, he was paying these tactless attentions to Antonia and thereby incurring Antony's furious ill-will.

Now, Dolabella, like so many others, was on the verge of bankruptcy; and as Tribune he proposed in the Comitia a revolutionary law by the terms of which all financial contracts might be annulled, all debts repudiated, and all payment of rent abolished. I think it is to be supposed that he had in view no more than a moratorium which would be followed in most cases by a settlement not wholly ruinous to the creditor; for Cæsar, during his last brief visit to Rome, had dealt with the matter of debt by promulgating a very moderate measure for the partial relief of debtors, and had thus shown himself opposed to drastic steps. But the mob whom Dolabella addressed, it seems to me, interpreted the proposal in no such manner: to them it was to be a grand assault upon the hated capitalists, a sweeping emancipation of the down-trodden from all the obligations which in these troubled times had become more and more difficult to meet.

It was to be the first step along the blissful highway of proletarian rule, the first step towards the seizing of the property and the money of the rich. The old order had been destroyed at Pharsalia; the People were the victors; and now they were going to receive the fruits of their victory. "Down with capital!" was the cry; and the moderate democrats who heard it shook in their shoes, for they knew that the price of mob-support was being demanded of them. They feared that the always dreaded contingency inherent in a democratic triumph—the releasing, that is to say, of the left wing of the party from the restraint of the right, was about to eventuate, and that that catastrophe was going to take place which is so often a consequence of a proletarian victory, namely revengeful poverty's blind destruction of the misused sources of plenty.

In all ages the constitutional democrats' most exacting task is the prevention of a retaliatory anarchy after the overthrow of conservative rule, so difficult is it to leash the forces which have been given their head during the process of the revolution. Cæsar, it appears to me, had not fully realized that his personal struggle with Pompey had become in effect a struggle between the People and their traditional rulers; and he had casually disappeared into Egypt at a time when every dictate of common sense should have required him to hold the reins tightly in his own hands in Rome itself.

He had left to Antony the hardest task of all, namely the maintaining of law and order in these days when the mob was mad with excitement at the rout of the class which had held it down. Cæsar, in fact, had viewed his victory as a personal triumph; but the People, on the contrary, regarded him as a Tiberius or a Caius Gracchus, a Catiline, the hope of the poor, the scourge of the rich, and, thinking that they understood his projects, they were not prepared to wait for him to come home to tell them how to profit by their success; they *knew* what to do. As far as they were concerned he had served his purpose; he had overthrown their rulers; and now they would take matters into their own hands under the leadership of this fiery young protégé of his, Dolabella.

Antony had given orders that no civilian was to carry a weapon in the city; but this rule was constantly being disobeyed, and Dolabella's followers were continuously fighting with the partisans of the more sober citizens. A socialistic revolution seemed imminent. The property-owners besieged Antony's house, urging him to save them; senators and politicians of the right wing of the democratic party demanded that he should take immediate measures for the protection of the constitution, telling him—as, indeed, he well knew—that Cæsar was a moderate, not a revolutionary. Antony sent for Dolabella to reason with him, but the hot-headed young man would not listen to common sense. Antony lost his temper, and a personal element of hostility was introduced by "the terrible suspicion," as Plutarch terms it, "that Dolabella had committed adultery with his wife." As a consequence of the quarrel Antony summarily divorced Antonia, furiously telling her to go to her lover; and at the same time he warned Dolabella that he would oppose the passage of the proposed law by force, if need be.

The Senate then formally charged Antony with the duty of protecting the State, and authorized him to use the military for that purpose. Thus when the time approached for the first reading of the bill by Dolabella, as Tribune, in the Comitia, Antony concentrated a force of troops in the Capitol, ready to march them into the Forum to keep order while the other Tribunes, who were on his side, should oppose the measure. But during the night before the eventful day, Dolabella collected the mob in the Forum, and barricaded the streets leading into it, so that the passing of the bill should be effected without opposition; and sunrise found him upon the rostra, the voters in readiness in front of him, and every entrance to the meeting held by an armed rabble.

Thereupon Antony led his men to the barricades, demanded admission, and, on this being refused, gave the order to his troops to take the place by storm. A furious fight ensued, and before Dolabella and the remnant of his mob took to their heels, eight hundred of them lay dead upon the ground together with not a few of the soldiers. It was an appalling catastrophe; but there can be no doubt that it saved Rome from anarchy, though whether or not this object could have been attained by other and less sanguinary means is a matter for speculation. Too little attention has been paid to the incident by historians; but a careful study of the situation will show, I think, that on that day the empire's fate hung in the balance.

Antony, however, soon had other troubles to deal with. The troops stationed in Campania mutinied because of their long-deferred discharge, and he had the greatest difficulty in persuading them to await Cæsar's return. Dispatches were presently received that a son of Mithradates had revolted in Asia Minor; and from Africa came news that Cato and the two sons of Pompey were in alliance with King Juba, and were gathering a formidable army. Yet month after month went by without any news of Cæsar, and, indeed, the belief began to spread that he would never return: he was a prisoner, they whispered, or was dead. [7] It was not until the late spring of 47 B.C. that at long last the silence was broken, and the tale of his adventures began to filter into Rome.

It will be recalled that Cleopatra and her brother Ptolemy, the children of Auletes, had succeeded jointly to the Egyptian throne, and had sent a fleet of sixty ships to the aid of Pompey; but they had then quarrelled, Cleopatra had been driven out of Egypt, and her brother, while at Pelusium on the north-eastern frontier of his kingdom, had been a party to Pompey's murder. Cæsar, therefore, had landed at Alexandria early in October, 48 B.C. to extract at least an apology from the Egyptian king for having at first aided Pompey, and an explanation of his conduct in afterwards having

[7] Dion Cassius, xlii, 30.

authorized his murder. With about four thousand men he had marched through a hostile crowd into the palace, which was situated on a promontory forming one side of the Alexandrian harbour; and thereupon, so the story went, King Ptolemy had hurried back to his capital to find out what on earth Cæsar meant by thus pushing himself into the royal residence. No sooner had the young monarch arrived, however, than he had found himself a prisoner in his own house, Cæsar, his unwanted guest, being his gaoler and the Roman troops being posted at all the gates.

A few days later the exiled Queen Cleopatra, whom rumour described as a clever and audacious little daredevil of some twenty years of age, had come to Alexandria by boat from across the eastern frontier, and had caused herself to be smuggled into the palace, so that she might lay her case against her brother before this great Roman, who was now evidently the autocrat of the western world. Seven years ago, when Antony had met her in Egypt, she had been a girl of no great attraction so far as he could remember; but now, it was said, she had grown into a charming and vivacious young woman, not outstandingly beautiful, but piquant and sparkling in a superlative degree, and having an extremely seductive manner and what Dion Cassius calls "a most delicious voice." [8]

Cæsar at this time was fifty-four; but his years, as Antony knew, had not greatly diminished his capacity to play the lover, and, after months of campaigning and travelling, it was evident that he had seized upon this royal young lady as his natural prey, and had seduced her within a few hours of her arrival, for the news stated that it would not be long now before she presented him with a child. Thereafter he had lived with her in the palace; her brother had escaped, and had besieged them both, which accounted for the absence of news of him in Rome; but after giving Cæsar a pretty bad time, and, on one occasion, having been within an ace of capturing him, the unfortunate young man had been killed in battle; and in March, 47 B.C., all Egypt had submitted, Cleopatra being declared Queen with her second brother, also named Ptolemy, who was only eleven years of age, as joint sovereign.

Such was the news. Communications between Alexandria and Rome were now re-established, and Antony fervently hoped that

[8] Dion Cassius, xlii, 34.

Cæsar would soon return to relieve him of his difficult task of keeping order; but the anxious weeks went by, and he showed no signs of hurrying himself. The delay was incomprehensible to Antony, for not only was Asia Minor in revolt, but Cato's forces in Numidia were ever increasing in numbers, and it was very apparent that the civil war was not yet over. Moreover, Cæsar must now have received the reports of the state of affairs at Rome, and must have heard of Antony's trouble with Dolabella.

At last, however, it began to dawn on him that Cæsar had made up his mind to wait in Alexandria until Cleopatra's baby should be born; [9] but history does not enlighten us as to whether it fell to Antony to report this explanation of the delay to Calpurnia, Cæsar's wife in Rome, or to hide it from her. It seemed that Cæsar, this time, was really in love; and Antony must have scratched his head in perplexity as he considered what the consequences might be. Would he divorce Calpurnia, and marry this charming *queen?* It was just the mad sort of thing he might do. Cleopatra was a pure Macedonian Greek, having not a drop of Egyptian blood in her veins to disqualify her from being received as a westerner by Roman society; she was the richest woman in the world; and there was a persistent rumour that in her own kingdom she had caused Cæsar to be recognized as her legal consort. But would such a union inspire him with the ambition to become a monarch himself? Would he overthrow the Republic on his return, found a sort of Egypto-Roman throne, and set up a dynasty with himself and this royal Cleopatra at its head? Or would he remain a democrat, a leader of the People, and forget this dazzling little enchantress who now had him in thrall? Antony was puzzled and extremely troubled.

In August, however, exciting news arrived in Rome. Early in July, just nine months after her meeting with Cæsar, she had presented him with a son whom she had named Ptolemy Cæsar, or, more familiarly Cæsarion; and immediately after the event the happy father had sailed for Asia Minor to deal with the rebellion there of the son of Mithradates. Shortly after that, dispatches arrived stating that he had utterly routed the rebels at Zela (Zilleh)

[9] My contention that Cæsar remained in Egypt until the child was born is fully discussed in Chapter vii of my *Life and Times of Cleopatra*. Appian (*Civil Wars,* ii, 90) says that he stayed in Egypt nine months, a fact which tallies with my conclusion.

in the north-east of Asia Minor early in August; and so rapid had been his journey thither and his offensive that he wrote to a friend in Rome delightedly describing his victory in the three famous words, *Veni, vidi, vici,* "I came, I saw, I conquered!" Thence he passed through Greece, crossed the Adriatic, and in the last week of September landed at Tarentum (Taranto), in the heel of Italy, where he learnt that the faithful Antony had caused him to be re-appointed Dictator for the coming year 46 B.C.

Hearing of his arrival the unhappy Cicero hastened from Brindisi, some thirty-five miles away, to meet him; and to his great joy Cæsar received him with the utmost kindness, embraced him, and went for a walk with him, telling him, no doubt, how glad he was that Antony had allowed him his life and freedom. Moreover, he authorized him to use the consular lictors; but, judging by subsequent events, the Dictator advised him to meddle no more in politics, and for some time after this the great orator devoted himself to those literary pursuits which, in spite of his weak character and the absurdities of his behaviour, have handed down his name to posterity in deathless renown. After all, artists in words should be neither required nor permitted to vie with men of action, lest the balance of their thought be tipped.

When Cæsar arrived back in Rome Antony received one of the greatest blows of his life: his hero reprimanded him for having employed unnecessary force in suppressing Dolabella. It was useless for him to explain to that cold critic how unavoidable the use of the troops had been, or to blame him for leaving a lieutenant so many months unsupported. It was useless to remind Cæsar of his devotion under the most trying circumstances. The Dictator looked icily at him, accusing him of having estranged the lower classes—the masses upon whom Cæsar relied in the last extreme. Antony had killed eight hundred democratic voters, eight hundred friends or relations of the rank and file of the Roman army: it mattered not how great had been the provocation—a terrible blunder had been committed.

Nor was a curtain-lecture all that he had to endure. Cæsar at once set about the rectification of the mistake, and in doing so humiliated Antony without mercy. He called Dolabella to him, and, knowing him to be the idol of the mob, publicly patted him on the

back. The young man's proposed law in regard to debts and arrears
of rent, he admitted, was somewhat too drastic, but it had been upon
the right lines; and now he himself drafted a measure by which the
payment of rent by the men of small means should be cancelled for
one year. He distributed presents of corn, oil, and actual money to
every man who was in any need; he gave free meals to the poor;
and he instituted a levy upon capital. He courted, in fact, the left
wing of his party, the extremists; and the moderates were left in bewilderment.

Antony bore his shame as best he could, but he was not going
to allow himself thus to be trampled upon by the man he had
loved and served with such devotion; and an incident which now
occurred showed that he was ready for a fight. Cæsar regarded
the property of Pompey as having been confiscated to himself,
and he at once put up the fallen leader's town house and furniture for auction. No wealthy man in Rome, however, would bid
for them, partly out of respect for Pompey's memory, partly for
superstitious reasons, and partly, it would seem, because the re-
serve-price was too high. Antony, thereupon boldly declared that
he would take charge of the whole property, and very soon he
had placed his servants in possession of the house and grounds.
Cæsar, finding him thus established, demanded a cash payment,
but Antony replied with the argument that the property was as
much his by right as Cæsar's, since he had helped to defeat Pompey.
"Why does Cæsar demand this money of me?" he asked. [10] "Was
he victorious without my help? No!—and he never could have been.
Why should not those whose common work the achievement is have
the booty in common?"

Cæsar was astounded, but he did not press the matter for the
moment; and soon Antony had converted Pompey's magnificent
mansion into a sort of pleasure-resort for all and sundry and was
giving away the furniture, plate, and linen to his guests with a
hand made lavish by his anger. In the cellars he found immense
quantities of wine, and the drinking-parties which he gave attracted
hundreds of bibulous friends to his doors. Every living-room became
a saloon, says Cicero, [11] and every bedroom a brothel. No man or
woman left his house without being loaded with gifts, and even

[10] Cicero: *Philippic ii,* xxix.　　　　[11] *Ibid.,* xxviii.

the slaves covered their beds with Pompey's richly embroidered counterpanes. "Nothing was locked up," Cicero adds, "nothing sealed, no list of anything was made; whole storehouses were handed over to the most worthless of men; actors seized on this, actresses on that; and soon there was hardly anything left."

Cæsar guessed, presently, that Antony was thus dissipating the unlisted contents of the house from motives of retaliation, so that there should be little left for him to demand back in lieu of payment; and when Antony at last offered to renew the auction, and placed on view a few of Pompey's old clothes and some battered metal plates and cups as a sample of what there now was to sell, Cæsar let the matter drop, apparently admitting that Antony had the laugh of him.

But, for Antony the quarrel was no laughing-matter. He loved Cæsar, and his always sensitive feelings were deeply hurt at the Dictator's treatment of him. In his bitterness he decided to retire altogether from public life; and when Cæsar set out in December to destroy Cato and the Pompeians in North Africa, Antony neither asked for nor received any command in the army or official position at home. He was a wounded and disillusioned man. Cæsar's attitude had permitted the rabble to abuse him with impunity, and with the upper classes he was not uniformly popular; [12] for some there were who dared not befriend one at variance with Cæsar, and some who honestly disliked his hectic kind of life, and in particular his having brought the actress Cytheris to live with him in Pompey's house now that he was once more a bachelor. [13] Yet the right wing of the democratic party knew that he had been badly treated and made a scapegoat by his chief; and there were plenty of others who liked the honesty and simplicity of his character, admired him for being perfectly open about Cytheris, laughed indulgently at their theatrical parties, appreciated his otherwise excellent taste and elegant mode of life, and, in general, deemed him a good fellow and a man of mark.

Cæsar's African campaign resembled most of his others in the

---

[12] Plutarch (*Antony*) quotes Cicero as saying that Antony was loathed by all respectable people at this time; but this is some of Cicero's venom from the Second Philippic, and is refuted by the speech of Calenus quoted by Dion Cassius at the beginning of Book xlvi.

[13] Cicero: *Philippic ii,* xxviii.

sense that it opened with his placing himself in a position of the utmost danger, from which he was saved by sheer good fortune, and that it ended in complete victory. He landed on the African coast, to meet an army reckoned at not less than fifty thousand men, with a force of only about three thousand, the others having been delayed in transit; and for some time his chances of escaping annihilation were slight indeed. At length, however, his missing battalions turned up, and he was able to march on Thapsus (Demass), a little African sea-port, where he encountered the enemy under the command of Metellus Scipio, the late Pompey's father-in-law. The Pompeians, in spite of a huge advantage in numbers, were routed after a stubborn fight, and the slaughter which followed was terrible. This time Cæsar showed little mercy: besides the many important officers killed in the battle, he put to death Faustus Sulla, Pompey's son-in-law, the son of the great Sulla; Lucius Julius Cæsar, Antony's first cousin, son of his uncle of the same name; and Afranius, the Pompeian general whom he had previously defeated in Spain; while Metellus Scipio, King Juba, and others committed suicide.

That strange and inflexible traditionist, Cato, whose narrow and militant career had been one long agitation against democracy, was at Utica, near the site of Carthage, when the news of the defeat was brought to him. He at once offered all the ships in the harbour to those who desired to make their escape, but stated that he himself would remain where he was. [14] That night at supper he drank heavily, as, indeed, he had been doing for some months, and then began to talk vehemently in praise of the Stoic philosophy which advocated suicide in the last resort as a means of preserving a man's mastery over adverse circumstances. He was very excited, and Plutarch tells us that in a fit of anger he hit one of the servants so resounding a blow with his fist that his hand was severely damaged. It was obvious that he intended to make away with himself during the night, and his friends therefore took his sword from his bedside; but when he discovered the loss he turned upon them irritably, saying "Why don't you bind my hands behind my back?—I want no sword to put an end to myself: I need only hold my breath, or knock my brains out against the wall." He insisted upon the sword being

[14] Detailed accounts of Cato's last hours are given in Plutarch's *Cato*, and Appian, *Civil Wars*, ii, 98.

returned to him, saying, when he had it again, "Now I am master of myself!"—and presently, finding himself anxiously watched, he asked whether they really thought they could keep a man alive against his will. "Can you give me any reason," he demanded, "to prove that it will not be unworthy of Cato, when he can find his safety in no other way, to ask it from his enemy?"

He then seated himself in his bedroom, and began to read the *Phædo*, Plato's treatise on the soul, until, at dawn, he lay down on his bed and slept. Then, being awakened by the singing of the birds outside and the light of the sun, and finding himself alone, he seized the sword and drove it into his stomach, ripping himself open so violently that his intestines fell out. At the sound of his first convulsive struggles his friends rushed into the room, and stared at him in horror as he lay now silently before them in a pool of blood, his eyes fixed inscrutibly upon their faces. A doctor was sent for, who attempted to close the wound; but while the man was turning to reach for the bandages, Cato suddenly tore the gash wider open with his two hands, pulled out the intestines again, and a few moments later expired.

Cæsar marched into Utica during the morning, and when he heard of his enemy's death he is said to have expressed sincere regret. "Cato, I grudge you your death," he exclaimed, "as much as you grudged me the privilege of giving you your life!" It may be added that during the next few weeks Cæsar spent some time in regulating the affairs of the neighbouring kingdoms of Numidia and Mauretania, and that this work having brought him into contact with Queen Eunoe, wife of the Mauretanian monarch, he took the opportunity to seduce her before he left for Italy. She was a dusky-complexioned Moorish lady, and he found her attractions so novel that he loaded her with presents, and for the time being forgot all about Cleopatra.

By July, 46 B.C., he was back in Rome again, where he celebrated a fourfold Triumph. The first day's proceedings were devoted to the commemoration of the already half-forgotten wars in Gaul; and at the head of the wretched captives walked the noble Vercingetorix who had surrendered to him, it will be remembered, at Alesia in 52 B.C. For six years he had been kept an obscure prisoner in Rome; and now, after being paraded through the streets, loaded with chains, he was taken at the end of the day to the Tullian dungeon beneath the Capitol and there put to death. The act was one of gross cruelty and barbarism, but while blaming Cæsar, one must not forget that at a Triumph the killing of a foreign prince taken in the wars was an ancient custom having its origin in propitiatory human sacrifice, and that deviation from this traditional course would have been far more remarkable than adherence to it. Rome was then quite uncivilized according to modern standards of humanity; and though Cæsar could be merciful to his fellow-countrymen, and even to foreigners on occasion, his leniency was dictated by policy rather than by any inborn regard for human life.

On the second day he celebrated his Triumph over Egypt, and in this procession Princess Arsinoe was led in chains through the streets. She was the younger sister of Cleopatra, but since she had taken sides against the latter in the late troubles at Alexandria, there was no objection to her being humiliated; and Cæsar did all that was necessary out of regard for Cleopatra by releasing her after this public ordeal. On the third day the victory in Asia Minor was commemorated; and on the fourth the Triumph for the recent African campaign was celebrated, the little son of the dead King Juba of Numidia being exhibited. This boy, because of his youth, was also spared, and lived to become a great scholar, being ultimately restored to his throne. [15] In this procession Cæsar had the bad taste to show a picture of Cato tearing open the wound in his stomach; and later, when Cicero published a little book in praise of Cato, Cæsar wrote a counterblast which he called *Anti-Cato:* it is now lost, but Plutarch says that it was a compilation of whatever could be said against that odd and violent personage.

Antony, so far as we know, took no part in these Triumphs, although his participation in that over the Gauls might have been expected, since he was one of Cæsar's chief officers in those campaigns. He seems to have been bitterly nursing his grievance at this time, and to have been so angry with Cæsar that the latter was ready to believe a rumour that he wanted to kill him. [16] What his future

[15] He subsequently married Cleopatra Selene, daughter of Antony and Cleopatra, and by her had a daughter Drusilla, who married Felix, the brother of Pallas, the great minister in the time of Claudius and Nero. (See my *Nero*, Chapter V.)
[16] Cicero: *Philippic ii*, xxix.

would have been it is hard to say—except that he would have assuredly drunk himself into an early grave—had he not, in about the autumn of 46 B.C., become intimate with Fulvia, the extremely strong-minded widow of Curio, who set herself the congenial task of reconstructing his life.

Fulvia, it will be recalled, had been married first to Clodius, Cæsar's turbulent protégé who was killed by Milo early in 52 B.C.; and then to Curio, another of Cæsar's men, who was killed in Africa in 49 B.C., as has already been related. Plutarch describes her as "a woman not born for spinning and household duties, nor one who could even be content privately to rule her husband, but was quite prepared to govern a governor or give commands to a commander-in-chief." She was now a woman of perhaps about thirty years of age, and was, by her first husband, the mother of two children, a boy, Clodius, and a girl, Clodia; and she seems to have felt that Antony, who had divorced his wife Antonia over eighteen months ago and was, aparently, no longer in love with Cytheris, nor had any legitimate children of his own, except one little girl Antonia, the daughter of the divorced Antonia, would be just the right husband for her and stepfather for her son and daughter. He was only thirty-seven years of age, and yet he had practically ruled the empire during Cæsar's absence. He had a great career before him, she thought; and this quarrel with his chief could easily be patched up. She knew how to handle Cæsar: she had done so with success—at least, I think we may suppose so—in the days when Clodius was trying his patience and when Curio was getting into scrapes. Cæsar was always ready to grant a favour asked by a good-looking woman; and it must have seemed to her that all Antony needed for his re-establishment in his chief's good graces was just such an intervention on his behalf by herself. He was really devoted to Cæsar at heart, and Cæsar had often shown how greatly he trusted him: surely she could bring them together again.

Antony, of course, was fated to fall into the hands of a restless, scheming, domineering woman of this kind. I have tried to show that he was a man of brains, yet in many ways was what history deems him—a simple, good-hearted giant; and in spite of his by no means negligible attainments in the world of culture and dilettantism, in spite of his fine leadership in war and capable rule in peace, he had just those weaknesses, those gentle qualities, that attraction towards the line of least resistance, which placed him inevitably at the mercy of feminine determination. When Fulvia decided to marry him, lift him out of the doldrums, stop him drinking, take Cytheris away from him, reconcile him with Cæsar, and make him once more the second man in Rome, and perhaps ultimately the first, it was beyond his power to prevent her doing so. Before the year was out she had made him bring his affair with Cytheris to an end, [17] and had married him; while before the following spring she had effected his reconciliation with Cæsar—but the story of the reunion must be held back for a moment while other matters of more immediate importance are recorded.

In the autumn of this year 46 B.C. Queen Cleopatra, and with her, of course, her baby, Cæsar's son, arrived in Rome as the Dictator's guest, and was given a suite of rooms in his house on the far side of the Tiber. Roman society was both intrigued and scandalised, and nobody could pretend to fathom Cæsar's intentions, for his movement towards the founding of a royal dynasty was not apparent to more than a few of his contemporaries until at least a year later. All that could be said was that the Queen of Egypt was his mistress, and the mother of his child; that he was evidently thinking of her as a possible wife; and that the situation created by such a union would be anomalous in the extreme.

It was to be supposed, of course, that such a marriage would mean that Cleopatra would abdicate her throne and would become the first lady of the Roman Republic, with Egypt, perhaps, as her private estate, administered by Roman officials—which is, in fact, what it did become under Augustus; but there was always the possibility, on the contrary, that Cleopatra would retain her crown, and that she and Cæsar would be regarded as sovereigns in Egypt at the same time that they were private persons in Rome. [18] It was even conceivable that Cæsar would attempt to establish a monarchy in Rome; but this possibility, as has been said, had hardly yet entered the minds of more than a few persons: it was too outrageous. True, Tiberius Gracchus had once been thought to be aiming at a

---

[17] Cicero: *Philippic ii*, xxviii. Cytheris afterwards became the mistress of the young poet Gallus.

[18] Suetonius: *Cæsar*, lxxix.

throne; so had Catiline; so had Pompey: kingship, indeed, was a familiar bogey to the Romans; but surely Cæsar, with his reiterated democratic ideals and his recent inclination towards the left wing of his party, the socialistic wing, had no such intentions.

A subject which Cleopatra's arrival also opened up, was that of the heirship of Cæsar's now vast estate. Would he recognize the little Cæsarion, Cleopatra's baby, as his son and heir? He had no legitimate son, and at present it was understood that he intended to adopt his grand-nephew, Octavian, the son of Atia, the daughter of his sister, Julia, who was now a youth of seventeen years of age. There was also a widespread rumour that he was going to acknowledge Brutus as his own son, for he had shown the greatest consideration for him after Pharsalia, and had now made him governor of Cisalpine Gaul. People had lately been saying that he thought the world of Brutus and that he had declared that nobody was so fit as he to be his heir [19]; but at this juncture the young man spoilt his chances by divorcing his first wife and marrying Portia, daughter of Cato and widow of Bibulus, Cæsar's old enemy, thereby linking his fortunes with the republicans—a step which his mother, Servilia, did her best to prevent, and which must have been a great blow to the Dictator. Thus, the question as to whether he intended to marry Cleopatra had this further interest, that it involved the matter of the heirship; and Antony for one, though it seems that he did not call to pay his respects upon the Queen, must have listened with attention to the gossip which told how Cæsar was showing a fatherly affection for the baby.

At about this time another matrimonial complication, which must here be mentioned, engaged the notice of Roman society. Cicero, it will be recalled, had for long been on bad terms with his wife Terentia, who was a cold, critical woman, incapacitated, it would seem, by sheer honesty from responding as he would wish to his heroics and his emotional outbursts. One feels that the years had opened her eyes to his shortcomings, and that she had no bouquets now to lay upon the altar of his vanity. But to Cicero flattery was as the breath of life, and there had lately come into his house a pretty little girl of fourteen, Publilia by name, who was his ward, and who thought him the most wonderful of men. Now Publilia was

[19] Plutarch: *Brutus*, 7.

not only adoring: she was also extremely rich; and it occurred to the orator, who was at this time sixty years of age, that if he were to divorce Terentia and marry this child, he would be able to replenish his much depleted fortunes, pay his many debts, recover something of his forgotten youth, and re-establish his position as a hero in his own home.

He therefore dismissed the elderly Terentia, and married his ward; but he soon found that the girl was violently jealous of his daughter, Tullia, and made a scene every time he paid the latter any attention. Tullia, who was going to have a baby, had recently been divorced by the scapegrace Dolabella, and was living at home; but shortly after her confinement she died, plunging Cicero into the deepest grief, whereupon the naughty little Publilia could not restrain her delight, and went about the house singing and smiling so happily that Cicero, observing her unseemly behaviour, promptly divorced her. It was a disastrous end to his domestic life; and thereafter he devoted himself to his literary work, pointing out to his friends how courageously he was behaving under his affliction. "After being stripped of all those public honours which I had won for myself by my unparalleled achievements," he wrote, [20] "the one solace which remained—my daughter—has been taken from me. But I am resolved to be strong amidst absolute despair."

In the winter of 46–45 B.C., Cæsar, having sent Cleopatra back to Egypt, loaded with gifts, [21] went off to Spain to attack the last of the Pompeians, who were concentrated there under Sextus and Cnæus Pompeius, Pompey's sons. Once more the campaign began badly, and Cæsar's army was very nearly starved into an ignominious defeat; but in March, 45 B.C., a desperate battle at Munda, in southern Spain, in which Cæsar escaped death or capture by the merest chance, at last ended in a victory, Cnæus being killed, with his chief general, Labienus, and Sextus sent flying. As soon as the news was made known in Rome a number of Cæsar's admirers decided to undertake the journey to Marseilles—where the victor was expected soon to arrive and to stay while attending to post-war business—to congratulate him and to escort him back to the capital; and, hearing of this, Fulvia persuaded Antony to hurry ahead as far as Narbo (Narbonne) on the Spanish frontier, where Cæsar was then

---

[20] Cicero: *Ad Familiares,* iv, 6; v, 13.   [21] Suetonius: *Cæsar,* lii.

staying, and to present himself at headquarters as a practical mark
of his willingness to go more than half way to meet him in the matter of their personal quarrel. Brutus and Octavian were of the party
which went to Marseilles; but it was Antony at Narbo "who was
the best received of any," and later, when they all set out on the
road back to Rome, "Antony was made to ride almost the whole
journey with Cæsar in his carriage, while in the carriage behind came
Brutus and Octavian." [22] The reconciliation, in fact, was public and
complete.

This settlement of the quarrel is as understandable as was its
cause. When Cæsar had returned to Rome from Egypt, he must
have found that people were somewhat doubtful of his democratic
ideals, since he had been living so many months in a luxurious palace
with a queen as his mistress; and when he had been told of Antony's
severity towards the socialistic extremists of the party, he had
thought it advisable to give a practical demonstration of his benevolent interest in the left wing by sitting heavily upon his unfortunate
lieutenant who represented the right. But since then he had come to
realize that Antony's attitude had probably been wise, and that, at
any rate, it was supported by the bulk of moderate opinion. He had
found, in fact, that the right wing of his party was much stronger
than he had realized; and since that wing was politically closest
to the conservatives, or Pompeians, with the shattered remainder
of whom he wished to live at peace, he was anxious now to face
about, reverting to his old dream of a coalition. Antony, he saw, was
regarded as a level-headed man who, while being a sound democrat,
would stand no nonsense from the rabble; and a renewal of his
friendship with him would thus help the political situation.

Moreover, Antony seemed now to have turned over a new leaf
in his private life. He had dismissed Cytheris and her theatrical crowd, and was married to the capable Fulvia, who, as the
wife of Clodius and then of Curio, had won Cæsar's esteem;
and hence there were high hopes that he would no longer be
deemed a black sheep by the respectable element in Roman society,
but would serve Cæsar's purpose as a factor in the union of the
two political camps—that union which alone could mend the wreck-
age of the now ended civil war. Cæsar's desired rapprochement with

[22] Plutarch: *Antony.*

the conservatives was so evident that Brutus wrote a letter to Cicero saying that the Dictator seemed actually to intend to set up a government on the old aristocratic lines [23]; and, this being so, I think it is clear that the quarrel with Antony required to be ended. And, after all, Cæsar must have felt that a man who could defy him as boldly as Antony had done in regard to the payment for Pompey's house would be safer as a friend than as an enemy.

Antony, of course, was very happy at the reconciliation, and as he jogged homewards in Cæsar's carriage his thoughts may well have turned gratefully to Fulvia who had persuaded him to take this fortunate step. He told himself that she was evidently a woman in a thosuand, and he made up his mind to pay back his debt to her by trying his best to be faithful to her. While the party was still two or three days' journey from Rome, Cæsar was obliged to stop off for a few nights at a certain city to attend to some business; and Antony therefore obtained permission to go on ahead, for he knew that Fulvia would be deeply anxious about him, and would be worrying herself as to whether the quarrel had been patched up or had been intensified by the step she had advocated. But when he arrived on the outskirts of Rome he dismissed his escort, and went into a little tavern where he wrote his wife a letter telling her that he loved her and that she need never fear that he would return to the arms of Cytheris.

He waited in hiding in this inn until it was dark, and then, muffling himself up in his cloak, he drove in a hired carriage to his house, and when the porter at the gates asked him who he was and what he wanted, he replied in a dramatic whisper that he was an express courier from Marc Antony. He was then led into the presence of Fulvia, to whom he silently and ominously handed the letter; but when she had read it and knew from it that he was not only safe but was full of love for her, she burst into tears, whereupon Antony threw off his disguise and flung his arms around her. [24]

This little joke of his, however, caused a good deal of trouble, for soon the story got about that he had come back secretly and in flight to Rome, and that Cæsar had been defeated. At length he was obliged to show himself at the Comitia, and to explain that

[23] Cicero: *Ad Atticum*, xiii, 40, 1.
[24] Cicero: *Philippic ii*, xxxi; Plutarch: *Antony*.

he had merely come on ahead in connection with some private business, and that Cæsar would presently arrive; but at a later date Cicero threw the incident up at him in a public speech, exclaiming, "O worthless man!—was it in order that a woman might see you before she hoped to do so, that you disturbed the city by nocturnal alarms and with terrors of several days' duration? My friends, mark the trifling character of the fellow!"

Cicero, of course, could never appreciate Antony's jokes, which generally had a touch of horseplay about them; but in this particular instance he failed to see what we can plainly see now, that Antony was wildly elated at the termination of his quarrel with the man he had idolised and at his coming return to public life. The estrangement had been a nightmare to him, and now that all was well again he wanted to dance a jig on the rostra in the Forum or turn cartwheels all down the Sacred Way.

CHAPTER X

Antony's Consulship, and the Death of Cæsar.

45-44 B.C.

In Cæsar's mind there was never rest: no sooner had he completed one task than his ambition set him another. He came back from Spain full of the idea of conquering Parthia, the mighty Oriental empire which was the only dangerous rival of Rome. Doubtless many of his officers had begged him to make the attempt to wipe out the stain of the defeat of Crassus, and to recover the legionary standards then captured by the Parthians; but he was impelled not so much by motives of this kind as by a romantic desire to open the fabulous East to Roman dominion and exploitation.

No one can understand the character of Cæsar who does not realize that with him accomplishment always stumbled impatiently along in the footsteps of vast and airy vision. Grand as were his achievements, his plans were grander, and were ever crowding out all satisfaction from his mind and urging him on to further efforts. He was always striving to touch with his practical hand the thing which his inner eye beheld; and time and again he imperilled not only his own life in so doing but also the lives of tens of thousands of his soldiers. Once, when he was a younger man, he had burst into tears because he had not equalled the record of Alexander the Great! and now at the age of fifty-seven he still desired with burning intensity to outdo all other men who had ever lived.

Parthia presented the most promising field for these ambitions. If only he could annex that great empire to Rome as he had annexed Gaul, the road would be open to India and the remainder of the known world. Alexander had marched through Persia into India;

but he, Cæsar, would do more than that: he would bring these teeming and wealthy lands under the perpetual sway of Rome, and he himself, the Dictator of Rome, would thus become Lord of the Earth, the autocrat of the entire human race. In all his campaigns he had plunged into the fray without thought of disaster, relying confidently upon his good fortune which never seemed to desert him; and in regard to Parthia he was certain that he would succeed where Crassus had failed. His luck was astounding; and he could not resist the feeling that the miraculous was ever at work in his behalf.

He began at once to make his preparations; and his first concern was the selection of a man who could safely be left in charge of the western world while he himself was swallowed up in the East. His choice fell upon Antony, in whose whole history there is no clearer indication of greatness, no more sweeping vindication of his character. It is obvious that Cæsar had by this time realized how loyally his lieutenant had served him during his absence in Egypt, and how successfully he had governed the country, in spite of the unfortunate affray with Dolabella in the Forum. He saw now that Antony was the strongest man in Rome as well as the most reliable; and, more than this, it must have become apparent that he was not merely a devoted follower but a colleague who would act upon his own initiative in a crisis.

Cæsar was to be Consul again for the coming year 44 B.C., and he proposed Antony to the electors as the candidate for the other Consulship, the plan being that Antony in Rome should govern the empire while he himself was away at the wars; and during the next few weeks the two men must have been closeted together for many an hour, discussing ways and means. Antony was nearly twenty years younger than Cæsar, and in these conversations must have treated him with the respect due to an elder and greater man [1]: but at the same time he stood up to him boldly, and was no more afraid now of taking an opposite view in a discussion than he had been of defying him during the time of their estrangement. Indeed, one may well suppose that it was just this independence of opinion in Antony which his senior liked, more especially since the word of Cæsar was

---

[1] Cicero (*Philippic ii,* xxxii) says he was very humble in Cæsar's presence; but the evidence from other sources contradicts this.

at this time absolute law and he was surrounded by people who made it their business to agree with everything he said and to approve of everything he did.

The complete overthrow of the last of the Pompeians in Spain had raised Cæsar's position to an unprecedented level, and during the last weeks of the year 45 B.C. he came to be regarded with more actual awe and reverence than had ever been bestowed by the Romans upon any one of their rulers at any time in their history. The growth of this public attitude towards him had been rapid and bewildering; and it is perhaps best exemplified by a reference to the letters of Cicero in regard to him.

A year ago the orator had boasted of Cæsar as a friend, and had even shown some patronage towards him; but now his awe of him clearly reveals itself. In the middle of December, 45 B.C., Cæsar came to dinner with him while staying in the neighbourhood of his country home; and after he had gone, Cicero wrote to Atticus [2] saying that the dread experience of entertaining so formidable a guest was one which, though it passed without mishap, he would shrink from enduring twice. "Cæsar," he said, "is not the sort of person to whom you would say 'I shall be most delighted if you will come again.' Once is enough!" An army of at least two thousand men accompanied him and bivouacked in the grounds, while his suite filled three dining rooms, and the servants' quarters were crammed with his slaves and retainers. It was not a visit, Cicero complains: it was a *billeting*.

Antony's election as Consul for the new year, and partner in Cæsar's autocracy, was greatly resented by Dolabella who had hoped that he himself, as the recognized leader of the extreme democrats, would be given some position of trust—even the Consulship, in spite of his youth [3]—untrammelled by the control of a man such as Antony who was not only a moderate but also his personal enemy. He was bitterly disappointed. He had believed that Cæsar, who had so severely punished Antony for his attack upon the mob, would this time leave a real representative of the People in charge: he had never dreamt that he would take Antony back into his confidence and place him in absolute power, which was tantamount to muzzling the left wing and putting all authority into the hands of the right. So

[2] Cicero: *Ad Atticum*, xiii, 52.   [3] Cicero: *Philippic ii*, xxxii.

great was his annoyance, that Cæsar was quite afraid of the young man, and once, when he had to pass the gates of Dolabella's house in the country, he ordered his guards to draw their swords and to close in around him as he went by. [4]

The mob, too, began to show some hostility to Cæsar, angrily complaining, I suppose, that he was going to leave them at the mercy of a Consul who had been responsible for the massacre of eight hundred of them; and so serious did their protests become that at last, to appease the socialists, Cæsar hit upon the novel compromise of proposing to make the hostile Dolabella vice-Consul for him in Rome during his absence, that is to say a sort of junior partner with Antony in the government, though without much real authority. But here Antony showed once more his fearless defiance of Cæsar. In a public meeting of the Senate he opposed the appointment of Dolabella with all his might, abusing him roundly and being abused by him in return; and, later, when the matter was being put to the vote in the Comitia, he forbade the proceedings on technical grounds, and Cæsar was obliged to abandon the idea,[5] thereby incurring Dolabella's passionate hatred.

It had not yet been decided at what date the Parthian campaign should be opened, and meanwhile Cæsar spent his time in putting in motion some of those schemes with which his head was filled. He sent for the astronomers whose work had interested him in Egypt, and set them to the difficult task of adjusting the calendar, the nominal seasons having fallen some eighty days behind the actual, owing to the ignoring for centuries of the fact that the length of the true year is a fraction of a day over the three hundred and sixty-five days which constitute the calendar year. [6] Next, he began to collect and codify all the existing laws of the Romans; he started to establish public libraries in all parts of Rome; he proposed to divert the course of the Tiber in order to drain the Pontine marshes, to cut a canal through the Isthmus of Corinth, to lay out a road

[4] Cicero: *Ad Atticum*, xiii, 52.

[5] Cicero, however, (*Philippic ii*, xxxii) suggests that Cæsar had already agreed with Antony that Dolabella should be dropped. I have followed Plutarch's *Antony*.

[6] The adjustment having been made, an extra day was added every fourth year, as we do now, it being supposed that the length of the year was 365 days, 6 hours. Actually, however, the year is 365 days, 5 hours, 49 minutes, and the error caused the calendar to be some days in advance of the seasons in 1582 when it was again adjusted by Pope Gregory XIII.

across the Apennines, to construct a great port at Ostia, to divide up the Campus Martius into building sites and to lay out a new campus at the foot of the Vatican hill. His building-projects were vast. He proposed, for instance, to erect a temple to Mars which should be the biggest and grandest thing of its kind in the world; and he began the construction of the huge theatre afterwards completed by Augustus and now called the theatre of Marcellus.

In all these undertakings Antony rushed about, busily helping him.[7] He was a happy man at this period, for not only was he enjoying his work, but his domestic life was also providing him with pleasurable excitement. At just about the time of his reconciliation with Cæsar his wife Fulvia had presented him with a baby son: they had named him Marcus Antonius, but familiarly they called him Antyllus, a shortened form of Antonillus, or "Little Antony." They were both very proud of him, Antony himself being always a family man at heart, and having often jovially declared that the more children he had, legitimate or otherwise, the better he would be pleased. Fortune, indeed, seemed to be smiling upon him; and both in his relations with Fulvia in his home, and in those with the Dictator at his office, he showed himself to be a contented and light-hearted companion. In one respect, however, his loyalty to Cæsar was beginning to be somewhat tried: the great man was now definitely considering the possibility of making himself actual monarch of the Roman world, and of this project Antony did not approve. It frightened him, because he felt that it might result in another catastrophic civil war—the republicans against the monarchists this time. He watched the growth of the idea in Cæsar's mind and was greatly troubled by it, even though its magnificence made its appeal to his dramatic sense. The two extremes of society—the proletariat and the conservative aristocracy—were opposed to any tampering with the republican constitution, and only the middle classes, it seemed to him, would be likely to accept the innovation. But Cæsar was in no mood to be corrected: the consciousness of his unlimited power had fevered his brain, and his cool, critical faculties had been overpowered by the imaginative and romantic qualities of his nature. He was, as it were, intoxicated by his fortune, and nothing could hold his moth-like thoughts back

[7] Dion Cassius, xlvi, 15.

from the bright candle of his dream of sovereignty. He wanted to
be King of the Earth; he wanted to found a dynasty, and to hand
on his glory to his descendants.

At this time Queen Cleopatra was once more his guest in Rome,
having returned from Egypt towards the close of 45 B.C., and
there can be little doubt that she played an active part in the development of these schemes,[8] and that her baby, Cæsarion, was
the heir whom Cæsar had in mind when he pictured himself as an
old man seated upon the throne of the world in the years to come,
after the boy had grown to manhood. Antony could see clearly
enough now that he wanted to make Cleopatra his royal consort,
and for that reason had called her back to Rome; and not only
he, but a great many other people, had already formed the same
opinion.

The Queen of Egypt was so obviously the right partner for
the would-be monarch. She was, as has been said already, a pure-
blooded Macedonian Greek of ancient and royal lineage, possess-
ing all the elegance and culture of that race which fashionable
Rome was then trying to emulate, and having as her background
the artistic and intellectual splendour of her city of Alexandria,
at this time the undisputed centre of Greek art and thought. She
was clever, witty and exceedingly fascinating, if not actually beautiful, and, being just four-and-twenty years of age, she still enjoyed the charming exuberance of youth. She was fabulously
wealthy, and she would bring as her dowry the vast riches of Egypt
with its growing trade with India and the Orient—those far-off
lands whose fabled splendours had so gripped Cæsar's imagination.

Antony, as Consul now and Cæsar's partner, must often have
met her, and must have been called upon to express polite admiration for her baby, whose parentage Cæsar did not deny, the child
having, indeed, a close resemblance to him.[9] Fulvia, too, must
have been a frequent visitor at the Queen's quarters, and one may
picture the two women comparing the merits of their babies, though
Fulvia, to be sure, was a more interested politician than mother,
and was more concerned with Cleopatra's doings in the field of in-

---

   [8] Cleopatra's return to Rome is shown by Cicero's letters, for he speaks of her
presence there, and departure after Cæsar's death.
   [9] Suetonius: *Cæsar,* lii.

trigue than in the nursery. But the situation was awkward both for Antony, and his wife, for they had also constantly to meet Calpurnia, Cæsar's legal spouse, who, no doubt, would have been very willing to tear Cleopatra's eyes out, more especially since she had no son of her own. Cæsar himself, however, was not conscious of embarrassment, and, feeling that he was above the law, blandly instructed a lawyer to draft a bill authorizing him, if necessary, to marry the Queen or anybody else without having to divorce Calpurnia,[10] of whom he seems to have been rather fond in his own way, though he did not pretend to be faithful to her or even to the two of them.

Antony and Fulvia had also to meet and consider Servilia. She had been Cæsar's mistress for years, and though she was nearly as old as Cæsar himself, she was still his good friend and had recently received from him the present of some great estates—as compensation, people said, for his having transferred his affections to her daughter, Tertia,[11] the child of her marriage with Junius Silanus and wife of that Cassius who was afterwards the chief of Cæsar's assassins. Servilia was the mother of Brutus, presumably the son of her adultery with Cæsar; and since it was quite likely that Cæsar might forgive Brutus his recent marriage and nominate him as his heir, in the event of his plans in regard to Cleopatra and Cæsarion miscarrying, the future of this now elderly lady was full of possibilities.

As the weeks went by Cæsar became more and more anxious to settle the question of an heir—an heir, that is to say, to his name and authority as well as to his fortune—for he felt that he must make a decision before he set out for Parthia; and Antony was doubtless brought into the discussion very fully, since, in the event of Cæsar's death while abroad, it would be he who, as Consul, would have to carry out the great man's last wishes. In Spain Cæsar had had with him his grand-nephew, the young Octavian, now eighteen years of age, who, as has already been explained, was the son of his sister's daughter, Atia; and on his return to Rome he had made a will in which he bequeathed his property jointly to this young man and two other grand-nephews, the sons of another of his sister's daughters. Lately, however, he had been staying with

[10] Suetonius: *Cæsar*, lii.   [11] *Ibid.*, l.

Phillipus,[12] Atia's second husband, where he had had the opportunity of taking another look at Octavian; yet still he was undecided as to whether to make him his successor.

Octavian was a rather pimpled and unhealthy youth with a chronic cold in his head [13]; and Cæsar, while admiring in him a certain courage and resourcefulness, does not seem to have thought him physically strong enough for the strain of public life. He decided, however, to give him a military training with a view to taking him on the Parthian expedition if his health should improve; and for this purpose he now sent him over to Apollonia, on the other side of the Adriatic, where the expeditionary army was being concentrated, and where he could complete his education under Greek professors.

Cæsar does not seem to have considered him a desirable heir to the sovereignty which he wished to establish, but in the event of his, Cæsar's, death in Parthia while Cæsarion was an infant, Octavian would perhaps be more suitable than anybody else as the heir to his name and estate, and at last after much hesitation, he made up his mind to add a codicil to his earlier will to the effect that Octavian should be adopted into his family and should assume the name of Cæsar.[14] He did not tell him of his intention, however,[15] for he obviously hoped to live long enough to see Cæsarion grown to manhood, in which case a new will would have to be made in favour of the latter; but Antony was undoubtedly in the secret, and perhaps approved of the nomination, for Brutus, the only likely alternative, was a rather critical and unfriendly personage. It was no good considering Cleopatra and her infant son at this juncture, Cæsar seems to have said: in due course the child would anyhow become King of wealthy Egypt, and that was fortune enough unless and until his father could win a throne for himself, marry Cleopatra, and make him heir-apparent to the sovereignty of the whole earth, with Rome and Alexandria as joint capitals of the world-wide kingdom.[16]

Antony was perplexed and troubled by all this talk of monarchy. Since their estrangement Cæsar had not been quite the hero

---

[12] Cicero: *Ad Atticum*, xiii, 52.   [13] Suetonius: *Augustus*, lxxx, lxxxi.
[14] Suetonius: *Cæsar*, lxxxiii.   [15] Suetonius: *Augustus*, viii.
[16] Suetonius: *Cæsar*, lxxix.

to him that he used to be, and he was now fully alive to the defects in his character—his rashness, his overweening ambition, and his growing arrogance. One day Cæsar told him that the learned men in charge of the Sibylline Books had found a prophecy therein which declared that Parthia would never be conquered except by a king, and that therefore this title ought to be conferred upon him, if only outside Italy. On another occasion, when some overzealous admirer had placed a royal crown on one of his statues and two Tribunes of the People had removed it and had sent the man to prison, Cæsar summarily dismissed them from their office. It is true that the commotion caused by this incident obliged him to deny in public that he was aspiring to the monarchy; yet the fact remained that almost daily he was permitting new honours to be conferred upon him which were the most palpable preludes to kingship.

Perhaps the most significant of these was the permission granted to him, at his own request, to be buried within the precincts of the city instead of outside the walls as the law enjoined; for in Alexandria Cæsar had seen the sepulchres of the Ptolemaic kings of Egypt grouped around the mausoleum of Alexander the Great in the heart of the city, and his imagination had leapt forward over the centuries to the hoped-for day when the visitor to Rome should be shown the tombs of the Cæsars, the sovereigns of the earth, similarly grouped around *his* burial place in the middle of the metropolis.

Other honours included the right to wear a triumphal robe on all state occasions, to be escorted everywhere by a bodyguard of senators and gentlemen, to sit upon a golden throne in the Senate, to ride in a sort of state coach, to have his portrait impressed upon the coinage, and so forth. It was decreed that a statue of him should be placed in every temple, and two on the rostra in the Forum; and finally his image was set up in the Capitol beside those of the seven kings who had ruled Rome before the days of the Republic.

But if these precursors of monarchy worried Antony he must have been even more perplexed by another and more extraordinary phase of Cæsar's increasing megalomania which now began to unfold itself. In Egypt the sovereign was regarded as a divinity, Cleopatra being an incarnation on earth of Isis-Venus; and Cæsar while in Alexandria had not only become accustomed to the idea

of having a goddess for his mistress but had found it not too preposterous to think of himself also as superhuman, for so the Egyptians regarded him, and so his invariable good fortune seemed to
indicate. His family traced its descent back to Venus; and Cleopatra, who *was* Venus on earth in the opinion of her subjects, may
well have hailed him as a fellow divinity and have imbued him
with the sense of his superiority to mortal clay. At any rate he
now began to assert his divinity, no doubt telling Antony with
a smile that he did so for reasons of state, but making it apparent
enough that he thought of himself at least as the *instrument* of a
higher power even though he had no very clear conception of the
nature of that power and was decidedly agnostic in his religious
beliefs.

By his commands, or with his consent, a decree was now pro-
mulgated raising him to the official status of a god, and a temple,
dedicated to him under the name of Jupiter-Julius, was ordered
to be built; while in the temple of Quirinus his statue was set up,
inscribed with the words "To the Immortal God." A college of
priests was established whose business it was to minister to his
divine nature, to celebrate annual festivals in his honour and especially to make sacrifices to him on his birthday, the name of
the month in which he was born being changed from Quinctilis or
Quintilis to Julius in his honour—whence comes our word "July."

It is difficult to say whether or not Cæsar took his deification
very seriously in his own heart, but the evidence seems to indicate
that, after his first bewilderment, Antony, at any rate, regarded
the matter as lightly as its political dangers would permit; and
when Cæsar asked him,[17] as fellow Consul, to undertake the duties
of Priest of this new religious order, one may imagine that he
slapped his thigh and gave his jovial consent. The nature of the
duties he would have to perform intrigued and amused him. The
priestly college belonged to the *Lupercal* order, that is to say it
was under the patronage of the god Lupercus, an ancient Italian
deity who was both the protector of the flocks against his servants,
the wolves, and also the lord of fecundity, in which aspect he was
identified with the Arcadian Pan. There were already two colleges of
this order, the Quintilian and the Fabian; and the new establish-

[17] Dion Cassius, xliv, 6.

ment was called the Julian, its members being termed *luperci Julii*. At the annual festival of Lupercus, held on the 15th of February, a crowd of naked boys from each of the colleges was wont to parade the streets, and the Priest in charge of them made his startling appearance stark naked, or wearing nothing but a loincloth of goat-skin. The ceremonies always began with the sacrifice of a goat and a dog, the former representing the goats of Pan and the latter the wolves of Lupercus. The Priest was then daubed with the blood, at which he was required to utter yells of laughter, and to go bounding away down the street brandishing a whip made from strips of the skin of these animals. With this he hit at every woman he encountered, this being supposed to endow her with fecundity: I may add that the whip was called the *februa*, a word still preserved in the name of the festal month, "February."

Antony, always proud of his magnificent figure, was highly diverted at the thought of appearing in this state of nature in the very Forum, for a Consul of Rome leaping about, naked and unashamed, would be a spectacle never before witnessed in the city. He was not sure, of course, that he would dare to enact these duties at the approaching festival; yet it could not be denied that in doing so while holding a Consulship he would have the sanction of religious law if not of custom. After all, the whole affair had something of the nature of a carnival, and at such a time, surely, even a Consul could unbend.

Meanwhile, during January and the early days of February, 44 B.C., new honours were conferred upon Cæsar. He was nominated perpetual Dictator and Censor of Rome, that is to say absolute ruler for the duration of his life; and he was given the official title of *Imperator*. This word, which signified a victorious military generalissimo, had always been a title of honour conferred by the army upon a leader who had been eminently successful in a major battle, but it had not yet assumed the monarchical meaning implied in our rendering of it—*Emperor;* and it is incorrect to say that Cæsar was the first "Emperor" of Rome in the modern sense of the word, for the term did not in his lifetime convey the idea of sovereignty. Still, it is not to be supposed that the title of *Rex*, or "King," was aimed at by him, for the word had an ill sound in Roman ears, and once when somebody in the crowd hailed him by that name there was such general consternation that he quickly called out "I am Cæsar, and no *King!*" Thus, it may be that he intended to raise the title of "Imperator" to the kingly significance it afterwards attained.

His growing regality and arrogance, as has been said, increasingly worried Antony, who racked his brains for a means of turning Cæsar's mind from the thought of monarchy [18] without incurring his violent displeasure. Instances of this arrogance were daily accumulating. On one occasion Cæsar received the whole body of the Senate without rising in the customary manner from his seat, and it was only when he was informed of the offence he had thereby given that he apologised by saying that he was suffering from an upset stomach and was afraid to stand up lest by so doing he should bring on an embarrassing spasm of the gripes. On another occasion he was heard to remark that whatever he said ought to be regarded as law, that the republican form of government was merely a name, and that he would never follow the precedent of Sulla in resigning the arbitrary powers of Dictator.

Cleopatra, too, was becoming rather presumptuous now that she believed her hopes of marriage to Cæsar and their joint elevation to the throne to be so near realization. Cicero, who paid an occasional call upon her, told his friends that he detested her and that her "insolence," as he described it, was hard to bear. Cæsar had recently caused a temple to Venus, his divine ancestress, to be erected in Rome; and now he ordered a statue of Cleopatra to be placed therein, as though she were an incarnation of that goddess, while, for circulation in Egypt, he allowed her figure to be impressed upon the coins in the guise of Venus, holding the little Cæsarion, as Eros, in her arms. Her haughtiness, therefore, is understandable; but none the less it gave great offence, and increased the sheer horror with which Cæsar was regarded by the old-fashioned republicans. He had by now pardoned all his former enemies of the Pompeian party, and had welcomed back to Italy those who had been in exile, even restoring much of the confiscated property; but he could never reconcile them to his autocracy, and his movement towards monarchy filled them with dismay. Antony was aware of their secret murmurs, and his fears for Cæsar's safety

[18] Dion Cassius, xlvi, 17, 19.

were intensified as he observed how many of his closest friends
were showing their disapproval and were hinting that the Dictator
was going too far and that his colleague in the Consulship ought
to tell him so.

At length came the day of the Lupercalia, and Antony, having
fortified himself with liberal potations of wine, presented himself
at the place of sacrifice stark naked except for the slip of goat-
skin around his loins, and rather drunk.[19] The people laughed and
clapped their hands to see their Consul thus enacting the time-
honoured rôle, and when, having been "blooded" and handed the
februa, he pranced away into the crowd, the women ran merrily
forward to receive from him one of those jovial blows he was delivering to right and left and incidentally to admire his splendid
physique. Here and there, however, a man or matron of the old
school turned away in pained disapproval; and amongst these was
Cicero, who asked what could be more shameful than this foolery
and this nakedness, and declared that Antony, even if he were
Priest of Lupercus, ought not to have forgotten that he was Consul
too.[20] How different this was, he sighed, to his own conception of
the Consular dignity! How the standards had been lowered since
this loose spirit of democracy had taken hold of men's minds!
What a dreadfully vulgar personage Antony was, he murmured,
turning his eyes from the roistering figure: what offence he must
be giving to the good old nobility!

Cæsar, clad in triumphal purple, was seated on his golden chair
upon the rostra, waiting to take the salute from the procession of
nude boys, when his colleague came bounding into the crowded
Forum, followed by the laughing mob, and pushed his way towards
the Dictator for the purpose of hailing him as patron lord of the
Lupercalia; but suddenly, so it seems, Antony observed in the
throng one of Cæsar's ardent admirers holding in his hand an im-
provised royal diadem ornamented with bay-leaves with which he
intended, perhaps, to crown one of the Dictator's statues, profiting
by the license of the merry occasion to do so with impunity.[21]
Instantly a daring idea presented itself to Antony—"who was

[19] Cicero: *Philippic iii*, v.   [20] *Ibid., ii*, xxxiv.
[21] Cicero (*Philippic ii*, xxxiv) suggests that Antony had brought the diadem with
him, but it seems more likely that he chanced upon it.

always ready for any audacious deed," as Velleius says, in recording the incident: [22] he would offer this diadem to Cæsar himself, here and now, and thus force his hand, obliging him to show the public whether or not he really desired to be king, and at the same time giving the masses the opportunity to reveal their own sentiments in the matter. If Cæsar were to accept it, the significance of his action could, if necessary, be explained away afterwards by referring to the jesting nature of the occasion or by saying that Cæsar had merely been allowing himself to be crowned as king of the festivities. If, on the other hand, he were to reject the diadem, the quietus would be given to the rumours that he was about to overthrow the Republic.

Antony therefore waved the diadem about and called out to those around him, laughingly declaring that he was going to put it on Cæsar's head to see what would happen. Some of the Cæsarian enthusiasts thereupon lifted him up onto the rostra, and, amidst a mixed din of laughter, cheers and groans, he harangued the people,[23] making a witty and non-committal speech which, so far as anybody could understand his meaning at all, conveyed a friendly rebuke to the Dictator for his dalliance with the thought of kingship.[24] He spoke of the great Consuls of the past who had built up the Republic; and, declaring that Cæsar had so greatly increased Rome's power that he was now regarded as autocrat by Gauls, Africans, Egyptians, and so forth, asked with a smile if he were also desirous of being autocrat over the Romans as well. The actual words of the speech are lost, but we are told that "they caused Cæsar to change his mind; they humbled him, and made him stop short, feeling a touch of alarm."

At the close of his harangue Antony held the diadem out to Cæsar, repeatedly thrusting it towards him and withdrawing it again, looking down at the crowd and then at the Dictator, as though asking whether or not they or he had a clear determination in regard to it. Some people cheered and clapped their hands, others shouted their disapproval, many were silent or merely laughed; and Cæsar,

[22] Velleius, ii, lvi.

[23] Cicero: *Philippic ii*, xxxiv; Dion Cassius, xlvi, 19.

[24] Dion Cassius (xliv, 19) quotes a contemporary speech to show that it was Antony's purpose to rebuke Cæsar.

annoyed by the levity of the crowd, and recognizing, too, its lack
of unanimity, at last angrily pushed the diadem away from him,
whereupon Antony shouted to the people, telling them to take notice
that the crown of king had been offered to Cæsar and that he had
refused it. "Thus," we are told, "by Antony's cleverness and con-
sumate skill an end was put to Cæsar's ideas of monarchy, the proof
of which was that from that time forward he no longer behaved
in any way as a king." [25]

But though Cæsar, after this incident, certainly did take care
to avoid the accusation of arrogance, and was perhaps making up
his mind to wait until he returned from Parthia before pressing
forward his plans in regard to the monarchy, a great many people
continued to eye him with suspicion and to complain of his despotism. They told themselves that the late Pompey had been quite
right to attempt to defend the Republic against this individualist,
and they felt now that the civil war had not been a fight between
the conservatives and the democrats, but one between the upholders
of the constitution on the one hand, and, on the other, this single
individual who, under the pretence of democracy, was scheming
for a throne. There followed, in fact, a revival of the Pompeian
party, a recrudescence of the old bitterness against Cæsar, a secret
regathering of those who had fought him in the field and had since
been pardoned, to whom were added those democrats who did not
desire to see the constitution upset.

Antony knew that this opposition was crystallising, and that
some sort of plot was being formed against Cæsar. He had even
been sounded cautiously about his own attitude, and had felt
himself obliged to tell those who spoke to him that under all
circumstances, he would remain loyal to Cæsar, even though he
did not approve of his actions. [26]

There were two men in particular whom he suspected of hidden hostility to the Dictator. One of them was the lean and hungry-
looking Cassius, the husband of Servilia's daughter, Tertia; the
other was this personage's brother-in-law, Brutus, Cæsar's supposed
son. Cassius had been serving under Crassus at the time of the Parthian disaster, but had escaped from the shambles, and later had
commanded a part of Pompey's fleet in the war against Cæsar, and

[25] Dion Cassius, xliv, 17, 19.   [26] Plutarch: *Antony*.

in the end had surrendered to him and been pardoned. Cæsar had magnanimously made him Prætor for the present year, 44 B.C., and had promised him the governorship of Syria in the coming year; but the man's hatred of his benefactor had recently been revived owing, I suppose, to Cæsar's notorious adultery with his wife, Tertia: [27] "I don't like Cassius," the Dictator once remarked. "He looks so pale: I wonder what he can be aiming at." [28]

Brutus was a man whose character puzzled Antony; but Cæsar, believing him to be his son, would hear no word against him. There are not many incidents in Cæsar's life, nor temperamental passages, which inspire in us any sense of sympathetic sorrow on his account: he was so self-sufficient, so fortunate, so absorbed in the pursuit of his ambitions, that he makes little demand upon our compassion. Yet the story of his relationship to Brutus is pitiful, and does supply just that touch of sentiment which is otherwise largely absent from the tale of his brilliant, adventurous, and steely career. He loved Brutus, but Brutus disapproved of him; and therein lay the Dictator's tragedy.

It will be recalled that in the civil war Brutus had taken sides with Pompey against Cæsar, and had been generously pardoned for doing so. Later he had married Porcia, the late Cato's daughter, and by thus renewing his alliance with the old conservative party had deeply offended Cæsar, who, nevertheless, forgave him once more. Recently rumours had reached the Dictator's ears, perhaps through Antony, that Brutus was plotting against him; but he would not believe them. "What!" he exclaimed, putting his hand upon his heart. "Do you suggest that Brutus will not wait out the duration of this little body of mine?" [29]—and it seemed to those who heard his words that even yet Cæsar was thinking of Brutus as a possible heir to his power and his name.

Actually, however, Brutus was anxious to disavow, in public at any rate, his relationship to the Dictator, for he could not tolerate the thought that he was illegitimate and had no right to his name, and he wished also to clear his mother's reputation of the aspersions which had so long been cast upon it. The founder of the family whose name he bore was the celebrated Brutus who overthrew the early kings of Rome and established the Republic; and he pre-

[27] Suetonius: *Cæsar*, 1.   [28] Plutarch: *Antony*.   [29] Plutarch: *Brutus*.

ferred this honourable lineage—which, though of plebeian caste, glittered with illustrious figures—to the patrician but less historically famous ancestry of Cæsar. It seems that he made a point of speaking of his descent from the great liberator, Brutus, and to Cæsar's affectionate and paternal advances he responded with a coolness which deeply hurt the elder man.

He was now forty years of age, a sallow-faced, thin, grave and silent man, rather conceited and self-centred, a considerable scholar, an eager student of philosophy, and a strict adherent to the old school of upright, temperate behaviour. His manner of speaking was curt and abrupt; but there was no such brevity in his thoughts, for he was in the habit of turning matters slowly over in his mind, submitting his every action to the tribunal of his conscience, and so carefully considering the moral principles involved that he must have often been an intolerable bore. Goodness, integrity, and righteousness are qualities so essentially spontaneous that a man who would behave in a high-principled manner, but whose conscience does not give him an instant lead, must of necessity be wanting in that social ease which is true virtue's passport and authority in a wicked world. But Brutus had no such ease: he was always torturing himself as to whether he should act in this way or in that, and, consequently, he was often a most tedious companion.

Lately he and Cicero had become fast friends, though there was this difference in the character of the two men, that the orator was a bland, professional exponent of outward righteousness whose inner thoughts were often mean and contemptible, whereas Brutus was a struggling disciple of traditional virtue, whose heart was fundamentally honourable. At this time Cicero had returned to his accustomed position upon the fence, unable to make up his mind which side of the political field most sweetly called to him. He wanted to be friends with Cæsar, that is to say with the paramount power, and would perhaps have stepped down upon that side of the fence had he been encouraged to do so; but neither Cæsar nor Antony bothered very much about him—indeed, Cicero was once kept waiting so long in an anteroom for an interview with the Dictator that his vanity must have been greatly hurt.[30] On

[30] Cicero: *Ad Atticum*, xiv, 1.

the other hand, the conservative party paid him great respect, but lacked the influence to help him to renew his past triumphs as a public character.

His friendship with Brutus, however, suited his two-faced policy; for Brutus was at once the favourite of Cæsar and a representative figure in that group which was most opposed to him. Together the two men bemoaned the Dictator's growing despotism; and in many letters exchanged between them the impotence of the republican government, which lay fawning at Cæsar's feet, was sorrowfully discussed. Cicero paid his friend the compliment, too, of dedicating some of his literary compositions to him, and amongst these was the *Tusculan Disputation*,[31] a work in which the author advocates suicide as an honourable means of escape from conditions, political or otherwise, which are intolerable.[32] Brutus, on his part, dedicated to Cicero a work of his on *Virtue*, which is now lost.

Antony watched this friendship ripen and knew that it boded no good for Cæsar. He felt, as has been said, that some secret organization, hostile to the Dictator, was in existence, yet could not lay his hand upon the culprits. At length it came to his ears that Brutus was being anonymously urged to give his support to some kind of movement which had as its object the ending of the autocracy. Unsigned messages had been found on Brutus's desk, in which such words as "You are asleep," or "You are not a true Brutus" were written; and at the foot of the statue of the first Brutus, who had overthrown the Roman kings, a note was discovered, reading "O that we had a Brutus now!"

It seemed unthinkable, of course, that this quiet and pedantic man would allow himself to be involved in any kind of murderous conspiracy against one who was his reputed father, and who was certainly his loving benefactor; yet the fact could not be overlooked that the character of Brutus was such as would be easily influenced by any suggestion that it was his duty to strike a blow for the Republic which had been the creation of the first Brutus. He took things so very seriously. Antony, I may add, did not know then that Brutus was capable of writing to Cicero, "To have more authority than the laws and the Senate is a right I would not

---

[31] Cicero: *Tusculanarum Disputationum.*   [32] Cicero: *Ad Atticum*, xv, 2.

grant to my father himself," and, again, "Our ancestors thought that we ought not to endure a despotism even if it were that of our own father" [33]—words which meant that, although he might perhaps really be Cæsar's son, he was prepared to resist any tampering by him with the constitution.

Meanwhile, Cæsar was absorbed in the preparations for the Parthian war. He had abandoned the idea of a monarchy, or rather, had postponed his plans until after the coming expedition; and it would seem that he had advised the disappointed Cleopatra to go back presently to Egypt and to await there his victorious return. He had planned to leave Rome for the East a day or two after the Ides of March, that is to say March 15th, and, during the first days of that month, he and Antony had a hundred matters to discuss together, since the latter, as Consul, was to carry on the government of the empire single-handed during the Dictator's absence.

It had been arranged that Cæsar should address the Senate, for the last time before his departure, on the morning of March 15th; and at sunrise on that day, therefore, Antony went over to the Dictator's house [34] so as to accompany him to the assembly, which was to meet in the early morning in the great hall adjoining the theatre built by Pompey in what is now known as the Campo di Fiore. To his surprise, however, he found Cæsar very reluctant to leave his room, declaring that he had a premonition that some sort of disaster would befall him. A few days ago a fortune-teller had implored him to beware of this particular date, the Ides of March; and though he had taken little notice of the warning at the time, the thought seems since to have occurred to him that the man might have had knowledge of some sort of plot against him and might have used his professional art of prophecy to convey this piece of actual information. Moreover, Calpurnia, Cæsar's wife, had had a very bad dream during the night, and had fancied that her husband was dying in her arms—an experience which may, perhaps, be accounted for by the fact that at supper on the previous evening the conversation had turned to the subject

---

[33] Cicero: *Ad Brutum,* i, 16, i, 17.

[34] For the following details see Plutarch (*Cæsar; Antony; Brutus*); Suetonius; Dion Cassius; Velleius; Appian; Nicholas of Damascus; etc.

of death and the Dictator had declared that a man's best end was a sudden one. Cæsar, in any case, was not feeling well, and long after the sun had risen and the hour of the opening of the meeting was past, he was still debating whether or not he should attend the Senate that day at all.

He had just asked Antony to go alone to the meeting and to postpone its business until the following day, when Decimus Brutus Albinus, one of Cæsar's most trusted officers, was ushered in, having come across from the waiting Senate to find out the cause of the delay. The Dictator told him that he had decided to remain at home that day, whereupon Albinus begged him not to give the senators any such cause for regarding themselves as slighted, particularly since on this occasion they were going to pass a measure which was of utmost importance. They had decided, he said, to authorize the Dictator to assume the status of King in all parts of the empire outside Italy itself.

At this piece of news Cæsar's heart must have leapt within him. At last his dream, which he had temporarily abandoned, was to be realized: he was to be *King!* He did not doubt for a moment that the next months would find him marching, like Alexander the Great, through conquered Parthia into India; and when these distant lands had been annexed to Rome he would be in very truth Autocrat of the Earth.

Antony, of course, must have been amazed at the news, for no such senatorial decision had been made known to him. It did not occur to him, however, that Albinus, Cæsar's old friend, was lying; and the fear of treachery, the thought that for a terrible, hidden reason the Dictator was being urged not to disappoint those who were so anxiously waiting for him, did not enter his simple mind. He must have seen only the satisfaction in Cæsar's face, the galvanizing of his tired body as he rose to his feet and, in the characteristic manner described by Cicero, ran his fingers through his now grey[35] and scanty hair, and adjusted his robes.

Albinus grasped his hand and led him towards the door, Antony following; and presently the three of them were being carried in their litters through the crowded streets. They had not gone far when Cæsar observed the fortune-teller who had given him the

---

[35] Dion Cassius, xliv, 49.

warning, standing at the roadside as he passed; and beckoning the man to him, he said with a smile, "Well, my friend, the Ides of March are come." "Yes," the soothsayer replied, "but they are not yet gone"; and, so saying, disappeared amongst the throng. A little later another man, holding a letter, pushed his way forward, and, on being allowed by the Dictator to approach—for it was his custom thus to receive the petitions of the poor—whispered to him, "Read this, Cæsar, alone and quickly," and pressed the document into his hand, where it still remained, unread, at the end of the journey.

Upon arriving at the steps which led up to the portico of the hall wherein the Senate was assembled, they alighted, and a certain personage who was a friend of the Dictator's kept him in conversation for a while, much to the evident perturbation of Albinus, who was talking to Antony but whose eyes were fixed anxiously upon Cæsar. Antony supposed that the renewed delay in the Dictator's entry into the Senate was the cause of this anxiety, and he was not surprised when, presently, Albinus left him and hurried up the steps into the building as though to remind Cæsar that he was already late enough. Cæsar took the hint and made his way into the building; but just as Antony was about to follow him he was hailed by a certain Trebonius, an ex-Consul and one of Cæsar's trusted generals, who now took him by the arm and began to tell him a long story.

Antony was impatient to enter the building, and was about to interrupt the surprising garrulousness of this old soldier, who may well have seemed to be a little intoxicated, when, suddenly, an outburst of shouts and cries within the hall fell upon his ears, and, a moment later, a number of frightened senators came running out through the doorway. Two or three of them, seeing Antony, called frantically to him to fly for his life: Cæsar had been assassinated, they gasped, and he, too, would be murdered unless he could make his escape.

Antony hesitated, but as he stood there, bewildered and unable to collect his thoughts, some of the assassins appeared at the doorway brandishing their daggers which were wet with blood; and at this, knowing that Cæsar was beyond his aid, he took to his heels, joining the crowd of flying senators and at last dashing with two or three fugitives up a side street and into the house of one of them.

Here, panting and horrified, he tore off his consular robes, and put on the clothes dragged from a startled servant, so as to be ready to escape in this disguise through the back premises if those who sought his life should burst into the house from the front.

While he waited in an agony of suspense he was given by his companions a breathless account of what had happened. While he, Antony, had been detained in conversation by Trebonius, who was evidently one of the conspirators, specially appointed to that task, Cæsar had entered the hall and had taken his seat upon his golden chair, whereupon a certain Tullius Cimber, a man whom the Dictator regarded as a loyal friend and to whom he had given the governorship of Bithynia, had approached him under the pretence of presenting a petition. Thereupon a crowd of other senators and high officials had gathered around him, pressing so close that Cæsar had ordered them sharply to stand back; and, at this, Tullius had snatched at his gown and had pulled it from him, while a certain Casca, whom Cæsar had recently made a Tribune of the People, had struck at his benefactor with his dagger, wounding him in the shoulder.

Then the whole pack had fallen upon him, and Cæsar, fiercely defending himself with his *stilus*, had fought his way to the foot of the statue of his old enemy Pompey, where, suddenly seeing his dear Brutus coming at him knife in hand, he had cried out in anguish, "You, too, Brutus, my *son!*" and had offered no further resistance, but had pulled his clothes across his face, as the old patrician custom required the dying to do, and had fallen to the ground pierced by countless wounds. Most of the conspirators were Cæsar's closest friends, and Antony must have been dumbfounded as the names of some of them were mentioned.

Presently news came that the conspirators, who numbered between sixty and eighty, had marched up to the Capitol and had barricaded themselves in; and during the afternoon the further report was received that it did not seem to be their intention to kill anybody else, on hearing which Antony resumed his consular dress and boldly sent for his lictors and soldiers to conduct him to the Forum. It was a dangerous proceeding, and he realized that he was taking his life in his hands, for he did not know the temper of the mob; but now that Cæsar was dead he was sole Consul, and actual ruler of the empire, and he felt that he must assert himself quickly if anarchy was to be prevented.

He was, in fact, ashamed of having gone into hiding at all; but, although he did not yet know it, the question as to whether or not he should be killed at the same time as Cæsar had indeed been vigorously argued by the conspirators, and he owed his life in the end only to the advice of Brutus. The others, led by Cassius, had all said that as Cæsar's friend, and as a man who had the army as his command, he ought to be put out of the way, especially since "his great physical strength made him formidable"[36]—the fact being that Antony could have thrown most of the assassins over his head. But Brutus, after turning the matter over and over in his mind, had argued on the contrary that "so gifted and honourable a man as Antony, and such a lover of great deeds,"[37] might perhaps be persuaded to come over to the side of "republican liberty," as they termed the object of their plot, and, anyway, by leaving him to function as Consul, they would show that they were out to defend the constitution, not to overthrow it.

It was probably in the dusk of early evening that Antony made his reappearance, and he must have found the streets silent and deserted. The conspirators were up in the Capitol, at a loss to know what to do, and the nervous citizens were for the most part locked in their own homes, shaking in their shoes and wondering what was going to happen, expecting at least some sort of street-fighting before the morning. He went straight to the Forum where a small crowd had collected, and there he was informed that the body of the murdered Dictator was lying in one of the public buildings. The assassins had at first intended to throw it into the river, but they had been too anxious about their own safety to carry out this part of their programme, and, in the end, three loyal slaves had borne the corpse to its present sanctuary. It may be supposed that Antony entered the building and looked down with sorrow and dismay upon the body of his murdered friend and colleague, afterwards making arrangements for a guard to be placed upon it; but what actually happened is not recorded. Thence he went to Cæsar's home, where he had a painful interview with the distracted Calpurnia, the widow, as a result of which she agreed to hand over to him, as Con-

[36] Plutarch: *Antony.*   [37] Plutarch: *Brutus.*

sul, all the Dictator's papers and letters, and all the money and valuables in the house; for there was considerable likelihood that the conspirators would raid the place.

Most of the night must have been spent in collecting these things and transferring them to Antony's house, and there could have been little sleep for him. Next morning, the 16th, he went again to the Forum, attempting to resume the business of state in his Consular capacity; and here he heard a full account of all that had happened. One very ugly fact then became known to him. When the assassins had swarmed out of the hall in which the murder had been committed, they had all shouted "Cicero!— Cicero!" [38] at the top of their voices; and it certainly appeared —though to this day it has never been proved—that the orator knew all about the plot and, thinking the return of the conservative party to power to be a certain consequence, had given it his blessing. A few hours after the assassination, moreover, Cicero had sent a letter to Basilus, one of the conspirators, then in the Capitol, congratulating him and saying how delighted he was [39]; and later in the day he had gone up there himself to see Brutus and his other friends, and to tell them how heartily he was with them. One may suppose that, in his colossal vanity, he had expected to be called upon to fill the consular vacancy left by Cæsar's death, and to act as Antony's senior colleague; and, indeed, it may well have been the intention of the conspirators, should they obtain the public ear, to obtain this post for him, for he was regarded by them as the sound and elderly exponent of the highest traditions of republican government, a man whose writings on the subject were masterpieces of literary eloquence—his *De Republica*, for instance, and his *De Legibus*.

But Antony now heard that the incorrigible Dolabella had also visited the Capitol, and hard on this news came the report that he, Dolabella, had induced the mob to vote him Consul in Cæsar's place, declaring that the dead Dictator had always intended him to be his deputy. Presently the young man appeared in the Forum and made a speech in favour of the murderers, and this was so well received by the crowd that Brutus and Cassius were induced to come down from their stronghold and give a public explanation of

[38] Dion Cassius, xliv, 20; xlvi, 22.   [39] Cicero: *Ad Familiares*, vi, 15.

their conduct. An escort of conservatives or impartial senators was provided for them, the general feeling being that the number of the conspirators, their high standing, and the earnestness of their views, entitled their two leaders to a safe-conduct and a hearing, while the urgent need to avoid civil war required a conciliatory attitude.

Brutus then made a short and very solemn speech, but it was received in such ominous silence by the main part of the crowd that he and Cassius were glad enough to retire thereafter to the Capitol again. Its reception was the first indication which Antony had had that public opinion was not in favour of the conspirators; and it emboldened him to adopt a stronger attitude. He therefore called a meeting of the Senate for the following morning, and went back to his house, where the leaders of the Cæsarian party appear to have discussed the situation with him until tired eyes and aching heads could no longer resist the demands of sleep.

On the morning of the 17th [40] the Senate met in the court of the Temple of Tellius, or the Earth; and here Antony's statesman-ship was tried to the uttermost, for while the majority of the sena-tors were in favour of commending the assassins for their patriotism in removing a man who had desired to overthrow the Republic, the crowd outside the gates had suddenly swung away from Dolabella's two-faced leadership, and was demanding the punishment of Bru-tus, Cassius, and their whole gang. Antony felt strongly that blood-shed was to be avoided at all costs, and he made a short speech advising a temporary amnesty, urging that no action should be taken either one way or the other until the will of the People was known. But he proposed that the office of Dictator, at any rate, should be abolished in view of the calamity it had brought about [41]; and this measure received general approval.

At this, Cicero rose to second the motion, advising that an "act of oblivion" should be passed, and that not only should the con-spirators be pardoned but also those who had supported Cæsar in his undoubted tyranny. This, of course, was a thrust at Antony; but the latter swallowed the insult with as good a grace as possible, biding his time until he could find out just how much public sup-port he could command. He was obliged, however, to go across to the Forum and to address the crowd, telling them to await the issue

[40] The date is fixed by Cicero: *Philippic ii,* xxxv.   [41] Cicero: *Philippic i,* 1.

patiently, and not to throw the nation into civil war. Thereafter, he returned to the senatorial meeting, where an amnesty of some sort was finally decreed, notice of it being sent up to the weary and disheartened men in the Capitol.

The hostility of a growing section of the crowd towards them, however, restrained them from leaving their place of refuge, and again that night they slept in the Capitol, while Antony worked until the small hours in an attempt to discover how far he could rely on the troops and on the officials and citizens to support him were he to turn at once upon the conspirators. It is obvious that he was eager to avenge the dead Dictator, yet the paramount necessity of the moment was to maintain peace.

Next morning, the 18th, it was agreed by the Senate that Antony should invite the conspirators once more to come down into the city; but having sent a message up to them, he received the blunt reply that they would only descend if both Antony and Lepidus, one of Cæsar's loyal friends who was in command of some of the troops in the city, should each send his son up to the Capitol as a hostage. At this, Antony seems to have consulted his strong-minded wife Fulvia, and, perhaps somewhat to his surprise, that capable woman at once agreed to send her baby Antyllus, now some eight or nine months old, up to the Capitol in the care of its nurse, but only on the condition that Cassius should spend the night in her house. A brief consultation with Lepidus induced that personage to act in a similar manner: he would send his infant son to the Capitol if Brutus, the other leader of the conspiracy, would sleep at *his* house. In other words, Brutus and Cassius were to be hostages for the good behaviour of the conspirators, and the infant sons of Antony and Lepidus were to be hostages for that of the Cæsarian party.

That night, therefore, Antony sat down to supper with Cassius as his guest—Cassius who was the murderer of his hero, Cæsar; and no more painful situation could well be imagined. The conversation of the two men during the meal appears to have displayed their concealed hostility, and it is recorded that Antony suddenly turned upon Cassius, saying, "Have you by any chance got a dagger up your sleeve even now?" "Yes, I have," Cassius replied, "and a big one, if you, too, should try to play the tyrant!" [42]

[42] Dion Cassius, xliv, 34.

Early the following morning, the 19th, the Senate met again, and Antony, addressing the assembly, proposed that Cassius and Brutus should each be assigned the governorship of a distant province, and should thus be sent away from Rome; and to this the senators agreed. The meeting then passed a vote of thanks to Antony for having staved off civil war, and "he left the Senate," says Plutarch, "with the highest possible reputation and esteem, for it was apparent that he had prevented a revolution, and had composed, in the wisest and most statesmanlike manner, questions of the greatest difficulty and embarrassment."

By this time, however, he had made up his mind to turn popular opinion definitely against the conspirators, for he had obtained possession of Cæsar's will, and knew that the contents would be sufficient to excite the People to an outburst of love for the dead man; and he therefore gave notice that he would read the will that afternoon, and, at the same time, in the teeth of the opposition of the conspirators and their friends, he boldly instructed his officers to prepare for the public funeral on the following day. He himself would speak the oration over the corpse; and if the gods should grant power to his words he would raise such a storm of hatred against the assassins that not one of them should escape. Rome was calmer now, and at last he could act as his heart dictated.

CHAPTER XI

Antony's Struggle to Prevent Civil War, and his Difficulties with Cæsar's Heir, Octavian.

44 B.C.

BRUTUS was the only one of the assassins who could be said to deserve sympathetic consideration, for Antony had now heard of the great mental struggle through which this slow-brained and studious personage had passed, and he could see that the unfortunate man had been actuated by motives as altruistic as they were misguided. When Cassius was first organising the conspiracy, so Antony was told, it was agreed that Brutus ought to be persuaded to join in the plot for the reason that his acquiescence would give almost a religious sanction to the plan,[1] and therefore the greatest pressure had been brought to bear upon him. In revealing the plot to him, for instance, Cassius had said: "Rome demands from you, Brutus, as an hereditary debt, the extirpation of tyranny"; and thus by approaching him as the genuine descendant of the great Brutus, the liberator of the nation from the rule of its early kings, the conspirators aroused in his heart that bright flame of family pride, which had but flickered within him so long as the stigma of being Cæsar's bastard was upon him.

But after he had entered into the plot, his conscience had given him no peace; and his mind had been so tortured by its silent arguments that sleep had left him, and at last his wife Porcia, Cato's daughter, had become aware that he was living in the anguish of a terrible secret, and in the end had persuaded him to admit her into it. Thereupon she, too, had been rendered sleepless and distracted, and on the fatal day she had nearly revealed the conspiracy by her hysteria. At the moment of the assassination, in fact, she was in a dead faint.

[1] Plutarch: *Brutus.*

Antony's determination to punish the murderers, however, was not influenced by these personal considerations, and he proceeded to bring about their ruin. Cæsar's will was read in his, Antony's, house in the presence of those of the Dictator's friends and relatives who were available; and, as has already been stated, it was found that he had left a great part of his fortune to Octavian, and smaller shares to his two other grand-nephews, and that Octavian had been asked to adopt the name of Cæsar. In the event of the two above-mentioned grand-nephews dying before him, their portions were to go to that same Decimus Brutus Albinus who had betrayed him, and to Antony—a mark of esteem which the latter must have deeply appreciated and which is yet another indication of his worth.

But the clause in the will which Antony's mind seized upon, and which was obviously his trump-card in the line of action he had decided upon, was that which bequeathed his beautiful gardens beyond the Tiber to the people of Rome as a public park, and a personal gift of three hundred *sesterces* [2] to every individual in the city —a sum which must have represented several weeks' wages to the working man. The size of the gift, however, was not its outstanding feature: the fact which was so valuable to Antony was that Cæsar had thereby shown his unfailing love for the People, and that the bequest would establish him in their memory as a loving father, a friend of the poor and the humble.

On the following day, March 20th, [3] the funeral took place— in spite of the passionate protests of Brutus and Cassius, who saw clearly enough that the public cremation of the Dictator would give occasion for a show of sympathy very detrimental to their cause. Antony, however, had been stubbornly determined to do Cæsar this honour. He had arranged that the body should be carried in state to the Campus Martius, where a pyre was constructed, close to the tomb of the Dictator's daughter, Julia, Pompey's wife; but the earlier ceremonies were to be performed in the Forum, and hither, seething with excitement, the crowds flocked. All day long the musicians played their dirges and solemnly beat their drums, while

[2] Suetonius: *Cæsar,* lxxxiii; Plutarch: *Brutus;* Dion Cassius, xliv, 35. See Ihne: *Römische Geschichte,* vii, 263.
[3] The date is not certain, but as Cæsar had then been dead for five days it is unlikely that the funeral was further postponed.

from time to time actors performed short scenes from classical plays chosen by Antony because of their bitter appropriateness to the occasion, one such being an excerpt from a tragedy by Pacuvius, in which the words "I saved those who have killed me" were repeated with telling effect.

At nightfall Antony, magnificent in his Consular robes, made his way to the Forum, determined to arouse the people to a whole-hearted support of the Cæsarian party, yet equally determined to prevent any riotous attacks upon the assassins, who had confined themselves to their houses in anticipation of trouble. His purpose—and in it he proved his statesmanship—was to maintain peace in this hour of turmoil, yet to excite indignation against the crime, so that in due course the conspirators might be brought to justice without a fight when Rome was once more tranquil.

On his arrival upon the turbulent scene, in the gathering darkness, the body of the Dictator was taken from its temporary mortuary, and, to the dissonant accompaniment of cries and mournful chanting, was laid upon an ivory bed covered with purple and cloth of gold, this being placed under a gilded catafalque which represented in small size the temple of Venus, Cæsar's divine ancestress. After the religious ceremonies had been performed, during which Antony himself intoned the funeral chant, a herald, instructed by him, recited to the crowd a list of the honours, both human and divine, which the Senate had conferred upon the Dictator, and censoriously repeated the oath so vainly taken by the senators to defend his person with their lives. Antony then mounted the rostra and addressed the now silent multitude in a speech which, though short, [4] was "in every way beautiful and brilliant," [5] and which was afterwards described by Cicero [6]—who, however, was not present when it was delivered—as a panegyric capable of arousing the most intense emotion. The text of the speech quoted by Appian and Dion Cassius is probably a later elaboration of what he said; but it seems that he referred tenderly to Cæsar's brilliance and goodness of heart, and spoke of the great benefits he had conferred on the people of Rome both in his lifetime and now by the terms of his will.

Then, carried away by his own eloquence and by his very gen-

---

[4] Suetonius: *Cæsar*, lxxxiv. [5] Dion Cassius, xliv, 35.
[6] Cicero: *Philippic ii*, xxxvi.

uine sorrow, he impulsively told his officers to bring him the blood-stained garments of the murdered man which had been exhibited at the head of the bier; and with these in his hands he turned again to his audience, dramatically showing them the rents made by the daggers, and the stains of the blood, the tears running down his face as he struggled to find words by which to vent the torrent of the emotions pent up within him these five days.

It had been arranged that at the end of his oration the funeral procession should set out for the Campus Martius to cremate the body, as the law decreed, outside the city's walls; but the crowd was so stirred by Antony's words that, as though the matter had been carried by vote, they determined with one consent to take the proceedings out of the hands of the officials and to cremate the corpse here in the heart of the metropolis. Some shouted out that it should be carried up to the Temple of Jupiter Capitolinus and there burnt in the holy-of-holies, the most sacred spot in Rome, even though in so doing the whole building would probably go up in flames; others declared that it ought to be burnt upon the spot whereon the murder had been committed.

But at length somebody proposed that the cremation should be carried out here in the Forum; and, instantly taking to the suggestion, the crowd seized upon chairs, benches, and any available pieces of woodwork, heaping them up into an enormous pyre, onto which the bier was presently lifted. Lighted torches were applied, and soon the body of the Dictator subsided into the flames, while the sparks shot up into the night, and the smoke rolled like a cloud across the face of the rising moon.

Many persons, moved by the general hysteria, tore off their outer garments and flung them into the blaze; military officers un-buckled their valuable breastplates and cast them upon the pyre; and here and there a weeping woman was seen to throw her jewels into the flames. On all sides people were sobbing passionately, beating their breasts, and wailing the funeral chants; and at length the fierce cry was raised that the houses of the assassins should be attacked and burnt, whereupon, in spite of Antony's alarmed protests, a rush was made for the pyre, and flaming pieces of wood were carried off by shouting and gesticulating men, who hastened away in the direction of the houses of Brutus, Cassius, and others. "It was you, Antony—*you*, I say," cried Cicero [7] a few months later, "who let loose those attacks! Abandoned men, slaves for the most part, hurled firebrands into our houses, and we were obliged to repel their onrush by our own unaided exertions; but it was *you* who set them on!"

Antony was in reality aghast at the emotional outburst his words had caused, which endangered the peace of the city, and he checked the rioting with the utmost severity, giving orders that those caught setting fire to any house should be summarily executed. Brutus, Cassius, and the others no doubt owed their lives to his prompt action; but there was one man at least who was not so fortunate. He was a Tribune of the People, named Cinna; and the mob, confusing him with Cæsar's brother-in-law, Cinna, the Prætor, who had lately made some disparaging remarks about Cæsar's moral life, pounced upon him and literally tore him to pieces, finally dancing off with his head stuck upon a spear.

On the following day there was further rioting, and the conspirators were again besieged in their homes, while the miserable Cicero, appalled to find that his ambitions and rash inclinations had led him to identify himself with the losing faction, sat behind the barred doors of his house, listening to the tumult outside and cursing Antony and all his works. Brutus, of course, was in despair. He had expected the majority of the senators and officials to commend the murder; and though a great many of them had certainly done so, and had made possible the technical amnesty which now existed, he had not reckoned with the People. Antony's speech at the funeral had been fatal to the murderers' cause; and it seemed likely that the popular party would now oblige them to leave Rome, even, indeed, if it did not exact from them the extreme penalty. Only Antony stood between them and public vengeance; and the question which fevered their minds was whether he, Antony, was strong enough to maintain peace, or whether he would not be more likely to be carried along on the tide of the mob's excitement, more especially since it was obvious that his own emotions would tend to lead him in that direction.

Dolabella had already fled from the city, [8] having lost his

---

[7] Cicero: *Philippic ii,* xxxvi.

[8] At least he is not heard of again for several weeks.

influence with the rabble by his having shown friendliness towards the conspirators; the Senate was divided in its views, and was much too frightened to be of any service to the cause of peace; and Cicero had proved himself to be far from the bold leader of republican thought his writings and his private conversation had led Brutus to expect him to be. The murderers, in fact, had supposed that they would have a solid backing of better-class opinion; they had pictured themselves grouped around the revered figure of Cicero, from whose inspired lips the doctrines for which they stood would pour in acceptable language; and they had supposed that Dolabella would swing the mob over to their side.

But Antony had wrecked their hopes. He had secured a public funeral for Cæsar against the opposition of all those who approved of the assassination; he had used the occasion to play upon the emotions of the People; and he had turned to overwhelming account the contents of the Dictator's will. True, he had managed to maintain order and to effect a sort of compromise during these perilous days—Brutus admitted that they had to thank him for *that;* but the stupefaction of the whole city had aided him, and now he seemed to be undoing the good work, and allowing the popular hysteria to carry him off his feet.

During the next few days one conspirator after another slipped out of Rome and went into hiding in the country. Albinus, by one of Cæsar's last appointments, had been given the governorship of Cisalpine Gaul; and, since one of Antony's measures in the emergency had been the ratification of all the Dictator's decrees, Albinus hastened to his province to take possession of it before his authority was repealed. Tullius Cimber, likewise, hurried off to Bithynia, of which Cæsar had made him governor. By the first week in April Cicero, too, had given up all hope of leadership, and had fled in despair to his villa on the Bay of Naples.

Shortly after this, a certain Herophilus, who had been banished from Rome by the Dictator, came back to the capital, and, wishing to gain the favour of the rabble, set up a sacred column on the spot where the body had been cremated, and, by arousing the religious frenzy of those who here made their devotions to Cæsar's divinity, attempted to incite the crowd to further acts of violence against the conspirators, as a result of which Cassius, Brutus, and

others were again besieged in their houses, these becoming so many
forts each defended by its household against the angry mob. A
critical state of affairs developed; but Antony acted with prompt
and justifiable severity. He caused Herophilus to be arrested and
executed, and thereby saved the city once more from anarchy.

He then authorized Brutus and Cassius to leave Rome, and
before the middle of April these two had fled to Lanuvium, a day's
journey to the south. Trebonius followed shortly afterwards, going as governor to the province of Asia Minor, that post having
been given him by the man he had helped to assassinate. At the same
time the leading members of the Cæsarian party also left the metropolis; and some time in April Queen Cleopatra packed up and set sail
for Egypt, taking with her the Dictator's little son, Cæsarion. She
must have been a broken-hearted woman; for, whether her expecta-
tions were based on fact or not, she had believed that her marriage to
Cæsar had been imminent and she had never for a moment doubted
that she would presently be seated at his side on the throne of an
Egypto-Roman kingdom whose bounds would be the ends of the
earth. Now, by the daggers of men she had often entertained at her
house, her position had been changed in an instant from that of prospective omnipotence to the mere sovereignty of a restless little
country across the seas—a sovereignty which a new and unfriendly
Roman government might soon send its legions to take from her.

To Antony she must have poured out her troubles, but he could
do nothing to help her: she would have to return to Alexandria and
bide her time until the Roman situation had clarified; but there can
be little doubt that her thoughts, fired by Cæsar's vision of world-
wide dominion, must have burnt with the desire to ally herself to
whatever new master of Rome the Fates might throw up out of
the existing chaos. In her own way she had loved Cæsar, but she
had loved his dreams still more; and the overthrow of all those
splendid hopes which had completely possessed her mind for these
last months must have left her more desolate than any words have
the power to describe.

Though history is silent upon the subject, it is not credible
that she could have gone back to her own country without first having attempted to enlist the good offices of Antony; and it may be
supposed that he had promised to do his best to help her to maintain

her position at least as sovereign of an independent kingdom. In him she may have already seen the future autocrat of the world; but his authority was by no means unshakably established, nor was he following, even with unsteady tread, in Cæsar's clear footsteps. He had been opposed to the Dictator's ideas of monarchy, and he had not yet so much as dreamt of aiming, himself, at that royal crown which Cæsar's hands had so nearly grasped. All his energies were directed at present to the sole purpose of maintaining peace under democratic rule in his distracted country, and the highest flights of his imagination carried him no further than the vision of himself as virtual Dictator for the next few years, governing the empire as the successor and representative of the murdered Cæsar. Some day, Cleopatra may have told herself, she would whisper into the ear of a new ruler of Rome the suggestion of a world-throne to be shared with her and perhaps to be handed on to Cæsarion; but whether or not that man would be Antony she could not yet determine.

It is possible that before she left she gave him money with which to maintain his cause, for he was undoubtedly collecting funds at this time by every means, straight or crooked, and Cicero, a few months later, demanded to know how it came about that Antony, who was heavily in debt on the Ides of March, should have been free of his burdens in April. [9] "There was nothing in the whole world," said Cicero, "which anyone wanted to buy that Antony was not ready to sell"; and though this, of course, was an exaggeration, there can be little doubt that the urgent need of money required as urgent a search for it.

King Deiotarus of Galatia and Armenia, a man who had sided with Pompey against Cæsar, and had been deprived by the latter of part of his dominions, offered a large sum of money for the restoration of these realms; and Antony very conveniently found amongst Cæsar's papers a memorandum which justified him in acceding to this monarch's wishes. Many people declared, of course, that it was a forgery; but the fact that Cicero had recently pleaded for Deiotarus in the presence of Cæsar, in an eloquent speech—*Pro Rege Deiotaro*—which is still extant, suggests that the Dictator may well have made a note to this effect.

[9] Cicero: *Philippic ii*, xxxvii.

Antony then produced another document, purporting to be a memorandum of the Dictator's, which was his authority for giving the rights of citizenship to the Sicilians—of course at a price; but here again one may suppose that such an action had been contemplated by Cæsar, very possibly at the instance of Cicero, who always had the interests of the Sicilians at heart, and it is well-known that the Dictator had aroused the anger of the conservatives in the past by his wide gifts of Roman citizenship outside Italy. Yet one cannot but suspect that Antony did juggle somewhat with the Dictator's papers; and the Senate certainly made the proposal that the documents should be placed in the charge of a special commission. [10] Antony, however, was not deterred by the common belief that he was resorting to forgery; and a little later he obtained a sum of money from the Cretans in return for granting them, again on the authority of Cæsar, future exemption from taxation. His justification is that he needed funds for the upholding of his authority, and for winning the support, for instance, of Cæsar's veterans; and it is certain that, while helping himself liberally enough in the usual Roman way, he spent the bulk of the money in what he conceived to be the public interest.

Towards the end of April the sessions of the Senate closed for the May vacation, and Antony decided to make a tour of the country south of Rome in order to feel for himself the pulse of the nation, and also to do a little recruiting in a quiet way. Brutus and Cassius had been attempting to undermine the Cæsarian cause in that part of Italy, and had been trying to gain the support of those old soldiers settled upon the land, whom Antony now wished to enlist; and Cicero, too, down in the neighbourhood of Naples, had lately been venting his disappointment by vilifying both the dead Dictator and Antony. The orator, at this time a sour, grey-haired man of sixty-three, was so embittered by his misfortunes that, while in public he maintained for his own safety a neutrality which included a treacherous show of friendship to Antony, in private he allowed himself to become extremely violent in his attacks upon the Cæsarians.

He now spoke of the murder of the Dictator as "the magnificent

---

[10] Cicero: *Philippic ii*, xxxix. Plutarch (*Antony*), however, seems to exonerate him from the charge of forgery.

banquet of the Ides of March," and regretted that he had not been invited to take part in it; he spoke of Brutus and Cassius as "heroes," and of Antony as a "drunkard" and a "reckless gambler"; [11] and, to quote a well-known editor of his private correspondence, [12] "he expressed a satisfaction at the assassination, which, after Cæsar's great generosity to him and his profuse, if not servile, acknowledgment of it, is nothing less than ferocious, so that no portion of the whole collection of his letters exhibits his character in so unpleasant a light." He fretted at the inability of the conspirators to take any action, and to Atticus he wrote, in April, "I fear me the Ides of March have given us nothing beyond the pleasure and the satisfaction of our hatred." [13] That hatred was intense, and gradually it focussed itself wholly upon Antony, the one man who stood like a hulking gladiator in the path of the assassins' advance.

Antony was able to leave Rome with some easiness of mind because his wife, Fulvia, and his two younger brothers, Lucius and Caius, were there to carry on his work and to keep him in close touch with events. Caius was now Prætor and Lucius a Tribune of the People, both having been given these appointments by Cæsar: they were men of no great distinction, but they were useful agents of their brother. Fulvia, too, was in these days an important factor in political life, and many of Antony's measures—for instance, the rehabilitation of King Deiotarus [14]—were thought to have been initiated by her.

Antony's mother, Julia, was still alive, and, being a member of the family of the Cæsars, was probably a strong supporter of a policy of revenge against the assassins, although her brother, Lucius Cæsar, was in favour of the Act of Oblivion. Antony's uncle, Caius Antonius, was also back in Rome now, after nearly fifteen years of exile on the island of Cephallenia, having been pardoned, it would seem, by Cæsar; but he could have had little liking for Antony, who had disgraced and divorced his daughter Antonia, it will be recalled, because of her misbehaviour with Dolabella. Indeed, Antony must have deeply offended the returned exile; for, a few weeks earlier, in a full meeting of the Senate, at which Caius Antonius was

[11] Cicero: *Ad Familiares*, x, 28; *Ad Atticum*, xiv, 4; xiv, 6; xiv, 3; xiv, 5.
[12] Jeans: *Life and Letters of Cicero*.
[13] Cicero: *Ad Atticum*, xiv, 12.   [14] *Ibid*.

present, Antony had lost his temper with Dolabella, and had publicly branded the fat young man and the unhappy Antonia as adulterer and adulteress. [15] Antony was very liable, always, to lose his
temper and to say more than he intended; and, anyhow, he was very
sore about this intrigue, for it was a reflection upon his own success
as a lover, a matter upon which he prided himself.

His tour of the south was very successful in its purpose, namely
that of arousing, and recruiting, Cæsar's ex-soldiers, and counter-
acting the propaganda of the conspirators; but, during the trip, he
seems to have combined business with pleasure in a rather unnecessarily reckless way. In spite of the gravity of the situation he gave
very gay parties in the cities he visited, and often drank too much.
At a charming villa near Casinum (S. Germano) on the inland
road to Naples, which had been confiscated from the author, Marcus
Varro, on the dubious authority of Cæsar's papers, he entertained a
party of guests, who all misbehaved themselves so thoroughly
that scandal said the floors were awash with wine, and the place full
of the laughter of actresses and prostitutes. At the break-up of this
riotous house-party he was carried to the neighbouring town of
Aquinum dead-drunk; and the inhabitants who had come out to give
him an official welcome heard only his snores issuing from behind the closed curtains of his litter. Reaction from the strain of
the terrible days through which he had passed, and freedom from
the controlling hand of Fulvia, had evidently been too much for
him.

While he was on his way back to Rome, bringing with him a
whole army of Cæsar's veterans, news was suddenly brought to
him that Dolabella had come out of hiding, and, declaring that he
was joint-Consul with Antony, had ordered the destruction of the
sacred column set up by the late Herophilus on the spot where the
Dictator had been murdered, was inciting the crowd against the
Cæsarians, and was being hailed with acclamation by the senators
who favoured the conspirators. Antony's brother Lucius had come
to verbal blows with the young man; and the city, it was said, was
once more in an uproar, the conservative element rallying round
Dolabella, as though he were the hoped-for saviour of their cause.
Upon hearing these tidings Antony was so stunned that he was after-

[15] Cicero: *Philippic ii*, xxxviii.

wards said by eye-witnesses to have fainted dead away, [16] though
it is more probable that he merely rested his befuddled head against
the nearest support, and shut his eyes in an effort to gather his wits.

Thereafter, he hastened to Rome, arriving towards the end of
May, and thoroughly scaring his opponents by marching the ex-
soldiers through the streets with drawn swords, their shields and
baggage bumping along behind them upon carts. But the whole
face of the situation was changed by the news which awaited him:
Octavian, Cæsar's grand-nephew and heir, had come to Rome, had
claimed his heritage, and had taken the name of "Cæsar."

Octavian had been at Apollonia when he received the news of
the Dictator's death, and a few days later he had crossed the Adriatic back to Italy, where, on disembarking, he heard for the first time
of the contents of the Dictator's will.[17] He then made his way quietly to Naples, which he reached on April 18th, and thence went
straight to his home, the house of his stepfather, Philippus, not far
away. Philippus was a cautious man, and strongly advised Octavian
not to claim so dangerous an inheritance, [18] especially since he was
only eighteen years of age. At present, he said, it was doubtful
which side would finally gain the upper hand; and in the event of
the conspirators obtaining control, Octavian's life would not be
worth very much if he were known to be putting himself forward as
Cæsar's successor.

Philippus suggested a visit to Cicero, who lived quite close,
and who, superficially, was neutral; and Octavian therefore went
over to see the two-faced old orator, and made himself as agreeable
as he could, [19] not knowing that Cicero was at this very time privately expressing his savage approval of the Dictator's murder. Octavian
wanted to adopt the name "Cæsar" at once, in accordance with his
great-uncle's wishes; but Cicero advised him not to do this, and so
did Philippus. The boy then startled them by announcing that he
was presently going on to the capital to see his mother, Atia, who
was still at her town-house in Rome; and not long afterwards he
made the journey there with so little ostentation that Antony, who,
of course, was informed of his movements, did not think the youth
was worth worrying about. It was only when he got back to Rome

---

[16] Cicero: *Philippic ii*, xlii.
[18] Suetonius: *Augustus*, viii.
[17] Velleius, ii, lix; Dion Cassius, xlv, 3.
[19] Cicero: *Ad Atticum*, xiv, 2.

that he was told how the daring youngster had proclaimed himself Cæsar's successor.

Octavian certainly did not lack courage, and in spite of his being a poor specimen of manhood, unhealthy, spotty, and somewhat effeminate in manner, he was unusually active both in mind and body, being a keen football-player, [20]—so long as he did not have to play in the sun, which hurt his eyes and made him sneeze—and keeping himself fit by long evening walks and runs. He belonged very decidedly to Rome's fashionable young intellectuals, spoke Greek fluently, tried his hand at writing plays and poems, and, like the members of the modernist movement today, cultivated an easy, vernacular style free from the sort of grandiloquence that Antony loved. He dressed untidily, allowed his fair, yellowish hair to fall into its natural waves without care, and was erratic about his meals, having a poor appetite and little sense of time. He had superb confidence in himself, was callous and inclined to be cruel, and, at this period of his life, was devoid of sex morality, being unpleasantly familiar both with men and women. [21]

Antony had only met him occasionally, and had never regarded him as a serious factor in the situation; but now the stories he heard about him were not a little alarming. Caius Antonius, the Prætor, reported that the young man had come to him at a public meeting, and, having asked to address the people, had promised the crowd that he himself would be responsible for the payment of the three-hundred *sesterces* to every townsman. Lucius Antonius, the Tribune, reported, likewise, that Octavian had addressed the *Comitia*, making the same promise, and uttering a bold and sincere panegyric upon the dead Dictator which had been much resented by Dolabella. Just before Antony's return, moreover, Octavian had almost caused a riot at a public function by asking to have Cæsar's golden throne brought out, [22] this being refused by some of the republican Tribunes amidst the loud applause of the senators.

The situation was almost ludicrously triangular. Antony, upholding the democratic cause in the name of the murdered Dictator, was aiming at the future discomfiture of the assassins and their con-

[20] Suetonius: *Augustus*, lxxxiii.　　　　　[21] *Ibid.*, lxviii.
[22] Cicero: *Ad Atticum*, xv, 3.

servative sympathisers so soon as the immediate danger to the nation's peace was averted; and he was bent on retaining the supreme power in his own hands as the late Cæsar's friend, Consular colleague, and trustee. He was in possession of the dead man's papers, personal valuables, and so much of his fortune, outside the share bequeathed to Octavian and his counsins, as could be realized; and Calpurnia, the widow, and most of Cæsar's relatives, regarded him as the guardian of their rights.

Dolabella, Antony's personal enemy, represented the other faction, and had now been confirmed by them in his office as joint-Consul, and was doing his best to have the conspirators restored to public favour. And now into these troubled waters this boy, Octavian, had come fishing, and would soon be asking Antony to hand over Cæsar's remaining money so that the bequests might be paid. Octavian, it was true, was rich enough to pay the legacies out of his own fortune, for his grandfather had been a millionaire money-lender; but it was not to be expected that he would thus impoverish himself.

Antony's policy was clear: much as it went against the grain, he would have to patch up his quarrel with Dolabella, and attempt to regain that position of impartiality which he had held in the first days after the assassination. The audacious Octavian would have to be squeezed out: there was no room for him in Rome.

A few days later Antony received from the young "Cæsar" a request for an interview, and, in a very bad temper, told him to come to his house—that same house which had once belonged to Pompey. [23] There he purposely kept him waiting in the ante-room for a long time, and at last, ordering him to be ushered in, asked him how he was and what brought him to Rome; but before Octavian had fully stated his purpose, which was to see to the carrying out of the terms of Cæsar's will, Antony cut him short with an uncomfortable laugh, and asked him somewhat blusteringly how at his age he dared to take up the responsibilities of this heritage, when, as he could see for himself, grown men who were tried in battle and were used to politics needed all their courage and their experience to cope with the dangerous situation. He advised the young man to settle

[23] For this interview see Plutarch: *Antony;* Appian, *Civil Wars,* iii, 14; Florus, iv, 4; Velleius, ii, lx; and Nicholas of Damascus, xxviii.

his business and get out of Rome as quickly as possible—before Dolabella, or somebody, murdered him, I dare say he said; and, giving him a patronizing pat on the shoulder, he hurriedly dismissed him before anything could be discussed.

The interview brought into Antony's puzzled mind the consciousness that Cæsar had known what he was about when he had made Octavian his heir. This was no ordinary youth: he had rather a sinister character and an opinion of himself which was disconcerting. The impression he left on the elder man was unpleasant, and Antony seems to have had the feeling that his own game of bluff, his attempt to scare his youthful visitor, had been a mistake. He ought to have overlooked his age, and to have bargained with him as with a man of affairs.

The next few days showed him clearly his error. It was reported to him that Octavian was openly accusing him of having betrayed the memory of Cæsar by taking no steps against his murderers and by allowing the amnesty—Cicero's famous Act of Oblivion—to remain in force. The young man had gathered a group of supporters around him, and was making violent speeches to the mob, urging them to take vengeance on the conspirators and to brush Antony aside as one who was too lukewarm to be their leader. He was declaring that he alone had the right to act in Cæsar's name, and he was telling the delighted crowds that he was prepared to sell everything he had to pay them the Dictator's bequest, which was being withheld from them only by Antony's mishandling of Cæsar's fortune. Cæsar had been the People's friend, but Antony was their enemy: he was a traitor, willing to hobnob with the assassins so that by a compromise he might keep the power in his own hands.

Antony was startled, and he at once counter-attacked by taking steps to prevent the ratification of Octavian's adoption into the family of the Cæsars when the measure should come before the Senate. At the same time he sent for Dolabella, and suggested that in the face of the common enemy they should compose their differences and work together. After all, I suppose he argued, Dolabella had once been Cæsar's devoted friend, and it was only because the Dictator, in the last months of his life, had slighted him that this quarrel had arisen which had led Dolabella now to throw in his lot with the conspirators. But had not Cæsar also quarrelled with An-

tony himself? They both knew what sort of man Cæsar had been,
and how he had dropped his friends mercilessly when they stood in
the way of his schemes; yet who could fail to admire him, and, now
that he was dead, what use was there in taking vengeance upon his
memory? Dolabella and Antony, as the two Consuls, ought to work
together for peace, and for the maintenance of that amnesty which
alone at present could secure it; and they should both do their utmost
to suppress this youth who was trying to throw the whole nation into
confusion.

Dolabella was a man without scruples, and he seized the opportunity of striking a bargain with Antony. His terms were quite
concrete: he said that at the end of his Consulship he wanted to be
made governor of Syria—the province promised to Cassius—for a
period of five years, so that, if circumstances should permit, he
might lead an expedition against Parthia and thereby gain wealth
and renown; and meanwhile he wanted a sum of money down.
Antony agreed to the terms, and thereupon Dolabella returned to his
Cæsarian allegiance, never again giving Antony any cause for anxiety about him.

The next thing to do was to reorganize the democratic party,
and to draft as many loyal partisans as possible into the Senate. At
the same time the sympathies of the left wing were enlisted again
by the framing of a new land law through the agency of Lucius
Antonius: its details are not known, but in general it was a socialistic measure, something in the nature of the law put forward by the
Gracchi, and it involved the setting up of a commission with power
to buy land and to distribute it, together with some of the public
domains, amongst the needy. [24]

Octavian retaliated by making overtures to the conservatives
or republicans; and the conspirators, seeing their opportunity, thereupon approached the young man and urged him to join forces with
them against their common enemy, Antony. They tried to persuade
him that although they had assassinated the Dictator, and although
he, as Cæsar's heir, had cause to regard them as family enemies,
nevertheless he and they had more in common than had he and the
democrats. They asked him to try to forget the murder and to unite
with them against Antony's party; and Octavian, in view of the

[24] Dion Cassius, xlv, 9.

dangers of his position, readily agreed to make this unholy alliance. It was a bewildering and ludicrous volte-face, and obliged him to show open friendship to those very men upon whom he had so recently demanded vengeance. But he was not embarrassed, at this period of his life, by any high principles, and his quarrel with Antony guided his actions with a far more compelling hand than that of his duty to the Dictator's memory.

Cicero and the conspirators—Brutus, Cassius, and all the others who had not left Italy—were now convinced that Antony intended to repeal the Act of Oblivion and set the law in motion against them as soon as circumstances should permit; and they were eager, therefore, to discredit him. Indeed, they heartily wished that they had killed him when they had killed Cæsar. It was owing to him that their cause was in such bad shape, and they were constantly blaming one another for having spared his life on the Ides of March. [25] One hopeful sign, however, had revealed itself, namely that Albinus, who had hurried from Rome to take up the governorship of Cisalpine Gaul, had reported that the legions there had accepted him in spite of his being one of the murderers of Cæsar. Another point in their favour was that Cæsar's Parthian expeditionary force which had seen a good deal of Octavian when he was with them at Apollonia, where they still were stationed, had tentatively offered its loyalty to him in his trouble with Antony, and might now follow his lead in making friends with the republican party.

But in spite of these reassuring signs they were depressed and anxious, and Cicero himself, who was always either in the heights or the depths, was at present in the abyss of despair. He did not realize, however, that Dolabella had wholly deserted them, and when it became known that the province of Syria had fallen to him, Cicero offered to go there with him as his chief-of-staff. The suggestion fell through, however, and the orator then began to consider the expediency of a private journey into Greece, his object being to retire from Italy until the troubles had blown over. His nerves had gone to pieces, and he longed for the quiet of some Greek retreat, where, amongst the philosophers, he might finish the charming book he was writing on the subject of Old Age. Moreover, he was at this time weighed down with debt, for he always kept up

[25] Cicero: *Ad Atticum*, xv, 11 and 12.

a style of living far beyond his means; and he longed to escape the increasing attentions of his creditors. [26] After much hesitation he sailed for Greece early in August, telling his friends that he was going to see the Olympic Games.

Meanwhile in Rome Octavian's mother, Atia, spread a curious story [27] in support of her son's position as Cæsar's sole representative. She said that before he was born, she fell asleep one day in the temple of Apollo, and dreamt that that deity in the form of a fascinating serpent had caused her to be unfaithful to her nuptial vow and had afterwards carried her procreative organs up to heaven to be blessed. That same day, moreover, her husband had the startling dream that the sun had risen from out of her midst, as though she were a range of mountains lying along the eastern horizon. This tale was passed around the city to the accompaniment of appreciative nods and exclamations, and it greatly increased the young man's prestige. He was given an ovation by the crowd at the public games in July; and when it so chanced that a comet was seen in the evening sky, and the quick-thinking Octavian had declared that it was assuredly the soul of Cæsar flying to heaven, the enthusiasm was intense. Octavian then caused a statue of Cæsar to be placed in the Temple of Venus, with a golden star above its head—much to the annoyance of Antony, who felt that by such actions the objectionable youngster was stealing his thunder.

To add to his troubles Antony was now having difficulty in dealing with Brutus and Cassius whose continued presence in Italy was a very disturbing influence upon the public mind. He proposed therefore that they should be sent abroad to supervise the purchase of foreign corn, a mission which it was the custom to place in the hands of men of standing. Brutus and Cassius, however, did not care to be thus disposed of: they had many friends in the Senate, and they were ever hoping that the republican party would become strong enough to effect their entire rehabilitation.

At length Antony sent them peremptory orders to undertake this mission, and in a letter to him dated August 4th [28] they replied in a tone which revealed their sullen and unbending attitude. "We have read your letter," they wrote, "which is insulting, intimidating, and

[26] Cicero: *Ad Atticum*, xvi, 2.   [27] Dion Cassius, xlv, 1.
[28] Cicero: *Ad Familiares*, xi, 3.

in every way an improper one for you to have written to us. . . .
Our personal sentiments are these. We are anxious to see you held in
dignity and honour if it be in a free Republic. We do not invite your
antagonism, but, nevertheless, we value our liberty of action more
than your friendship. You should therefore consider again and again
what you are doing, and what your power is able to accomplish; and
be sure you bear in mind not how long Cæsar lived, but how short a
time he was able to behave like a king."

This last remark was intended as a warning to Antony not to
attempt to play the autocrat; and the letter in general had the
effect of making him reconsider the matter of the corn-buying mission, for he was not yet ready to come to blows with the conspirators:
the danger from Octavian was too much of a menace to his own
position to permit him to think of himself as all-powerful. Octavian
was his most serious enemy; and his quarrel with this youth seemed
likely to wreck all his plans. His friends were constantly telling him
to beware of his young rival; but the more they did so the angrier
he became.

At length Cæsar's old soldiers made up their minds to oblige him
and Octavian to compose their differences and work together for
the good of the State; and they therefore marched in a body to
Octavian's house. The young man thought that his last hour was
come when he saw this army approaching, and, having shouted
orders for the gates and doors to be bolted, he fled to the roof. But
when, to his great relief, he heard the soldiers cheering him, he
crept downstairs again and presently received the leaders of the
demonstration, who told him in no ambiguous terms that he and
Antony had got to shake hands.

The soldiers, it seems, then marched to Antony's house, who
doubtless fled, likewise, to the roof or the cellar, so uncertain was
the temper of the populace, and so prepared had he to be at all
times to save his skin. It was a nerve-racking life. When he understood their purpose, however, he sullenly consented to meet Octavian; and amidst the cheers of the veterans he and his embarrass-
ingly young rival exchanged visits and agreed to work in harmony.

At about the same time Antony came to an agreement with
Dolabella—in their capacity as fellow-Consuls—in regard to the
distribution of provincial governorships at the end of the present

year, 44 B.C., or earlier, if necessary. Dolabella, as has already been said, was to have Syria for five years, and was to be permitted to set out for that province in the early autumn. Antony chose for himself Cæsar's old province of Cisalpine Gaul—northern Italy, that is to say—it being so close to Rome; and it was arranged that Albinus, who was already there, should be transferred to Macedonia, while the troops then in the latter country should be transferred to Cisalpine Gaul to serve under Antony who proposed to hold that governorship, likewise, for a period of five years. Brutus was to be got rid of by being given the governorship of the island of Crete; and Cassius was to be sent off as governor, it would seem, of Cyrene.

Now it so happened that Cicero's voyage to Greece had been delayed by storms, and at length, after a bad tossing at sea, his ship had been driven back to the Italian coast, where several days were passed in port waiting for better conditions and a favourable wind. Here, however, he received news from his friends that the Senate had been convened for September 1st, and that there was hope then of gathering so strong a body of senators of republican views that Antony's plans might be brought to nothing. A copy of the letter of Brutus and Cassius to Antony was also shown to him, and he was told that Antony had seemed to take it so to heart that he was likely to abandon his pugnacious attitude and to aim at some sort of compromise. Moreover, Cicero was informed that his departure for Greece had been regarded as a sign of cowardice, and that he was thought to have but repeated his unfortunate flight of fourteen years earlier when his behaviour in regard to the Catilinarian conspirators had made him dangerously unpopular. Even his friend Atticus wrote to him in bitter sarcasm, saying, "Very well, then, *go*, and desert your country: it is quite right in the man who said he was not afraid to die for the fatherland!" [29]

After renewed hesitation and indecision, therefore, he made up his mind to abandon his journey, and to return to Rome for the purpose of encouraging his party at this moment when Antony seemed to be amenable, and also in order to attempt to detach Octavian from his new alliance. It was a bold step; but he had been stung by the imputation of cowardice, and for once in his vacillating career—and this, indeed, was one of the great moments of his life—

[29] Cicero: *Ad Atticum*, xvi, 7.

he rose to the occasion with a courage which goes far to outweigh his former weakness in history's estimation of his character.

"I see," he had already written to Atticus, "that I shall run some risks, but I cannot help thinking that it may lie in my power to do some good for the State." [30] When he was warned that Antony might force him into subserviency, he replied, "I know a better way than that" [31]—meaning suicide; and when it was pointed out that he might be driven into exile he answered, significantly, "I look to another haven which lies handier to my time of life: all I wish is that I may reach it leaving Brutus in prosperity and the Republic re-established." [32] It is hardly to be supposed, of course, that he seriously contemplated suicide—that sequel of political defeat which Roman thought had made customary, for there was considerable reason for hope that his party would come successfully through this period of its difficulties; yet the risk of disaster in some form was present, and his fine words had a closer relation to actuality than was usual with him.

He arrived back in Rome on the last day of August and Antony was irritated to find that he received a great welcome from the conservative party, and that Octavian, too, paid his respects to him. The Senate, however, was to meet next morning, September 1st, and Antony determined to snub the interfering old orator on that occasion by putting forward various measures adverse to the conspirators' interests which the senators, he believed, would be obliged to pass. One of these—a measure likely to delight the crowd —was the proposal that public prayers and supplications should be made to the spirit of Cæsar as to the immortal gods, [33] for the Senate had already, before the assassination, acknowledged his divinity, and the senators could hardly go back now on their former admission, much as many of them might wish to do so. It gave Antony the greatest pleasure to contemplate the discomfiture of Cicero, who would of course be present in the Senate on the morrow, and would have either to acquiesce in this measure or to oppose it publicly, in which latter case the mob would be at his throat. It was a clever trap laid for him, and Antony looked forward with enjoyment to the hour when it would be sprung.

[30] Cicero: *Ad Atticum,* xiv, 13.   [31] *Ibid.,* xv, 3.
[32] *Ibid.,* xiv, 19.   [33] Cicero: *Philippic* i, v, vi.

But Cicero was not so easily caught. On his arrival at his house his friends warned him of Antony's plans, and a hasty conference of the conservative party led to the decision that Cicero and the majority of his colleagues should refrain from attending the sitting of the Senate. Next day, therefore, most of the senatorial chairs were unoccupied, and a note was received from Cicero saying that owing to the fatigues of his journey he was confined to his bed.

Antony was furious, and his anger was increased when the rumour reached him that Cicero had refused to come because he feared that violence would be done to him by the Consul's soldiers. [34] In a passion of rage and disappointment he addressed the nearly empty House, saying that this rumour was a dastardly slander and belief in it an insult. The conservative senators, he declared, had placed an unbearable slight upon him and the Senate by absenting themselves at this opening meeting of the new session; and he would not tolerate it. He would use all his Consular powers to oblige Cicero to come; and therewith he gave orders that locksmiths and masons should be sent at once to the orator's home to break open its doors, while soldiers should bring him by force, or, failing to find him, should burn his house to the ground.

The senators were shocked and frightened, and begged him to calm himself; and at length Antony cooled down sufficiently to countermand these wild orders, and to accept sureties for the orator's good behaviour. But he declared that he would never forgive him; and, indeed, all men realized that day that the quarrel between the Cæsarian democrats and the anti-Cæsarian republicans had entered upon its crisis.

The issue was clear: on the one side was Antony, the representative and would-be preserver of the dead Dictator's absolutism, the defender of that paradox—a democratic autocracy, and with him the unwilling Octavian, forced now to play second-fiddle; on the other side were the conservatives and the conspirators, led by Cicero, representing the old republican ideals and bent upon the recognition of Cæsar as a tyrant justly slain. Antony stood for the rescinding of the Act of Oblivion so soon as public calm could be established; Cicero stood for the maintenance of that amnesty. Antony had the People solidly behind him so long as their sympathies

[34] Plutarch: *Cicero.*

were not divided by any disagreement between him and Octavian in the matter of leadership; Cicero was sure of the support of the conservative upper classes.

It was to be a fight now to a finish between the republicans and the democrats. Antony's blood was up, and he guessed that Cicero, usually so cautious, was in a similar state of ebullience; but in Octavian lay the danger. How long would that pale-faced and sinister young man consent to occupy a back seat?

CHAPTER XII

Antony's Departure from Rome where Cicero was Delivering the Philippic Orations Against Him and his Failure to Wrest Cisalpine Gaul from Albinus.

44–43 B.C.

On the following day Cicero, elegantly dressed, and with his grey hair carefully combed and scented, [1] attended the Senate, having announced beforehand that he would deliver a speech in defence of his attitude and would make certain suggestions in regard to the future conduct of affairs—at which announcement Antony at once decided to absent himself, on a like plea of ill-health, in order to show as much contempt for Cicero's proposals as the orator had yesterday displayed for *his*. The speech was afterwards published, as also were the thirteen others against Antony which Cicero delivered during the following weeks; and they are now known as the *Philippics*, a name given to them a few years later because of their similarity in form to the orations of Demosthenes against Philip.

In this the First Philippic Cicero, with his habitual vanity, began by telling the senators—and there must have been a pretty full House to hear him—that it was he himself who had laid the foundations of peace after the assassination by proposing the Act of Oblivion, though he admitted that Antony had played quite a distinguished part at first in promoting good will, as also had Dolabella. Then, had come the sad change, and the orator had gone away in disgust, only to return at once, however, when he heard that Brutus and Cassius, whom he said that he dearly loved, had obliged Antony by their firmness to be less truculent. But having returned, he had found by the events of yesterday that Antony was hostile to

[1] Dion Cassius, xlvi, 18.

him, and had made his, Cicero's, quite excusable absence from the Senate a *casus belli*. Antony, he declared, had a right to be angry if he had said anything against his private morals, but not on account of his having expressed his political views. As a matter of fact, he said, he was quite prepared to allow all Cæsar's laws to stand, and even to wink at Antony's use of the dead Dictator's memoranda, since the dividing line between what was Cæsar's and what was Antony's could not be drawn. "Men have been recalled from exile," he smiled, "by a dead man; the freedom of the city has been conferred not only on individuals but on entire nations and provinces by a dead man; our revenues have been diminished by the granting of countless exemptions by a dead man. Nevertheless I will uphold these measures which have been brought from Cæsar's house on the authority of a single individual—a very excellent individual, I admit." Cicero saw, in fact, that the rejection of any part of Cæsar's arrangements would mean also the repudiation of his assignment of provinces to some of the conspirators—Cisalpine Gaul to Decimus Brutus Albinus, for example—and he had no wish to upset these or any other of the measures which were of advantage to his party.

He then went on to admonish both Antony and Dolabella for what he considered their high-handedness, and to warn them that people were saying they were only anxious for their own enrichment. "Of course," he added with the unctuousness of a politician, "I myself cannot be induced to suspect that Antony has been caught by the desire to acquire money. Every one may say what he pleases, but we are not bound to believe such a thing; for I never saw anything sordid or anything mean in him. I know his uprightness, and I only wish that he had been able to escape all such suspicion."

Next, growing more bold, he warned Antony against the use of armed force, but remarked that it was hardly necessary to emphasise the point. "If the fate of Cæsar," he said, "does not influence him to prefer to be loved than to be feared, no speech of mine will have any effect on him. No one can be happy who behaves in such a way that he may be assassinated not only with impunity but even to the great glory of his slayer."

Having uttered this thinly veiled threat that if Antony did not compromise with the conspirators he would be murdered, Cicero wound up by saying that he himself was not afraid to die. "I have lived long enough for the course of human life," he declared, "and for my own glory. Yet, if any further years are granted to me, they shall be given to the service of the Senate and of the Republic."

This speech, with its rather brutal hint of murder, was reported to Antony, whose opposition was thereby stiffened towards the conspirators and towards their pernicious doctrine of assassination as a cure for supposed political ills. He could not abide Cicero, regarding him as treacherous in the extreme; and the orator's eloquence, with its plausible expression of high-principle, nauseated him. During the next week or two he refused to speak to Cicero when they met; and when he heard that Octavian, on the contrary, was showing friendliness towards the orator, flattering him and calling him Father of his country, he broke off all relations with that young man also. He was not surprised, therefore, when he was told that Octavian was plotting against his life; and though he could obtain no absolute proof of the truth of the report, he was sufficiently assured of its correctness to denounce him, and Cicero also, in a speech, now lost, which he delivered before the Senate on September 19th.

The sensation it caused was immense; and Atia, Octavian's mother, implored the boy to leave Rome, but without success. Death was in the air: its dark shadow was menacing the lives alike of Octavian, Antony and Cicero; but all three were keyed up to deeds of daring at this time, and not one of them had any intention now of running away. Dolabella, however, took the opportunity to set out for his new province of Syria while Antony still had the power to support his claim upon it: the problems in Rome were too difficult for him, and he was eager to seek his fortune in Parthia.

At this time some of the legions in Macedonia were about to sail back to Italy, having been ordered by Antony to come over so as to be ready to accompany him to Cisalpine Gaul at the close of his Consulship; but he was not aware that Octavian, who had made friends with many of their officers while he was in Apollonia, had just sent them a secret message, telling them of his troubles in Rome, and begging them to give their support to him as Cæsar's rightful heir and not to his rival. Antony, whose thoughts were usually those of a soldier, felt that he would be much more comfortable with these legions at his back; and he therefore decided to go down to

Brundusium (Brindisi) to meet them on their arrival, and to march them to the capital before the conspirators who were scattered about southern Italy could tamper with them.

In the second week in October, at the close of the senatorial sessions, he and his wife, Fulvia, set out for the south; and shortly afterwards both Octavian and Cicero left Rome—Octavian for the purpose of gathering some more of Cæsar's ex-soldiers as a sort of bodyguard in case of trouble with Antony, and Cicero only for the purpose of obtaining an interval of quiet after the excitements of the previous weeks, so that he might get on with his literary work. But when Antony had reached Brundusium and had presented himself to the troops on their disembarkation he was surprised to find that the officers of at least one legion—the Martian—greeted him with little warmth. He could not understand it, and, ordering them to be paraded, made a speech to them promising them the usual rewards, and reminding them that he was their dead general's former colleague and present representative.

They laughed in his face. They called him "traitor," shouting that he had usurped Octavian's heritage, and that Octavian would give them far greater rewards than those just offered. For a moment it must have looked as though they would kill him there and then.

Antony's rage was unbounded. He stormed off to the house where he was staying, calling to him all those officers of the other legions and auxiliary cavalry whom he could trust, amongst these being several of his old friends of the Gallic cavalry with whom he had served in Syria, Egypt, and Gaul. They told him that Octavian's agents had been trying for weeks past to detach them from Antony's authority, and they gave him a list of the officers who were disloyal. Fulvia, it seems, was present during this conference, and her anger was more terrible than her husband's. Furiously she urged him to have no mercy on the rebels; and we have to picture her with flashing eyes and gesticulating arms, calling down curses on these men who were so near to ruining the cause.

Orders were given for the arrest of the disaffected officers. They were dragged before Antony, summarily tried, and condemned to instant execution. Loyal swords flashed, and the heads of the culprits rolled one after the other across the floor. Fulvia was in an hysterical condition, and, screaming her imprecations at the men who were being butchered, she approached so close to them as they died that she was drenched with their spurting blood. To Antony her behaviour must have been an appalling revelation; and it is to be supposed that his ultimate estrangement from her began to take shape from this day. In spite of the violence of his temper, and the severity which he sometimes displayed in dealing with a situation of this kind, in spite, too, of his bouts of drunkenness, he was a cultured, sensitive man, far removed from the savage—easy-going and humane, in fact, on most occasions; and there must ever have remained in his mind the disgusting picture of his wife's face [2] and clothes dripping with blood, and her feet paddling in that scarlet river.

Antony's violent action cowed the disloyal troops, and they accepted the orders which were now given them to march northwards along the east coast of Italy to Ariminum (Rimini), on the borders of Cisalpine Gaul, where they were to await Antony's arrival as governor of that province at the close of his Consulship two months hence. With a small force of the more trustworthy troops, the nucleus of which was the Fifth Legion, known as the *Alaudæ* or "the Larks," he then marched towards Rome, his troubles with the conservatives and the conspirators being now relegated to the background in the more immediate crisis of his quarrel with Octavian.

That young man, who had recently attained his nineteenth birthday, [3] was in the meantime touring the south-west, recruiting Cæsar's ex-soldiers, and tempting them, by heavy bribes, from the lands whereon they were settled. A letter from Cicero to Atticus [4] reveals Octavian's plans.

"A letter for me from Octavian reached me on November 1st," he wrote. "He has great schemes. The ex-soldiers of Casilinum (Capua) and Calatia, near by, he has entirely brought over to his side, and no wonder, since he offers them five hundred *denarii* apiece! He proposes to go the round of the other military settlements: obviously what he has in view is to put himself at the head of an army to fight Antony; and so I see that in a few days we shall be under arms. Who, however, is to be our leader? Think of Octavian's name! [5]—think of his age! And he writes to ask that in the first place

---

[2] Cicero: *Philippic iii*, ii.   [3] On September 23rd.   [4] Cicero: *Ad Atticum*, xvi, 8.
[5] He means, think of the conspirators being led by a Cæsar!

I will grant him a strictly private interview. Surely it is childish if he supposes that this could possibly be private; and I have written to tell him that what he asks is neither necessary nor practicable. He sent a friend of his to me who brought the news that Antony was moving towards Rome with the Fifth Legion, borrowing money from the towns, and marching under flying colours. He wanted to ask my advice as to whether he should go to Rome with three thousand ex-soldiers, or occupy Casilinum and intercept the advance of Antony, or go to meet the legions from Macedonia now making their way northwards by the coast-road along the Adriatic, whose sympathies are, he hopes, all for him. In short he offers himself as our leader, and thinks it will not be right for us to fail him. I myself have recommended him to go to Rome, because it seems to me that he will there have not only the poor rabble of the city on his side, provided that he has proved his sincerity, but also the good men."

Octavian took his advice and marched the newly recruited veterans towards Rome; and a few days later Cicero wrote as follows to Atticus. [6] "Every day I have had a letter from Octavian asking me to take up his cause, and be a second time the saviour of the Republic, and to come at once to Rome—which I am afraid to accept and ashamed to refuse. He certainly has acted and is acting with vigour. He is bringing a large force to Rome, but then he is the merest boy. He thinks that the Senate can be convoked in a moment. But who will attend? Or, where everything is so precarious, who will make an enemy of Antony? Yet, boy though he is, the country-towns seem to be marvellously in favour of him. At Teanum (Teano), for instance, the good-wishes were astonishing. Could you have believed this?"

Octavian reached Rome on November 10th, and camped his men in the open ground near the Temple of Mars, on the Appian Way outside the city walls; and day by day he made public speeches against Antony, calling him a traitor to the dead Cæsar. But clearly the only traitor was the young man himself, for he was now in open alliance with Cæsar's murderers, and was not only flattering Cicero to the skies, but was already making friendly overtures to Decimus Brutus Albinus, the man who had lured the Dictator to his doom, and who was now governor of the province of Cisalpine

[6] Cicero: *Ad Atticum,* xvi, 11.

Gaul from which Antony wished to remove him. This was too much for Octavian's army of veterans to swallow: they had been enlisted to oppose Antony, but they had not bargained for an alliance with the assassins of their old leader. They began to desert to the other side; and at the same time the republicans in Rome were by no means in favour of this union with the obviously treacherous heir of the dead tyrant, and showed no enthusiasm for him.

Meanwhile, the melancholy and wrong-headed Brutus, the arch-assassin, had left Italy and had gone to live in Athens, where, while giving most of his time to a serious study of philosophy in the schools of Theomnestes and Cratippus, he made his secret preparations for the war with Antony which he felt to be inevitable. He had no intention of taking up the governorship of Crete which had been assigned to him, and was hesitating whether or not to seize the province of Macedonia which had been promised him by Cæsar and to which he had therefore as much right as Albinus, for example, had to Cisalpine Gaul. He did not at all approve of Cicero's relations with Octavian, and wrote to him with great bitterness pointing out that it would be just as bad to have Octavian in power—the heir of the man they had murdered—as it was to have Antony, and saying indignantly that it seemed as though Cicero had no objection to living under the tyranny of an autocrat so long as that autocrat were not his personal enemy, Antony. All Cicero cared about, he declared, was his own comfort, but he, Brutus, refused to be a slave to any man, friend or foe.[7]

But while Octavian's position was thus uncertain, the angry Antony was approaching Rome with the faithful Larks and with his loyal Gallic cavalry. The Larks, it should be mentioned, were recruited in Gaul, the legion having been first raised by Cæsar in that country in 55 B.C. The upstanding feathers which they wore on their helmets suggested the tuft of a lark, and perhaps their singing abilities also provided a reason for their nickname. They were a rough lot of fair-haired giants; and having known Antony in the Gallic wars and having witnessed his wild bravery in battle, they loved him, and were prepared to die for him.

From time to time on his march Antony issued proclamations or made speeches denouncing Octavian, belittling his ancestry, and

[7] Plutarch: Brutus.

attacking his moral character. He said he knew for a fact that
the Dictator had had improper relations with him, as also had one
of Cæsar's generals in Spain, the well-known Hirtius [8] who was one
of the Consuls-elect for the coming year and now belonged to
Cicero's party; and he made constant jokes in regard to Octavian's
effeminate ways, calling attention to the fact that the youth was
regularly in the hands of the *ustriculæ*, or lady-barbers, whose business it was to remove the hair from his legs and to make them soft.

This, of course, was a case of the pot calling the kettle black,
for Antony's own effeminate youth was notorious, even though he
had now passed to the opposite extreme, and was a very man
amongst men. Moreover, Antony had spoken with disdain of
Octavian's mother, Atia, as a provincial woman from a small town,
her home being in Aricia (Riccia), a few miles south of Rome,
although his own mother, Julia, had spent her childhood in the
same place; and, anyhow, as Cicero remarked [9] in answer to this
insinuation of provincialism, what right had Antony to talk in
this fashion when his own wife, Fulvia, came from the small town
of Tusculum (Frascati), and was the daughter of a man named
Bambalio, so called because he had an impediment in his speech
and was more or less half-witted? Antony's purpose, however, had
been to show that Octavian was neither by birth nor character de-
serving of especial reverence; and he was much too angry just now
to avoid that kind of imputation which had the nature of a boomer-
ang. The hurling of abuse intended to sting was a recognized part
of ancient hostilities, just as it is today in the East; and nobody
troubled to ascertain the truth of the accusations.

Antony arrived in Rome on or about November 20th, and sent
the troops who were with him to Tibur (Tivoli), some sixteen
miles north-east of the city, retaining on the spot only the ex-
soldiers whom he had previously recruited—a force apparently
much larger than that still loyal to Octavian. He then convened
the Senate for the 24th, issuing a warning that those senators who
failed to attend would be regarded as his enemies; but, suddenly,
on the 23rd, he seems to have heard that his rival's agents were
busy at Tivoli, and therefore, postponing the senatorial meeting
until the 28th, he hastened off to the camp of the Larks and their

---

[8] Suetonius: Augustus, lxviii.   [9] Cicero: *Philippic iii, vi.*

auxiliaries, to address them and if necessary to outbid any offers of money which Octavian might have made them. But while he and his merry men were banqueting [10] and drinking damnation to his rival, he received a staggering blow: dispatches arrived from Rimini informing him that the Martian Legion, whom he had so severely punished at Brindisi, had declared for Octavian. They had detached themselves from the remainder of the troops from Macedonia who were still loyal, or, at any rate, undecided—these consisting in the main of the Second, Fourth, and Thirty-fifth Legions—and were marching back towards Rome.

During the next four days he remained at Tivoli, not knowing what to do for the best, since the reports from Rome were most alarming, and his friends seemed to think that there would be an immediate landslide in favour of Octavian. He hardly dared to enter the city for fear that he would be murdered; and yet at all costs he must be present at the meeting of the Senate on the 28th, lest his absence should give his rivals the opportunity to say that he had deserted his Consular post and was no longer fit to hold it.

The meeting was to take place in the Capitol, and while he was turning over in his mind some means of reaching that building without running the gauntlet of a mob now in all likelihood suddenly headed against him, a friend reminded him of a secret passage, an old tunnel burrowed by the Gauls in their attack upon the citadel in 390 B.C., which led up into the cellars beneath the senatorial hall.[11] Instantly he made up his mind to enter the city, with some of his Gauls, under the cover of darkness during the night of the 27th, to make use of this tunnel, and quietly to take his place in the Consular chair on the morning of the 28th. It was quite likely that he would be assassinated; but his courage always rose as his fortunes fell, and he preferred the risk of death to the certainty of the disaster which would result from his absence.

On the morning of the 28th the senators, including Cicero, who had arrived on the previous day, trooped into the Capitol, eagerly asking one another what news there was of Antony, and discussing what would happen if he should not put in an appearance. The atmosphere was electric with the menace of a political earthquake; and

[10] Cicero: *Philippic iii*, viii.
[11] *Ibid.*

Cicero was elated at the prospect of being able to propose the deposition of his enemy. Then, suddenly, as though by a miracle, Antony appeared before them, bland and unafraid, and took his seat, presiding thereafter over the business of the day, and saying no word about his or Octavian's position. It may be, as Cicero afterwards thought, that he had intended to test the opinion of the House by denouncing his youthful rival; but towards the close of the meeting a terrible message was brought to him which must have driven any such thought from his head. It informed him that the Fourth Legion had followed the example of the Martian and had gone over to Octavian; and with sinking heart, but with outward calm, he wound up the day's affairs, dismissed the assembly, and rejoined his waiting bodyguard of Gauls.[12]

He believed that the news of this second mutiny was not yet known in Rome, but he realized that as soon as it was circulated the still hesitating mob would probably declare for Octavian, and Cæsar's veterans might unite under the young man's standard. Only the Gallic Larks and the Gallic cavalry could be relied on; and he saw at once that his one hope lay in seizing with their help the province of Cisalpine Gaul, of which he had assigned himself the governorship at the coming close of his term as Consul. The Senate, however, had not yet officially confirmed that appointment, and the question which now agitated his mind was whether he had the time or the power to have it ratified and to get out of the city before the landslide.

The action which he took was perilous in the extreme. He knew that most of the senators would be leaving dangerous Rome for the security of their suburban or country homes during the day, and he therefore sent private messages to those of them whom he could trust, calling them to an emergency meeting of the Senate that evening, while those whom he could not trust he allowed to depart uncalled.

As a result of this maneuver he found a thinly-attended but friendly assembly awaiting him at the close of the day; and, quietly addressing them, he said—so I suppose—that in view of the danger of a clash between the troops loyal to him and those siding with

[12] Cicero (*Philippic iii,* iv) speaks of Antony bringing "armed barbarians" into the Senate.

Octavian, he proposed to set out for Cisalpine Gaul at once, so that he should be there, ready to take over the governorship from Albinus, at the close of the year. He asked them therefore to be so good as to ratify the allotment of that province to him, and at the same time to give the province of Macedonia to his brother Caius Antonius, after which he proposed that the other governorships for the new year should be assigned by drawing lots in the usual way. All this was nervously agreed to; and at the end of the meeting he found himself in possession of the papers authorizing him to go to Cisalpine Gaul.

Meanwhile, he had sent an invitation to those of the ex-soldiers who did not wish to desert him, to come with him to Tivoli that night, and he had told them to muster quietly and under cover of the darkness at a certain place. Then, putting on the armour and the scarlet cloak of a general, he set out for the rendez-vous, not knowing how many of the veterans would be there; but, to his great relief, he found that the bulk of them had remained loyal, and soon he and a satisfactorily large force were marching under the stars along the highroad to the north. His wife, Fulvia, did not accompany him, for at this period the great ladies of Rome were seldom in any danger of violence; but for greater safety she and her children went to stay in the house of one of Antony's chief supporters in the city.[13]

During the next two or three days deputations of senators and persons of importance came to him at Tivoli, urging him to try even at this eleventh hour to come to terms with Octavian, but his brother, Lucius, who had joined him, was violently opposed to any reconciliation; and Octavian, on his side, had been so elated by the mutiny of the two legions that he felt able, with the support of Cicero's party, to force the quarrel to an issue. Nothing came, therefore, of these negotiations; and Antony set out for Cisalpine Gaul early in December, at the head of the Larks, the Gallic cavalry, most of Cæsar's ex-soldiers, and certain units of the garrison of Rome. His purpose was to effect a junction with the Second and Thirty-fifth Legions now at Rimini, and, with this army at his back, and his papers of authority in his hand, to take peaceable possession of his new province, to assume command of

[13] Cicero: *Philippic xii*, 1.

the seven legions stationed therein, and to send Albinus home. Later on, it might be necessary to do what Cæsar did—cross the Rubicon, and march on Rome.[14]

But Octavian and Cicero, working together, sent messengers to Albinus, promising him that if he could induce the army under his command in Cisalpine Gaul to declare for Octavian and to resist Antony, they would give him all the help in their power and would send the two legions who had deserted Antony's cause, and who were now nearing Rome, to attack their former general in the rear. Cicero's letters to him were couched in the most flattering terms; and in one of them,[15] after referring to the murder of Cæsar as "that great deed of yours, the greatest ever done in the history of mankind," he said: "I pray that you will for ever set the Republic free from the tyranny of a king, and make the last act of your drama suitable to the first." In another letter [16] he wrote: "We hope and trust that as you have set free the Republic from a monarch, so now you will from a monarchy." Albinus replied that he would most certainly do his part, and hold his province against Antony.

The majority of the members of the Cæsarian party in Rome, meanwhile, mistrusting Octavian and greatly resenting his alliance with Cæsar's assassins, showed so strongly and so unexpectedly their sympathy with Antony that Octavian suddenly decided to leave the city, put himself under the wing of these two legions who had come over to his side, and remain with them outside Rome. At the same time several of the most important Cæsarians set out to follow Antony, being unaware that Albinus would resist his advance, and thinking that Cisalpine Gaul, which was so near to and yet so far from Rome, would be a more comfortable place than the disturbed metropolis. These movements left the Capital more or less in the hands of Cicero and his republicans, and the elderly orator thus found himself in that position of authority for which he had longed unceasingly ever since the days of his Consulship.

To him it was clear now that Antony was doomed, and that Octavian would in the end embrace the cause of the republicans

---

[14] Cicero: *Philippic iii, i.*   [15] Cicero: *Ad Familiares,* xi, 5.
[16] *Ibid.,* xi, 8.

and would make his permanent peace with Cæsar's murderers. He was overwhelmingly elated. The democrats would almost cease to exist as a party; the conspirators would at last be recognized as having saved the State, and would once more take their place in Roman political life; while Cicero himself would stand for a second Consulship and would be for many glorious years the revered leader of the nation. He felt that he must strain every nerve to destroy Antony, whom he had disliked for many years and for the last two months had hated with burning intensity. He had recently composed a long tirade against him; and this he now decided to publish. The abuse of Antony contained in it was, of course, wildly exaggerated; but he felt that he was justified in placing every possible weapon at the service of his eloquence in his battle with the man whose destruction meant his own aggrandisement and the victory of his own political party.

The composition is now known as the Second Philippic and is one of the fiercest and most violent pieces of writing which antiquity has handed down to us. Cicero begins by indulging in that self-praise for which he was notorious, and which Plutarch describes as a nauseating disease whereof he could not be cured. His opening paragraph contains the exaggerated boast that during the last twenty years no man has done ill by the Republic without having to cross swords with him, and none has survived that encounter; and now he asks how Antony could have dared to court that invariable fate. "Am I to think that *I* have been despised?" he asks, and adds in astonishment: "I see nothing in my life, or in my influence in the city, or in my exploits, or in the abilities with which I am endowed, which Antony could despise! Did he think that it was easy to disparage me in the Senate?—a body which has testified in favour of many illustrious citizens that they have *governed* the Republic well, but in favour of me alone, that I have *saved* it!"

He then goes on to praise his own Consulship, about which Antony had made some disparaging remarks, and he says that there was not a senator in those days who did not regard him as the very salvation of his life. Only Clodius and Curio had ever dared to criticise it, and he warns Antony that their misfortunes and violent ends await him likewise, especially "since there is now that in his house which was fatal to each of them," meaning the ill-omened Fulvia, the widow of both these men.

Antony, he proceeds, had often accused him of having instigated the murder of Cæsar, and in reply he declares his regret that he was not one of "the gallant band" who undertook "that glorious deed, the greatest exploit ever performed in all the earth." The reason why Brutus and the assassins shouted the name of Cicero after the murder was committed, he explains, was simply that, having done something which they deemed to be noble, they naturally wished to call all men to witness that they were imitators of the great Cicero's noble exploits. But he adds that if he had been one of the conspirators he would most certainly have seen that Antony had perished too.

Presently he passes on to a devastating review of Antony's career from his youth up—how he had behaved like a female prostitute when he was a boy, "until Curio stepped in, and settled him in a steady and durable wedlock"; how he was the friend of the riotous Clodius; how his actions in regard to Cæsar caused the war with Pompey; and so on. He admits that he has to thank Antony for sparing his life after Pharsalia, but of course, he adds, "I was sacred in the eyes of the legions, because they remembered that the country had been saved by me." He describes Antony's public career thereafter as being that of a drunkard and a libertine, which reached its shocking climax when he appeared naked and drunk in the Forum during the Lupercalia, and offered Cæsar the crown. What can be more disgraceful, he asks, than that Antony, who tried to place the crown on the head of the man deservedly slain on that account, should himself be allowed to live?

Next, he points out what damage was done by Antony's speech at Cæsar's funeral; and, afterwards, how he seized Cæsar's money, forged his papers, and behaved himself like a tyrant. Throughout the whole composition he speaks of him as a sort of madman, a drunken fool, and a reckless gambler; and he calls him in one place a "brute-beast," and in another says that he is "devoid of all sense and all feeling." Finally, he asks whether Antony can possibly think that he will not meet the fate of the Dictator. "If men could not tolerate Cæsar," he says, "does he think that they will tolerate *him?*"

"As for myself," he writes in conclusion, "I defended the Republic as a young man, and I will not abandon it now that I am old. I scorned the sword of Catiline, and I will not quail before Antony's. No!—I will cheerfully expose my own person, if the liberty of the Republic can be restored by my death. To me, indeed, death is now even desirable, after all the honours I have gained, and all the great deeds I have done."

A string of lies of this sort demanded an answer; and presently an ex-Consul named Quintus Fufius Calenus, who had been one of Cæsar's generals, and had fought side by side with Antony, got up in the Senate and made a vigorous reply which has been preserved.[17] "I would not have Cicero's innate impudence go without a response," he said, "nor would I have his private enmity against Antony accepted in place of what is to the common advantage. Ever since Cicero entered politics he has been continually causing disturbances one way or the other; and now he insults and abuses Antony, whom he was wont to say he loved, and makes friends with Octavian, the heir of the man he was instrumental in murdering. And, if he gets the chance, ere long he will murder Octavian also. For the man is naturally untrustworthy and turbulent, and has no ballast in his soul, and is always stirring things up and twisting this way and that. He is a juggler and impostor, and grows rich and strong from the misfortunes of others, blackmailing them, dragging and tearing at the innocent as do the dogs."

He then gave a picture of Cicero's youth on his father's farm, and asked how one who was accustomed to live with the pigs can dare "to slander the youth of Antony who had the advantage of tutors and teachers such as his high rank required." Cicero, he said, is one of those lawyers "who are always waiting, like the harlots, for a man who will give them money, and who pry into people's affairs to find out who hates whom, and who is plotting against whom. How much better it would have been if he had been born a stammering Bambalio (like Fulvia's father) than that he should have taken up such a career." "He is always jealous of his betters," he went on, "always toadying to important people, telling them that he is their only true friend, pandering to their fears or their conceit, and 'fawning upon them.'"

[17] Dion Cassius, xlvi, 1–28.

Antony's life, meanwhile, he declared, had been noble, and of the greatest value to the State. At the Lupercalia he cleverly destroyed Cæsar's chance of obtaining the crown by forcing him to reject it in public. "That is the great service which was done by this man whom Cicero calls uneducated; and no such service has been done by this clever, this wise Cicero, this user of much more soft-soap than honest wine, this man who lets his robes drag about his ankles to hide the ugliness of his legs. We all know those long, soft clothes of his, and have smelt his carefully combed grey locks!"

He then referred to the disgraceful manner in which Cicero had divorced his wife, and married a little girl for her money; and he accused the orator of having lived a whole life of secret impurity, and even of having committed incest with his own daughter, Tullia —an accusation which is probably quite as untrue, one may suppose, as are his own slanders upon Antony. Besides this he declared that Cicero in former years had lived on the proceeds of his wife's amours, and that he had recently been paying court, presumably for the sake of money, to an old woman of incalculable years. "This sort of talk is not to my taste," he explained, "but I want Cicero to get as good as he gave."

Next, he spoke of Cicero's actions in the matter of the Catilinarian conspiracy, of which he is "interminably prating," as having been worthy only of the strongest censure. He then defended Antony's behaviour after Cæsar's death, and said that he had made use of the Dictator's money and papers in a perfectly proper manner. "What man is there," he asked, "surpassing Antony in esteem or excelling him in experience? Which of the two seems to be in the wrong—Antony, who is now at the head of troops legally allowed him by the Senate, or Octavian, who is surrounded by a force privately raised?—Antony, who has left Rome to take up the governorship given to him by the Senate, or Albinus, who will prevent him from setting foot in that province?—Antony, who keeps our soldiers together, or those soldiers who have deserted their commander?"

"I warn you, Cicero," he said in conclusion, "not to show a spitefulness like a woman's, nor because of your private hatred of Antony to plunge the whole city again into danger."

On December 20th Cicero, thirsting for revenge, delivered before the Senate his Third Philippic, in which he proposed that Octavian and Albinus should be commended for the steps they were taking against Antony. "Octavian," he said, "though a mere boy, has held fast with an incredible and godlike degree of wisdom and bravery during this time when Antony's dangerous folly has been at its height; and he has collected a trustworthy force of ex-soldiers, and has spent his own fortune in doing so, or rather, I should say, has invested it in the Republic. We ought to feel the greatest gratitude to him, for who does not see that if Antony had come unopposed to Rome from Brindisi he would have committed all manner of horrors? The man who at Brindisi ordered so many gallant and virtuous men to be executed, and whose wife's face was notoriously bespattered with the blood of men dying at his and her feet, would have spared none of us, especially as he was coming here much more angry with us than he had been with those whom he butchered there. But from this calamity Octavian delivered the Republic by his prudence in gathering a force of his own."

He went on to praise the Martian and the Fourth Legions for having declared for Octavian, and he congratulated Albinus for having refused to hand over Cisalpine Gaul to Antony who seemed, he said, to be behaving as though he were a king. "All slavery is miserable," he declared, "but to be a slave to a man who is profligate, immoral, effeminate, and never sober, would surely be intolerable. Indeed, on that day when Antony, in the sight of the Roman people, harangued the mob, naked, perfumed, and drunk, and tried to put a crown on his colleague's head, he lost his right to the Consulship and to his own freedom." He must never be allowed to assume the governorship of Cisalpine Gaul, "that province which is the flower of Italy, the bulwark of the Roman empire, the chief ornament of her dignity."

Cicero's son, Marcus, it should be mentioned, was now in Athens with Brutus, and, although only twenty-one years of age, was already a hard drinker and a disreputable character—a fact which Antony had not failed to tell the world. Cicero's nephew, too—the son of his brother Quintus—was a bad character, and had come under Antony's verbal lash; and now the orator attacked Antony for making such accusations, and asked how "this gladiator dared to put such things in writing." "He ought to be put to death," he exclaimed; "and what good man will not demand his execution, since on his death depends the safety and the life of every good man?"

He went on to describe how Antony had come into the Senate through the tunnel beneath the Capitol, and how he had then fled to Tivoli, after seeing to the distribution of the provincial governorships. "But now we plant our feet firmly on the ground," he cried, "and take possession of that liberty of which I have been not only the defender but even the saviour. For long I have borne our misfortunes without cowardice and not without dignity; but who can any more endure this most foul monster? What is there in Antony except lust and cruelty and licentiousness and audacity? Of these materials he is wholly made up; and are we to bear the shameful tyranny of this profligate robber? What crimes he has committed since the death of Cæsar! He has emptied his (Cæsar's) well-filled house, has pillaged his gardens, and has transferred to his own mansion all their ornaments. While carrying out two or three measures beneficial, I admit, to the Republic, he has made everything else subservient to his own gain: he has put up exemptions and annuities for sale, has released cities from their taxes, has freed provinces from subjection to the Roman empire, has restored exiles, has passed forged laws in the name of Cæsar," and so forth.

"And now," he continued, "when his fortunes are desperate, he has not diminished his audacity, nor, mad that he is, has ceased to proceed in his headlong career of fury. He is leading his mutilated army into Cisalpine Gaul, with one legion, and that, too, wavering. He is more like a matador than a commander, a gladiator rather than a general." His brother, Lucius, he said, is just as bad as himself; but the Romans, surely, will never admit them again into the city. Antony, he pointed out, would soon be hemmed in, attacked in the rear by Octavian, and in the front by Albinus. Now was the time to act.

"I entreat you," he cried to the senators, "seize this opportunity. You know the insolence of Antony, you know his friends, you know his whole household; and to be slaves to such lustful, wanton, debauched, profligate, drunken gamblers, would be infamous." Therefore, he proposed that the two Consuls-elect, Hirtius and Caius

Pansa, who would come into office on January 1st, should be empowered to make an end of Antony.

Having concluded this impassioned speech, every word of which betrayed his fear of Antony and his trembling eagerness to bring about his death, he left the Senate, and went to the Comitia, assembled in the Forum, where he delivered another furious oration, now known as the Fourth Philippic, in which he urged the crowd to declare Antony a public enemy, and to give their allegiance to himself, to Albinus, and to Octavian—that boy "whose actions belong to immortality, the word 'youth' applying only to his age." "Antony," he declared, "is not an enemy with whom it is possible to make peace: he is a savage beast; and since he has fallen into a pit, let him be buried in it! Crush him, as, by my diligence, Catiline was crushed!" The corollary, though unspoken, was clear: if Antony were not crushed Cicero's life would now be in danger, for his libels had been unpardonable.

On January 1st, 43 B.C., the new Consuls, Hirtius and Pansa, both Cæsarians who had joined Octavian's party, came into office; and on that day Cicero addressed his Fifth Philippic to the Senate, directing his aim mainly at Calenus who had defended Antony, and had later suggested that negotiations should be opened with him. That course, Cicero declared, would be madness, for Antony was a scoundrel, who would sell the whole Republic for money, in which nefarious business he was aided by his wife, Fulvia, who, herself, had held a very auction of provinces and realms, and she and he had collected so much money that, if it were available for distribution, there would not be a poor man in Rome.

He advised his hearers to put their trust fully in Octavian: "I venture to pledge my word for him to you and to the Roman People," he said. But upon Antony he called down the wrath of heaven, repeating once more a list of his supposed crimes. He declared, moreover, that Antony had sold the office of judge in the Roman courts to all sorts of men who supported him: "dancers, musicians, and, in fact, the whole troop of his boon-companions, have been pitchforked onto the bench, so that infamous men whom no one would care to have in his house have been made judges."

He told the Senate that on that famous day, September 1st, he had declined to attend the meeting because he knew that An-

tony was going to kill him. And now it was proposed to open negotiations with this inhuman monster! No, indeed!—he must not
be *asked* to retire from the borders of Cisalpine Gaul: he must be
compelled to do so. "We must reject the slow process of negotiations," he insisted. "With this man we must wage war—war, I
say, and that instantly."

To Cicero's great disappointment, nevertheless, a deputation
was sent to Antony, and two days later, on January 3rd, the
orator delivered his Sixth Philippic, this time to the Comitia in
the Forum, in which he repeated his abuse of Antony, and the
demand for war against him, calling him now not a human being
at all, but a sinister and fatal beast. Daily he became more intent
on overcoming the better judgment and consequent hesitancy of
the senators, who knew that Antony was not what Cicero declared
him to be, and who felt that the old orator, now in fear of his life,
was pursuing his personal quarrel to exorbitant lengths.

In the Seventh Philippic, addressed to the Senate, he attempted
to contradict a rumour that Antony was prepared to come to terms;
and he declared that, in any case, a scoundrel such as he would
never abide by such terms. "Beware lest you let this foul and
deadly beast escape," he cried. "I have at all times been an ad-
viser of peace," he added, "and, indeed, the whole of my career
has been passed in warding off the danger of war. Thus I have
arrived at the highest honours; yet I, a nursling of peace, do not
wish to have peace with Antony."

His passionate eloquence at last prevailed, and the Senate half-
heartedly authorized the new Consul Hirtius and Octavian to
march forth with the Martian and Fourth Legions and such other
troops as they could collect, so that by their display of force in
Antony's rear they might induce him to surrender. Pansa, the other
Consul, meanwhile remained in Rome with orders to try to recruit an army, either voluntarily or by conscription.[18] A week
later Hirtius and Octavian arrived outside Rimini, on the east
coast of Italy near the frontier of Cisalpine Gaul, where they
found that Antony was encamped at Bononia (Bologna), two days'
march to the north, while Albinus was at Mutina (Modena), a
day's march further back into Cisalpine Gaul.

[18] Cicero: *Ad Familiares*, xi, 8.

To their surprise it was seen that neither Albinus nor Antony seemed to have any desire to begin real hostilities. Antony was making some pretence of besieging Modena, and his outposts were close under its walls, behind which Albinus was casually preparing for the expected siege; but meanwhile negotiations were in progress between them, and Antony was offering terms to his opponent. Hirtius and Octavian thereupon pushed on as far as Forum Cornelii (Imola), a few miles south of Bologna, and there encamped, leaving Antony's force unmolested between them and Albinus. At the same time the delegates sent from Rome to treat with Antony had found him ready to avoid hostilities if possible, and were on their way back to the capital with his terms, which were that he would be willing to accept the governorship of Gaul Proper for five years in exchange for Cisalpine Gaul—a proposal indicating clearly enough that he did not feel sufficiently strong to fight Albinus on his front and Hirtius and Octavian in his rear, and preferred a temporary respite in quiet and interesting Gaul.

This news threw Cicero into a frenzy. Antony, now his deadly enemy, might escape, and come back to Rome at some future date to settle accounts with him, which meant the violent death of one or other of them. The Senate was inclining towards moderation —Calenus, in fact, was insisting on an amicable arrangement; and now that Octavian had left the city the few remaining friends of Antony were winning a daily increasing party to the side of peace. In a passion of anger and anxiety, therefore, he delivered his Eighth Philippic to the Senate, urging war, which, indeed, he declared had already begun.

Resorting now to the most outrageous falsehoods he said that Antony intended to massacre the people of Rome. "He promises our very houses to his band of robbers," he cried, "for he says he will divide the city amongst them; and he will give them any lands they desire. His officers are marking out for themselves the most beautiful houses, gardens, and estates at Frascati and elsewhere; and those most clownish of men—if, indeed, they are men and not animals—are borne along on their vain hopes as far as the Bay of Naples"—where Cicero's own favourite estate was situated.

How could Calenus suggest a peaceful agreement at such a time, he thundered? "Does he call slavery a desirable peace? Or is it because he expects to be a partner in Antony's dominion? When I was a boy I was acquainted with the father of Calenus, who was a man of strict virtue and wisdom; and I remember that he used to give the highest praise to the man who killed Tiberius Gracchus. But Calenus himself would not have approved of his father's opinion. Yet surely whatever is rotten in the body of the Republic ought to be cut off so that the whole may be saved."

In conclusion Cicero proposed that all the soldiers serving under Antony should be given until the end of February to leave him and to come home, failing which they should be regarded as outlaws; and he implied that Antony himself should be either put to death or sent into exile.

The Ninth Philippic followed shortly afterwards, in which he urged again "that the audacity of Antony be branded with infamy." But a few days later news was received more or less simultaneously in Rome and in the military camps in the north that Brutus had quietly collected a force in Greece and had suddenly marched into Macedonia, of which province Caius Antonius, Antony's brother, had taken up the governorship. Caius had been forced to retire to Apollonia on the Adriatic coast, and one of his legions had surrendered to Cicero's son, Marcus, who was serving under Brutus. A force of cavalry, too, which was marching through Greece on its way to join Dolabella in his new Syrian province had surrendered to Brutus.

This startling news put a new, or, rather, a stronger complexion on matters, for now the assassins of Cæsar, as represented by Brutus in Greece and Albinus in Cisalpine Gaul, had joined fully in the fight; and more than ever Octavian's party was linked with the murderers of the man whose heir he was. To Antony the tidings were almost like a death-knell, for his right flank would now be attacked as well as his front and rear; to Cicero they were like the trump of victory; but to Octavian they must have been a source of anxiety, for he could see his own cause soon swamped in that of the conspirators.

Pansa at once summoned the Senate, to move a vote of thanks to Brutus; but Calenus urged that Brutus had acted without proper authority. Thereupon Cicero made a speech, which is known as the Tenth Philippic, wherein he spoke of his "excessive delight" at the news, and his disgust with the sturdy Calenus. "Why does Calenus alone oppose the actions of Brutus and his troops—men whom we ought almost to worship?" he demanded. "The glory of Brutus is divine and immortal—such patience; O God, such moderation; such tranquillity under injury! I saw him myself when he was leaving Italy for Greece; and O, what a sight was that!—heartrending not only to men but to the very waves and shores. The saviour of his country departing, while its destroyers were remaining there! But Brutus bided his time, and when he saw that Macedonia would be a refuge for Antony in defeat, he invaded that country, and thus hemmed him in."

"Macedonia is now ours," he went on. "The legions there are all devoted to us, and, above all, Brutus is ours—a man born for the Republic by some special destiny. But I see what Calenus means: he is afraid that those of Cæsar's ex-soldiers who are on our side will not endure the thought of Brutus having an army. Yet what is the difference between Brutus and Albinus?— what reason is there that the former should be an object of suspicion to these men who are already pledged to help the latter? The ex-soldiers were the first to put themselves under the authority of Octavian; afterwards the Martian legion checked Antony's mad progress; then the Fourth Legion crushed it. Being thus condemned by his own troops he burst his way into Cisalpine Gaul, pursued by the armies of Octavian and Hirtius; and afterwards Pansa recruited more reinforcements against him here. Why then should there be any objection because the army of Brutus has thrown its weight into the scale, to assist us in overwhelming these pests?"

In February, further news was received from the east, disquieting this time to Cicero, and cheering to Antony, Dolabella had passed safely through Greece, and had reached Smyrna, where Trebonius, the man who had detained Antony in conversation while Cæsar was murdered, was governor. Dolabella had requested permission to pass through his province on his way to Syria; but Trebonius had refused, whereupon Dolabella had surprised the city by night, and had captured and killed him.

Calenus agreed that Dolabella had been wrong to do this, es-

pecially as the report stated that Trebonius had been murdered under revolting circumstances; and he was the first to censure him.
Cicero then delivered his Eleventh Philippic, in which he proposed
that Cassius, the original leader of the plot against Cæsar, who
had been given the province of Cyrene, but was claiming Syria,
should be ordered to bring Dolabella to justice. Cassius was at that
time in Palestine at the head of no less than eleven legions, collected
from all the provinces round about, and even from Egypt where
Antony had allowed troops to remain to protect Cleopatra's throne;
and it was felt that he would have no difficulty in avenging Trebonius.

Dolabella was Cicero's son-in-law, of whom the orator had
often spoken in terms of superlative esteem; but now he began his
speech by saying that "Dolabella and Antony are the very blackest
and foulest monsters that have ever lived since the birth of man—
unprecedented, unheard of, savage, barbarous." Describing the
murder of Trebonius, he stated that Dolabella "had examined
him with scourges and tortures for two days as to where the public
money was concealed, and then had cut off his head, which was
carried about, fixed on a spear, while his body was dragged through
the streets and thrown into the sea." The report was probably quite
true, we may suppose, for Dolabella was a young villain with
whom Antony had made a friendly compact only out of dire necessity; but Trebonius, it has to be remembered, was also a murderer, and deserves little pity beyond that evoked by his sufferings. Indeed, a letter which he had just received from Cicero,[19]
wherein a gloating reference was again made to "the magnificent
banquet of the Ides of March," introduces a dark hue of ferocity
into our picture of him which goes far to obscure any appeal in it
to our compassion.

Cicero then made his proposal in regard to Cassius, but opinion
was much divided in regard to the man who had originated the
conspiracy against Cæsar; and Cicero could not well insist, "for,"
he said, "the mention of his glorious achievements is not yet acceptable to every one," and particularly not to Cæsar's ex-soldiers.
"But I think," he added, "that we ought not to consider these
veterans so much: rather we should look to the new recruits." Most

[19] Cicero: *Ad Familiares,* x, 28.

of the veterans, indeed, were heart and soul for Antony because of this very alliance of Octavian with the assassins.

In March, when spring had come, Antony began seriously to lay siege to Modena, and when news reached Rome that Albinus was hard pressed, the Senate again suggested that negotiations should be opened. Cicero's Twelfth Philippic was delivered in opposition to this move. "What terms can be possibly offered to this polluted and impious traitor?" he asked. "Are we to give him Gaul and an army? That would not be making peace but deferring war."

In the end the suggestion was dropped, and the Consul Pansa set out with the four legions he had recruited, to join Hirtius and Octavian. Antony now realized his great danger, for Modena held out against him stoutly; and when Hirtius and Octavian sent him a message to report the coming of that deputation which had since been abandoned, he wrote to them expressing his willingness for an accommodation, and telling them that they were acting against the true interests of the State in allying themselves with Cæsar's murderers. The letter, a very sincere and straightforward document, written in the bitterness of his heart, was forwarded to Rome, and Cicero thereupon delivered his Thirteenth Philippic, imploring the senators not to come to terms with Antony and his companions —men "whose breath reeks of wine," nor with Fulvia, "who is not only most avaricious but also most cruel."

He then read certain paragraphs from Antony's letter, which were as follows:—

"When I heard of the death of Trebonius," Antony wrote, "I was not more rejoiced than grieved. It was a matter of proper rejoicing that a wicked man had paid the penalty due to the ashes of the most illustrious Cæsar, and that the divine power of the gods had been manifest before a year was out by the chastisement of the assassins already inflicted in some cases and impending in others. That Dolabella should have been pronounced an enemy because he has put an assassin to death, and that Trebonius, the son of a fool, should appear dearer to the Roman people than Cæsar, are circumstances to be lamented." Here Cicero put in the comment that the father of Trebonius was no fool, but a most worthy man; and, anyhow, he asked, how could Antony reproach any one with mean birth when he himself had had children by a freedwoman, Fadia, his first love?

"But it is the bitterest thing of all," the letter went on, "that you, Hirtius, who used to be marked out for Cæsar's kindness, should have deplored the death of one of his murderers. [20] And you, too, Octavian, my boy, you who owe everything to his name, are taking pains to have Dolabella condemned, and to effect the release of this murderer, Albinus, from my blockade, in order that Cassius and Brutus may become as powerful as possible once more in Rome."

Then came a number of disconnected quotations, amongst which appeared the contemptuous remark: "You have the defeated Cicero for a general"; and on this the orator's amusingly conceited comment was: "I do not mind his calling me 'defeated,' for it is my fate that I can be neither victorious nor defeated without the Republic being so at the same time." These quotations are summed up in Antony's indignant words: "You have enlisted my soldiers and many veterans under the pretence of intending the destruction of those men who murdered Cæsar; and then, contrary to what they expected, you have led them on to attack their general and their former comrades."

"But consider, both of you," the letter proceeded, "whether it is more becoming for you to seek to avenge the death of Trebonius or that of Cæsar, and whether it is more reasonable for you to meet me in battle—in order that the old cause of the Pompeians and conservatives, which has so frequently had its throat cut, may be revived once more by you—or for us to agree together so as not to be a laughing-stock to our enemies, men who will count the destruction of either you or me gain to them. Are we to provide them with a spectacle which, so far, Fortune herself has taken care to avoid? —the spectacle of two armies, which belong to one body, fighting each other with Cicero as the master of the show, a man who has won both of you with the same flattery as that with which he used to boast that he had deceived Cæsar."

"However," he added, "I am quite resolved to brook no more insults either to myself or to my friends, nor to desert that democratic party which Pompey hated. If the immortal gods assist me,

---

[20] The last words of this sentence have been added to fill a lacuna.

as I have faith that they will, I shall continue on my way in happiness; but if another fate awaits me, I have already a foretaste of satisfaction in the certainty of your punishment. In conclusion, this is the sum of my feelings: I will forget your past insults if you will forget that you offered them, and if you are prepared to unite with me in avenging Cæsar's death."

Early in April news was received that Caius Antonius, Antony's brother, had surrendered to Brutus in Macedonia; but Brutus himself was in some difficulties, for he had very little money at his disposal, and was already exhausted by his exertions in the field, and longed to be back amongst his books in Athens if not in Rome. Moreover, he had had a long talk with his prisoner, Caius, and had been greatly disturbed by what he had said. [21] Caius had told him that Cicero was not to be trusted to bring peace to distracted Rome, but only everlasting war between the democrats and republicans; and he had pointed out how honest and simple a man Antony was, and how willing to make that peace which Cicero and Octavian were jeopardising. As a result of these talks, Brutus not only gave Caius his liberty, but joined with him in writing to Cicero proposing a general armistice. Cicero, of course, was furious and wrote very sharply to Brutus, telling him that energetic prosecution of the war, and not sentimental talk of peace, was the thing to be desired.

Meanwhile, Antony's letter to his opponents had been ignored, and in desperation he decided to hurry south and attack Pansa before he could effect a juncture with Hirtius and Octavian. He therefore left his brother, Lucius, to keep the latter engaged, while he himself secretly marched off with the Second and Thirty-Fifth Legions and a body of cavalry to waylay Pansa. But his move was discovered, and the Martian legion was dispatched to meet and reinforce Pansa, with the result that when Antony made his attack he found himself fighting not only the newly recruited legions but also this legion of war-tried soldiers who were thirsting for revenge upon him for the executions at Brindisi.

A fierce battle ensued [22] in which Pansa was mortally wounded, and the Martian legion was routed, the whole enemy force thereafter making its way in disorder towards Modena. Hirtius there-

---

[21] Cicero: *Ad Brutum,* ii, v.
[22] The battle is described in Cicero: *Ad Familiares,* x, 30.

upon marched to the relief of the fugitives, leaving Octavian to defend the camp against Lucius, in which undertaking he was entirely successful since the attack was no more than a feint to cover Antony's movements.

Antony, then, beating off a flank attack by Hirtius, marched back to his main army before the walls of Modena, more depressed by his losses than pleased by his success, but thinking that Hirtius and Octavian would take some time to collect the scattered remnant of Pansa's legions and to reorganize themselves. Hirtius, however, decided to attack again at once, in an attempt to break through Antony's army and to join forces with Albinus in Modena.

On April 21st, 43 b.c., Hirtius at the head of the Fourth Legion advanced on Antony's camp which was defended by the Larks (the Fifth Legion), and at the same time Albinus made a sortie from Modena. It was a day of alternating hope and despair for Antony, who rushed from one danger-point to another, cheering on his men, and exposing himself with his usual recklessness in battle; but at last the Larks were victorious on both fronts, and Hirtius was killed—a fact of which Antony, however, was unaware, as also he was of the seriousness of Pansa's wounds. Octavian then hastened to the rescue, but though he fought with personal gallantry, and was involved in the thick of the battle, he was driven off by the Larks; and at the end of the day both he and Albinus retired, leaving the sweating and exhausted Antony with his camp itself intact but with a sadly depleted force, the slaughter on either side having been terrible. There was no singing of the Larks at that sunset.

During the night Antony counted his dead and reviewed the situation. He did not know how greatly the enemy had also suffered, and, as has been said, he was unaware that Octavian was now their only surviving general, Hirtius being dead and Pansa dying. He was hopeless of victory and believed that next day Hirtius, Octavian and Albinus, acting together, would overwhelm him; and therefore in the darkness he gave the order for a retreat towards the west. Lepidus, the man who had helped him to keep order in Rome after Cæsar's murder, and who was now governor of Gallia Narbonensis (Southern France) was apparently a staunch adherent to his party, in spite of Cicero's attempt to terrorize him; [23] and An-

---

[23] Cicero: *Ad Familiares*, x, 27.

tony felt that his only hope lay in joining forces with him, now that Macedonia, on the east, was in the hands of Brutus.

Thus, on the following day Octavian found his enemy's camp deserted, and at once joined hands with Albinus. Antony and his shattered army had silently marched away.

CHAPTER XIII

Antony's Alliance with Lepidus and then with Octavian; and the Turning of the Tables upon Cicero.

43 B.C.

THE news of the battle and of Antony's precipitate retreat caused the most profound sensation in Rome. Cicero, of course, was overjoyed. He did not suppose for a moment that there was any chance of his enemy escaping: Octavian and Albinus would hunt him down, surely, without any great difficulty. The republican party was enthusiastic, and a crowd of its supporters congregated around Cicero's house to give him an ovation. When he appeared before them, smiling, bowing, and waving his hand, they insisted upon carrying him through the Forum and up to the Capitol and back, cheering him and hailing him as their rightful leader. It was the greatest hour of his life, the crown of his career; and as he stood in the Temple of Jupiter Capitolinus, returning thanks to the gods, the tears of pride flooding his eyes, and his vain old heart thrilling to the chant of triumph, he must have been completely unaware of the inherent dangers of his position. Had any soothsayer told him then that this high tide of his destiny was to be followed immediately by the ebb which was to carry him headlong to his pitiful doom, he would have laughed at him.

He was so transported by his own success and by the triumph of his party that he began on the instant to turn from his alliance with Octavian. The heir of Cæsar had served his purpose, and it only remained now to take the young man by the shoulders and to propel him with benevolent but determined hands into that obscurity from which he had come. The triumph, in Cicero's opinion, was the triumph of himself and of the cause of those republican conspirators who had destroyed Cæsar. Antony, Cæsar's representative and political successor, was in flight; and Octavian, Cæsar's adopted son, must be sent about his business with no more than polite thanks for his aid. Rome, he felt, belonged now to himself, the wonderful Cicero, to Decimus Brutus Albinus, to Cassius, to Brutus, to the whole "gallant band" of Cæsar's assassins, and to the faithful republican party. The democrats were done for: there was no place for them nor for Cæsarians of any kind, whether they were adherents of Antony or of Octavian.

At Cicero's instigation, unprecedented thanksgiving-festivals were decreed, and the highest honours were voted to Albinus whose promotion to the position of Commander-in-Chief of all the Roman armies was at once proposed. But for Octavian no such rewards were forthcoming. "Practically every advantage," says Dion Cassius, "which had been given to Octavian at Antony's expense was now voted to others at Octavian's expense; and they even undertook to overthrow him, setting his supporters at variance with one another and with him." [1]

But if Octavian's democratic friends were thus slighted by the triumphant republicans, Antony's were openly insulted, and went in danger of their lives. Julia, his now elderly mother, and Fulvia, his violent wife, were doubtless hooted and jeered at; and the five children of his household must have been in danger of rough handling. Four of these children, it will be recalled, were Clodius and Clodia, Fulvia's little son and daughter by the late Clodius; Antonia, Antony's daughter by the divorced Antonia; and Antyllus, Antony's son by Fulvia. The fifth was a baby in arms, the little Julus Antonius, a second son presented by Fulvia to Antony. His prominent supporters, too, such as Calenus, were threatened with a terrible doom. Yet it is evident that a great part of the mob was still loyal to him; [2] and, indeed, the Senate itself was not wholly with Cicero, nor in these first days of excitement could they make up their minds to pronounce the death-penalty upon Antony.

This hestitation induced the orator to deliver his Fourteenth Philippic, the last of the furious series. "You vote a Thanksgiving,"

---

[1] Dion Cassius, xlvi, 40. Ferrero (*Greatness and Decline of Rome*) does not agree that Octavian was already cold-shouldered; but I do not think that there can be the least doubt about it.

[2] Cicero: *Philippic xiv*, vi.

he protested to the senators, "and yet you do not name Antony an enemy. O, very pleasing indeed to the immortal gods will our Thanksgivings be with this omission, very pleasing to the spirits of our fallen soldiers! Antony, the foulest of all bandits, is still in arms against us, and, although hastening to his destruction, still threatens all of us. Remember, I entreat you, what we have been fearing during these few days: which of you have been able to look at your children or your wives without weeping?—which of you have been able to bear the sight of your homes?—when all of us were dreading a miserable death at Antony's hands, or meditating an ignominious flight. And shall we hesitate to condemn him now that he is in our power?"

He implored them to listen to his advice, reminding them of his right to speak as the hero of the hour. "Yesterday," he said, "the Roman People carried me in triumph to the Capitol; and in my opinion it was a just, a genuine triumph, for if at a time of such general rejoicing they address their congratulations to one individual, surely that is a proof of his worth. It is indeed against my will that I remind you of this, but my indignation makes me boastful, which is very contrary to my usual habit."

He then went on to say that lying rumors had been spread that he intended to make himself Dictator. "The idea of anyone being so wicked as to invent such a tale!" he cried. "Am I, who defeated and overthrew and crushed Catiline, a likely man myself to become a tyrant?" All he wanted, he declared, was to see the war continued to its end—the death of Antony. "Remember that, last December, I was the main cause of our recovering our freedom; that from January until this very hour I have never ceased to watch over the Republic; that it has been by my letters and my exhortations that all men in every part of the empire have been aroused to the protection of our country; and that I have always called Antony a public enemy, and have been opposed to any pretence of a peace which would be fatal to us."

He next turned to the praising of the victors, speaking first of Albinus, to whose succour the others had gone, then of the dead Hirtius, next of the wounded Pansa, and finally of Octavian, but using no superlatives in reference to the last-named such as he had lavished upon him in his precious speeches. And in conclusion he asked that a magnificent monument should be erected to the Martian Legion which had deserted Antony, and that the services of the Fourth Legion should also be recognized although its casualties had been slight.

Not long after the delivery of this speech, however, came the disconcerting news that Pansa was dead, that Albinus, unaccountably delayed, had marched away in pursuit of Antony only after the latter had had at least two days' start, and that Octavian had remained at Bologna, having been unwilling, or having failed to persuade his men, to take to the highroad. It looked as though Antony had made good his escape, and Cicero was deeply mortified to find that his pæans of triumph had been sung too soon.

Antony, indeed, had got clean away. Marching with his brother Lucius at the head of what remained of the Larks or Fifth Legion, the Second and Thirty-Fifth Legions, the Gallic and other cavalry, and the veterans of Cæsar, he had taken the road north-westwards to Parma, which he reached on April 23rd. The town shut its gates to him, and as a punishment he pillaged it, some of the inhabitants being killed in the confusion. He then moved on to Placentia (Piacenza), and thence through Comeliomagus (Cicognola) to Dertona (Tortona) which he reached on the 28th. The road he had taken was the main inland route to Gaul, and had led him in a wide arc into the mountainous and desolate country behind Genoa. Now he had to march southwards and westwards and to cross the Maritime Alps, so that he might reach the coast and proceed along what is today the Italian Riviera; and it was here that the most perilous part of the journey began.

No army would have followed him into those rocky passes amidst the barren hills had the troops not loved and trusted him. He explained his plans to them: after crossing the mountains they would make their way beside the sea, through Nicaea (Nice), Antipolis (Antibes), and the other towns of the modern French Riviera, to Forum Julii (Fréjus, near St. Raphæl), near which city Lepidus was stationed with seven of Cæsar's old legions. Lepidus had been Antony's friend in the past, and even if he were now to wish to declare for the other side, it was probable that his legions would join up with Antony whom they had learnt to love in the wars in Gaul, and who had such a large force of Cæsar's ex-soldiers with him. Possibly the troops under Plancus, another of Cæsar's old generals, and brother of one of Antony's officers, who were now in the neighbourhood of Lugdunum (Lyons), would also join with them; and thus with an invincible army they would march back to Italy and carry all before them. Everything depended on the attitude of Lepidus and his men; but this risk Antony's battered and weary troops were willing to take, and with dogged courage they began, on April 30th, their ascent into the mountains.

"Antony in this march was overtaken by distresses of every kind," writes Plutarch, [3] "and the worst of all was hunger. But it was his character in calamities to be better then than at anytime; and in misfortune he was most nearly a virtuous man. It is common enough for people when they fall into great disasters to discern what is right and what they ought to do; but there are few who in such extremities have the strength to obey their judgment, and a good many are so weak as to give way to their habits all the more, and are incapable of using their brains. Antony, on this occasion, was a most wonderful example to his soldiers. He, who had just quitted so much luxury and sumptuous living, made no difficulty now of drinking foul water and feeding on wild fruits and roots. Nay, it is related that they ate the very bark of trees, and, in passing over the Alps, lived upon creatures which no one before had ever been willing to touch."

He refused to shave or to have his hair trimmed so long as his men were in danger; and thus dirty and unkempt he trudged along all day, keeping step to the marching-songs of his dust-covered Larks, and eating with them as they sat under the stars around their camp-fires at night. It was urgently necessary that they should force their pace, in order to keep well ahead of the pursuing army; and there must have been many lamed stragglers, or men wounded in the recent fighting, who were left by the roadside, being unable to keep up with the hurrying host. On the other hand, however, some new recruits or useful camp-followers were collected on the way by the commandeering of gangs of slaves who chanced to be working in the territory through which they passed; and, indeed, as Albinus reported to Rome, [4] "Antony snapped up every kind of human being he came across."

[3] Plutarch: *Antony*.   [4] Cicero: *Ad Familiares*, xi, 10.

At last the weary and hungry troops came streaming down the mountain slopes to Vada Sabbatia (Vado Sabazia) on the sea-coast; and here, to Antony's joy, he was met by a large force of Cæsar's ex-soldiers of the old Seventh, Eighth, and Ninth Legions, who had been re-enlisted by one of his officers, Ventidius Bassus, too late, however, to help him at Modena. Upon hearing of his retreat these men had bravely marched by the lower route to join him, thus displaying a devotion to him and to his cause, even in defeat, which speaks highly for his personal character.

Being thus reinforced, Antony sent his brother Lucius ahead with the cavalry to Fréjus, which he reached on May 8th; and he himself meanwhile marched along the rocky coast with the infantry, arriving at Fréjus on May 15th, a little over three weeks after the departure from Modena. Here, to his dismay, he was told that Lepidus, on whose friendship he was relying, and who was encamped about a day's march inland, was showing every sign of regarding him as an enemy. As a matter of fact, Albinus had written to Cicero immediately on discovering that Antony had marched away, saying: "I beg you to send a despatch to Lepidus in order to prevent such a weathercock as he is from having a chance to ally himself with Antony and renew the war."[5] Cicero had done so, and had demanded this general's loyalty in such stern terms that Lepidus had decided to support the republican party, more particularly since Antony appeared to be on the run. Plancus, also, was said to be definitely hostile, and, though Antony did not know it, had just written to Cicero,[6] saying that he and Lepidus had agreed to work together to crush the fugitive.

At the same time Antony began to hear something of the movements of Albinus. Octavian had undoubtedly caused this general the greatest concern by refusing to join with him in the pursuit, and, actually, Albinus had written bitterly to Cicero,[7] saying: "If Octavian had been willing to listen to me and to cross the mountains with me I would have been able to corner Antony, and make an end of him; but Octavian is no more willing to take orders from others than his army is willing to take orders from *him*." Albinus had finally abandoned the attempt to catch up with the retreating enemy, and had

[5] Cicero: *Ad Familiares*, xi, 9.   [6] *Ibid.*, x, 11.
[7] *Ibid.*, xi, 10.

headed inland for the Alpes Graiæ (the Little St. Bernard) or the Cottiæ (Mont Cenis), with the idea of joining hands with Plancus who was moving along the valley of the Isère towards him.

Matters looked very bad, and Antony decided that the best thing to do would be to march his men close up to the army of Lepidus and to encourage them to renew old friendships with the soldiers of Cæsar now serving therein, particularly with those of the Tenth Legion who had known Antony well in the Gallic wars and remembered him as their beloved Cæsar's closest and most trusted friend. After a rest of a day or two at Fréjus, therefore, he made the journey inland, and pitched his camp on the near side of a little brook called the Argenteus, on the far side of which the army of Lepidus was entrenched; but whereas Lepidus took the precaution of keeping his troops behind their earthworks as though expecting a siege, Antony boldly displayed his desire for friendly overtures by telling his men not to dig themselves in, but to try to fraternise with the soldiers on the other bank of the stream.

The orders of Lepidus, however, were strict; and for more than a week Antony's efforts were frustrated. At length in despair he went down to the edge of the little river, and began to harangue the soldiers on the other side, who crowded together to listen to him. He had not yet shaved or cut his hair; and these men stared in amazement at the well-remembered, mighty figure of their old commander, who looked like a tragic Hercules as he stood before them, with his unkempt beard, his untidy locks, his travel-stained clothes, and his battered armour over which he had flung a dark cloak as a kind of symbol of mourning. Antony, as has already been said, was something of an actor; but the rôle he was now playing was so true a representation of his terrible plight that his sincerity was not in question. No sooner, however, had the matter been reported to Lepidus than he gave orders for the bugles to be blown so that Antony's voice might not be heard; and presently, with a gesture of despair, the unfortunate speaker was obliged to abandon his efforts and return to his tent.

That night, however, two soldiers, presumably of the Tenth Legion, disguised themselves as women, and, coming across the stream, managed to obtain an interview with Antony, who told them an indignant story of how he had attempted to carry on Cæsar's work, how he had wanted to bring the assassins to justice, how Octavian had allied himself with the murderers of the great Dictator, and how, after the defeat at Modena, Antony had felt that his only refuge was with the troops of Lepidus, Cæsar's and his own old comrades. The two men then revealed to him the fact that the Tenth Legion at any rate, and probably the rest of the army, were ready to kill Lepidus and put themselves under Antony's command, but that their desires were held in check by those of their officers whose sympathies were on the other side. They advised him to attack the camp next day, and promised that they would do all they could to stir up a mutiny.

To Antony, their message was like the voice of the immortal gods: it was like a repeal of his death-sentence; and with joy in his heart he sent them back to their fellows, telling them to do no injury to Lepidus, and promising that on the morrow he would ford the stream, and, even though it should cost him his life, demand an interview with their general.

He was as good as his word. Next morning, at the head of his men, he waded across the water, not knowing in the least whether an arrow or a javelin would end there and then his troubles; but before he had splashed his way half across the brook he saw the soldiers on the other side gathering to welcome him, holding out their hands to him, and breaking down the palisades which had been set up to defend the bank against attack. A few moments later he was in their midst, and he and his men were being hailed as long-lost friends.

Lepidus was in bed at the time, but without waiting to put on his general's apparel, he hastened to the spot and threw his arms around the huge and bearded Antony. It would seem that he had been wavering for several days, but now the unanimity of his troops, and the realization that he would probably be murdered if he did not recognize the claims of Antony, had decided him. Antony saw at once that the camp and the whole army was his, yet he treated Lepidus with the utmost civility, calling him "Father" when he addressed him—for he was an elderly man—and insisting that he should retain the chief command of the united forces.

The jollification which followed was marred by one tragic incident. A certain officer, named Laterensis, had done his best during these last few days to keep Lepidus and his army faithful to the republican cause; and now when he saw Antony acclaimed he drew his sword and killed himself in their presence.

Subsequent events moved along an almost inevitable course. Lepidus at once wrote an apologetic letter to the Senate saying naïvely that pity for Antony had been too much for himself and his soldiers; and when this horrifying message was received in Rome in the early days of June, Cicero voiced the consternation of his party by demanding that he should be declared a public enemy. Lepidus, however, had many friends in high places: his wife was the daughter of Servilia, and was thus sister of Brutus and of Tertia, the wife of Cassius; and he had a brother, moreover, in the Senate who was a faithful supporter of the republicans. Thus it was not until the end of June that Lepidus was condemned—his brother being one of those who voted for this measure, and not until the middle of July that he and his army received the notification of the fact.

Meanwhile Decimus Brutus Albinus had joined hands with Plancus at Grenoble, and they were thus in command of an army as big as that of Antony and Lepidus. From Rome the worried Cicero sent express messengers to Brutus in Macedonia and to Cassius in Syria, ordering them to march home to Italy as quickly as possible; and Sextus Pompeius, the son of Pompey the Great, was given command of the Roman fleets. Sextus was then a man of thirty-two years of age, who had maintained an independent fighting-force in Spain during the long period of exile which had followed the death of his father, but had been pardoned by Antony after Cæsar's murder, and had more recently been invited back to Rome by Cicero.

Octavian was still remaining inactive in Cisalpine Gaul, having made no move since the battle of Modena; but Cicero now cunningly proposed that he should be given the nominal command of the republican armies, so that the various legions which had sentimental associations with the late Cæsar should feel that they still had Cæsar's heir at their head in spite of the fact that they were no longer serving the cause of the democratic party. The power of Octavian's name as the Dictator's heir was immensely valuable to the republicans in their struggle with Antony; and

CICERO

Capitol Museum, Rome

CLEOPATRA

British Museum

Cicero, in the altered circumstances, was not prepared yet to relinquish the use of it, much as he wished now to be rid of the tiresome young man himself.

Cicero, though painfully anxious, had no reason to despair. Apart from Octavian, Albinus had ten legions; Plancus, now linked with Albinus, had five legions; Asinius Pollio, governor of Spain, who seemed to be loyal to the republicans, had three legions; Brutus in Macedonia had raised some seven legions; Cassius in Syria had at least ten legions; and there were other legions in North Africa and elsewhere who were apparently on their side. Nearly forty legions, in fact, were at the disposal of the republicans, against the fourteen under the command of Antony and Lepidus, and the two which were with Dolabella in Syria.

But Brutus did not obey the orders to come to Rome. He was not a man of war, and, anyhow, he had no wish to have any dealings with Octavian: he was willing to join forces with Albinus, his fellow conspirator, but not with Cæsar's heir. He preferred to await the coming of Cassius. Cassius, however, had his own troubles to delay his return. Dolabella had been trying to wrest the province of Syria from him, and, with his two legions and many local levies, was at Laodicea (Ladikiyeh) on the Syrian coast, not far south of Antioch. However, at about this time, Cassius overwhelmed him, and Dolabella brought his stormy life to a close by killing himself, after which Cassius began his slow march towards Italy.

Octavian's attitude towards the republicans, however, gradually changed during this period of his idleness in Cisalpine Gaul. He realized that he was tolerated by his soldiers solely because he was the Dictator's heir, and he saw that the republicans were only using him to retain the loyalty of Cæsar's old legions. More and more he disliked the thought of being allied with the Dictator's assassins; more and more he mistrusted Cicero. A story was current in Rome that he, Octavian, had treacherously killed Hirtius at Modena, stabbing him from behind in the thick of the fight, and that he had poisoned Pansa. Tales of this kind [8] must have seemed to him to have been invented by Cicero's party to discredit him.

He began to wonder whether he were not on the wrong side, whether, in fact, he would not be in a more dignified position if he

[8] Suetonius: *Augustus*, xi, xii.

were to make his peace with Antony, who was, in any case, still so formidable. Some of the troops who had fought under him at Modena came from the town of Nursia (Norcia), between Rome and Cisalpine Gaul; and the townspeople had there erected a monument to their fallen comrades, bearing an inscription which said that they had died in the cause of liberty. Octavian now asked himself whether the cause of liberty had indeed been promoted by this battle; and, deciding, in his new temper, that it had not, he sent orders to these Nursians to obliterate the inscription. [9] Then, when Lepidus privately wrote to him suggesting an alliance, he made up his mind to drop Cicero and the republicans at the first opportunity. The decision was rank treachery, but to us it is understandable and can be excused to some extent on the grounds that he was still a boy, and that an eleventh-hour recantation was better than the pursuing of a course forced upon him at a time of great danger to himself.

The two Consuls, Hirtius and Pansa, being dead Octavian now conceived the idea of having himself made Consul for the remainder of the current year, there being more than one precedent for the attaining of that position before the prescribed age; and a deputation of his officers thereupon went to Rome to demand the Consulship for him. Cicero had expected to be asked to accept a second Consulship, but this was not to the taste of Octavian, who proposed therefore that the other Consul should be his cousin, Quintus Pedius, one of Cæsar's grandnephews who had been remembered in his will, but who, being a timid man and desirous of keeping out of trouble's way, had handed over his share to Octavian, saying that he had enough money of his own. Pedius was popular with the mob, because in 48 B.C., he had brought about the death of Milo, the man who had killed Clodius, the People's idol. Milo had gone into exile after the murder of Clodius, but had afterwards returned to Italy at the head of a band of outlaws; and Pedius had been instrumental in destroying him, thereby winning the approval of the rabble.

The republicans, however, could not tolerate the idea of Cæsar's two grandnephews being Consuls, and Octavian therefore marched his troops to Rome to make his demands in person. Cicero, of course, was distracted; and when the young man entered the city, and, after

[9] Suetonius: *Augustus*, xii.

a dramatic and public reunion with his mother, Atia, and his half-sister, Octavia, held a reception of his supporters, the orator refused at first to pay his respects to him. At last, however, he called upon him, whereat Octavian made the cold remark that Cicero was the very last of his supposed friends to do so. On August 19th the boy was elected Consul with his cousin Quintus Pedius as his colleague; and thereupon [10] the heart-broken Cicero retired to his country house at Frascati. The bright-hued bubble of his dream of personal power and glory had burst.

At about the same time the legions which Cicero had summoned home from North Africa arrived at the capital, having disembarked at Ostia, the port of Rome; and these men, being old soldiers of Cæsar, joined with Octavian's own forces in demanding that he should take a strong attitude against the republicans and the conspirators, and in begging him to ally himself with Antony. Thereupon he felt the time had come for him to declare himself as a democrat and as the Dictator's avenger; and he immediately forced through the Senate a bill repealing the Act of Oblivion, and imposing the punishment of exile and confiscation of their property upon the assassins—Brutus, Cassius, Albinus, and all the others. It was a complete democratic and Cæsarian coup, and the party of the republicans collapsed.

Pollio, on hearing of the edict, at once placed his three legions from Spain at the disposal of Antony and Lepidus. Plancus followed suit, and handed over three of his five legions. The ten legions of Albinus deserted him, four of them going to Antony and six to Octavian. Thus Antony and Lepidus suddenly found themselves in command of twenty-four legions and at least ten thousand auxiliary cavalry.

Albinus, exiled, and deserted by all but ten men, fled into the mountains disguised as a Gaul, cursing Octavian who had so suddenly betrayed him; but it was not long before a brigand chieftain captured him and his party, and sent a message to Antony to know what he should do with his important prisoner. Antony had for long determined to hound every one of the assassins to death, and for Albinus in particular he had no mercy in his heart—the man who had so infamously coaxed Cæsar to come to the Senate to be killed,

[19] The exact date is not known, but I think it must have been at about this time.

and who afterwards had caused Antony such miseries by resisting his
claims to the governorship of Cisalpine Gaul. He therefore sent
back word that the prisoner should be killed; but when Albinus was
informed of his fate and was told to prepare to die the wretched man
lost his nerve and burst into loud lamentations, whereat one of his
faithful officers, Helvius Blasio by name, set him an example in
fortitude by quietly committing suicide before his eyes. An hour or
so later a messenger was on his way to Antony carrying Albinus's
head wrapped up in a parcel.

At the end of September Antony and Lepidus began their march
back towards Italy with seventeen legions, the others having been
left to garrison Spain and Gaul; and they sent messengers on ahead
to Octavian to tell him that they were prepared to make an alliance
with him, apparently on condition that he showed his good faith
by causing the Senate to annul the decrees by which they had been
made public enemies. This was done, Octavian's soldiers, in fact,
demanding it [11] out of their love for Antony; and a meeting was arranged which was to take place on a tiny island at the confluence of
the rivers Rhenus (Reno) and Lavinius (Lavino), not far from
Bologna.

Octavian, who arrived first at the rendez-vous, took every precaution against treachery. He built two bridges, the one linking the
island with the eastern bank of the river where his troops were encamped, and the other joining it to the western bank, where Antony's
men were to be quartered; while on the island itself he erected a tent
in which the terms of the alliance could be discussed. Messengers
passing to and fro between him and Antony effected an arrangement
as to procedure: Antony, Octavian, and Lepidus would leave their
troops at a little distance and would each advance to the water's
edge with a bodyguard of three hundred cavalry, after which
Octavian from the one side would cross the bridge onto the island
unattended, and from the opposite side Antony and Lepidus, separ-
ately and alone, would cross to the meeting-place by the other
bridge. All three were to be unarmed.

On the appointed day, which was at the end of October, 43 B.C.,
the three generals made their appearance as arranged, and, leaving
their escorts of cavalry, walked towards the bridges; but here they

[11] Dion Cassius, xlvi, 52.

hesitated, Antony fearing an ambush, and Octavian fearing Antony. Lepidus, however, overcame the difficulty by boldly crossing the bridge and making a rapid inspection of the island and of the large tent which occupied most of its small area. Having satisfied himself that nobody was there in hiding he beckoned to Antony and Octavian to join him, and this they did, walking warily towards one another, and at last embracing in the manner which etiquette required. This embrace gave each of them an opportunity to feel for a hidden weapon upon the person of the other, and the action was at once so apparent that they abandoned all concealment of it and openly felt each other all over with their hands. Then the three of them entered the tent.

They were a remarkable trio. The mighty Antony, now clean-shaven once more, was a man of forty, as muscular and as bull-necked as any gladiator, yet having that easy grace of carriage and that lordly air of assurance which made him always so conspicuous. Octavian, who had recently attained his twentieth birthday, and had grown a little beard, was still a pale, unhealthy, untidy youth, wor-ried-looking and older than his years, yet decidedly handsome and having the appearance of an aristocrat. Lepidus must have been over sixty years of age, but still had a thick crop of grey hair: he was a quiet, polite, gentlemanly personage of ancient patrician family, rather lazy, and having little strength of character visible in his kindly face, but a good deal of tact observable in his manner.

For two, or perhaps three, days this interesting trinity sat for hours in the tent, approached only at command by their servants, reviewing the whole situation, and adjusting their viewpoints one to the other. Antony's position was unquestionably the strongest: he had ruled Rome single-handed both during Cæsar's absence and after his death, and he was accustomed to command. He was great-ly beloved by the army; and although his drinking-bouts and his lapses into periods of idle and dissolute living had caused him to be regarded with apprehension by the more solid elements of Roman society, his ability to play the man in times of difficulty had raised his reputation to great heights. In general he was the most popular figure of the age, and the fall of Cicero and the republican party had removed all his enemies from his immediate path.

This being so, he dominated the conference, and was in a

position to oblige Octavian to accept only that share of the power now in their hands which he himself did not want. It was agreed that the three of them should form a Triumvirate which was to last five years, each having the title of Triumvir, and that the government of Rome and Italy should be conducted by them in concert, but that the rest of the empire should be parcelled out between them into three spheres of influence. Brutus, Cassius, and the other conspirators were in control of Greece and the eastern dominions; but the rest of the world outside Italy was theirs to divide. Antony demanded and received as his share Cisalpine Gaul and all that part of Gaul Proper which Cæsar had conquered. Lepidus was given control of Gallia Narbonensis (Southern France) and Spain. Octavian took Sicily, Sardinia, Corsica, and North Africa, the least important of the three divisions.

It was agreed that while Lepidus should remain as their acting partner in Rome with three legions to support him, Antony and Octavian should each command an army of twenty legions—forty in all—and should set themselves to the immediate task of overthrowing the conspirators and reconquering Greece, Asia Minor, Syria and the other parts of the eastern empire. Octavian undertook to resign the Consulship which he had held for the last two months or so, and that office was to be given to the heroic Ventidius Bassus in reward for the service he had rendered to Antony in bringing three legions to his aid. The Consulships for the following year, 42 B.C., were to be held by Lepidus and Plancus. It was finally agreed that Octavian should cement his alliance with Antony and the democratic party by marrying Clodia, Antony's step-daughter, the daughter of his wife Fulvia by her earlier marriage with Clodius, that violent demagogue who had met his death in 52 B.C.

The girl was probably no more than about twelve years of age or so, and it may be said in anticipation that the marriage was never consummated; but its political significance lay in the fact that Clodia's father was remembered as the hero of the popular party, the beloved leader of the People. She was the darling of the mob; and, in marrying her Octavian linked himself not only with Antony's household, but with the masses. In fact, I think the union must have been suggested by Octavian rather than by Antony, for the former profited by it, politically, more than the latter.

Then came the question of the punishment of the chief men in the republican party, the leaders in the movement which had caused the death sentence to be passed first upon Antony and then upon Lepidus. Antony, of course, was not going to show any mercy to Cicero, the man who had frenziedly demanded his death in those terrible Philippics which had poured such filthy and such lying abuse upon him; and now he insisted that the old orator should be put to death. The quarrel between the two men had passed beyond the limits of any possible accommodation: Cicero had done his passionate best to kill Antony, and now Antony would kill Cicero. It was a case of tit for tat.

Lepidus, on his part, was determined to revenge himself upon his brother who, as a senator, had voted for the death sentence against him proposed by Cicero; and he now demanded that this brother of his should die. Octavian, meanwhile, wished to be revenged upon Lucius Cæsar, Antony's mother's brother, who in some way now forgotten had worked against the interests of the young man, and had thrown in his lot with Cicero.

It was arranged, therefore, that these three men, and about a dozen others, should be immediately executed [12] without trial. A terrible list of some three hundred [13] republicans was then drawn up, at least a hundred of whom were senators; and it was agreed that these unfortunates should be put to death as soon as the absolute authority of the Triumvirate had been established. The mob in Rome which had always hated the capitalists and the aristocrats, and had lately begun to idolise the memory of Cæsar as the friend of the People, was thirsting for vengeance; and this wholesale slaughter of the republicans was expected to delight them. The precedent set by Sulla was closely followed, and just as he had proscribed all the important men in the democratic camp, and had practically wiped that party out, so now, with equal savagery, it was to be the turn of the democrats to make a clean sweep of the republicans.

An ugly feature of this shocking proscription was the fact that since the property of the condemned was to be confiscated, and

---

[12] The authorities disagree as to the number in this first batch of victims, some saying twelve and others seventeen.

[13] These numbers also vary, and I here follow Plutarch's *Antony*.

since the Triumvirate was in urgent need of funds with which to pay the promised rewards to the legions, many of the victims were selected because of their wealth. The Triumvirs not only desired vengeance for Cæsar's death and for their own past misfortunes, they not only wished to establish the democrats and the Cæsarians as the sole rulers of the empire: they also wanted money; and the urgent need for it, rather than the particular guilt of the persons chosen for the extreme penalty, compelled them to write name after name into that awful list.

The conference seems to have ended about November 1st or 2nd, but for a few days longer messengers passed between the three Triumvirs, and visits were exchanged, while final plans were made. At last, orders were sent to Pedius, the Consul in Rome, to carry out the immediate execution of the first small batch of the condemned; and these instructions were received by him shortly before the middle of the month, giving him a shock which threw him into a state of extreme nervous agitation. With dismay in his heart he issued the necessary commands, and within a few hours the heads of four of the victims were brought to him. That night, while search was being made for the others, the wildest panic broke out in the city, and Pedius, breathless with anxiety, was obliged to go about the streets, attempting to calm the people, to check the bloodthirsty ferment of the mob, and to prevent a wholesale flight of republican senators and officials. Next morning, on his own authority he issued a statement saying that these few men were alone to be proscribed, and that nobody else need have any fear. Throughout the day he was besieged by persons asking for further information or for protection, and so great was the general excitement that he himself was keyed up to a pitch which his constitution could not endure. He had not closed his eyes all night, and the horror of the duty imposed upon him of searching for and carrying out the execution of Cicero and other men so recently great, drove him almost frantic. Before the day was out his overtaxed heart stopped, and he fell dead.

Cicero and his brother Quintus were at Frascati when runners brought the news that both of them were condemned; and therewith in bewildered anguish they fled towards the sea, hoping to find a boat to carry them to Brutus in Greece, and when the soldiers arrived at the house their prey had disappeared. Meanwhile another band of soldiers was chasing the proscribed Lucius Cæsar through the streets of Rome. He took refuge at last in the house of his sister Julia, Antony's mother; and when the search-party demanded admittance, she barred their way, crying out: "You shall not kill him until you have first killed *me*, the mother of your general!" Lucius, it will be recalled, had been proscribed by Octavian; and it may be that Antony had sent secret word that he was to be allowed to escape: at any rate the soldiers retired, and Julia kept her brother safe in the house, and ultimately he was pardoned by Antony, much to Octavian's annoyance. [14]

On November 24th Octavian entered Rome, bringing with him one legion; on the 25th Antony marched into the city with a similar force; and on the 26th Lepidus arrived, also with one legion. On the 27th a law was passed confirming the establishment of the Triumvirate for a period of five years, namely until the close of the year 38 B.C.; and therewith the proscriptions were published, a reward being offered for the head of each man named in the list, and the penalty of death being decreed against those who should aid in the escape of any of them.

Then followed scenes the like of which Rome had not beheld since the time of Sulla—scenes as terrible as those enacted in the French Revolution. Some of the victims fled in disguise, and not a few of them made their escape. Some hid themselves in the hypocausts under the rooms of their houses, the low tunnels, that is to say, through which the hot air from the furnaces was radiated in winter beneath the floors; and some crept into the drains and public sewers. Some defended themselves in their homes, and died fighting; others were killed by their slaves, though there are one or two cases on record in which a slave dressed himself in his master's clothes and perished in his stead; while yet others, frantic to be done with the horror of their suspense, killed themselves or hastened to meet their executioners.

A certain elderly man of wealth flung all his valuables into the street, so that the townspeople rather than the Triumvirs might possess themselves of his treasure; and then set his house on fire, and threw himself into the flames. In a few cases wives betrayed the husbands whom they disliked; but in general it is said, the

[14] Suetonius: *Augustus,* xxvii; Dion Cassius, xlvii, 8.

women were more faithful to their men than the sons were to their fathers, there being a remarkable number of instances in which the younger generation turned upon the elder, [15] a fact which perhaps indicates that the youth of Rome was violently Cæsarian.

Daily the soldiers passed through the streets to the Forum carrying sacks of heads which were to be exhibited upon the rostra; but whereas in the days of Sulla it was the upper classes who gloated over the spectacle of the slaughter of the leaders of the People, now it was the mob and the popular party who cheered the arrival of every new consignment of these severed heads of the aristocrats and the republicans, regarding them with almost religious frenzy as a bloody sacrifice to the spirit of the divine Cæsar, the People's lost leader. Democracy had triumphed, and Antony, Lepidus, and Octavian were hailed as their deliverers from the rule of the conservatives who had murdered their hero and had trampled upon their liberties. The money confiscated from the wealthy victims was to be distributed amongst the common soldiers —this the rabble knew, and they hoped that some of it would also come their way. A democratic redistribution of the riches of the capitalists was taking place; and the crowds hooted and groaned their delight as each new head of a rich man was added to the ghastly array.

Antony and Lepidus, it is said,[16] were easily persuaded to pardon some of the proscribed, or to wink at their escape; and the youngest of the Triumvirs was occasionally induced by his half-sister Octavia to spare those who had aroused her pity. But, in general, Octavian was far more ruthless than his two colleagues; and his pitilessness is sometimes described as having been very close to madness, an attitude, however, which may perhaps be accounted for by the fact that he was painfully aware of being suspected by the masses because of his former alliance with Cicero's party. He wished to prove himself the most ruthless avenger of the dead Dictator, the true inheritor of Cæsar's leadership of the People; and, being so young, he was more fully carried away by the popular clamour than were either of his more experienced colleagues.

Meanwhile, Cicero and his brother Quintus, as has been said,

[15] Velleius, ii, lxvii.
[16] Suetonius: *Augustus*, xxvii.

had fled from Frascati. Their plan was to make their way southwards to the island of Astura (Torre d'Astura) at the mouth of
the river of the same name, where Cicero had a villa. The distance was no more than thirty miles, and the slaves were sufficiently
attached to the family to be trusted to carry the two fugitives
thither in their litters; but as they approached their destination
the brothers began to realize a fact which had been overlooked in
the hurry of their departure, namely that a great deal of money
would be required to bribe those persons whose help they might
need. It was therefore suggested that Quintus should go back to
get the money, it being the custom of the time for every man of
means to keep a chest or jar of gold coins concealed in some part
of his house in case of emergencies; and this task Quintus bravely
undertook, the two brothers bidding goodbye to one another with
many tears, for they must have known that there was very little
hope. Quintus, in fact, sealed his fate by his courageous action;
for his slaves betrayed him, and he and his son were both killed.

Cicero reached Astura without mishap, and, too frightened to
wait for Quintus, immediately boarded one of his own ships and
sailed with a favourable wind as far as Circæum (Circello), about
half way between Rome and Naples. He was, however, completely
unnerved by his terrible situation, and could make up his mind
neither to proceed nor to wait for his brother, nor yet to put an
end to himself. All his life he had found it hard to come to a decision in a crises, and now his hesitation and perplexity were more
pronounced than they had ever been before. According to the code
he had always preached, his means of escape was suicide; and at
last in a burst of courage he ordered his men to put him ashore
and to carry him back to Rome. He would make his way secretly,
he said, into Octavian's house, and there kill himself before the
altar of the household gods of the Cæsars, thereby, as the popular
belief declared, bringing a curse upon the persons of the family of
the young scoundrel who had delivered him over to Antony's vengeance.

But after he had gone a short distance along the road to the
capital, fear seized him and he went back to the ship, whereon
he was taken to Caieta (Gæta), near Formiæ (Mola), where he
had another house, "an agreeable retreat," says Plutarch, "where,

in the heat of summer, the Etesian winds are so pleasant." Here, once more, he insisted upon landing, crying in the last sorry exercise of his imperishable vanity, "Let me die in the country I have so often saved." There was a little temple of Apollo in the grounds of this villa, overlooking the sea; and as his ship approached the shore a number of black crows arose from the trees around it and with a great cawing and flapping of wings alighted on the rigging. This was taken to be a sign that a further voyage by this particular vessel was likely to end in disaster, Cicero, being thus confirmed in his determination to land; and, going ashore, he entered the house, and flung himself down upon a bed, soon falling asleep from sheer exhaustion.

As he slept, the crows cawed dismally around the open windows, and one of them even entered the room, upon seeing which the faithful slaves determined to take him from so ill-omened a place. Arousing him, therefore, they persuaded the bewildered and frightened man to get into his litter so that they might carry him to another vessel moored some distance along the coast; but while they were making their way under the trees by a path which led through the grounds, the local soldiery, informed of his arrival, hastened to the house, and, receiving no answer to their summons, broke the door open and entered.

There was a young manumitted slave, a studious youth, named Philologus, who lived on the estate and in whose education Cicero had taken a personal interest. The officer in command of the soldiers asked him where his master was, and the terrified Philologus gave the required information, whereupon the soldiers ran off in pursuit of their victim. Cicero heard their shouts in the distance; and suddenly, in the realization that the end was nigh, his fear left him, and his composure came back. He told the slaves to put down the litter and when they had done so he sat quietly in it, his elbows on his drawn-up knees, his left hand stroking his unshaven chin, and his tired eyes fixed thoughtfully upon his approaching executioners. It is evident that he was utterly weary, and yearned with all his heart to be dead.

The officer, sword in hand, ran at him; and Cicero with perfect dignity bent his head and extended his neck to receive the blow. "Of all his misfortunes," wrote Livy, "death was the only one that he bore like a man." [17] His slaves turned away covering their faces, as the sword fell.

Orders had been given that the orator's right hand, with which he had written the Philippics, should be struck from the body as well as the head; and when these were brought to the Triumvirs in Rome Antony uttered an uncomfortable laugh, and, to put the best face upon a shameful business, cried "Now there can be an end of our proscriptions!"—at the same time telling his men to place the head and the hand upon the rostra with the rest of the collection, that all men might know the penalty of double-dealing and lies. But when they brought Philologus forward to receive his reward, Antony angrily ordered him to be handed over to Pomponia, Cicero's sister-in-law, the wife of Quintus, and this frenzied woman is reported to have put him to death with fiendish tortures. Fulvia, however, was more savage than her husband, and it is said that she took hold of Cicero's severed head, spat at it, and thrust one of her hairpins through the tongue which had maligned Antony.[18]

Some years later, when Octavian had become the Emperor Augustus, he happened to come upon a youthful member of his family who was reading one of Cicero's works, and who immediately hid the book, thinking that the Emperor would be displeased. But Augustus demanded it of him, and having turned the pages over thoughtfully, reading a paragraph here and there, handed it back, saying "My child, this was a great orator; a great orator, and one who loved his country well."

[17] Livy, quoted by Seneca: *Suasoriarum*, 6.
[18] Dion Cassius, xlvii, 8.

CHAPTER XIV

The War against Brutus and Cassius, and the Destruction of the Republican Party.

42 B.C.

"THERE was," writes Plutarch, "much simplicity in Antony's character. He was slow to see his faults, but when he did see them he was extremely repentant and ready to ask pardon of those he had injured. He was severe in his punishments, but prodigal in his acts of reparation; and his generosity was much more extravagant than his severity. His banter or abuse, for example, was sharp and insulting, but the edge of it was dulled by his readiness to accept any kind of repartee, and he was as willing to be sworn at as he was to swear at others."

Dion Cassius, writing more than two and a half centuries after these events, describes Antony as being the most ruthless of the three Triumvirs at the time of the proscriptions [1]; but Suetonius who was separated from the period by over a hundred year less than this, and is the better authority, is emphatic, as has already been said, that Octavian was the only one of the three who showed no wish to bring the massacre to an end. Antony, in fact, appears to have been the first to feel shame for his atrocious behaviour; and at any rate there can be no doubt that he alone retained his popularity with Rome's democracy, whereas Octavian was detested. People made insulting jests at the expense of the young man [2]; they accused him of being so fond of fine furniture and Greek antiques that he would condemn a man in order to get hold of his

---

[1] So does Velleius, but it was this historian's policy to show Augustus, in whose circle he moved, in the best light, and to malign Antony; and therefore his evidence is not to be accepted. He accused Antony, in any case, chiefly of having shut for ever Cicero's "divine lips"; but the Philippics were not divine—they were devilish.

[2] Suetonius: *Augustus,* lxx.

coveted collections; and they declared that he used to get drunk and then cruelly add names to the lists of the proscribed.[3] Antony, on the contrary, when he was intoxicated, seems to have beamed upon the world in ineffable goodwill; and Plutarch, in his comparison between him and Demetrius, describes him under the influence of wine as being like Hercules deprived of his club and his lion's skin, and as wanting only to have a game with somebody.

A personage who played an important part at this time was Sextus Pompeius, the son of Pompey the Great. As has already been recorded, he had been placed by Cicero in control of the Roman fleet; and now he managed to retain possession of a good many of the ships of war, adding to the numbers under his command by seizing merchant-vessels and enrolling vagabonds and criminals to act as their crews. He is described as being quite illiterate, and his language is said to have been shocking[4]; but he was a brave man, and his exploits as a pro-republican outlaw, an old-fashioned Pompeian turned pirate, won him much renown.

He took complete possession of Sicily, putting the governor to death; and he issued a proclamation far and wide, offering sanctuary to all proscribed persons or republicans who could make their escape to him from the mainland. He seized the corn-ships which were coming to Rome from Egypt and the east, and caused something like a famine in the city; he attacked the forces of the Triumvirate wherever he encountered them; and at length he sent his ships close in to the Italian shore to pick up the fugitives, and, for any help given to them, offered rewards double the size of those offered by the new government for their heads. His activities caused great apprehension in Rome, but for the moment the Triumvirs could take no serious steps against him.

Meanwhile, a wave of adoration of Cæsar's memory was sweeping the country; and though Octavian was much disliked, and was regarded as an unpleasant and intrusive representative of the great dictator, Antony was hailed by the old soldiers, by the mob, and, indeed, by the bulk of the democrats and Cæsarians, as his true successor in the leadership of the People, and as his avenger. Everybody was begging him to prosecute the war against Brutus and Cassius with all speed, and to hunt down every one of the assassins.

[3] Seneca: *De Clementia*, i, ix.   [4] Velleius, ii, lxxiii.

A temple was erected to Cæsar's divinity upon the spot in the Forum where his body had been cremated, and the hall in which he had been murdered was closed to the public as a mark of detestation of the crime.

Ventidius Bassus was now Consul, and enjoyed great popularity not only as the man who had come to Antony's aid after Modena, but as one of Cæsar's old soldiers. He had once been a simple mule-owner, but had been raised to high office by the Dictator; and the townspeople looked upon him as a fine instance of Cæsar's democratic indifference to a man's origin, and of Antony's loyalty to the same ideals in promoting him to the highest honours. The People, in fact, felt that they were truly in power; and in their idolisation of the memory of their dead leader they rallied round Antony, the chief of the Triumvirs, and urged him on to destroy the remaining republican forces in the east.

Antony, however, had been away from the metropolis for a year; and now that the cessation of the executions was offering him the opportunity to forget his months of hardship by enjoying in peace for a while the comforts of his beautiful house in Rome, and all the amenities of city-life, he was in no hurry to be off to the wars again. His affection for his wife Fulvia, it is true, had not been revived by his long absence from her; and he can hardly have been happy in sharing his home with so forceful and so violent a woman, "in whom there was nothing feminine but her figure," as Velleius says,[5] and whose ambitions for his ultimate autocracy gave him little rest. Yet he was able to elude or exclude her fairly frequently, and to make merry with his friends; and his parties became once more the talk of the town. Often the doors of his house, people complained, were shut in the face of magistrates and officials, and yet were opened to actors and actresses, dancers, jugglers, and drunken guests; and he was accused of spending in this manner some of the money confiscated from the slaughtered republicans. Octavian, in fact, called at last for an account and a proper division of these spoils, for "it was clear that nothing would ever be enough for Antony,"[6] whose wild generosity and "lavish gifts to his friends and fellow-soldiers" quickly scattered the fortunes which fell into his prodigal hands.

[5] Velleius, ii, lxxiv. [6] Plutarch: *Antony.*

It is necessary now to turn to the affairs of Brutus, who, after deep thought, had recently sealed his quarrel with the Cæsarians by putting Antony's brother, Caius, to death in cold blood, as a matter of principle and in retaliation for the execution of Cicero. Brutus was no sentimentalist, and one may say of him, perhaps, that, like many puritans, he was capable of striking at his worldly-minded opponents with all the venom of years of self-denial. He had little respect for individual human life, his own not excepted: he stood for a certain system of constitutional government, and his narrow intolerance drove him sometimes to extremes of heartlessness wholly foreign to the essential sanity of true rectitude.

On hearing that Antony contemplated an invasion of Macedonia in the spring, he decided to retreat with his army eastwards into Asia Minor and there join hands with Cassius; and having learnt that the latter intended to make an attack upon Egypt, where Cleopatra had declared her adherence to Antony's cause, he sent him a letter begging him to give his sole attention to the coming fight with the Triumvirs, as a result of which a meeting at Smyrna, in Lydia, north of Ephesus, was arranged.

Brutus, now some forty-three years of age, was a man whose lofty motives, though wrong-headed, were never in doubt; and even Antony admitted that he was the only one of Cæsar's assassins who acted as he did out of an earnest belief in the righteousness of the republican cause.[7] Brutus was, indeed, weighed down by his sense of responsibility, and by his strained consciousness of the principles for which he stood. He suffered from melancholia, and his nights were often sleepless, and his pillow wet with his tears, as his slow and pedantic mind reviewed the duties which he believed a stern Providence had imposed upon him. His nerves were in a very bad state: more than once he experienced a definite hallucination; he was, at this time, always very close to tears; and the news of the deaths of Cicero and so many of his friends was almost unable to be borne.

His meeting with Cassius, however, heartened him somewhat, for between them they now had a pretty big army, and there was a fair chance of victory. Cassius was a clever general and one of forceful, aggressive character: he was not an idealist; he was a

[7] Plutarch: *Brutus.*

practical man, impelled by a hatred of his enemies which Brutus could never feel, and inspired by a desire for personal power and wealth which he must have had difficulty in concealing from his self-denying colleague. Cassius, in fact, supplied the driving force in their united activities; but it was faith in the patriotic and disinterested motives of Brutus that sustained the spirit of the legions. The men were fascinated by his complete sincerity: he was like a holy-man leading a crusade for the rescue of the fatherland from the rule of the democrats. Yet he did not preach hatred: of Antony he said only that his punishment was already sufficient in having such a treacherous colleague as Octavian,[8] who would one day turn upon him—"in which," Plutarch remarks, "he proved to be no bad prophet."

The plans of the two generals were simple. There were two areas of doubtful loyalty in these eastern dominions which they controlled, namely, the island of Rhodes off the south-west corner of Asia Minor, and Lycia, the state on the mainland east of it. These would have to be subdued before they could comfortably march back to Macedonia to give battle to the Triumvirs; and it was agreed that Cassius should undertake the former campaign, Brutus the latter. Both enterprises were successful; but Brutus was much shaken by the effects of his attack upon Xanthus, (Gunik), the Lycian capital, for nearly the entire population of the city committed suicide before his eyes, being suddenly possessed by an almost incredible frenzy which Plutarch aptly describes as a sort of "ravenous appetite to die." Not only men and women, but even children, plunged into the flames of the burning houses which they themselves had fired, or hanged themselves, or leapt from high walls to the ground, or stabbed themselves and each other to the heart. One woman was seen to set fire to her house, and then with the torch still in her hand, and her strangled baby suspended around her neck, to hang herself from one of the blazing beams.

Brutus was appalled. Mounting his horse, he galloped around the walls of the burning city, crying out to the inhabitants that he would not harm them, and holding out his hands to them, imploring them not to die, the tears running down his cheeks as he

[8] Plutarch: *Brutus*.

did so. But none would listen, and in the end, out of the entire population, less than two hundred were able to be restrained from self-destruction by the Roman soldiers to whom Brutus had offered a reward for every Xanthian saved.

The two generals rejoined one another at Sardis (Sart), near Smyrna, and, crossing the Hellespont, marched into Thrace. At about this time the overwrought Brutus experienced another hallucination. Late one night he was seated alone in his tent, deep in thought, a dim light burning in a lamp beside him, when suddenly he saw a figure standing silently in front of him. "Who are you?" he called out. "What do you want?" The apparition replied, "I am your evil genius, Brutus: you shall see me again at Philippi." "Very well then," Brutus calmly replied, "I shall see you there."

Next morning he told Cassius of his experience, but that unimaginative man laughed the matter off, saying that he did not believe in ghosts, and that he only wished he did, for then he might believe also that the spirits would aid them in their coming fight. "Your mind," he said, "is in an excited and abnormal condition, because you are tired out. Not all we feel or see is real; for the senses are most slippery and deceitful, and the brain is quick to put them in motion and to stimulate them without any real occasion of fact. Just as an impression is made upon wax, the consciousness can easily of itself produce and assume every kind of shape and figure, as is evident from our dreams: it is ever in activity, and this activity produces these fantasies and creations." [9]

But Brutus was not comforted. His brain was dark with the menace of impending doom; and this strange experience indicates that, deep in his subconscious mind, he was not always so sure of the righteousness of those principles which had caused him to murder the Dictator. The clear, guiding light of his conscience sometimes grew dim, leaving him in the darkness of doubt; and it was then that he wondered whether, after all, he was not being consigned to disaster by some flaw in his reasoning, some awful fallacy in the whole argument of his life, some delusion, which in his tent he had visualised as his evil genius.

Meanwhile, the light-hearted Antony had sent eight legions

[9] Plutarch: *Brutus.*

across the Adriatic from Italy to Macedonia, and had suddenly extricated himself from the pleasures of Rome to put himself at the head of twelve more legions which were waiting at Brindisi for him to lead them over the sea. Octavian, acting in concert with him, now attempted to recapture Sicily from Sextus Pompeius, so as to prevent an attack upon the transports by that piratical commander's nondescript fleet; but in this he was wholly unsuccessful, and Sextus remained a menace to the expedition. Then, while Antony was waiting for the opportunity to slip across, an enemy fleet under Murcus, a renegade Cæsarian, made its appearance before Brindisi, and thereafter blockaded the transports in the harbour throughout the spring and early summer of 42 B.C.

Antony made several daring attempts to break the blockade, but failed to do so. Octavian, however, at last brought his ships from Sicilian waters, and drove Murcus off; and the two Triumvirs were thus enabled to sail over to Dyrrhachium (Durazzo), on the other side, with their army.

But here Octavian fell sick and had to take to his bed, though the nature of his complaint is unknown. He was an unhealthy young man, and though the lower part of his face, as has been said, was at this time covered by a youthful beard, his visible features revealed the weakness of his constitution. Suetonius [10] says that his left hip and leg used often to give him trouble, that he suffered from gall-stones, that his liver was liable to be out of order, and that he had the itch: in the autumn he was usually feverish, in the spring he complained of pains in the neighbourhood of the diaphragm, when the wind was from the south he always caught a cold in his head, in the heat of summer he was prostrated, and in winter he could endure neither the sun nor the chill of the shade, and while not daring to go out into the glare except with a broad-brimmed straw hat to protect his head, had to guard himself from the cold by wearing a thick toga, four tunics, a shirt, a flannel chest-protector, and swathings around his thighs and legs. It is understandable, therefore, that he was incapacitated by his exertions in the great heat of summer.

Brutus and Cassius were now marching westwards along the coast of Thrace towards that narrow doorway into Macedonia

[10] Suetonius: *Augustus,* lxxx–lxxxii.

which is situated between the mountains and the sea, where lay the plains of Philippi overlooked by the city of that name. A few miles to the west was the fortress of Amphipolis (Ienikeui), and to this important point the first eight of Antony's legions had been despatched to hold the enemy in check; but in September at the approach of the republican forces, the commander sent urgently for Antony to come to his support, whereupon the latter, leaving Octavian at Dyrrhachium, marched the other twelve legions as fast as he could to Amphipolis, which he reached in time to bring Brutus and Cassius to an unexpected halt. The speed of this march is said to have been almost unbelievable; but Antony had learnt from Cæsar the value of speed.

Brutus then camped his army at the foot of the mountains, a little south-east of the city of Philippi, while Cassius placed his forces a short walk to the south, at the edge of a marsh which passed down to the sea; and the two camps were joined by a palisade and entrenchments. A little stream, the Gangas, running down from the hills, supplied them with water; and the whole of Thrace behind them, and their ships which could unload in the neighbouring harbours, provided them with food.

Antony then divided his forces, taking up his own position with half his army in front of the camp of Cassius, near the sea, and leaving to Octavian, when he should arrive, the command of the other half which faced the camp of Brutus. The sickly young man turned up some ten days later, but he was too ill to be of any service. The republican army was slightly smaller than that of the Triumvirs, but was better equipped; and in fact, the officers serving under Brutus, being of far more elegant taste than those under the democratic Antony, wore armour and used weapons richly ornamented with gold and silver, while even the soldiers each carried quite a little fortune on their persons in this manner.

Far into October these armies confronted one another. Brutus was anxious to hasten a pitched battle, but Cassius believed that delay was to their advantage. Antony was also ready to fight it out at once, before the cold weather set in; and he did his best to tempt Cassius into the open, particularly by beginning to construct a road across the marsh between him and the sea for the purpose of turning his position, and, so it seems, by letting him know that reinforcements for the Cæsarians would soon be on their way from Italy.

At last, one day towards the end of October, Brutus persuaded his colleague to give battle on the morrow; and that night, having made all his arrangements, he showed himself more cheerful than he had been for many weeks, though Cassius, on the contrary, was depressed and silent, declaring that he did not like this hazarding the future of his country on one big battle. Brutus, however, expressed his determination either to conquer or to kill himself. "Indeed," he said, "I already gave up my life to my country on the Ides of March, and I have lived since then a second life solely for her sake. If Providence does not give us the victory, I shall die quite content with my lot." In this he was not, like Cicero, uttering fine-sounding words: he was entirely in earnest, and the belief that the crisis had come seemed to lift a dead weight from his melancholy heart.

Next morning, Brutus was the first to begin the attack,[11] which was directed against Octavian's entrenchments in front of him; and his troops were so eager to take the offensive that they went forward in a disorderly but overwhelming swarm, cut to pieces Octavian's advance-guard of two-thousand newly recruited Spartans, nearly annihilated his Fourth Legion—one of those which had deserted to Octavian from Antony the year before, drove back the rest of his forces onto the open ground, and, getting quite out of hand, gave themselves up to the plunder of Octavian's camp. What happened to Octavian himself is a mystery. In his own memoirs, according to Plutarch, he said that a friend of his had had such a bad dream about him that, to please him, he had consented to leave the camp that day, before he knew that an attack upon it was contemplated; but the fact that his litter was found a little distance away pierced by arrows and spears, indicates that he had fled after the battle had begun, and had escaped on foot when he was pursued. Brutus, at any rate, thought that he was dead, and some of the victorious soldiers declared, in fact, that they had seen him surrounded and killed—which suggests that he had had the narrowest of escapes.

[11] For the account of the fighting see Plutarch's *Brutus,* which seems to be better than the somewhat different version given by Appian, *Civil Wars,* iv, 110.

Meanwhile, Cassius had attacked the Cæsarian forces in front of him, at a time when Antony himself was supervising the road-making across the marshes, and was more or less off his guard. Antony managed to get back to his camp, however, beat off the assault, and soon counter-attacked, leading his men in a wild onslaught upon the republican position. This was completely successful, and soon the camp of Cassius was being as thoroughly plundered by Antony as Octavian's had been by Brutus.

Brutus, returning from his victory, saw with dismay what had happened to his colleague, and sent his cavalry across to his aid. Cassius, who in his flight had halted on the high ground behind his lost camp, observed these men bearing down upon him in the distance, and dispatched one of his officers, Titinius, a dear friend of his, to find out whether they were comrades or foes. This officer quickly recognized them, and at once rode forward to greet them, being soon surrounded by them and hearing from them the news of their victory over Octavian. But when Cassius saw Titinius thus swallowed up by the oncoming cavalry he jumped to the fatally mistaken conclusion that these troops were Cæsarians, and that they had killed or captured his lieutenant.

He was too shattered by Antony's capture of his camp to be able to form a proper judgment, and thinking that the supposedly hostile force would soon overwhelm him, he cried out "O, that I should have lived to see my friend taken by the enemy before my very face!"—and immediately ordered his servant, Pindarus, to kill him. Pindarus, who was also quite frantic, at once raised his sword and with one blow cut his general's head off; but when, a few minutes later, the relieving cavalry arrived, and the mistake was discovered, the man took to his heels in horror, and was never seen again. Titinius, however, regarding himself as in part to blame, stabbed himself and fell dead across his general's headless body.

Then came Brutus, flushed with his own victory, and intent on reassuring Cassius; but when he found his colleague's corpse lying decapitated in the midst of the astounded cavalry, he burst into tears, and presently gave orders that it should be secretly carried away, so that the army should not be unnerved by a public funeral. Antony, meanwhile, had just heard of Octavian's defeat and flight, and had called his men back to defend their camp. Thus, the fighting ceased, Cassius being dead with some eight thousand of his men, and the loss of his camp, on the one side; and Octavian having disappeared, on the other, his camp plundered, and nearly twice that number of his soldiers slain.

For some hours Antony assumed that the republicans were victorious, and, with heavy heart, he must have made all arrangements to retreat; but after nightfall, to his vast surprise, Octavian turned up safe and sound, and the news of the death of Cassius was brought in, whereupon he boldly announced that the battle would be continued on the following day, and he spent the hours of darkness in steadying his own forces and reorganizing those of Octavian.

Brutus, meanwhile, behaved with a savagery which can only be accounted for by the overwhelming excitement of the time, and by the shock of the death of Cassius. He had captured a host of slaves in Octavian's camp, and, having apparently no higher sentiments than any other Romans in regard to the rights of slaves, gave orders that these wretched prisoners should all be slaughtered. The few soldiers and other free-men who had been taken, however, he released,[12] with the exception of Volumnius, a comic actor, and Sacculio, a clown, whose business it had been to entertain Octavian's camp. Brutus was too puritanical to show any mercy to persons connected with the stage, and when he was told that these two were facing their perilous situation with jests and wry smiles, he indignantly gave orders that they should be flogged and sent back, naked and bleeding, to the Cæsarians; but later, changing his mind at the instance of Casca, the man who had struck the first blow in the murder of Cæsar, he had them put to death. He then gave a promise to his soldiers that in the event of victory he would lead them to the wealthy cities of Thessalonica (Salonika) and Sparta, both of which had sided with Antony, and would allow them to kill, rape, and plunder to their hearts' content. The apparent collapse of his moral character in this hour of excitement is a matter of astonishment.

Next day, however, rain fell in torrents, and Brutus would not

---

[12] So Plutarch says; but Dion Cassius, xlvii, 48, says that both the republicans and the Cæsarians killed most of their prisoners.

come out to fight, although Antony sent some of his men close up to the republican camp to shout rude remarks at him in an attempt to goad him into action. Several days then elapsed, during which there was an exceptionally early spell of wintry weather; and the fact that Antony's men were entrenched on low-lying ground which first became a quagmire and then froze, caused much hardship and many complaints. Every day, however, they were expecting the arrival of large reinforcements from Italy, and a great convoy of much-needed winter supplies; and Antony can hardly have been altogether sorry that the battle was delayed.

Now, however, came a terrible shock. Messengers arrived in the Cæsarian camp, bringing the news that disaster had overwhelmed this convoy. The ships had been attacked at sea by Murcus and Cnæus Domitius Ahenobarbus, and two entire legions and all the supplies had been lost. One of these lost legions was the Martian, that same which had deserted from Antony to Octavian after its punishment at Brindisi; and the only satisfaction which Antony could derive from the appalling tidings was that these men had, from his point of view, got their deserts. This Ahenobarbus,[13] it may be mentioned, was the son of Lucius Domitius Ahenobarbus, Pompey's general at Pharsalia whom Antony had slain in that battle. Cnæus had been present at Pharsalia, and had afterwards been pardoned by Cæsar; but he had now returned to the republican cause, for, his mother having been the sister of Cato, he was the uncle of Porcia, the wife of Brutus.

Antony now felt that he had only two alternatives—either to retreat or to bring on an immediate battle before the news of this disaster should reach Brutus. That same day,[14] however, by a coincidence, Brutus made up his mind to fight on the morrow; and, having made the necessary preparations, he retired to his tent, where, it is said, that same apparition which had visited him once before again made its appearance and stared at him, this time without speaking. Brutus, indeed, was in so overwrought a condition that it is by no means improbable that he believed himself to have received this second and promised visit from the spectre: his state

---

[13] He was the great-grandfather of the Emperor Nero.
[14] The date is not known, except that it was twenty days after the first battle of Philippi.

of mind must have been conducive to such an hallucination. He
had recently received news that his wife Porcia, whom he had left
in Italy, was dead [15]; and this, too, had unnerved him.

But what was more ominous was that a swarm of bees had that
day settled upon one of the legionary standards, and a report had
also gone about that one of his officers had found to his astonishment that his arm was sweating attar-of-roses, nor did this sweet-
smelling oil cease to ooze out of the pores of his skin, so it was said,
even after the arm had been wiped many times. One cannot avoid
the thought that Antony's agents were in the camp, spreading such
rumours, though why a supposed phenomenon of this peculiar kind
should have been thought to indicate disaster is not now known.
There certainly were, however, traitors at work among the soldiers of
Brutus, for next day, when he drew up his army for battle, a trusted
cavalry officer named Camulatus suddenly whipped up his horse
and galloped away to Antony across the open ground.

It was at about three o'clock in the afternoon that Brutus gave
the signal for the onslaught, and soon his men had driven in the
Cæsarian left wing commanded by Octavian; but the right wing,
under Antony, responded by a charge which broke through the
opposing forces and took Brutus's victorious legionaries in their
rear. A great but not very sanguinary route of the republicans then
followed, and by nightfall Brutus's army was in full flight.

Several of the younger officers, following the aristocratic tradition, fought to the last, and died gallantly. Cicero's son, Marcus,
brought his brief and rather disreputable career to a close in a
whirl of desperate bravery; Cato's only son, Marcus, who was
the brother-in-law of Brutus, pulled off his helmet and shouted his
name, thus successfully attracting the enemy's weapons against
him; Lucullus, the son of the general whom Pompey succeeded in
the war against Mithradates, and of Servilia, sister of Brutus's
mother of the same name, fell fighting courageously; and Lucius,
the nephew of Cassius, was also killed.

As Brutus rode from the field in a dazed condition one of his
staff officers, a certain Lucilius, who was riding a little behind,
noticed a body of Antony's Gallic cavalry approaching through the
gathering darkness; and, in a brave attempt to save his general,

[15] See the last paragraph of Plutarch's *Brutus*.

he slowed his horse and allowed himself to be taken prisoner, telling his captors that he was Brutus. "They believed him," Plutarch writes, "mainly because he begged so earnestly to be taken to Antony and not to Octavian, as though he feared the latter but could trust the former"—and I quote the remark for the reason that it reveals Antony's high reputation for what we should now call good sportsmanship and compares it with Octavian's unpopularity.

The Gallic troopers brought their prisoner to Antony, who, on hearing of his approach, stood scratching his head and wondering what sort of attitude he ought to adopt towards him, being evidently greatly embarrassed now by his earlier declaration that he would hound all Cæsar's assassins to their deaths. He was sorry for Brutus, and in this hour of triumph he wanted to deal generously with all men; and thus when he saw that the prisoner was not Brutus he seems to have been decidedly relieved.

"You may be quite sure," said Lucilius, saluting Antony, "that Brutus will never be taken alive. I cheated your men so as to save him, and I am ready to take the consequences."

At this there were angry exclamations on the part of the soldiers, but Antony held up his hand for silence. "I see that you are annoyed at being deceived," he said to them, "but in my opinion you have made a capture better than you expected; for you were looking for an enemy, and you have brought me a friend. The truth is, I was not at all sure how to deal with Brutus if you had brought him in alive; but I am quite sure what to do with this man." And, so saying, he went over to him and embraced him. "It is better to have such men as Lucilius our friends than our enemies," he smiled.[16]

Meanwhile Brutus had escaped with a few of his officers, servants, and friends, including the philosopher Volumnius, who afterwards wrote the story of these events which is now lost but is the basis of Plutarch's account. In the darkness they crossed a stream, and came to a halt amongst the trees and rocks on the other side, where Brutus, looking up at the stars, solemnly quoted some lines of poetry, calling down a curse upon the author of his misfortunes, and, having drunk some water brought to him in a helmet, seated himself under the projection of rock, which screened him from the

[16] Plutarch: *Brutus.*

cold night-wind, to consider his position. There was little hope for
him: the Cæsarian troops were round about, and could be heard
on the far side of the stream. One of his servants, in fact, was
wounded while fetching water; and an officer who was sent to try
to find out in what direction the main army had fled fell into the
enemy's hands and was killed.

At last, some time after midnight, Brutus decided to put an
end to himself, and whispered to his personal servant, asking him
to strike the blow; but the man burst into tears and refused to do
as he was bid. He then made the same request to Volumnius and
others, begging them to help him to drive his sword into his heart;
but at this they all suggested that they should, rather continue
their flight. "Yes, indeed," said Brutus, "we must make our escape,
but not with our feet: with our hands"—meaning that death by
suicide was a more honourable course. Presently, in the darkness,
he was heard to quote the following lines,[17] which did, in fact,
provide a close parallel to his tragic life:—

"Unhappy Virtue!—you were but a name, while I
   Who have been Fate's plaything,
   Thinking your godhead real, have vainly followed you."

He then stood up, and shook each man by the hand, his expression being described by Volumnius as one of great happiness.
He told them what satisfaction it gave him to think that none of
them had deserted him, and he declared that his situation was far
more to be desired than that of his enemies, because he would
leave behind him a reputation for high principle which his con-
querors would never be able to acquire, and because posterity
would certainly regard his cause as just and good, and theirs as
wicked. Only a few days previously he had written to a friend
saying how happy he was that the end of his troubles was near,
for he would either be victorious in the battle or would kill himself, thus by the one means or the other obtaining the rest he so
much needed; and it seems that he was now indeed eager to close his
ill-balanced account with Fate, and have done with life's bad

[17] Dion Cassius, xlvii, 49, puts into his mouth these words, which, in Nauck's
Fragmenta Tragicorum Græcorum, are given as Fragment No. 374.

business. In sudden haste, therefore, taking only two or three of his best friends with him, he withdrew himself a short distance from the others, and, with the aid of one of them, plunged his sword into his heart.

Next morning Antony was conducted to the spot where the dead general had been found, and, taking off the rich, scarlet cloak which he was wearing, he laid it gallantly over the corpse. Octavian, however, presently arriving upon the scene, insisted that the head should be severed from the body in the customary manner, and sent to Rome to be placed at the foot of Cæsar's statue,[18] and to this his colleague seems to have been obliged to agree, although insisting on his part that the decapitated body should be cremated with all honour, and handing out a sum of money for the purpose. A funeral pyre was erected, and a few hours later, with great pomp, the body was consigned to the flames; after which Antony gave orders that the ashes should be sent to Brutus's mother, Servilia, for burial.[19] It was generally supposed that Brutus was Cæsar's own son, and it was remembered that the Dictator had been very fond of him; and thus Antony's reverent treatment of his remains was more in accord with Cæsarian sentiment than was Octavian's severity.

A few of the important prisoners were put to death; Favonius, a stern puritan who was generally nicknamed "Cato's Ape" because he emulated the austerity of that unbalanced personage, was executed by Octavian's orders; and by Antony's the only son of the orator Hortensius was beheaded for his complicity in the death of Caius Antonius, Antony's brother. A number of other commanders committed suicide. Livius Drusus, father of Livia who afterwards married Octavian and became the mother of the Emperor Tiberius, killed himself in his tent; Quintilius Varus, who had been captured and pardoned by Cæsar in his war with Pompey, put on his full dress as a general and all his decorations, and obliged his servant to run him through with his sword; and Antistius Labeo, a famous lawyer who had been one of Cæsar's assassins, dug his own grave and, stabbing himself, fell into it.

[18] Suetonius: *Augustus,* xiii.
[19] See Plutarch's *Antony,* and *Brutus.* In the last paragraph of his *Comparison between Brutus and Dion,* he says that the last rites were splendid.

Brutus's stepson, Lucius Bibulus, son of Pompey's old admiral by Porcia, the daughter of Cato who had afterwards married Brutus, surrendered to Antony and was pardoned by him, as were Quintus Horatius Flaccus, the afterwards famous poet, and several others who gave themselves up or were captured. But many, of course, fled, and were not again heard of for many a day; and it may be mentioned that Murcus and Ahenobarbus, commanding the enemy fleet, put to sea as soon as the news of the battle reached them, and took to a roving, piratical life, the former in conjunction with Sextus Pompeius, and the latter independently. Most of the defeated troops, meanwhile, went over to the Cæsarians, and thus completed the extinction of the republican cause.

It is an interesting commentary on the relative positions of Antony and Octavian in popular esteem that when the prisoners who were brought in after the battle were paraded before the two Triumvirs they saluted Antony with respect, but cursed and spat at Octavian.[20] The young man, indeed, seems to have been generally detested, and, realizing the fact, he behaved with great cruelty to some of those prisoners who had been unlucky enough to pass under his jurisdiction and not Antony's. One condemned man, for example, begged that his body should not be left unburied, and to this Octavian replied, with a sneer, "That matter may be left to the birds to decide"; while in another case where a father and son both pleaded for their lives, Octavian coldly told them to draw lots, and the father having drawn the fatal lot and having been instantly beheaded, the son promptly killed himself also. Octavian was only twenty-one years of age, and to us his youth may excuse him, since we know that he developed into a praiseworthy man; but to his contemporaries, who knew not how he would shape, the spectacle of his pale and spotty face, his cold, cruel eyes, and his sour unhealthiness, must have rendered his severity absolutely odious.

In the ensuing weeks the incoming news of what was taking place in the meantime in Rome caused Antony to thank the gods that he was in far-off Macedonia, and not in the capital. Not only the third Triumvir, the easy-going Lepidus, but also Lucius, Antony's brother, who was Consul-elect for the coming year, had

<hr>

[20] Suetonius: *Augustus*, xiii.

passed entirely under the domination of the strong-willed and terrible Fulvia. Acting in the name of Antony, she had established herself as the real ruler of Rome, and, in the words of Dion Cassius,[21] "neither the Senate nor the People dared transact any business contrary to her pleasure." The indecisive Lepidus, indeed, was entirely discredited, and both Antony and Octavian were at one in their wish to eliminate him as soon as possible. It was agreed between them that they would divide the rule of the empire without including him at all in their arrangements: they would, in fact, oblige him to retire into private life.

Of the troops under their command, several legions would have to be demobilised, and of the remainder Antony proposed that he should have the command of seventeen, while Octavian should take fifteen—including the three to be filched from Lepidus. Antony would take over the province of Gallia Narbonensis from Lepidus and add it to his portion of the empire; and Octavian would take Spain from him. For the present the question of the government of the east—Greece, Asia Minor, Syria, etc.—was left undecided; but Antony now made up his mind to travel through this part of the empire not only to eradicate the influence of the republicans from these regions, but also to raise money. He was glad of the excuse to remain away from Rome and Fulvia; and he was very ready to agree that Octavian should go alone to the capital.

He felt quite confident that the young man would there pass like everybody else under the dominance of Fulvia; for not only had he played a very secondary part in the war and had by no means derived any credit from it, not only was he extremely unpopular, but his health was so bad that his early death seemed quite probable, and was anticipated with unconcealed pleasure by most people.[22] Octavian, indeed, was hardly to be reckoned with as anything more than a nominal factor in the situation; and when Antony parted from him at about the end of the year, sending him back to the intrigues of Rome while he himself set out to tour the more tractable Greece and the east, he did not really expect to see him again: either he would die a natural death at no distant date, or Fulvia would strangle him, metaphorically or actually.

Antony knew himself now to be really the only ruler of the

[21] Dion Cassius, xlviii, 4.   [22] Ibid., 3.

Roman world; and he turned to his new task with relish. The cities of Greece and the east were delightful places to visit; and he was sorely in need of relaxation. He was at this time forty-one years of age, and, after months of active life in camp, he was physically in excellent shape; while the consciousness that he was not only supreme but was immensely popular, particularly with the troops, was in these days an unfailing stimulant to his mind. The Philippics of Cicero had been uttered wholly in vain: his reputation had gloriously survived them, while the two battles of Philippi had crowned his military career, and had greatly increased his prestige as a brave and gallant soldier. The world, in fact, was at his feet; and with a light heart he dismissed from his mind all thought of the masterful Fulvia and the sinister Octavian.

OCTAVIA

Louvre

OCTAVIAN

Copenhagen

CHAPTER XV

The Meeting of Antony and Cleopatra at Tarsus, and His Winter with
Her in Alexandria.

41–40 B.C.

It was very urgent that Antony should collect money during
his tour, for immense sums were needed with which to pay off the
disbanded soldiers and to meet the requirements of those still under
arms; and it was therefore expected that crushing fines would be
imposed on those provinces or semi-independent kingdoms which
had given their support to Brutus and Cassius, and that taxes
would be collected all round with great severity. But the business
of satisfying the demobilised troops was a task which Antony had
shifted, with some cunning, onto the shoulders of Octavian; and
in his present mood of happy benevolence he was not prepared to
exert himself unduly, nor, by intolerable exactions, to jeopardise his
chance of making popular the democratic Cæsarian cause in Greece.

During the early weeks of 41 B.C. he marched a part of his
army southwards through Thessaly and down to Athens, in which
charming city he so greatly enjoyed himself that instead of imposing taxes he made lavish presents to it. Like all educated
Romans he could speak Greek fluently, and he amused himself and
delighted the Athenians by often attending the public debates between philosophers and men of learning, and showing an intelligent
interest in their arguments. Brutus, who, it will be recalled, had
resided for a long time in Athens before making his fatal incursion
into Macedonia, was remembered there as a studious and scholarly
man; and the city's intellectuals were surprised to find that the
new master of the Roman world, in spite of Cicero's Philippics,
which, of course, they had read, was also a person of education,
who had not lost on the battlefield that approximation to learning
and taste which had enabled him to hold his own amongst the shin-

ing lights of Cæsar's famous galaxy. He was always asking to be shown their ancient buildings and works of art; he patronised their artists and scholars; and he gave proof of a genuine appreciation of their traditions which warmed their hearts in these days of their city's decline. Sports and games were taken very seriously in Athens, and Antony also gave much pleasure by his interest in the athletic contests and the races to which the people flocked. His own enormous physical strength aroused their admiration, while his easy manners and his friendliness made him immensely popular. People spoke, too, of his fairness and impartiality in matters in which he had to give judgment; and they were much flattered to observe his pleasure when in gratitude they hailed him as a true Philhellene, a lover of Greece, and, in particular, a lover of Athens. Greece still stood for artistic elegance, and it is the fact that when Antony was not fighting or playing the fool he displayed strong leanings towards the cultured life, a tendency which he was pleased to see recognised.

In spite of this, however, there must have been an occasionally observable touch of the honest Philistine in him, a slight indication of that pleasant and shameless practicality which reveals itself sometimes in the modern tourist who is a little tired of the reverence for ruins. We all know the story of the returned traveller who recalled Rome to mind as the place where the buildings were so out of repair; and a somewhat similar story is told of Antony by Plutarch. The people of Megara, a city some twenty-six miles west of Athens, famous for its antiquities, invited him to come over to see their celebrated Senate-house; but when, after conducting him over the venerable edifice, they asked him what he thought of it, he replied, "Well, it isn't very large, and it is extremely ruinous. . . ." People were a little shocked, too, when he proposed to have extensive repairs carried out in the hoary temple of the Pythian Apollo [1]; but, after all, there is not much to be said in defence of an undue admiration of the mere action of time and its pulverising effect upon builders' materials.

In the spring, when the smiling landscape was bright with wild-flowers, and all the world seemed gay, he went north into

[1] At least, I think the point of Plutarch's reference to the repairs is that people were shocked.

Thrace, and, having left one of his generals as governor of Greece and Macedonia, marched with a small and happy army to the Hellespont and thence into Bithynia, which had become a Roman province on the death of its monarch, Nicomedes the Third, the friend of Cæsar. Here he remembered the purpose of his mission, and collected whatever money he could lay his hands on, "while," as Plutarch says, "kings waited at his door, and queens vied with one another in sending him presents and in endeavouring to appear most charming in his eyes." His tour now became a kind of royal progress, splendid, sumptuous, and magnificent; and as he passed on he left behind him the mingled encomiums of those he had entertained or by whom he had been fêted, and the groans of those into whose treasure-chests his tax-collectors had dipped their greedy hands.

Great artistic geniuses—actors, singers, musicians, and dancers —joined themselves to his company. Anaxenor and Xuthus, famous throughout the music-loving Asia Minor, travelled with him; Metrodorus, the celebrated dancer, attached himself to his ever increasing suite; until what Plutarch describes as "a whole Bacchic rout" seemed to move along in his train, "far outdoing in their licence and their folly the pests who had followed him out of Italy." It is needless to say that Antony was soon drinking heavily again; and the unfortunate fact that when he was drunk he was prodigal in his generosity, caused a great deal of suffering of which, it is said, he was wholly unaware. His friends, for instance, would ask him for estates which they untruthfully declared had no surviving owners; and on one occasion he gave his cook the house of a wretched citizen of Magnesia whom he incorrectly believed to be dead, this being a tipsy reward for a particularly good supper.

Thence he came to Ephesus, where, in view of the reputation which had preceded him, the women met him dressed as nymphs and Bacchantes and the men and boys as satyrs and fauns, wreathed with ivy, and singing his praises to the accompaniment of drums, harps, flutes, and other instruments. In their songs they hailed him as Bacchus or Dionysus, a deity who was not only the god of the vine, but was the Joy-bringer, the gentle Spirit of Peace and Love—"and so Antony was to some," says Plutarch, "though to far more he was the Devourer and the Rioter." In this city he

passed his time in the former capacity, enjoying a Bacchic round
of festivities; but before he left he assumed the latter rôle for
just sufficient length of time to issue an ill-considered command
that the annual tax should at once be collected throughout Asia
Minor, in giving which orders he overlooked the fact that the
tax of the previous year had only just been paid. Thereupon a
certain citizen came to him and told him in plain language that
this was sheer robbery. "If you are going to collect two years'
tribute at once," he said, bitterly, "you can doubtless give us a
couple of summers and harvests. If the last tax has not been
paid to you, ask your collectors for it; if it has, and is all
gone, we are ruined men." It is said that Antony was touched to
the quick by these words, and cancelled his orders with generous
apologies; for, as Plutarch points out in this connection, "he
was quite ignorant of most things that were done in his name—
not that he was careless, but that he was so prone to trust frankly in
all about him."

It was probably while at Ephesus that he made the then apparently casual decision which changed the whole course of his
life. For some reason not made clear by classical writers, he
sent a messenger across the sea to Egypt to tell Queen Cleopatra
that he desired to see her. Plutarch thinks that he wished her
to answer an accusation that she had given assistance to Cassius
in the late troubles; but this seems to be contradicted by the
fact that Cassius, when in Syria, had wanted to bring Egypt by
force over to his side before he ventured to join Brutus in the west,
and by the statement of Appian [2] that Cleopatra had sent ships
to help the Triumvirs. Moreover, it is extremely unlikely that
Cleopatra would have sided with the murderers of Cæsar, the
father of her boy Cæsarion, who was now nearly six years of age,
having been born in July, 47 B.C.; for it must have been obvious
to her that if the party of Brutus and Cassius came into power they
would show little consideration for the woman who had shared
Cæsar's dreams of a Roman monarchy.

It appears most probable that Antony wished to ask the Queen
for money, and also to speak to her regarding the possibility of
bringing the young Cæsarion onto the scene as the Dictator's right-

[2] Appian: *Civil Wars*, iv, 74.

ful heir. The murdered hero's own little son, his only known son now that Brutus was dead, might be made a very important factor in the situation. He was said to resemble his father closely; and if, in two or three years' time, he were brought to Rome and shown to Cæsar's old soldiers, they might rally round him to the complete extinction of the unpopular Octavian, who was, after all, but the Dictator's grand-nephew. Antony perhaps saw himself as the future guardian of the boy, ruling the empire as a sort of regent; for, as will presently become apparent, that was undoubtedly the position at which he afterwards aimed.

The adoration of the memory of Cæsar, and the actual worship of his divinity, were now at their height in Rome. Antony owed much of his popularity to the fact that he had unswervingly pursued the chief assassins to their deaths; and the dislike of Octavian was largely due to his having, on the contrary, allied himself for some time with them. Cæsar's spirit, in fact, dominated the Roman world; and Antony could not overlook the tremendous potentialities inherent in the existence of this child, this sole and genuine offspring of the celestial hero of the People.

At any rate, whatever the motive might be—and it was certainly political—Antony was anxious to see Cleopatra again after this lapse of three and a half years since the day when she had fled from Rome. Her age was now twenty-seven, and he had heard that she had matured into a most attractive and clever woman: indeed, he remembered that when she was Cæsar's mistress she had impressed him as a witty and talented young lady, and he was evidently not a little intrigued by the thought of renewing his acquaintance with her. She had not married, and he must have wondered whether she had remained romantically true to Cæsar's memory, or whether there was any foundation for the vague stories he had heard that she had indulged in various secret love-affairs with the gentlemen of her court. [3]

His messenger was a diplomatic young man named Quintus Dellius, who had been the companion of Dolabella in Syria, had fallen into the hands of Cassius whom he had unwillingly served,

[3] Perhaps, however, these stories were not yet in circulation; for the characterization of the Queen as an immoral woman was largely the outcome of later propaganda.

and now was on Antony's staff. He was instructed, it seems, to bring back the Queen's reply, after which a rendez-vous could be arranged at some seaport city further to the east which Antony intended in any event to visit; and it may be said in anticipation that Dellius was able to convince her that his master was, as Plutarch records, "the gentlest and kindest of soldiers," and that she need have no fears. It is said, however, that she showed no inclination to hurry herself, and that the mission of Dellius was followed by a considerable number of letters from Antony and those of his officers who had known her in Rome; and these no doubt gave her news of his movements, so that she might know where to find him when at last she should decide to cross the sea.

Meanwhile Antony proceeded on his gay and leisurely way eastwards, passing through Phrygia, Galatia, and Cappadocia, and so coming down into Cilicia, to the city of Tarsus, which he appears to have reached in August or September. Tarsus, the Tarshish of the Bible, stood on the river Cydnus, twelve miles back from the open sea. It was a city famous for its schools of oratory and philosophy, and it had produced and was producing so many celebrated men of learning [4] that its general atmosphere was academic and scholarly in the highest degree. Antony had made a point of visiting it because it had been a place much honoured by Cæsar, and in consequence of its loyalty to the Cæsarian party had been savagely punished by Cassius. Antony now offered what reparations he could, and instead of gathering money from the city, made generous presents to it, just as he had done in the case of Athens.

It may well be supposed that here, as in Athens, he played the part of the dilettante, patronising the above-mentioned schools, visiting the places of antiquarian interest, and curtailing the exuberant activities of his theatrical entourage. Queen Cleopatra, however, who had decided to make her visit to him during his sojourn here at Tarsus, had heard from Dellius and others a great deal about the Bacchic reception given to him at Ephesus, and about the spectacular nature of his whole progress through Asia Minor. She was deeply interested in him, and in his almost miraculous ascent through difficulty and disaster to supreme power. To her he must have seemed to be more than a play-actor, and his tour a sacred carnival rather

---

[4] St. Paul also was born there a generation later.

than a mere show: she recalled, no doubt, his behaviour at that never-to-be-forgotten Lupercalia, when he had pranced almost naked and in a sort of inspired and momentous frenzy, through the Forum—she had been in Rome at the time, and must have had an account of it from Cæsar, if, indeed, she had not witnessed his strange and eventful antics herself from some window; she remembered that he used often to comport himself as a Hercules, thus impersonating his legendary ancestor; and she had heard more than once of late that people were speaking of him with affectionate awe as an incarnation of some deity.

Now, in her own country she was herself an actual divinity, and Cæsar had presented her to Rome as an incarnation of his own mythical ancestress, Venus, placing her statue, it will be recalled, in his new temple dedicated to that goddess, and allowing her likeness to be impressed upon her coinage in the guise of Isis-Venus. She therefore made up her mind to play the rôle of Venus to Antony's Dionysus—not altogether in fun, not altogether in consideration of its spectacular value, but in a large measure because the custom and mental outlook of the age enabled her, in spite of her reason's ridicule, to think of herself in some sense as a goddess and of Antony as a God. After all, Cæsar was now Jupiter-Julius, and in the fiery guise of a comet he had been seen in the starry night-sky rushing to heaven: why, then, should not this new superman, this new master of the Roman world, who had so miraculously arisen, be also a deity, as Ephesus had evidently deemed him?

But in this seat of learning as has been said, Antony had discarded his celestial rôle; and when the news was suddenly brought to him one afternoon by runners from the coast that Cleopatra's fleet had been sighted, and that she was sailing up the river to the city, he assumed his most dignified posture, and gave instructions that the city's Forum should be prepared for a formal reception. He dressed himself in his official robes, and, when the time came, went in state to this place, seating himself upon the magistrate's throne, his glittering company of officers and officials about him, the learned professors and venerable elders of the city on his either hand, and a great array of soldiers holding in check the excited crowds. [5]

[5] The account of the meeting between Antony and Cleopatra is given in Plutarch's *Antony*.

As he sat waiting, however, he noticed that one by one his immediate company excused themselves and left him, and that gradually the crowd was melting away. Making puzzled enquiries, he found that Cleopatra's ships had arrived at the quay near by, and that the vessel upon which she was travelling was so marvellously decorated that the sight was drawing the whole city to the waterside. Hastily he sent her a message, little short of a command, that she should come ashore to be received formally by him, and that afterwards, since it was already dusk, she should accompany him to his official residence to attend the state banquet which he had ordered to be made ready.

By the time that her answer was received he was almost alone in the darkening Forum, save for his staff and the wondering soldiers. She sent word that she would prefer to receive him and his friends on her ship, and to give him dinner there instead; and at this, Antony appears to have been completely nonplussed, not knowing what was the dignified thing to do. The enthusiasm of the crowds, however, relieved him of his embarrassment, for they trooped back into the Forum, shouting out that Venus herself had come to feast with Bacchus, and that he must certainly betake himself to the quay to greet her and to see the marvellous sight.

He therefore complied with their wishes, cancelled his banquet, and walked with great dignity down to the mooring-place. Darkness had now fallen, and the sight which met his eyes was indeed astonishing. The hot September night being still and windless, the illuminations which Cleopatra had provided for the occasion were seen at their best: the whole deck of the royal vessel was ablaze with candles, arranged in squares, circles, and other patterns; and in their steady light the Queen could be seen reclining under a golden canopy backed by a still spread sail of purple linen. Around and about were half-naked boys, impersonating Cupids, and maidens scantily attired as nymphs of the sea: the sailors had all been sent below, and these youths and girls were so posed at the rudder, at the helm, and about the rigging, as to suggest that they were the fairy crew of a fairy ship. There was an orchestra, too, playing the haunting music for which Egypt was famous; and here and there stood a priestly figure burning sweet-smelling incense.

When Antony went aboard, and greeted the Queen in these

fantastic surroundings, he found that she herself was dressed in
the guise of Venus, that is to say she was wearing the soft and
shimmering robes of that goddess and her elaborate headdress.
She was a small, dainty little creature, radiant, rather than beautiful, but having a charmingly moulded face, an abundance of soft,
dark hair, a fascinating mouth, thoughtful, wide-set eyes, and a
general appearance of breeding which justified her rather prominent
though finely chiselled nose. He was charmed by her personal appearance, and yet I fancy that he must have felt a little embarrassment at the theatricality of her studied pose and at her carefully
staged tableau; for, as we shall presently see, she very quickly
changed her tactics.

Antony, it has to be remembered, had had so much to do with
the theatre and with all sorts of professional actors and actresses
—his former mistress, Cytheris, in particular—that by now he must
have been quite incapable of being bewitched by the histrionics of an
amateur, however splendidly presented. He could admire her display as a work of art; but he could not respond to it in the same unnatural vein, and, indeed, it would seem that the more ardently she
enacted the part of the voluptuous goddess the more uncomfortable
he became, and the more he felt himself to be a practical, vulgar
man. As so often happens when a would-be enchantress plays her
romantic part before a man of the world, his response was discon-
certingly close to laughter. His identification with Dionysus, after
all, had not been of his own seeking; and he was not prepared to
sustain the rôle for the sake of supporting this young lady in her
own celestial impersonation.

"She, perceiving that his joking behaviour was broad and vulgar," says Plutarch, "and that it savoured more of the soldier than
the courtier, soon responded in the same manner"; and though that
writer is here referring to the following day, one may suppose that,
being a quick-witted woman, she did not take long to step out of
her rôle and to explain it as a piece of fun, or as something intended
for the eyes of the people. At any rate, she had made herself look
charming: that was enough, and for the rest, she had to admit, as
many a young woman has had to do, that her intended effect had
been ruined by its contact with the armour of a middle-aged man's
experience. Antony was now forty-two: he had reached the age at

which plain-dealing on the part of the other sex is more appreciated than the cleverest acting.

History does not tell us more of that first meeting after these three and a half years; but we are informed that on the next night, or the night after that, Antony entertained the Queen in return, and that on this occasion she herself behaved as jovially and as naturally as he did, capping his improper stories with her own, passing ribald remarks upon the cooking, teasing him about the dearth of sparkling conversation, and generally treating him like an old friend and boon-companion. This bantering, outspoken woman was far more to his taste than the languorous Venus of the night of her arrival; and he was quite captivated by her.

"Her actual beauty," writes Plutarch, "was not in itself so remarkable that none could be compared with her, or that no one could see her without being struck by it; but the contact of her presence, when one got to know her, was irresistible. The attractions of her person, combined with the charm of her talk, and the distinctive character of all she said or did, was something bewitching. It was a pleasure merely to hear the sound of her voice, especially as she could pass from one language to another, and could speak without an interpreter to Ethiopians, Bedouins, Jews, Arabs, Syrians, Persians, and many others," not to mention Egyptians, Greeks, and Romans.

On the following night Cleopatra entertained Antony at another banquet, and on this occasion the entire floor of her vessel's saloon was carpeted with roses so thickly packed that they formed a sort of sweet-smelling mattress. For some weeks she remained at Tarsus with him, and at length she suggested that he should visit her at her capital, Alexandria. Antony was in any case going to continue his tour from Tarsus on into Syria and Palestine, where he expected to arrive in November or December; and from Palestine it would be a simple matter to cross the desert into Egypt, and he felt that he could spend his time very profitably there during the winter months. I imagine that at first he merely thought of exacting a handsome sum of money from the Queen in return for a promise of Roman support for her on her always precarious throne; but gradually, it seems to me, a larger plan presented itself to his mind, and he was eager to study the resources of her country, financial, military, and naval, and to enroll her as an active ally in his future schemes.

There was every reason for him to avoid going back to Italy for the present; for he must have been most anxious not to involve himself in the difficult situation which had there developed. Octavian had unexpectedly recovered from his illness and was now not only unlikely to die young, but was proving himself quite capable of asserting his authority even though it were in opposition to that of Antony's self-appointed representatives—Fulvia, his wife, and Lucius, his brother, who was one of the Consuls for this year 41 B.C.

It had been Octavian's thankless task to try to settle the demobilised soldiers on the land, and to satisfy their demands both for profitable acres and for payment of the money due to them; but, having no available funds for the purpose, he had been obliged to ask the municipalities and private landowners in certain districts to find room for the veterans on their estates and to supply them with their initial stock. This, so Antony heard, had caused an uproar; and Lucius, supported by Fulvia, had opposed the plan, saying that the grants to the ex-soldiers should be suspended until Antony returned to look into the matter. [6] Octavian, on his part, had angrily declared that Lucius was not acting in accordance with Antony's wishes in taking the part of the threatened landowners against the soldiers; and to mark his disapproval of Fulvia, whom he regarded as more to blame than Lucius, he had divorced her daughter, Clodia, Antony's step-daughter, whom he had married at the time of the establishment of the Triumvirate, and had sent her back, still a virgin, to her mother.

The upper classes had for the most part decided that Lucius was quite right in opposing this spoliation of the rich for the benefit of the disbanded troops, and in demanding that no such drastic measures should be taken until Antony had been consulted and had had time to raise money in the east. Lucius had thus become the hero of the moneyed classes and what remained of the republican party, and the enemy of the veterans; but with one section of the latter he had retrieved his popularity by suggesting the compromise that lands should be found for those soldiers who had been loyal to

[6] Dion Cassius xlviii, 5–7.

Cæsar's memory from the first, and who had actually fought at Philippi.

Matters had then passed out of control. The veterans in some cases had forcibly seized the lands which Octavian was trying to obtain for them, and had come to blows with the owners, who relied on the support of Lucius; and there were indications that actual warfare would break out between the two parties. Lepidus, the discredited third Triumvir, meanwhile, had played so ignoble a part that he had been brushed aside in the general commotion, and was no longer of the least importance. According to the dispatches which Antony received, however, it seemed that Fulvia was the stormy petrel, and was encouraging these disturbances in order to oblige her husband to return to Italy, [7] not only so that he should be once more under her control but also that he might be forced to quarrel with Octavian whom she now passionately desired to destroy— if only in revenge for his insult to her daughter.

Antony, however, did not want to quarrel with Octavian at the moment, and, indeed, had honourable scruples in that regard, since, after Philippi, he had made an amicable agreement with him, binding so long as the Triumvirate should last, and since, moreover, he had the interests of the veterans at heart himself, and was most anxious to avoid being involved in the difficulties consequent on their demobilisation until he had collected sufficient money to satisfy in cash their just demands. That was the crux of the matter: money. By hook or by crook he would have to raise money; and, at the moment, Egypt seemed to him to be the most likely source of the gold he needed. Cleopatra's kingdom was immensely wealthy; and I think he must have seen that he could probably persuade her to raise the required sum with which to satisfy the veterans in the hope that thus she would pave the way for their recognition of Cæsarion as Cæsar's true heir.

He knew that Cæsar had intended to marry her and to make her his consort upon the world-throne which he had desired to establish; he realized that the dream of such a throne for her son still haunted her thoughts; he saw that a goal of this kind was to her the only hope for her dynasty, since its alternative fate would probably be extinction, and the annexation of Egypt by Rome, at no dis-

[7] Appian: *Civil Wars*, v, 19.

tant date. If, then, he could induce her to place all her resources at
his disposal in return for a promise that he would act as guardian
to her son and that he would launch him, when he was of age, into
the adventurous sea of Roman life as the heir of the adored Dictator,
he would not only be able to return to Rome with enough money
to win the gratitude of the ex-soldiers, but would ultimately be able
to place in the field a formidable rival to Octavian. It was necessary,
then, for him to get to know the young Cæsarion, and, if he should
prove to be a promising boy, to arrange for his education in Rome.

It was some such plan, I think, which led him to accept Cleopatra's invitation to visit her in Egypt. It is true that he had found
her to be a most entertaining companion now that she had dropped
her celestial pose and had come down to earth, so to speak, with
such an uncompromising impact, and it is certain that he had already
entered into amorous relations with her in his own light-hearted way;
but I do not think that he was as yet at all deeply in love with her,
nor she with him. He was a very fine figure of a man and she was
greatly attracted, no doubt, by him: she was an exceedingly charming young woman, and he was greatly intrigued by her. But world-
events were too serious just now for the consideration of them to be
relegated to the back of the mind; and neither he nor she could
forget that they were leaders in momentous movements. Both were
bent on obtaining from the other certain material advantages. There
was no room yet in their hearts for sensational romance.

After Cleopatra had left Tarsus, Antony moved on to Daphne,
near Antioch, in Syria, and later into Palestine, whence, having
made certain dispositions in regard to the Jewish government, [8] and
having apparently sent most of his troops back into Asia Minor, he
crossed the desert into Egypt, and so arrived at Alexandria probably
in December. The Egyptian capital was at this time the most important city in the world, with the exception of Rome, and not even
Rome could rival it as a seat of learning and a centre of intellectual
and artistic life, in which respect it had long since taken the place
of Athens. In character it was predominantly Greek; and although
the population was very mixed and contained Egyptian, Syrian,
Jewish, and many other elements, the language, dress, and habits
of the upper classes were Greek, as also was the city's architecture.

[8] Josephus: *Antiquities of the Jews,* xiv, xiii, 2.

It had been founded by Alexander the Great to serve as a Greek port on the conquered coast of native Egypt; but Cleopatra's ancestor, a Greek general who had made himself King of Egypt after Alexander's death, had converted it into the capital of the country, and he and his descendants had there ruled for the last three hundred years over the people of the Nile, with whom they had no more real or penetrating connection than Englishmen in India today have with the natives of that country, or the early settlers in America had with the pacified Redskins. Cleopatra, as has already been pointed out, was not an Egyptian: she was a Macedonian Greek, enthroned in a Greek palace, and living a Greek life in a Greek city which had little concern with the native Egyptian nation other than that of governing it and drawing enormous wealth from it.

The palace stood upon the Lochias promontory, on the east side of which the rocks and sandy coves fronting the city extended into the distance, while on the west was the harbour protected from the open sea by the long, low island whereon rose the famous Pharos lighthouse, then regarded as one of the wonders of the world. This lighthouse, built two centuries earlier, was a white marble structure, nearly six hundred feet in height, and having a beacon-light visible for thirty miles out to sea.

The city was full of magnificent buildings, the Temple of Serapis (the Jupiter of the Egyptians) being without a rival. The Museum, which was what we should now call a university, was the greatest institute of learning in the world, its particular subjects of study being medicine, astronomy, mathematics, and literature; and its famous library contained nearly half a million books. The mausoleum in which lay the body of Alexander the Great, in a coffin of gold, was one of antiquity's most revered monuments, and around it were the splendid sepulchres of Cleopatra's royal ancestors. The Forum, the theatres, the Hippodrome or racecourse, the Gymnasium, and the famous arcaded Street of Canopus, were amongst the other architectural marvels; and the public parks and gardens were celebrated.

The Alexandrians carried on an immensely prosperous trade with the Mediterranean lands. Egypt has been called the granary of the ancient world, and corn was exported to Rome and elsewhere in great quantities. The linen trade was extensive, and the material of which the sails of ships were made came nearly all from here. Perfumes, incense, and oils were exported, and many manufactures such as glass, pottery, and paper (papyrus) were sent across the seas. Gold, copper, and ornamental stone were extracted from the eastern Egyptian deserts; and works of art of all sorts were carried over to the European markets, while Greek and native Egyptian artists and craftsmen were everywhere in demand.

Over this wealthy Greek city, and over the teeming Egyptian race dwelling in the Delta and the Nile Valley beyond, Cleopatra ruled in strangely solitary splendour. Her two brothers, who had in turn been her consorts, [9] were both dead, the one having been killed in 47 B.C. in the war which was waged when Cæsar was in Alexandria, and the other having died early in 44 B.C. just before the Dictator's assassination. Her now exiled sister, Arsinoe, and her little son, Cæsarion, were the only other surviving members of the royal family; and it appears that the boy was all the world to her. It is indeed remarkable that after Cæsar's death she had not married, but had for these three and a half years and more remained in lonely control of her kingdom; and the explanation must be that she was waiting for that new master of Rome to arise who would take the place of Cæsar as the protector of her boy and as the aspirant to the world-throne to which Cæsar had wished to elevate her, and of which she had never ceased to dream.

Antony was now that master: he seemed to her to be the hero for whom she had been waiting so patiently, watching with anxious eyes the movement of Roman affairs. Until lately she had hardly supposed that the expected man of destiny would prove to be this Antony, Cæsar's jovial colleague; but now that she had come to know him in Tarsus, and had seen his popularity and his power, she was convinced that in him lay all her hopes. Her attitude to him differed from his to her in this respect, that whereas he sought to make use of Egypt's wealth for his own political ends, offering in return to promote the future interests of her son in the arena of Roman ambition, she, on her part, regarded Antony as the destined ally and husband for whom she had waited, and saw no reason why he should not create with her

[9] She had been "married" to each of them, according to the Egyptian custom of brother-and-sister marriages in the royal house; but this was an empty formality.

that Roman throne which Cæsar had so nearly succeeded in found-ing. Her line of action was quite clear to her: she would have to excite his admiration for her regal power and her boundless resources of wealth, and at the same time she would have to win his actual love as she had won Cæsar's.

When she had captivated Cæsar, it should be pointed out, she had been no more than twenty-one years of age, and had been a wayward, capricious, audacious little creature, whose pluck had greatly appealed to him. She had been driven out of Alexandria by her brother, it will be remembered, and when the Dictator had taken possession of the palace she had managed to penetrate the enemy's lines and to be carried into Cæsar's room rolled up in a carpet. He had promptly seduced her, but she had so won his affec-tion that he had remained with her until her child was born, it will be recalled, and then had renewed his relations with her in Rome. There she had perhaps become a little vain and haughty, as Cicero had found her; but the disaster of Cæsar's death, and her consequent flight back to Egypt, had knocked all the vanity out of her, and now, as her twenty-eighth birthday approached, she was a woman of much deeper character. There is no reliable evidence that she was less moral than most other women of the time; [10] and, in any case, it is not for us to sit in judgment upon her if it be true, which is questionable, that she had not behaved with continence during these years of her solitude. She must have been very lonely.

It must be admitted that the writers of antiquity have por-trayed her character in ugly terms, presenting her as a lewd and vicious enchantress, ambitious, ruthless, and cruel; but if we remember that she ultimately *did* make the bid for a throne in Rome, that the attempt was wrecked by Octavian, who himself became the first Emperor, and that the writers of the imperial age not unnaturally placed the blame upon her for the unaccountable behaviour of the popular Antony, we can easily see that they would be prone to describe her as a siren and a courtesan, the slave of her passions.

Actually, Cleopatra was not altogether the cause of Antony's downfall; and in the light of this unavoidable conclusion the Queen's character takes on a fairer aspect. To understand her we

[10] See my *Life and Times of Cleopatra*.

must think of her at this time as a woman struggling to prevent her country being annexed by Rome, and audaciously meeting that danger by aiming at no less than an Egypto-Roman crown, a world-wide sovereignty, which was, she hoped, to be established for her and her son, Cæsar's child, by the aid of Cæsar's kinsman, friend, and representative—Antony. Let us admit that she was ambitious, scheming, and unscrupulous; let us admit what nobody denies, that she was brilliant, energetic, courageous and tenacious; yet in the absence of any but vague and prejudiced gossip about her, we must surely receive the conventional stories of her immorality with the greatest caution.

Like many of her ancestors she was a woman of refinement and culture, a true Greek in her artistic and intellectual equipment; and as soon as Antony arrived she set herself to the task of dazzling him with the brilliance of her court, and shaming him out of those less elegant kinds of entertainment in which she had participated in Tarsus. Here in Alexandria she was surrounded both by genuine scholars and artists and by fashionable and wealthy intellectuals who seem to have combined the art of good living with the rarer accomplishment of clever conversation; and Antony at once found himself the guest of honour, and, indeed, the dominant figure, in a scintillating company such as he had not known since the days when he was a member of the famous bevy of talent over which the astonishing Cæsar had presided. It is true that he was a simple soul, and was as happy in a rough company of soldiers as he was, in other mood, in the society of the elegant; but here in Cleopatra's gay capital there was a Greek spirit of light-heartedness in these men of brains which nothing in Rome could match; and its effect upon him was like that of wine. It seems that he had never before so thoroughly enjoyed himself.

Very soon he proposed that Cleopatra and the most brilliant of his new friends should form themselves into a society or club which should be called the *Amimetobioi*, or "Inimitable Livers"; and, the idea being well received, Antony became the chief "Inimitable," with the Queen as his colleague. Each member of the club in turn entertained the others, all vying with one another in their attempts to stage the perfect party. As an instance of the length to which these efforts were carried, Plutarch mentions the fact that on one occasion a visitor to the royal kitchens saw no less than eight wild boars in different stages of being roasted whole, not because the company was large, but because the cooks, having no idea of the hour at which Antony and Cleopatra would choose to dine, were obliged to employ this method of ensuring that the pork would be cooked to a turn.

Antony, however, was incorrigibly boisterous, and the Queen did not neglect to meet his chronic high spirits with a revival of her own. "Were he disposed to mirth," writes Plutarch, [11] "she had at once some new amusement or delight to meet his mood: at every turn she was with him, and let him escape her neither by day nor by night. She played at dice with him, drank with him, hunted with him; and when he exercised himself in arms, she was there to see. At night she would go rambling with him to disturb and play pranks on people by knocking at their doors or windows, she and he being both disguised in servants' clothes; and from these expeditions he often came home very scurvily answered and sometimes even roughly handled, though most people guessed who he was. However, the Alexandrians in general liked it all well enough, and joined good-humouredly in his frolics and jokes, saying they were much obliged to him for acting his tragic parts at Rome and reserving his comedy for them."

It is hardly necessary to say that she was now his habitual bed-fellow. She made no secret of it; and, since in her own country she was above the law, she allowed her subjects to recognize in Antony her chosen consort, who, though having another wife in Rome, was here by the special sanction of the gods united to her, just as the divine Cæsar had been. Thus, when it became known that she was again going to become a mother, nobody was either surprised or shocked.

She herself, no doubt, was happy to think that a definite link between herself and Antony would thus be created, which might cause him to regard an ultimate legal marriage with her almost as a duty; but he, on his part, was not prepared to admit any such obligation. Perhaps he would divorce Fulvia and marry the Queen one day; but he was a busy man, and this little holiday in Alexandria

[11] Plutarch: *Antony.*

would presently end, and he would have to return to Rome to pursue his destiny. The thought had probably been implanted in his mind by now that his fortune might lead him to that throne of which Cæsar had dreamed; but the time had not yet arrived. For the present he was only prepared to offer Cleopatra his protection on her own Egyptian throne, and his guardianship of her boy, Cæsarion, whom he had found to be a promising child; and in return for this protection he was going to avail himself of Egypt's wealth. But for the rest, his future was in the lap of the gods.

One service, however, he was able to perform for the Queen, namely the removal of two pretenders to her throne. Her sister Arsinoe, that same princess who had been led through the streets of Rome in Cæsar's Triumph, had from childhood never ceased to plot against her; and it seems that she had given what help she could to the enemies of the Cæsarian party in the hope that their victory would lead to the dethroning of Cleopatra. She was now residing in Asia Minor, having found sanctuary with the priestesses of Artemis; and the Queen asked Antony to give orders for her execution. This he did, for she was unquestionably a dangerous enemy; and she was despatched at the steps of the altar where she was serving, the High Priest of Artemis being arrested as a conspirator against the Cæsarian cause, and a general clean-up of this nest of treason being carried out. The other pretender was a man who claimed to be that brother of Cleopatra who had really been killed in his war with Cæsar: he seems to have been in league with Arsinoe, and was trying to raise an army in Phoenicia at the time when Antony's agents seized him and put him to death. An ambitious Egyptian general, named Serapion, who had helped them both, was also executed.

The close of 41 B.C. found Antony at the height of his enjoyment of Cleopatra's splendid hospitality; but, probably in January or February of the new year, 40 B.C., he received belated despatches [12] from Rome, giving him an account of what had occurred in Italy since last he had had news, in the autumn.

The opposition of Lucius and Fulvia—supported by the men-

---

[12] News travelled from Rome to Alexandria very slowly in wintertime, for shipping was then disturbed by the dangers of rough seas, and dispatches were generally carried around by land, through Macedonia, Thrace, Asia Minor, and Syria.

aced landowners—to Octavian's intended appropriation of lands for the disbanded veterans, recorded earlier in this chapter, had at length developed into open hostilities, and the former had gone out into the country to recruit an army. At length Lucius had forcibly seized upon Rome, and had made a speech in the Forum, proposing that Octavian should be declared a public enemy, that the Triumvirate should be ended, and that Antony should be asked to return to Rome and to assume the post of Consul for 40 B.C., with special powers for the pacification of the country. These proposals may be described as an attempt to form a coalition between the democrats and the remnant of the republicans; and it is evident that Lucius and Fulvia had supposed Antony to be ready for a reconciliation of the two parties in opposition to the bullying Cæsarianism of the ex-soldiers. Octavian, however, with the aid of the veterans, had gained the upper hand, and had obliged Lucius to retire to Perugia, where he had soon been closely besieged; while Fulvia had taken up her headquarters at Præneste (Palestrina), and not only had assumed command of a military force, but had actually dressed herself like a general and had buckled on a sword. [13]

She was smarting under the now unconcealed insults of Octavian, and she had believed that she and Lucius, by declaring that they were carrying out the wishes of her absent husband, could rouse the country against the young man, and could clear him out of the way, so that she, Lucius, and Antony should be in complete control of the empire. Octavian, very wisely, had stated that he had no quarrel with his friend and colleague, Antony, but only with this turbulent couple, who, though Antony's wife and brother, were really acting against his interests: in fact, he seems to have said, he and Antony were both good democrats, having the welfare of the poor soldiers at heart, while Lucius and Fulvia had become traitors to the party, and were leaguing themselves with the old republicans, the conservatives and the aristocrats.

Antony, of course, was extremely troubled by this news; and, in the words of Plutarch, "at last arousing himself with difficulty from idleness, and shaking off the fumes of wine," he made preparations for his departure. He must have been furious with Fulvia and his brother Lucius for having thus recklessly jeopardised his cause by

[13] Florus, iv, v.

this premature attempt to pick a quarrel with Octavian; and one may suppose that his intention was to hasten back to Italy, to repudiate his wife, and, with Cleopatra's money and such funds as he could raise elsewhere, to satisfy both the veterans and the landowners, thus gaining personal credit for the ending of the quarrel, re-establishing his endangered position at home, and relegating Octavian once more to the background.

But now came another piece of news, this time from Syria, which was even more disconcerting. After the battle of Philippi a good many Roman fugitives had taken refuge in Parthia; and one of their number, Labienus, the son of the Pompeian general killed at Munda in Spain in 45 B.C., had persuaded the Parthians to invade Syria and Cilicia, his reckless aim being, apparently, to crush Antony and thus to pave the way for a future return of the republicans to power. A great invading army had crossed the Euphrates, and was marching on Antioch in northern Syria, and such Roman troops as were in that part of the country were in full retreat. The attack was a complete surprise.

With such dangers threatening him, Cleopatra had no wish to keep Antony in Alexandria. Egypt itself was safe from a Parthian invasion, for the Egyptian army, aided by the Macedonian troops permanently stationed in the capital, and the Roman soldiers who had been there ever since the days of Gabinius, could be relied on to hold the eastern Egyptian frontier. With a sudden sinking of her heart the Queen must have realized that Antony was not the undisputed master of Rome that she had supposed him to be. She had been too hasty, perhaps, in staking her all upon him; for he had yet far to go, and much lost ground to retrieve, ere he could think of championing her cause and that of Cæsarion before the Roman world. Her attitude towards him is revealed in an anecdote related by Plutarch. During the idle days shortly before his departure, he used to go out fishing with the Queen; but having been unlucky in his catches, he jokingly engaged some divers to descend unseen into the water and to fasten large fish onto his hook one after the other, so that he appeared to be the most wonderful of fishermen. Cleopatra, however, detected the trick, and sent a diver down with a salted fish, which Antony drew to the surface amidst great laughter, whereupon the Queen said to him: "Leave the fishing-rod, Antony, to us poor little sovereigns of Egypt: *your* game is cities, provinces, and kingdoms!"

Early in March, 40 B.C., he set sail for the city of Tyre, on the Syrian coast, with a small fleet, leaving Cleopatra to bring into the world, when her time should come, the offspring of their happy nights together. Neither he nor she could tell when they would meet again.

CHAPTER XVI

Antony's Return to Rome; His Marriage to Octavia; and His Maneuvers for Political Unity.

40–39 B.C.

WHEN Antony arrived at Tyre he was dumbfounded to find the city already in a state of siege. The Parthians, advancing with wholly unexpected speed, had swarmed over Cilicia, Syria, and Palestine, and the Roman troops in this particular neighbourhood had retired headlong within the impregnable Tyrian walls. Fortunately they were here quite safe for the present; for though they were thus besieged by land, they had command of the seas and were unlikely to run short of food. Antony therefore decided that he must hasten by ship to Greece and mobilise his army; and one may suppose that he promised to return as soon as he had cleared the Parthians out of Asia Minor. Tyre could hold out indefinitely; Egypt was pretty safe; Syria and Palestine could be reconquered when the time came. The danger-point was in Asia Minor, for there was nothing to stop the Parthian advance through Cilicia to the Hellespont. Thither it was obvious that he must go.

He sailed by way of Cyprus and Rhodes to Ephesus, at the other—the western—end of Asia Minor; but meanwhile the Parthians under Labienus had marched along the coast and were heading for the same city. In anticipation it may be said that their rapid advance was finally checked in Caria, the province just to the south of Ephesus; for here the three cities of Stratonicea (Eski-Hisar), Mylasa (Melasso), and Alabanda (Arabissor), held out against them, and, with the aid of Roman troops, blocked their way.

At Ephesus Antony received a full account of the troubles in Italy, and for a while he must have been distracted. Fulvia and

Lucius seemed to have ruined his prestige in Rome, and his hopes of returning there to settle triumphantly the dispute between them and Octavian—between the landowners and the veteran soldiers—had to be abandoned. He had no money to take home; and money was the essential factor. The funds which he had expected to receive from Cleopatra had been greatly reduced, I suppose, because of the needs of the Queen herself in placing her country in a state of defence against the Parthians; and whatever amount he *had* been able to procure from her was now required for the war against these invaders here in Asia Minor. Moreover, matters, in any case, had gone too far in Italy to be so simply set to rights.

It will be recalled that Octavian had shut up Antony's brother, Lucius, in Perugia, and had wrecked his and Fulvia's foolish attempt to rid themselves of him by forming a militant coalition of democrats and republicans. After a long but hopeless siege Perugia had surrendered early in March; and Octavian, being anxious not to rupture his relations with Antony for good and all, had allowed Lucius to go unmolested into retirement, at the same time, however, showing the utmost severity to the other prisoners, sentencing great numbers to death, and, to those who implored his mercy, making but one invariable reply: "You must die." [1] It was said that he had actually selected three hundred of the half-starved citizens, and had slaughtered them before the altar of the deified Cæsar on the anniversary of the Ides of March, as a sort of human sacrifice; but we may infer from the words of Suetonius that this story lacked confirmation.

Antony's family, and the few of his highly-placed officers who had lent support to this armed movement against Octavian, had been allowed to betake themselves unmolested out of the country, for Octavian had persisted in his refusal to annoy his colleague by punishing any one of them, and, indeed, his troops would never have allowed him to harm a relative or friend of the popular Triumvir. Antony's mother, Julia, now a woman of over sixty, had taken fright, however, and had crossed the sea to Sicily, where she had placed herself under the protection of the gallant and picturesque Sextus Pompeius, who was still leading his sea-roving life as the pro-republican commander of an independent fleet. The ill-starred

[1] Suetonius: *Augustus*, xv.

rising had been to a certain extent republican in character, and at any rate it had had the sympathy of the republican exiles to this extent, that Sextus was very willing to give sanctuary to the refugees, being in this instance glad also to put Antony under an obligation to him. Fulvia, meanwhile, had been escorted by three thousand of Antony's Gallic cavalry to Brindisi, where, breathing fiery threats of vengeance, she was preparing to take ship for Greece to join her husband.

Octavian had then returned to Rome, where he was now in absolute control, and, so Antony heard, was behaving himself with great brutality, maintaining a diplomatic pretence of fidelity to the Triumvirate, but quietly taking his revenge on all the lesser supporters of Lucius and Fulvia, putting many of them to death, some even by torture. To satisfy the veterans he was pursuing his policy of placing them upon the lands confiscated without any compensation from their rightful owners, most of whom were beggared by these now wholesale transactions; and all the upper classes —both republicans and right-wing democrats—were looking to Antony to come home to save them from this detestable young man, [2] who was only maintaining his position by such pandering to the unruly ex-soldiers.

Octavian was at this time in his twenty-third year, and his so far strangely successful struggle against sickness and opposition had hardened him into a man of unpleasant and cruel character. He was leading an unnatural life of anxiety and excitement, and the condition of his nerves was such that he could not sleep properly at night, and by day had often to distract his mind by throwing the dice and gambling for heavy stakes. Eating or drinking offered no temporary deliverance from his worries, for he had little appetite, and more than two or three cups of wine upset his stomach [3]; but, as is often the case with the sickly, his thoughts turned with great frequency to the gratification of his passions, many ugly stories being told of him in this regard, and, indeed, the widely believed reports that he had been perverted in his sexual tastes as a youth

[2] Ferrero (*Greatness and Decline of Rome,* iii, xiii) describes Octavian at this time as "a monster incarnate" and "the abomination of Italy"; but this seems an overstatement.

[3] Suetonius: *Augustus,* lxxvi, lxxvii.

are only to be discredited on the grounds that now in manhood he
was so addicted to common rape or adultery.

He was never free of his fear of Antony's popularity, and the
fact that for this reason he had been obliged to let Fulvia, Lucius,
and others go unpunished, must have been a constant irritation to
him. He knew, too, that he was hated by the upper classes, and
only tolerated by the army because he gave them what they demanded; and his own unpopularity was making him sly and morose.
Moreover, Italy was at this time almost in a state of famine, largely because Sextus Pompeius was preventing the safe arrival of
corn-ships from abroad; and his inability to cope with this master
of the seas was a source of continuous annoyance to him, more especially since the people blamed him, rather than Sextus, for all
their miseries, and openly prayed for Antony's return.

In this connection it may be mentioned that one day about
now Octavian gave a party to eleven of his friends, at which the
ladies dressed themselves as the goddesses Juno, Vesta, Minerva,
Ceres, Diana, and Venus, and the men as the gods Jupiter, Mars,
Mercury, Vulcan, and Neptune, while he himself appeared as
Apollo. The blasphemy, and the reported obscenity of the proceedings, were greatly resented, and the jesting remark was widely circulated that the scarcity of corn was due to these gods having eaten
it all up at this notorious entertainment. Very truly Octavian was
Apollo, people said: not Apollo the Preserver, however, but Apollo
the Tormentor, the Death-dealer, in which aspect that deity was
propitiated in flagellatory rites in certain parts of the city. [4]

These things Antony heard while he was at Ephesus, where he
stayed throughout April and May, energetically organizing the resistance to the Parthian advance; and then, in the latter month, came
the news that Octavian had opened negotiations with Sextus Pompeius, sending the latter's mother, Mucia, (one of Cæsar's former
mistresses, it will be remembered,) to him with proposals for an accommodation. The overtures, however, were unsuccessful, apparently because Sextus demanded full rehabilitation for the republican
refugees in return for the cessation of his attacks upon the corn-
ships. In June further disquieting news reached Antony, this time
of the death of Calenus, his old friend and defender against Cicero's

⁴ See Martial, xi, 15, 1.

attacks, who had been in command of his legions in Gaul. Octavian was reported to be hurrying thither to take control of these legions; and though he could be said to be doing so on behalf of the Triumvirate, it was apparent that he was in reality about to attempt to seduce this army from its allegiance to Antony.

The Parthian advance appeared now to be finally checked; and Antony, whose energies were concentrated upon the preparations for an offensive which should drive them out of Roman territory, came to the conclusion that his best course would be to go into Greece so as to be nearer to Italy in case of any trouble with Octavian in regard to the raising of troops. He therefore crossed over to Attica, and arrived at Athens towards the end of June; but meanwhile Fulvia had reached this city in her flight from Italy, and thus they met again. There is no clear evidence of what happened at that meeting, but it seems [5] that, while his wife furiously lashed out at him for his now notorious intrigue with Cleopatra, he as angrily attacked her for the mess she had made of his affairs in Italy. There was evidently a violent quarrel, for Fulvia did not remain long with her husband, but went to Sicyon (Vasiliko),[6] a little to the west of Corinth, and some eighty miles from Athens; and there she seems to have abandoned herself to despair, caring not whether she lived or died.

Two or three weeks later Antony's mother arrived from Sicily, bringing an offer of friendship from Sextus Pompeius, and a proposal that they should unite against Octavian. An agreement of this kind would have been extremely advantageous to Antony, for, in the difficulties of his situation, the taking of the republican refugees under his benevolent wing would have been very helpful to him; and in any case Sextus would be a useful ally, since he was in command of so powerful a fleet. But Antony, in spite of his many faults, was a man of honour, and he did not feel able to break the pact he had made with Octavian. He therefore sent a reply saying that he was grateful for the offer of friendship and that he would avail himself of it if Octavian should play him false; but that if Octavian should, on the other hand, remain faithful to the terms

---

[5] Appian: *Civil Wars*, v, 52.

[6] Dion Cassius, xlviii, 28. Plutarch's statement that Fulvia was at Sicyon *on her way* to meet Antony seems incorrect.

of the agreement ratified after the battle of Philippi, then Antony
would do his best to bring about an amicable agreement between
all three of them.

In August Antony received news which confirmed his growing
suspicion that Octavian was trying to hamper him in his preparations for the offensive against the Parthians. The unscrupulous
young man had managed to obtain the support of the legions of
the late Calenus in Gaul, and, having placed them under the command of one of his own friends, had returned quietly to Rome.
This was a definite breach of their agreement, for Gaul was Antony's province, and the troops therein were supposed to take their
orders from him alone; and Octavian's only possible justification
would be that his action had been designed to prevent these legions
from raising a rebellion of their own [7] now that their commander
was dead. Octavian, however, evidently realized that his behaviour
would appear to Antony to be hostile; and he therefore took the
friendly step of appointing Antony's brother, Lucius, to the governorship of Spain,[8] in spite of the fact that a few months ago
they had been at each other's throats. I do not know of the existence
of any evidence as to what then became of the turbulent Lucius;
and it would seem that he did not long survive this quick change
in his fortunes.

Octavian, however, was very worried on hearing of the overtures Sextus Pompeius was making to Antony, and at length decided to renew his own overtures to him. Sextus was married to
the young daughter of a certain Lucius Scribonius Libo, a man of
important plebeian family who had a sister, Scribonia. Scribonia
had already been married twice and was the mother of two children, but she was now a widow; and although she must have been
considerably older than Octavian, that harassed young opportunist conceived the idea of taking her to wife in place of the repudiated Clodia, and of thus uniting himself with the family of
the dangerous Sextus. True, Sextus was the son of Cæsar's old
enemy, Pompey, and had himself held command under Cæsar's
murderers; but Octavian was entirely without principle in his
political orientations. He therefore sent his confidential friend,
Cilnius Mæcenas—the afterward well-known patron of Virgil and

[7] Appian: *Civil Wars*, v, 60–63.   [8] *Ibid.*, 54.

Horace—to negotiate this curious union by which he would become the uncle of the sea-rover's wife; and within a few weeks the marriage took place—to the mingled anxiety and amusement of Rome.

Antony's response to this action was immediate. He wrote to Sextus inviting him to reopen the subject of an alliance on the basis of the rehabilitation of the republican refugees; and he also came to an agreement along the same lines with Domitius Ahenobarbus, the other independent sea-rover, promising him immunity from punishment as one of the conspirators against Cæsar, in return for his support. Ahenobarbus was probably able to show that he had not actually taken part in the murder of the Dictator; and Antony, so far the implacable hounder of the assassins, was glad to wink at whatever guilt was really his—a compromise which leads Dion Cassius to remark that in difficulties of this kind "those in power decide nothing in accordance with principles of justice, but determine on friend and foe merely as their passing needs demand, regarding the same men now as enemies and now as allies according to the exigencies of the moment." [9]

So far there was no actual rupture between the two Triumvirs,[10] but Antony was quite sure that Octavian would be ready enough to come to blows if he were to feel that such hostilities held for him any hope of success, and he was determined to forestall him. Early in September, therefore, he set sail for Italy with a strong force of loyal troops, seized Sipontum (Siponto), on the coast, north of Brindisi, and then proceeded to invest the latter port. At the same time Sextus Pompeius, always ready for an adventure, landed a small body of troops to the south, and also took possession of Sardinia. Octavian at once despatched a force under the command of his young friend Agrippa, which succeeded in beating Antony's men out of Sipontum; but at the same time Antony defeated Octavian's troops who were marching to the relief of Brindisi.

These movements, although attended by bloodshed, were regarded by both sides as simple maneuvers for position, not as actual warfare; for neither the one leader nor the other dared to begin another civil war. Both wished to show that they were ready

<hr />

[9] Dion Cassius, xlviii, 29.   [10] Velleius, ii, lxxvi.

for a fight, if fight there was to be, but each wished to avoid striking the blow which would carry the scuffle beyond the bounds of
this perilous but not envenomed game of tit for tat. Antony was
saying that so long as Octavian did not definitely break the pact
renewed between them after Philippi, and so long as he gave what
help he could in the preparations for the campaign against the
Parthians, he, Antony, had no desire to go to war with him; and
Octavian, on his part, was saying that not Antony but Fulvia
was the enemy of peace.

At that critical juncture Fulvia suddenly died at Sicyon: nobody knows how she came to do anything so beneficial to peace,
and, strange to say, the suggestion that one or other of the Triumvirs had administered a dose of poison was never advanced;
but the effect of her death was astonishing in its instantaneousness.
Octavian immediately wrote to Antony saying that the cause of
his fears was now removed, and apologising for having interfered with the legions of Calenus in Gaul; and Antony responded
by apologising for Fulvia's behaviour, and saying that the blame
for all the unpleasantness was entirely hers. In a few days—that
is to say, in the early part of October—the two Triumvirs met
in the camp outside Brindisi, and a new pact was made between
them; while their troops shouted and clapped their hands in enthusiastic approval, and all Italy breathed again.

The agreement was of the most novel and far-reaching character. Octavian was to be sole ruler of the western empire—Italy,
Dalmatia, Gaul and Spain; and Antony was to be autocrat of the
entire eastern empire—Greece, Macedonia, Thrace, Asia Minor,
Syria, and Cyrenaica in North Africa; while the feeble Lepidus
was to be allowed to retain control of the remainder of North
Africa west of Antony's dominions. Octavian was to hand over
the legions of Calenus, and a distribution of the other forces was
to be made so that he and Antony should have from sixteen to
eighteen legions each, while Antony was to be allowed to enlist
new recruits in Italy if the Parthian War made it necessary to do
so. Both sides agreed that Sextus Pompeius should be dropped,
and that force should be used jointly against him if he were re-
calcitrant. Finally, it was arranged that Antony should marry
Octavian's half-sister, Octavia, whose husband, Marcellus, had

recently died: it is true that Octavia was the mother of two infants and was about to give birth to a third,[11] but the latter exigency was a disqualification which would be removed shortly, and which need cause no delay to the marriage.

Octavia, of course, was not consulted in the matter. She was an unemotional, kindly, nice-looking young lady of about twenty-five years of age, whose virtue was beyond reproach, and who is described by Plutarch as "quite a wonder of a woman." Her brother was devoted to her, as she was to him; and it is said that she made his clothes for him,[12] and looked after him like a mother. She belonged very definitely to that category of the female sex which is typified by sweet and patient subserviency to the male, and which, for that reason, is described as virtuous by men of narrow outlook. To Antony, however, who had once capitulated to the stirring ambition of the masterful Fulvia and had lately been captivated by the courageous and vital Cleopatra, she must have seemed—if the epithet be not too strong—somewhat bovine. He can hardly have looked forward with much pleasure to domestic life with her, for passive feminine goodness can be exceedingly exasperating; but at least he could feel that she would not interfere with his freedom, except in so far as her gentle chiding might some day bring the blush of shame to his cheek. At any rate she was comely, and, indeed, Plutarch declares that she was more pleasing to the eye, at first sight, than Cleopatra, whose charm lay in her brilliancy and in that quality which is now commonly termed "sex-appeal," wherein, one may suppose, Octavia was somewhat lacking.

The marriage had been forced upon Antony to a great extent by the soldiers who saw in this union a guarantee of peace; and there can be little doubt that, while he was not really in love with the Egyptian queen, his mind was never quite free of her memory. Indeed, at this time she must have been very much in his thoughts, for he had just received news that she had presented him with twins, a boy and a girl, whom she had named Alexander Helios and Cleopatra Selene, the "Sun" and the "Moon." They had been born in September, and their arrival must have recalled very clearly to his mind those romantic nights in early winter when the splendor of the Alexandrian palace and the intoxication of Cleopatra's en-

[11] Dion Cassius, xlviii, 31.   [12] Suetonius: *Augustus,* lxxiii.

ticements had combined to make life for him an enthralling dream.

But the vast expanse of the ocean today lay between them, and even though she were now nursing at her bosom the babes which were his, even though she were sustained in her loneliness by the expectation of his return, the picture of her must have had little substantiality in his busy thoughts. Unquestionably he would go back one day to her, temporarily or even permanently; but for the present it was to her interest as well as to his that he should climb the difficult path of his ambition without her charming companionship. It was his business first to conquer Parthia, and to extend the Roman dominions to the very frontiers of India; then, returning to the west in the glory of these conquests, he would unite the warring political factions in the capital, and would so outshine Octavian that the perpetual rulership of the entire empire would perhaps pass into his hands. After that the next step would possibly raise him to that dreamed-of throne, Cleopatra being then at his side, and Octavia divorced. Until that great day, however, the Queen would have to remain an absent helper and friend, and the memory of her an unsubstantial vision to warm his nights by Octavia's placid side.

As soon as the agreement with Octavian was signed and sealed the two Triumvirs made their way to Rome, both riding in triumph into the city, escorted by tumultuous crowds of townspeople and soldiers; and the marriage was celebrated with prolonged public festivities which had hardly terminated when the bride's confinement took place.

The people then demanded that peace should be made with Sextus Pompeius, so that his raids upon the corn-ships coming to Rome should be ended, and the menace of famine removed. Public opinion turned in favour of this outlawed son of Pompey the Great, and soon the very mention of his name was received with loud applause. At the Circenses, the annual races and contests held in November, it happened that the statue of Neptune was carried around the course in the religious procession which opened the day's sport; and at sight of it the crowd cheered and clapped, for the house of Pompey was said to trace its descent back to that god. Antony and Octavian thereupon removed this statue from the procession, and were in consequence hooted. A dangerous riot ensued, in which Octavian lost his self-control, implored the mob to do him no hurt, and rent his clothes in despair, while Antony cursed and swore at the rioters and vainly defied them and their brickbats.[13] They escaped only with difficulty, and were obliged afterwards to promise that negotiations would soon be opened with Sextus.

Meanwhile, Antony turned his attention to the Parthian menace, and having appointed Domitius Ahenobarbus to the governorship of Bithynia, Asinius Pollio to that of Macedonia for the coming year, and Munatius Plancus to that of Asia Minor, made Ventidius Bassus governor of Syria, and gave him the command of the large army he had prepared for the attack upon the Parthian invaders. Asinius Pollio and Plancus, it will be remembered, were the former generals of Cæsar who had thrown in their lot with Antony during his final struggle with Cicero: they were both men of culture who had once been members of Cæsar's brilliant circle, and although Plancus was too fond of the gaieties of fashionable life to leave much of a name for himself in history, Asinius Pollio was a true patron of the arts and himself a distinguished poet, dramatist and scholar. I mention the fact because it is an indication that Antony was maintaining his own position as a patron of the arts, and that his officers and intimate friends, like Cæsar's, were largely drawn from Rome's intellectual and artistic circles. Ventidius Bassus, however, was a man of very different stamp: he had risen from the lowest ranks, had won Cæsar's esteem, and afterwards had endeared himself to Antony by his fidelity and help after the disaster of Modena. He was a brave and brilliant soldier; but since, as a youth, he had been taken prisoner in the civil wars of 89 B.C., he must have been old enough to be Antony's father.

In parenthesis it is necessary to speak here of the two great poets, Virgil and Horace; for at this time they were already known to Antony and must have received his patronage while he was in Rome. Virgilius Maro (Virgil) was born in Cisalpine Gaul in 70 B.C., and was at this time about thirty years of age. His small family estate had been seized by Octavian and handed over to some ex-soldiers during those wholesale confiscations after the battle of Philippi which had caused the rising engineered by Fulvia

[13] Dion Cassius, xlviii, 31.

and Lucius; but Antony's friend, Asinius Pollio, had taken up his case, and, through the good offices of Mæcenas, had obtained compensation for him from Octavian. Virgil had already composed some poems of importance, and Antony's former mistress, Cytheris, had recited them in the theatre with great success; and though his famous works were still to be written, he was now recognised as one of the coming men in that world of literature which so greatly interested Antony.

Quintus Horatius Flaccus (Horace) was five years younger, having been born in southern Italy in 65 B.C. He had been at Athens during the time when Brutus was organizing there his coming campaign; and he had taken part in the battle of Philippi, and thereafter, as has already been mentioned, had fled before the Cæsarians' victorious pursuit. Antony, however, had pardoned him, and he had returned to Italy, only to be deprived of his paternal domain by Octavian during that same confiscation of lands for the benefit of the ex-soldiers. His friend Virgil now introduced him into the society of the great, and with the help of Mæcenas he was able to obtain employment in Rome. At this time he had just composed his first important Satire, the subject of which is an indication of the lax morals of the age: it is a discussion as to whether a young man should confine his amorous attentions to professional prostitutes or to other men's wives.

The close of the year 40 B.C. found Antony still in Rome, working in outward harmony with Octavian, with whose half-sister, Octavia, he had now begun his conjugal life. Her baby by her husband, Marcellus, had been born at the end of October or early in November, and already at the end of December or beginning of January fecund Nature had once more delegated her for motherhood in the following autumn. Antony, it should be observed, was ever proud of his productivity, and used to say that, like his ancestor, Hercules, he wished thus to propagate his race in many lands nor cared to confine his hopes of progeny to any one woman. Already he had many illegitimate children by Fadia and others; a daughter, Antonia, by his first wife of the same name; two sons, Antyllus and Julus Antonius, by Fulvia; the twins, Helios and Selene, by Cleopatra; and now Octavia was to perform her hurried part in the perpetuation of his healthy and vigorous line.

He was, of course, eager to get back to Asia Minor to direct the operations against the Parthians, but affairs in Rome required his presence, and in particular the promised treaty with Sextus Pompeius had to be arranged—a treaty which was in effect a step towards the unification of all political parties, since Sextus was sheltering so many political refugees. Antony had lately come to feel that a coalition of democrats and republicans such as Cæsar had once aimed at was the most desirable form of government; and he was evidently now working towards this end. Sextus, however, did not respond very willingly to the first negotiations, and Octavian was none too eager in the matter, since the refugees loathed him; and thus the spring of 39 B.C. had gone by before the two sides came seriously to business. Messages, thereafter, passed slowly between them, conveying terms and modifications of terms, until at length in the summer a full agreement was arrived at and a meeting arranged for the signing of the treaty. This meeting took place at Misenum (Miseno), the important naval base at the northern end of the Bay of Naples.

Both sides feared treachery, and while Antony and Octavian placed themselves in a commanding position upon the quay, surrounded by their bodyguards and backed by a great army which lined the shores in both directions, Sextus took his stand upon a breakwater separated from them by one of the narrow mouths of the harbour, his huge fleet covering the sea behind him, the decks of the ships being crowded with his soldiers. Across the few yards of intervening water the Triumvirs and the famous outlaw exchanged their salutations, and made their protestations of friendship to one another, after which the documents to be signed were conveyed by boat from one side to the other.

The terms of the treaty were simple, and one can plainly see in them Antony's efforts to heal the old sores left by Pharsalia and Philippi, and to unite the two political parties. From Octavian's western empire, Sicily and Sardinia were conceded to Sextus—who already occupied these islands—as territory to be governed for five years by him on behalf of Rome; and from Antony's eastern empire, the northern coast of the Peloponnesus—Achaia, that is to say [14]—was handed over to him, obviously because Octavian had not been willing to cede any territory unless Antony did the same. Sextus undertook to add no more ships to his fleet, to give sanctuary to no refugees from Italy, and to interfere no more with Rome's corn-supply. The Triumvirs, on their part, agreed to extend a free pardon to the political fugitives, runaway prisoners or slaves, and all the others who had collected under the standard of the sea-rover, with the exception of any of the actual assassins of Cæsar who might have obtained sanctuary with him. Certain of the republican refugees, who had fled to Sextus after Philippi, were to receive compensation to the extent of a quarter of their confiscated property; and some were to be given office as Tribunes or Prætors in Rome. Sextus himself was to receive an indemnity for the loss of his father's property, and at the end of the five years was to be one of the Consuls.

As soon as the signed documents had been exchanged between the contracting parties, a great shout was raised by the men on either side, for at long last the remaining menace of political warfare was removed, and the fugitive republicans and other outlaws would be able to rejoin their families. The cheering is described by Dion Cassius as having been "tremendous and inextinguishable," and with charming exaggeration he adds that the hills shook thereat and several people died of fright or from concussion. Many of the refugees who had come over in the boats of Sextus dived into the sea and struck out for the shore from which they had been exiled, while their friends swam to meet them, "hailed them while swimming, and sank under the water with them as they embraced." For the rest of the day and far into the night the vociferous reunions continued, while here and there the sounds of lamentation told of someone's discovery that a relative on the other side was no longer living. "Those who could get no news of their loved-ones," says Dion, "were like maniacs; or, on learning the worst, they would tear their hair and rend their clothes, calling upon the lost by name as if they had just died and were lying there before them." [15]

[14] The whole of the Peloponnesus, and northern Greece south of Thessaly, was included by the Romans in the province known as Achaia; but it seems that only the actual little region of Achaia itself was now ceded.

[15] Dion Cassius, xlviii, 37.

Meanwhile, the Triumvirs and their new ally drew lots as to which should entertain the others to supper, and the lot having fallen to Sextus, Antony asked him where the meal would be served. "There," said Sextus, pointing to his flagship, which had now been moored at the quay; "that is the only house that Pompey has inherited from his father"—and as he spoke he gave a meaning glance at Antony, who, it will be remembered, was now in possession of the former mansion of Pompey the Great in Rome. Wine flowed freely at the supper, and presently, says Plutarch, Sextus began to make jokes about Antony's love-affair with Cleopatra, which Antony, being benevolently intoxicated, took in good part. All were making merry when suddenly Menas, the captain of the ship, whispered to Sextus: "Shall I cut the mooring-ropes and make you master not only of Sicily and Sardinia, but of the whole Roman empire?" Sextus remained silent for a while, and during that silence the lives of Antony and Octavian, all unknown to them, hung in the balance. Then he replied: "You could have done it without telling me; but now it is impossible. I cannot break my word."

On the two following days Sextus was entertained ashore first by Antony and then by Octavian, and so promising did the alliance seem to be that the three men decided to make it more binding by some new marriage between the families. Now Sextus had an infant daughter, who was the niece of Scribonia, Octavian's wife; and Antony's new wife, Octavia, had a little son of about four years of age, the child of her previous husband, Marcellus. This boy was both Octavian's nephew and Antony's stepson, and what, therefore, could be more agreeable than that he should complete the circle by becoming Sextus's son-in-law? The fact that the girl and boy were not yet out of their nurseries was some hindrance to their marriage, of course; but there was no reason why they should not be formally betrothed, and this ceremony was therefore performed at once. Everybody was in the highest spirits; for the return of the republican outlaws, their compensation and the promise of office made to them, was an indication that a new spirit of political toleration was abroad, and that Cæsar's old dream of a coalition of all parties had been successfully revived once more.

It was generally felt in Rome that Antony had been the moving spirit in this pacification of the country, and though he had been unable to do much to alleviate the bitterness felt by the landowners dispossessed by the ex-soldiers, the blame for that injustice was laid wholly upon Octavian, whose unpopularity was increased by the return of the exiles—men who hated him for his treachery after Modena, when he had suddenly turned upon them and had joined Antony, and for his cruelty after Philippi. Antony, at any rate, had never been treacherous, they said, and had seldom acted with cruelty. Both political parties liked him as greatly as they disliked Octavian; and this attitude was so frequently expressed by voice and gesture that while Antony went about his business unarmed and unattended, smiling good-naturedly upon all men, and hobnobbing alike with rich and poor, Octavian was morose and nervous, dreading assassination and seeing dangers everywhere.

A certain inoffensive gentleman named Pinarius was one day making some shorthand notes of a speech then being delivered by Octavian, when the latter thinking he was a political enemy gathering material for a later verbal attack, ordered him to be arrested; and on the man resisting, a soldier ran him through with a sword before Octavian's eyes. On another occasion a Prætor named Quintus Gallius approached him, carrying a writing-tablet under his cloak: Octavian thought it was a dagger, and had him put to torture in order to find out whether he belonged to any group of conspirators. He was never seen again.[16]

In the month of September two interesting events occurred. Octavian celebrated his twenty-fourth birthday, and thereupon shaved his chin for the first time,[17] giving a great public entertainment to celebrate the event. As has already been said, it was the custom in Rome for young men to allow their natural beards to grow untouched until at some age, generally soon after twenty, they and their relatives deemed the time to have come for their entrance into the sedate and clean-shaven company of their elders; but it seems that only now did Octavian feel that his career could dispense with the prerogatives and the palliations of youth. The other event was the confinement of Octavia, and the birth of a daughter, whom she and Antony named Antonia. (I may mention

[16] Suetonius: *Augustus*, xxvii.   [17] Dion Cassius, xlviii, 34.

in passing that the girl was ultimately married to Lucius Domitius Ahenobarbus, the heir of that Ahenobarbus who had just been reconciled to Antony; and the son of this union was the father of the Emperor Nero).

The good Octavia was now mother or stepmother to no less than nine children—Antony's eldest daughter, Antonia, the child of his first marriage; his two sons by Fulvia; Fulvia's two children, Clodius and Clodia, the latter being the repudiated wife of Octavian; Octavia's own boy and two girls by Marcellus; and this new baby, Antonia. Pompey's house on the Palatine, where they lived, must thus have been a lively place enough; and what is known of Antony's character permits us to suppose that he enjoyed the racket, and endeared himself to these occupants of the nursery. He was not happy, however, at this time; for he could not overcome a distaste for the company of Octavian who, as his brother-in-law as well as his colleague, was frequently a guest at his house. The young man was invariably the winner, and Antony the loser, in any friendly contests or games in which they indulged —in cock-fighting, for example, or dice-throwing; and, in fact, the phenomenon was so remarkable that Antony at length consulted an Egyptian fortune-teller about it, who, having evidently a deep insight into men's characters, advised him to keep clear of Octavian, since, he declared, there was something in Antony which instinctively feared and mistrusted him. "When you are away from him," the soothsayer explained, "your spirit is proud and brave, but when he is present it becomes depressed." [18]

There was, indeed, something coldly masterful in this remarkable young colleague of his, something unpleasantly domineering, which suggested that his phenomenal rise to be, at twenty-four, the acknowledged ruler of the western empire was due to more than good luck. He had done innumerable things which ought, by every rule of the game, to have consigned him to limbo: he had been a traitor and a turncoat, he had appeared to run away in battle, he had mercilessly put men to death; and yet here he was with half the Roman world under his command. It is true that in all their joint actions in affairs of state Antony was still the stronger partner; but he experienced increasing difficulty in sup-

[18] Plutarch: *Antony*.

pressing Octavian's independence. Like some phantom of a night-mare which rebounds after every blow, interminably beaten down only to rise again unharmed and threatening, so Octavian must have presented himself to Antony's troubled mind as a menacing, contemptuous figure, endlessly overwhelmed yet ever indestructible, continuously defeated yet always the ultimate, sneering victor.

It may be supposed that the healthy-minded, robust, and simple Antony watched with perplexity the seemingly undeserved good-fortune of his unclean and sickly colleague. The frigid grey eyes of the younger man, with that unblinking stare of which he was beginning to be so proud;[19] the cruel little mouth; the sallow, pimpled face; the untidy, fair hair; that perpetual, sniffling cold in the head—these characteristics, one may suppose, were begin-ning to get upon Antony's nerves, more particularly because they were so inexplicably associated with a certain dignity and power and with this irritating disdain of the fortunate for the unlucky. We who look back upon these times from a distance of nearly two thousand years, and who know that Octavian became in the end an outstanding benefactor of his country, and a strong, puri-tanical ruler—a hypocrite always, but, like many a hypocrite, a pillar of the state—can see the cause of Antony's perplexity and sense of frustration; for in this ailing and iniquitous youth we behold the potentialities which transformed him into the revered Augustus, and we know that Antony was baffled by a brain and a will-power greater than his own. To him, however, this was not apparent; and the annoying consciousness that Octavian was the incurable cancer in all his plans came to assume an uncanny sig-nificance.

The treaty with Sextus Pompeius, however, spared Antony the necessity of having to remain longer in Rome. His work there was done. He had accomplished by statesmanship what Fulvia and Lucius had so disastrously failed to accomplish by their rash re-sort to arms. The rehabilitation of the republican exiles had put the necessary check on Octavian's activities, for there was now quite a large body of men in office who were opposed to his par-ticular brand of Cæsarianism and were hostile to the man him-self; and thus Antony felt that he could return to Greece with his

[19] Suetonius. *Augustus,* lxxix.

mind at ease in regard to the probable developments in the capital. The Senate was like clay in his hands, and, indeed, he had created so many new senators in conjunction with Octavian that the House had little character, opinion, or prestige, and could be relied on to do what it was told.

Some time in October, therefore, as soon as Octavia was able to travel, he set out with her and the baby for Athens, carrying with him a senatorial decree ratifying in anticipation all the dispositions he should make while absent from Rome.

CHAPTER XVII

The Enforced Renewal of the Triumvirate, and Antony's Departure for
the East, and Reunion with Cleopatra.

39–36 B.C.

Upon Antony's arrival at Athens he received the most welcome
news in regard to the struggle with the Parthians. Not in vain had
he devoted weeks and months of his time to the organisation of a
trustworthy Roman expeditionary force; nor had he been mistaken in his choice of a general. The doughty old Ventidius Bassus
had led his army, in the spring of 39 B.C., through Thrace and
across the Hellespont into Bithynia, whence, in the summer, he
had marched southwards through Galatia; and at this the Parthians under Labienus, who were still in occupation of the southern coast of Asia Minor, had hastily withdrawn into Cilicia, near
the Syrian frontier.

Some time in September Ventidius had come to grips with Labienus amongst the Taurus Mountains and had utterly defeated
him. The Parthians had fled into northern Syria and thence eastwards to the Euphrates; whilst Labienus had escaped in disguise
into Cilicia, but shortly afterwards had been captured and executed
as a traitor—a Roman in command of Rome's enemies. Thereupon
the other Parthian armies in Syria had also withdrawn to the Euphrates, all Syria and Palestine being once more opened to the
Romans, the siege of Tyre raised, and the highroad to Egypt re-
established. Thus, in one brilliant campaign, the invaders had been
entirely cleared out of Antony's eastern empire.

Antony was elated, and ordered public feasts and thanksgivings to be celebrated throughout Greece and Asia Minor. In Athens
itself he caused great festivities to be held; and at the races and

games he astonished everybody by discarding the dress and circumstance of a military ruler and by acting, himself, as steward, appearing in the square-cut gown and white attic shoes of that office.
Moreover, so thoroughly did he perform the steward's duties that
whenever he considered the two champions in any combat to have
fought long enough he entered the ring, took them by the scruff
of the neck, and separated them, his own exceptional strength en-
abling him to do so with loudly applauded ease.

Having sent orders to Ventidius to remain in Cilicia, probably
at Tarsus, during the winter, and having promised to join him
there in the spring, he settled down to reorganize the eastern empire and particularly to give his attention to the improvement of
conditions in Greece.[1] So greatly was he beloved that on all sides
the people revived the legend that he was Bacchus or Dionysus come
to earth; but it should be pointed out that in doing so they were
not identifying him merely, or even at all, with the rollicking and
tipsy god of wine, but rather with that gentle and benevolent
spirit of goodness and happiness which was this deity's most
widely recognised aspect. In this connection I think it will be as
well to remind the reader that a few generations later, when the
story of the beautiful life of Christ was spread throughout these
parts, the people at once identified Him with Dionysus; and, in
fact, the date of our Christian Epiphany—January 6th—is none
other than the date of the great Dionysian festival.[2] Evidently there
must have been some exceptional qualities of sweetness in Antony's
disposition, or, at any rate, in the side of his character shown to
the Greeks, which thus caused them to associate him in their minds
with that same diety to whom they afterwards found a resemblance
in Jesus of Nazareth.

A curious story, by the way is related by Dion Cassius[3] that
at the great festival of Athena, the patron goddess of Athens,
when it was customary to celebrate her mystical betrothal, the
Athenians invited Antony to play the male rôle in his aspect as
the incarnate Dionysus, and that he agreed to do so, insisting, how-

---

[1] Dion Cassius's remark (xlviii, 39) that he tried to impoverish those cities of
Achaia which were to be handed over to Sextus Pompeius, is against all the
evidence.

[2] Weigall: *The Paganism in Our Christianity*, Chap. xxii.

[3] Dion Cassius, xlviii, 39.

ever, that his celestial bride should bring him a dowry, or, in other words, that Athens should make him a handsome present for his services on the occasion.

This winter in Athens marks a considerable change in Antony's political views, or, rather, it marks the putting into execution of a policy which had perhaps been developing in his mind ever since he had come under the influence of Queen Cleopatra in Alexandria. Like Cæsar, Antony had been a democrat, but, again like Cæsar, he had begun to consider the possibility of converting his popularly sanctioned autocracy into actual monarchy. In his dreams of the expansion of Roman power into the Orient he had realized the disadvantages of holding his authority simply from the Senate in Rome for a limited number of years; and he had begun to feel that his interests could not well be developed by a system under which he himself was a temporary ruler served by governors of provinces and other magistrates appointed for short periods. Something more permanent was required.

Here in the eastern empire many of the provinces were accustomed, or had been in the recent past, to the idea of monarchy, and even the Roman mind, he believed, was almost ripe for the acceptance of a king, although expressed opinion was still opposed to such a thought. The two Consulships of earlier days provided a now unwieldy form of government, and, in fact, their power had already been destroyed by the superimposing of his and Octavian's joint autocracy. It had once been suggested that Cæsar should be actual king outside Italy; and Antony saw no reason why that permanent position of regal authority should not ultimately be his. In the meantime, he felt that he should be supported not by temporary provincial governors but by petty kings each at the head of a local government made strong by the removal of the exigencies of frequent change; and in pursuit of this policy he now decided to play the part of King-maker upon the grand scale.

The country of Pontus, at the north-east corner of Asia Minor, had been without a monarch since the death, in 47 B.C., of Pharnaces, the successor of that Mithradates who had fought against Rome, as recorded earlier in this book; and now Antony restored the monarchy, giving the crown to Darius, the son of Pharnaces. The mountainous land of Pisidia, just to the west of Cilicia, had never fully admitted Roman authority; and here Antony established a certain Amyntas as king. Upon the empty throne of the neighbouring territory of Lycaonia he placed an officer named Polemo, who had taken an active part in the defeat of the Parthians: he was the son of Zeno, a famous orator of Laodicea. At about the same time he recognized as King of Judæa that afterwards celebrated Herod who was still alive at the time of the birth of Christ and who figures in the Gospel story.[4] He also gave his patronage to the kings of Thrace, Galatia, Cappadocia, Paphlagonia, Upper Cilicia and elsewhere, who had all been expecting extinction by Rome rather than support, being the last left of the dynasts; and of course he confirmed Cleopatra in her sovereignty of Egypt.

Antony himself, meanwhile, was unquestionably adopting an attitude towards life and a manner of living which were those of a Hellenised potentate rather than of a Roman magistrate. The transformation in his person is noticed by some of the ancient writers, and, indeed, they are inclined to exaggerate it in order to present a picture of him in keeping with the tradition, which later grew up, of his having ultimately become a typical oriental; but actually the change was slight, though noticeable, and was, I fancy, no more than that which we might observe today in a man of northern race who had taken up his abode in a Latin land—an Englishman or American living in Paris, for example.

In many respects he was following a course already pursued by Cæsar. Conventional and conservative Romans—men of Cicero's or Cato's stamp—had always regarded Cæsar as "a dangerous man," one who had broken with traditional Roman habits, and had become somewhat foreign in his ideas; and the case of Antony was very similar, with this addition, that he was rather fond of theatrical display, enjoyed dressing the part, liked a splash of colour. His entertainments were sumptuous; wine, women, and song were to be found wherever he went; and his house was always open to actors and actresses, dancers and musicians, artists and men of letters—clever and talented people of all kinds, in fact—to whom he played the host with prodigal generosity. Yet he did not lose the common touch, and almost to the end was adored by his

[4] *Matthew*, ii.

soldiers and by the masses, the secret of his popularity being his unbounded sympathy, his easy manners, his simplicity, and just that democratic attitude which the stiff-necked Roman aristocrat believed to be incompatible with the maintenance of prestige.

The beginning of the year 38 B.C. brought Antony an astounding piece of news from the metropolis. Octavian had divorced his wife Scribonia upon the very day on which she had borne him a daughter, Julia. He said he was quite tired out by her peevishness [5]; but there were two more palpable reasons for the separation. In the first place he wished to sever his connection with the family of Sextus Pompeius, against whom he had made up his mind to launch an attack at the first possible opportunity; and Scribonia, it will be remembered, was the sister of Sextus's father-in-law, and had been married to him to create an alliance between the Pompeian and Cæsarian houses. In the second place he had fallen in love with another man's wife.

This lady was the beautiful and talented Livia, daughter of the republican Livius Drusus who, it will be recalled, had committed suicide in his tent after Philippi. She was the wife of Tiberius Claudius Nero, an important person of ancient lineage who had taken up arms with Lucius and Fulvia against Octavian, had later fled to Sextus Pompeius, and thence to Antony, and had been one of the exiles rehabilitated by the terms of the treaty of Misenum. To her husband she had borne one son, who was named Tiberius, and ultimately became Emperor of Rome. Octavian had fallen in love with her some time ago; and now, when she was going to have a child in about three months time, either by him or by her husband, a divorce was arranged so that she might marry her lover. The husband, apparently, was quite agreeable to the arrangement, and not only attended the wedding and formally handed Livia over to Octavian, but also gave her a dowry as though he had been her father.

It is to be supposed that Octavian believed Livia's unborn baby to be his, for it is difficult, otherwise, to understand for what reason he married her thus in haste when she was in this condition; yet no such explanation was put forward by ancient writers, and when, in the spring, the child was born and proved to be a boy, Octavian

---

[5] Suetonius: *Augustus*, lxii.

named him Claudius Drusus Nero, and sent him with his compliments to Livia's former husband, at the same time placing it on record that the latter was the infant's father. Yet gossip seems to have implied that Octavian was the real parent; for the remark was widely repeated, and passed into a proverb, that in the families of the great the children are born in three months.[6]

Rome was scandalised by the marriage and its circumstances, and Octavian was regarded as a very unpleasant young scoundrel. The gods, too, were outraged, and, in fact, the goddess Virtus fell off her pedestal flat on her face [7]; and when the priests took her down to Ostia to purify her in the sea, she tumbled into the waves and was with difficulty recovered.

But if Antony was astonished at the news, his surprise was turned to anger when he received the intelligence that Octavian had followed up his divorce from Scribonia by persuading the forces of Sextus Pompeius in Sardinia to desert their leader and to hand that island over to him with sixty ships and many men. Sextus at once reported to Antony that Octavian had broken the treaty, and therewith the angry sea-rover began again to attack the Roman shipping. Octavian then wrote to Antony asking him to come at once to Brindisi to discuss the situation, declaring that the fault lay with Sextus who had himself broken the treaty in various little ways.

Antony was furious. He was just about to start for Cilicia to join Ventidius Bassus, having heard that the Parthians were making a new incursion into Syria; and the dislocation of his plans thoroughly upset him. With all possible speed he raced back to Italy, determined to stop the expected fight [8]; but to his great annoyance Octavian was not at Brindisi to meet him. He therefore wrote very sharply to him telling him to behave himself and to respect the treaty with Sextus; and therewith he sailed back to Greece, and at once set out for Cilicia, hoping to reach the army in time to lead them against the enemy.

He arrived there in June, only to find that Ventidius had already marched into Syria to attack the Parthian invaders and

---

[6] Dion Cassius, xlviii, 44.

[7] Ibid., 43.

[8] So Appian, *Civil Wars,* v, 79, which contradicts Dion Cassius, xlviii, 46.

had overwhelmed them at Gindarus in the land of Cyrrhestice, that area of northern Syria above Antioch which lay between Cilicia and the Euphrates. Pacorus, the son of the King of Parthia, had been killed, and so many thousands of his men with him, that the Romans were justified in regarding the victory as full revenge for the destruction of Crassus and his army at Carrhæ, sixteen years earlier. Ventidius had then pushed on to the city of Samosata (Samosat) on the Euphrates, the capital of Commagene, Parthia's ally, and had laid siege to it.

Antony must have been bitterly disappointed at having arrived too late to take command of these operations; but he hastened on to Samosata, where he and Ventidius spent the summer in fruitless siege operations which were terminated at last, probably in August, by the surrender of the beleaguered King of Commagene on terms. Antony then went south to Palestine in order to establish Herod upon the throne of Judæa which had been seized, with the aid of the Parthians, by that same Antigonus, the son of Aristobulus, against whom he, Antony, had fought in 57 B.C. The authorities in Jerusalem, however, refused to receive Herod, and submitted to a siege, during which, according to Josephus,[9] Antony took the opportunity to make a brief visit to Egypt to see Cleopatra and to make the acquaintance of the twins, who were now just two years old.

It is unlikely that he went to Alexandria. It is more probable that Cleopatra came by ship to some point, such as Pelusium, near her eastern frontier, to meet him; and their time together was necessarily brief, for Antony had just heard that Octavian had begun hostilities against Sextus Pompeius, and he was most anxious to get back to Greece or Italy in order to set this matter to rights. It can hardly be supposed that the Queen received with much enthusiasm the man who had deserted her to marry Octavia; and one may suppose that the meeting was charged with all those potentialities of domestic storm which are usually present when an errant lover returns to the unmarried mother of his children. Antony's excuses, however, seem to have been as masterly as Cleopatra's tact; and though history does not offer us any guiding light through the dark channels of their brief reunion, we may

---

[9] Josephus, *Antiquities,* xiv, xv, 9. Plutarch, however, does not mention this visit.

suppose that Antony's approach to their inevitable compromise was illuminated by many vows of fidelity. Doubtless he told her that he would have nothing more to do with Octavia, or at any rate that he would begin to do something about their divorce.

Returning to the siege of Jerusalem, he gave orders to his new governor of Syria, a certain Caius Sossius, to lend all possible aid to Herod in his efforts to capture the Jewish throne; and therewith he and Ventidius Bassus hastened back to Greece. Having arrived at Athens towards the end of September, he found the patient Octavia and her baby awaiting him; and the fact that a few weeks later she learnt that she was once more to become a mother indicates that her warm-hearted pleasure at seeing him again had quite overcome his resolve to keep her at arms' length. It was now that he heard the news of the warfare which had been waged between her brother and Sextus Pompeius during the summer; and her disappointment and anxiety in this regard may well have obliged him to refrain from adding just now to her unhappiness.

Octavian had attacked the latter's province of Sicily, and had been completely defeated at sea off that ill-omened rock, Scylla, which, with the neighbouring Charybdis, was the bane of the sailor. He had behaved despicably in the fight, and, losing his head as was his habit, had gone ashore in the midst of the fight,[10] leaving his men to the mercy of the enemy and of the tempest which had arisen. His fleet had been sent to the bottom, and thousands of his men drowned. Octavia, who loved her brother deeply, must have been heartbroken at the news; and it was not in Antony's sympathetic and generous nature to turn from her at such a time.

Hard on the heels of these tidings there arrived at Athens an embassy from Octavian, headed by Mæcenas, and including the poets Horace and Virgil.[11] The object of the mission was obvious. The five years originally ordained for the duration of the Triumvirate would end at the close of this present year, 38 B.C., and Octavian, after the fiasco of his campaign against Sextus, saw no hope for himself except in its renewal. Without Antony's patron-

---

[10] Appian: *Civil Wars*, v, 85.
[11] The embassy's journey is described by Horace, *Satires*, i, v.

age he would be completely discredited, and would have to retire from public life, at any rate for the time being. He was eager,
therefore, to place his version of his trouble with Sextus before
his elder colleague, to excuse himself, to minimise the seriousness
of his defeat, and to put forward the advantages of a continuance
of the existing arrangements. He was thoroughly frightened, and
his perpetual dread of Antony's popularity was increased almost
to panic by the spectacular successes of the latter's army in the
east, of which he had just received the news.

Antony, however, was not willing to commit himself. The
ball was at his feet: fortune had suddenly showered her blessings
upon him, and the goal of his ambitions was within sight. His
young colleague and rival was disgraced, but his own reputation
had risen to unexpected heights. For some time he had been considering the possibility of invading Parthia, and of putting into
execution the plan of campaign which Cæsar had worked out and
of which Antony had probably found all the memoranda amongst
Cæsar's papers. There remained now only the realization of this
dream of conquest in the east; and after that the pathway to his
sole autocracy, to his absolute rulership of the entire Roman empire, east and west, would be open to him. This time, surely, Octavian would fail to weather the storm.

Antony's first move was to send Ventidius Bassus to Rome
to celebrate the Triumph which the Senate and People had accorded him with enthusiasm; and thus, on November 27th, the aged
general went in procession through the streets of the capital. That
Antony did not go himself to Rome to take part in the Triumph
seems to have been due to some extent to his desire to allow Ventidius to have full credit for the victory, for, as Plutarch remarks,
Antony wished him to receive the glory.[12] But there was another
reason which kept him from going to Rome, namely his anxiety
not to be drawn into any discussion of the future with Octavian:
he did not wish to meet him just now; he wanted the troublesome
young man to sink into the quicksands of his ignominy, and he
knew that in Rome he would be obliged for decency's sake to give
him a helping hand.

[12] The suggestion of Dion Cassius that Antony was jealous of him is a later in-
vention, and has no foundation.

When the Triumvirate should come to an end on January 1st, 37 B.C., a few weeks hence, Roman law and custom prescribed that the retiring parties should remain outside the capital until further arrangements had been made. Lepidus was in Africa, and well out of the way; and if Antony were to remain in Greece, Octavian would be obliged to follow suit and to retire from the city. Antony would then wait awhile until Octavian's rustication had completed his political collapse; and thereupon he would ask the Senate to transfer some of Octavian's legions to him to serve in the Parthian expedition which he was now planning for the following autumn. The Triumvirate being ended, Octavian would have no authority to hold back these troops; but Antony, meanwhile, would have caused himself to be appointed by the Senate as Commander-in-Chief of the Parthian campaign, and would therefore have a right to their use.

That, at least, is how I interpret Antony's decision to remain for the winter in Athens: in a word, he could not go back to Rome without being drawn into a renewal of this bargain-making Triumvirate. Octavian, however, with equal cunning, decided to retain command of his troops by the simple expedient of assuming, likewise with the consent of the Senate, the position of Commander-in-Chief in another campaign against Sextus Pompeius; and thus on January 1st, 37 B.C., both he and Antony allowed their positions as Triumvirs to fall into abeyance in place of these appointments as generals, respectively, of the expeditionary forces against Parthia and Sicily.

Now Antony was seriously in need of the extra troops, and his annoyance must have been extreme when he found that Octavian's proposed renewal of the war against Sextus Pompeius had provided justification for their withholding. He, Antony, was entitled to recruit soldiers in Italy, but what he wanted was the trained veteran legions; and soon, it seems to me, he realized with dismay that nothing short of another bargain with Octavian could obtain them for him. He would have to offer his former colleague some of his ships—which he himself did not require for his inland campaign—in exchange for the legions he needed; but when this compromise was suggested, Octavian made the stipulation that the Triumvirate should in that case be renewed, and to this Antony replied by postponing the discussion of that matter until April or May, that being the latest date to which the mobilisation for the autumn campaign against Parthia could be held over.

Meanwhile, during the early months of 37 B.C. Antony, from his headquarters at Athens, enthusiastically organized his forces for the coming invasion of the Orient which had so taken hold of his imagination, and administered his empire, keeping himself informed of Octavian's movements and watching with bitter disappointment the amazing young man's recovery from his disaster. He was told that a new fleet was being built in the Bay of Naples to take the place of that destroyed by Sextus; and presently it became apparent that soon Octavian would have no real need of the ships which Antony was offering him in exchange for the legions. As week after week went by, the position of affairs, so favourable to Antony in November, became equalised as between him and his rival: Octavian's prestige recovered, and soon there was little doubt that he would in the end overwhelm Sextus Pompeius as fully as Antony hoped to overwhelm Parthia.

By May Antony was exasperated, and determined to go to Brindisi to see Octavian and to force him to hand over the required legions. He therefore sailed across the Adriatic with a large fleet, taking with him Octavia, who was expecting her baby in about four months' time. But when he arrived before Brindisi the authorities in that city took fright, thinking that he had come over with intentions hostile to Octavian, and refused to allow him to land. Antony therefore sailed on to Tarentum, a port at which he had reason, apparently, to expect a friendlier reception; and there he waited for Octavian to come to him. Octavian, however, was now in a truculent mood, and would do nothing until Antony had agreed to renew the Triumvirate; and the letters exchanged between them seem to have breathed the defiance of both.

At last Octavia intervened, and persuaded her angry husband to let her go to her brother to arrange a meeting. To this he agreed, and it was by her exertions that a complete rupture was avoided. With tears and lamentations she told Octavian, in the words of Plutarch, "that from being the most fortunate woman on earth she was in danger of becoming the most unhappy, for as yet the eyes of everyone were fixed upon her as the wife and sister of the two great commanders, but, if rash counsels should prevail, and war ensue, she would be reduced to hopeless misery, since, whichever side won, she would be the loser." At this, Octavian agreed to meet Antony, and came in state to Tarentum, where, with much pomp and ceremony, the two men dined together and composed their differences.

It was agreed between them that the Triumvirate should be renewed for five years, dating from January 1st, 37 B.C.; that the promise of a Consulship for Sextus Pompeius at the close of the period of their treaty with him should be rescinded; that Octavian should hand over to Antony twenty-one thousand soldiers, and that Antony should deliver to Octavian one hundred and thirty ships in exchange [13]; and that, to cement the bargain, Octavian's infant daughter Julia, the child of his divorced wife Scribonia, should be betrothed to Antyllus, Antony's son by Fulvia. Lepidus, the third Triumvir, was allowed to retain office, simply to save trouble.

This agreement was a veritable climb-down on Antony's part, for it placed Octavian once more in undisputed authority in the western empire. Again Antony had found it impossible to get the better of him; again this discredited rival of his had miraculously extricated himself from his difficulties, and had turned defeat into victory in such a way that the elder man could but regard him with superstitious awe. Octavian's good fortune was uncanny.

Antony at once gave orders for his new troops to begin their long journey to Syria, and with such ships as remained under his command he set out for Greece. By the time that he reached the island of Corcyra (Corfu), however, he had made up his mind to postpone his Parthian campaign for some months, and to concentrate his army in Syria in preparation for an offensive in the spring. Thither he would go at once, if only to be as far away as possible from Octavian. He was exasperated beyond endurance by affairs in Italy, and by the frustrations which there always met him. He could not stand the sight of the gentle Octavia, in whom he daily saw the depressing reflection of her brother; and suddenly he told her to go back to Italy, protesting, in excuse, that as she was so soon going to

[13] Appian: *Civil Wars*, v, 95.

have a baby she would be more comfortable there. He wanted to be free; to leave behind him all incumbrances; to be rid even of his children.

His eldest daughter, Antonia, the child of his first marriage with his cousin of the same name, had recently been betrothed to the son of Lepidus, the third Triumvir, and it seems that she was already with her future father-in-law. Fulvia's children, Clodius and Clodia, appear now to have been housed elsewhere. His own two sons by Fulvia, Antyllus and Julus, had been with him in Athens, and could now be handed over to Octavia, who would look after them until he could send for them to join him in Syria. As for his little daughter, Antonia, the child of Octavia, her place was obviously with her mother and her uncle Octavian; and he now told his wife to take her back to Italy, nor did he care greatly if, as proved to be the case, he should never see her again.

Octavia was complacently obedient to his wishes. During these last months she must have found him increasingly difficult; and the anticipation of a quiet life alone with her children may well have made its appeal to her disturbed mind. She did not realize, when she bade him farewell, that he was shaking from off his shoes the dust of the west, and was hastening with outstretched arms to the adventurous east. She was unaware that she had no part in the bright visions which lured his thoughts away from the paralysing rebuffs, the lame and impotent conclusions, of his dark struggle with her brother; and she was happy in her ignorance of the fact that he was going out of her life for ever.

Historians have never asked themselves a simple question which may well have presented itself to the reader. Why, during the greater part of the course of the Triumvirate, was Antony content to engage himself in the affairs of the east and to leave Rome and the west to Octavian? Why had he not concentrated his efforts all along upon establishing his authority in the capital? Why, when he might have fought it out with his rival, as Cæsar did with Pompey, had he now turned his back upon Rome as though the metropolis and its affairs were not worth the struggle? In my opinion the answer is to be found in the statement of Suetonius that Cæsar had often thought of transferring the capital of the entire Roman world to Troy, in northwestern Asia Minor, or to Alexandria, [14] and that Rome was not a city "suitable to the grandeur of the empire." [15]

Antony, in fact, who had been Cæsar's confidant, and, after his death, had possessed himself of all his memoranda, seems to have believed with him that the future capital of the Roman dominions ought to be situated in some part of the world more central than Italy. A glance at a map will show that Athens was geographically a better centre than Rome; and now that Antony had hopes of bringing Parthia and the Orient under Roman sway, and adding the eastern dominions of Alexander the Great to the regions which he already ruled, the transfer of the seat of government to Asia Minor or even to Alexandria seemed desirable. Antony had travelled extensively. Gaul and the countries northwest of Italy were regarded by him as barbarous territories, and even Spain and the western coast of North Africa were not of first-rate importance. But east of Italy, in that empire which he now administered, there were the wealthy and ancient cities and lands of Greece, Macedonia, Thrace, Asia Minor, and Syria—and, south of Syria, Egypt—which together formed a teeming hive of human activity; and in relation to them Italy was as it were a mere western outpost. In this rich and busy eastern area he had made himself fully acquainted with mighty cities such as Athens, Ephesus, Tarsus, Tyre, and Alexandria; and Italy had become to him but a faraway limb of this pulsing body.

I think there can be little doubt that he desired to found a new capital, possibly in Cilicia, that region being equidistant from Greece and Egypt, from Italy and Parthia, and practically the centre of the known world. In this new Rome he intended to establish the Senate and the government, and perhaps his own throne; and thus Italy did not hold so important a place in his thoughts as might now be supposed. He turned his back upon it without regrets, glad, indeed, to put seas and kingdoms between himself and the exasperating Octavian. For a brief period in the previous winter he had thought that the time had come for him to add Rome and the west to his sphere of authority; but he had been disillusioned, and now he would have to wait for that consummation until Parthia was his, and until the entire eastern empire, from Greece in the

[14] Suetonius: *Cæsar*, lxxix. [15] Suetonius: *Augustus*, xxix.

west to the Indus in the east, from Scythia in the north to Ethiopia in the south, was consolidated into one vast realm such as Alexander the Great had dreamed of and planned.

His brain was full of such visions as he sailed now over the summer seas towards Syria. But during his journey, says Plutarch, "the mischief that had long lain dormant, his love for Cleopatra, which wiser thoughts had seemed to have lulled and charmed into oblivion, upon his approach to Syria gathered strength again, and broke into flame; and, like Plato's restive and rebellious horse of the human soul, flinging off the harness of good counsel and breaking completely loose, he sent for her to come to him in Syria." This, doubtless, is something of a misinterpretation of his state of mind, for his love for the Egyptian Queen could not at this time have been overwhelming. Yet his repugnance to all that he had left behind him in the west, and his memory of his happy days in brilliant Alexandria three years and more ago, must have combined to fill his heart with the warm consciousness of Cleopatra's importance in his life.

There was today a place for her in his plans. That old prophecy which declared that Parthia would be conquered by a "king," and which had had such influence upon Cæsar, was always in his mind, it would seem; and he knew that Cleopatra, unable to conceal the fact that he was the parent of her twins, had made the knowledge palatable to her subjects by speaking of him as her legal consort—legal, that is to say, by Egyptian royal prerogative. In Egypt, in fact, he was almost a king, and there was no reason why he should not regularise that position by some arrangement with Cleopatra tantamount to a marriage, which should make of him an actual monarch in that country while leaving him still Triumvir in Roman eyes.

Such a marriage, geographically restricted in its legal acceptance, would be a first step towards that wider sovereignty which was now his ultimate ambition. After all, everybody knew that Cæsar had intended to marry Cleopatra; and it was common knowledge that she had termed him her royal and divine consort in Egypt, the earthly and celestial father of her son, Cæsarion. Now, therefore, that he, Antony, had turned his back upon the west, and was definitely committed to the Parthian adventure and thereafter to the creation of a great empire of the east, there was every reason why he should legalize his position as the sovereign lord of Cleopatra's realms while retaining his position as the democratic Triumvir of the eastern Roman world. In Greece and Asia Minor he was widely accepted by the masses as a kind of deity, an incarnation of Dionysus; and in Egypt Cleopatra had already covered their union with a mantle of divinity similar to that which she had cast about her previous union with Cæsar. It would be all to the good now to capitalise that royal and celestial position in his dealings with the east, just as Alexander the Great had done when he accepted his identification with the Egyptian god Ammon.

At the time of his previous association with Cleopatra he had felt that Cæsarion, her son by Cæsar, was the most important factor in the situation; for this youth might be put forward one day as the true heir of the Dictator in place of Octavian. But since that time, by the unaccountable workings of Fate, Octavian's position as Cæsar's successor had been unexpectedly consolidated, if only by the years and by the accustoming of the public mind to this view of his claims upon their allegiance. Yet there was still something to be said for Antony's assumption of the position of guardian and stepfather of Cæsar's only son, who was now ten years of age; and the boy's existence would certainly serve to make a closer connection with Cleopatra more understandable in Roman eyes.

Thus, in sending for the Queen and in inviting her to meet him in Syria, it was not so much a revival of his passion for her which was the incentive, as it was her usefulness to him. She was now thirty-one years of age, and the mother of three children, and he was forty-six, had been married three times, and had enjoyed the charms of many mistresses. Yet, even so, he must have been prompted in part by his affection for her, or, rather, by the memory of her brilliant and alluring companionship. He wanted, I suppose, to make amends to her for his treatment of her; he wanted her to know that his marriage to Octavia had been a political necessity which had now outgrown its value. The Queen had been so faithful to him in her loneliness; and at their recent meeting she had been so justified in her rebukes. Apart from all other considerations, she must have been, so to speak, on his conscience.

He reached northern Syria early in September, and took up

his headquarters at Antiochia (Antioch), a pleasant city some twenty miles back from the sea. Here he received news that the siege of Jerusalem had at last been brought to a successful conclusion, and that Antigonus had surrendered to Herod and his Roman allies. [16] Shortly afterwards the defeated monarch was brought to him at Antioch, where Antony ordered him to be kept in captivity; but later, at Herod's request, the unfortunate man was beheaded, after having been scourged and crucified [17] as a vicarious sacrifice, I presume, of the kind mentioned by Philo of Byblus [18] and others as being prevalent amongst the peoples of Syria and its neighbourhood.

The fall of Jerusalem released a considerable Roman force; and Antony now decided to take the first step in his Parthian campaign by sending an army of six legions and their auxiliaries, under Publius Canidius Crassus, into the Caucasus to open the northern route into Parthia, this being the route which Cæsar had planned to follow in his proposed campaign of 44 B.C. [19] Marching northeastwards across the eastern edge of Asia Minor, this army was to move into Iberia (southern Georgia), and thence south-eastwards to the plateau of Erzeroum, where it was to winter preparatory to the invasion of Media, the sister-state of Parthia.

It was towards the end of September when Cleopatra arrived at Antioch; and in the absence of any ancient account of the meeting itself, the apparent fact can only be recorded that she and Antony wasted no time in entering into a businesslike discussion of the general situation, as the result of which an agreement of the most far-reaching character was made between them. He and she were to be married according to Egyptian law, and the union was to be regarded as binding upon them, although it would not be recognized as legal in Roman law, nor would necessitate the divorcing of Octavia. By the legalising of his position as Cleopatra's consort, Antony would become actual king of Egypt; but it was agreed that he would not assume this title, reserving it, in fact, for Cæsarion when the boy

---

[16] For accounts of the siege, see Josephus: *Antiquities,* xiv, xvi, and Dion Cassius, xlix, 22.

[17] Dion Cassius, xlix, 22.

[18] Eusebius: *Preparatio Evangelica,* i, x, 29. See my *Paganism in Our Christianity,* Chap. vii.

[19] Suetonius: *Cæsar,* xliv.

should come of age. Instead, he chose to be called *Autocrator*, a Greek word signifying an absolute personal ruler or autocrat, and corresponding more or less to the Latin term "Imperator." Thus, while he would be "King" to Cleopatra's subjects, he was to be "Autocrator" throughout his eastern empire, yet would still be a democratic "Triumvir," a chief magistrate of the Republic, in Roman eyes. It is to be presumed, however, that he stated privately his intention of establishing in the end a throne for himself from which he and his successors would rule the entire Roman world—the whole earth, in fact, if his plans of conquest did not miscarry; and it seems to me that in order to benefit by Cæsar's worshipped name and authority, he was prepared to regard Cæsarion, Cæsar's only son, as the heir-apparent to this future throne.

It was agreed, also, that all the wealth and power of Egypt should be placed at his disposal in the colossal undertakings he had in mind; and in return he now proposed to extend Cleopatra's dominions so that they should be stretched around the east end of the Mediterranean. Nearly all Phoenicia and Syria and a great part of Cilicia should be hers, together with Cyprus and a part of Crete. Tyre and Sidon were to remain outside her authority, and Judæa, Herod's kingdom, was to be independent; but she was to have Damascus, Jericho, and the strip of country east of the Jordan, while Egypt's ancient claim to Sinai and northern Arabia was to be recognised.

History tells us nothing of the manner in which this agreement was ratified or the marriage performed; [20] but the event was celebrated by the striking of coins upon which their two heads were represented, she being Queen and he Autocrator and Triumvir. Moreover, Cleopatra introduced a new dating of the years of her reign: she was now beginning her fifteenth year as Queen of Egypt, but she spoke in future of this year as the first of her larger sovereignty; and thus on a coin minted six years later we find an inscription giving that date as the "21st, which is also the 6th year" of her reign.

The gift of all this territory is said to have been very dis-

[20] That some sort of marriage took place at this time between Antony and Cleopatra was first shown by Letronne, *Recueil des inscriptions grecques et latines de l'Egypte*, ii, 90; and then by Kromayer, *Hermes*, xxix, 584. See also Ferrero: *Greatness and Decline of Rome*, iv, i.

pleasing to the Romans of the west, "for," says Plutarch, "although Antony had bestowed great kingdoms upon several private persons, and had taken away the thrones of many kings, nothing stung the Romans as did the shame of these honors paid to Cleopatra, their dissatisfaction being increased also by his public acknowledgment that her twins were his; yet he, who knew how to put a good colour on the most discreditable action, now excused himself by saying that the greatness of the Roman empire lay more in giving kingdoms than in taking them away." Cleopatra, however, was not altogether satisfied with the arrangement; and she is said to have pleaded so hard to be given also the kingdom of Herod, the cities of Tyre and Sidon, and the land of Arabia, that Antony had to speak very sharply to her. [21]

One gets the impression, in fact, that this beginning of their renewed life together was not altogether idyllic. Antony was busy with his preparations for the Parthian campaign, and this enormous undertaking must have caused him the greatest anxiety. Yet Antioch was a charming city in which to spend the winter; and, being famous for its art and learning, it provided, no doubt, a pleasant setting for that kind of elegant existence which both he and she so much enjoyed. At any rate, in spite of worries and distractions, their intimate life together was happily renewed; nor was it disturbed by the news which presently arrived from Italy, that in the autumn Octavia had given birth to a daughter, whom, like her previous child by Antony, she had named Antonia. By the beginning of the new year, 36 B.C., Cleopatra found that she, too, was once more to become a mother.

By March all was in readiness for the campaign, and Antony set out from Antioch, marching north-eastwards, at the head of his legions. Cleopatra accompanied him for the first hundred and fifty miles; but at Zeugma on the Euphrates she turned back, probably owing to her condition, and began the return journey to Egypt, there to await the birth of her child and the hoped-for news of Antony's triumphant progress. It was hard to say when he and she would meet again, for the conquest of the Orient might occupy two or three years: there was no telling what would happen, and it might even be that he would never return.

[21] Josephus: *Antiquities*, xv, iii, 8, and xv, iv, 1.

The task he had set himself was one which, if victoriously carried out, would place his name alongside that of Alexander the Great; but if he were to fail, his death and the slaughter of his army would be a more likely consequence than a successful retreat. It was an appalling risk that he was taking; and the fact that he was prepared to take it, and to endure the inevitable hardships of the campaign, is an indication that at this time he was neither the chronic drunkard nor the luxury-loving libertine, nor yet the love-sick loon, which history has supposed him to have been. He was—the fact must surely be obvious—a man in perfect health, keen, ambitious, and extremely active in mind and body; and as he watched Cleopatra's cavalcade moving away on the road back to Antioch and the south, it may be supposed that he turned to the task before him with an eager heart not so greatly weighed down by his bereavement as elated by his vast hopes.

CHAPTER XVIII

The Great Parthian Adventure, and Antony's Movement towards Sovereign Power.

36–33 B.C.

THE fact that in the previous spring Antony had been so impatient to obtain from Octavian the extra legions he required for the Parthian expedition indicates that he had planned to open the campaign in the autumn; and the choice of this time of year suggests that he had intended to take the southern route into Parthia, marching down the valley of the Euphrates through Mesopotamia to Babylonia and thence to Ctesiphon, one of the Parthian capitals, for in these parts winter was the only tolerable season for campaigning. The fact that he himself took up his headquarters in Syria suggests, too, that he had expected to follow this southern route. But when the delay in Italy had forced him to postpone the expedition until the spring he had altered his plans and had chosen the northern route through Armenia and thence down into Media to the city of Ecbatana, for the reason that here in the north the summer season was more suitable for warfare.

When he reached the Euphrates at Zeugma, therefore, and first came into touch with the enemy outposts, they must have wondered whether he would advance up-stream to join his advance-guard already sent into Armenia, or whether he would move down-stream towards Ctesiphon. Antony, himself, was perhaps even yet not absolutely decided, for there seems to have been some delay here, and some uncertainty in regard to the plan of campaign, which led Plutarch to suppose that Antony was a man in love, unable to think of anything but his passion for Cleopatra. He seems, however, to have had little doubt that he should take the northern route, more especially since his general in Armenia had reported that Artavasdes, the King of Armenia, was prepared to co-operate with him, having a private quarrel with his namesake Artavasdes, King of Media, the Parthian ally.

The Parthian empire included within its wide bounds an area as big as that of the entire Roman world. Mespotamia, and ancient Assyria and Babylonia, formed its western wing; Persia, Carmania, and Gedrosia (Beluchistan) were comprised in its southern territory; and Bactriana (Bokhara) and those states which lay on the near side of the Indus, over against northern India, constituted its eastern possessions. Parthia (Khorassan) itself lay in the midst of these, just to the east of Media, and south-east of the Caspian Sea. It was a vast territory to conquer; but Alexander the Great had done so, and Antony was sure that he could achieve with his great Roman army the same success which Alexander's smaller force of Greeks had achieved three centuries earlier.

It was the middle of April, 36 B.C. when he set out upon his march northwards. Moving up the valley of the Euphrates, he passed through Samosata, the city which he and Ventidius Bassus had besieged in the previous campaign, and so came to Melitene in Cappadocia, and thence to Satala in northern Armenia Minor, which he reached in early June. He then proceeded into Armenia where, at the end of that month, he made his juncture with the troops which had been sent ahead; and here he proudly reviewed his whole army prior to the southern advance into Media. Not less than a hundred-thousand men were now under his command, the bulk of these troops being Roman legionaries amongst which were many of his veteran Gauls.

Polemo, whom Antony had made King of Laodicea, had recently been transferred by him to the throne of Pontus, the kingdom in north-eastern Asia Minor which adjoined Armenia; and this monarch was now here with a small but useful contingent of troops. King Artavasdes of Armenia was also in the camp, having placed in the field sixteen thousand horsemen,[1] these being extremely valuable because they were roughriders trained in the Parthian method of warfare, namely that of shooting with bow-and-arrows from horseback. Artavasdes himself proved to be most helpful and friendly: he was a man who had been educated as a Greek, and, being in-

---

[1] Plutarch: *Antony*.

clined to literature, had written some passable Greek plays and also a number of historical works. His people had received the Romans very hospitably, and were glad to open their country to them as a base of operations against their hereditary southern enemies, the Medes. A matter of great satisfaction to Antony, moreover, was the fact that a number of Parthian nobles had come into Armenia with offers of aid, having quarrelled with the King of Parthia, Phraates, a man of great cruelty who had begun his reign by murdering his father and most of his relations.

The frontier between Armenia and Media was formed by the river Araxes (the Aras), and Antony's army crossed this river about the end of July. Antony himself pushed rapidly forward with the main army to the city of Phraaspa, some forty miles north of Ecbatana, his object being to overwhelm these two important centers in the first rush, and thence to move eastwards into Parthia or southwards to Ctesiphon. He expected to take Phraaspa by assault, and he therefore left his baggage-train and his great siege-engines to follow him with an escort of ten thousand men or more, including the King of Pontus. But when he reached the city, in the middle of August, he found it strongly defended, and, to his great disappointment, he was obliged to prepare for a siege.

Meanwhile, the Parthian monarch, Phraates, had come up from the south with his host of mounted archers; and, hearing that Antony at Phraaspa was separated from his siege-train, which was now at Gaza, fifty miles to the north, he made a wide detour and suddenly fell upon it. The result was a disaster for the Romans which ruined Antony's hopes. All the siege-engines were destroyed, the baggage was lost, King Polemo of Pontus was captured, and nearly all the ten thousand men of the escort were slaughtered together with their general. On hearing the news, Antony at once hastened back with all the troops he could spare; but he found only dead men and the wrecks of his engines. He then learnt that the King of Armenia who had been advancing behind the siege-train, had at once fled with his sixteen thousand horsemen, and was now on his way back to his own country.

Antony would have been wise to have accepted his misfortune and at once to have marched his army back to Armenia; but the effect of the catastrophe upon him was that of angering him into the determination to fight it out. Such was his nature: the more formidable the enemy the more stubbornly he desired to hit back. Returning to Phraaspa he settled down to starve it into surrender; but owing to the fact that King Phraates and his Parthian and Median horsemen were hovering around the outskirts of his camp, he himself was almost as closely besieged as was the city he was besieging. He had to fight for his food in the country round about; but though he attempted to force the enemy into a pitched battle on the one side or to take the city by assault on the other, he failed to bring about a major engagement of any kind.

September went by, and, when the approach of cold weather in October and the difficulty of obtaining food had reduced him and his troops to the verge of despair, he made an elaborate and carefully planned movement to jockey the enemy into the open. Taking ten legions and all his cavalry he went a day's march from the camp, and when, as he expected, he was followed by the enemy, he suddenly turned upon them. As a result of the surprise, however, he killed no more than eighty of them and took only thirty prisoners, the fact being that the Parthian and Median horsemen were altogether too nimble for him, and prided themselves on their equal ability to swoop down on their opponents and to gallop away to safety. He was exasperated by his failure, and when he returned to the siege-lines and found that there had been a sortie which had put some of his men to flight, he angrily punished the cowardice of those who had fled by imposing upon them the old Roman penalty of "decimation," that is to say, the execution of one in every ten of the delinquents, the victims being drawn by lot. This severity checked a tendency to mutiny which would have meant disaster to the whole force; but if it startled the men into the endurance of their hardships with outward courage, it did nothing to relieve the inward depression of them all. The retirement of the King of Armenia from the campaign, with his sixteen thousand cavalry, was an irreparable loss, for these men would have been of the utmost service in dealing with the evasive enemy horsemen, their methods of fighting being similar.

At length the Parthians proposed an armistice, and to this Antony responded by saying that if the eagles captured from the legions of Crassus at Carrhæ in 53 B.C. were returned to him, and if the prisoners then carried off were released, he would take his departure. The Parthian King, however, rejected these terms, and merely sent word that if Antony would leave the country at once his retreat would not be molested.

In the deepest dejection, therefore, as the winds of winter began to whistle about the camp, Antony accepted this offer, consoling himself as best he could by the thought that he would recuperate in Syria and recommence the campaign next year. His sorrow and shame, nevertheless, were so great that he refused to address his men to acquaint them with the news which to them must have been so welcome. "Some of the soldiers," Plutarch writes, "resented this behaviour on the grounds that it slighted them, but the greater number understood the cause and pitied him, finding in it a reason why they on their part should treat him with even more respect and obedience than was their usual habit."

Antony had intended to march back by the way he had come, the road passing through open country; but a certain friendly chief of the Mardi—a people living in that part of Media which lay along the southern shore of the Caspian Sea—who had served with the Romans throughout the campaign, earnestly advised him to make for the mountains on the eastern side of Media and to follow the upland highway northwards to the frontier of Armenia, for in so doing he would prevent an attack by the Parthian horsemen who could maneuver at will on the level plains but were useless in the rugged hill-country. That such an attack was contemplated by the treacherous King Phraates, he declared, he had no doubt. Antony did not know whether or not to believe the man, but when he offered to allow himself to be shackled during the march, so that he could not escape if treachery were suspected, his good faith was recognized and his advice taken.

The retreating army therefore headed for the mountains; and three days later, when they were fording the river Amardus (the Sufeid), presumably near the town of Batina (Sultanieh), where it runs at the foot of the hills, they were attacked by the Parthians, as their guide had predicted. Antony's Gallic cavalry, however, saw that these wild horsemen got as good as they gave; and the encounter had the value of putting him on his guard and taught him to flank his heavy infantry with his archers and light cavalry. A few days later, however, an officer named Flavius Gallus took his men too far away in pursuit of the enemy who had again attacked the column, and, being ambushed, suffered a very serious defeat. Three thousand Roman and Gallic cavalry-men were left dead upon the ground, while five thousand were wounded. An even greater disaster was only averted by Antony's prompt action: he personally led out the Third Legion, and drove off the enemy. Flavius Gallus was brought in with four arrows shot through his body, and died a few hours later.

After this engagement, Plutarch tells us, "Antony went from tent to tent to visit and comfort those of the defeated men who were left alive, and was not able to look upon them without tears and a very passion of grief. They, however, seized his hand with happy faces, bidding him go and see to his own needs and not to worry about them, calling him their Emperor and their general, and saying that if he himself fared well they were safe. Never, indeed, in all these times can history point to a general at the head of a more glorious army, whether you consider their strength and youth or their patience and endurance in hardships and fatigue, while as for the obedience and loving respect they showed towards their general, and the unanimous feeling amongst humble and great alike, whether officers or common soldiers, that they preferred his good opinion of them to their very lives and existence, it is not possible that they could have been surpassed even by the Romans of old. For this devotion to Antony there were many reasons: his nobility, for instance, his frank and open manners, his generous and magnificent mode of life, his familiarity in talking with everybody, and, at this time in particular, his tender-heartedness in visiting and pitying the wounded, joining in all their pain, and furnishing them with all things necessary, so that the sick and disabled were even more eager to serve him than those who were well and strong."

Upon the next day Antony thought it would be only right to address the troops; and in order to show them how deeply he felt their sufferings and the loss of so many brave men he put on a mourning-garment, and went, unshaven and with tear-stained face, to the platform. But his anxious staff-officers stopped him, insisting that he should don his general's scarlet cloak; and this he finally consented to do. "There was no man of his time like him," says Plutarch, "for carrying his soldiers with him by the force of words," and on this occasion he made an impassioned speech, praising those who had fought well in the recent skirmishes, and reproaching a particular contingent which had shown signs of panic. At this the men of the latter called out that they were ready to undergo decimation or any other punishment so long as he would forgive them and not thus shame them; whereupon Antony flung his hands upwards to heaven, and, closing his eyes, uttered a prayer, saying that if, to balance the great blessings he had received, any misfortunes were in store, he implored the gods to pour their wrath upon his head alone, and to spare his soldiers.

Day after day the weary and underfed army made its way along the mountain road, while the Parthians and Medes shot at them from behind the rocks, and killed the stragglers. It was difficult to forage for food under these conditions, and the men had often to be content to eat the roots of wayside plants or anything else which seemed to be edible. Unfortunately, several men cooked and ate a certain herb, and were poisoned thereby. Its effect was said to be that of causing them to lose their reason, so that, like men enchanted, they wandered about, moving stones from place to place, or engaging vaguely in other useless tasks, until at last they collapsed and died.

Antony was the life and soul of the retreat, and from time to time he was heard to exclaim, "O, the Ten Thousand!"—as though proudly comparing their journey to that of the Greeks under Xenophon. Solely by the power of his personality he preserved the spirit and the discipline of his men; but at length a series of new misfortunes broke down their endurance and there was a serious mutiny. One night, while they were camped, several soldiers made themselves sick by drinking at a stream the water of which was brackish, and Antony, having failed to dissuade others from drinking, gave orders for the march to be resumed, there being better water a short distance ahead, so the Mardian guide had told him, and an attack by the enemy from the rear being expected. The night march which ensued was trying to the nerves of everybody; and at last some of the men revolted, beginning to plunder the baggage of their officers and even seizing Antony's own belongings. The noise and confusion caused by their behaviour led Antony to suppose that the enemy had attacked them, and were in their midst; and to him this seemed to be the end. Calling aside one of his freedmen, Rhamnus by name, he obliged him to take an oath that at a given signal he would kill him and cut off his head, burying it so that it should not fall into the hands of the Parthians; and, in fact, he was about to give this signal when he learnt the true cause of the disturbance.

Thereupon he called a halt, and took the necessary steps to restore order; but at break of day they were again attacked, a severe fight taking place, in which, however, the Romans were victorious. It now became necessary to descend into the plains and to cross a river; and here Antony expected another battle, but to his surprise the enemy allowed them to make the crossing unmolested, and, indeed, made signs to them from a distance as though bidding them farewell, thereafter unstringing their bows and riding away southwards. For the remainder of their journey they were not attacked, and six days later they crossed the Araxes and attained the friendly soil of Armenia. Here the men kissed the ground in their excitement, and there were scenes of intense emotion, the soldiers embracing one another and shedding tears of joy, while Antony himself received an ovation.

The retreat from Phraaspa had occupied twenty-seven days, and during that time the Romans had beaten off the enemy on no less than eighteen distinct occasions. The total losses of the whole campaign, including those incurred in the overwhelming of the siege-train, were twenty-four thousand dead, of whom a large part had died of sickness. Now, since ten thousand of these had been massacred on that one occasion, and three thousand on the occasion of the ill-advised action of Flavius Gallus, Antony could console himself with the thought that his unavoidable losses—the ordinary casualties of the war—had not been more than eleven thousand men, which was not excessive. His depression was thus relieved by the hope that he would be able to make a second invasion in the following year, and that, having now learnt the tactics of the Parthians, he would be able to prevent a repetition of his two major disasters. If only he could recruit a force of mounted archers in Armenia, or train his own Gallic cavalry in the Parthian methods, he would have a chance of success.

For this reason he forbore to punish the Armenian King for his desertion, but, wishing to use him to better purpose next time, marched through that country with flags flying, so to speak, making light of his retreat and giving out, apparently, that he would resume the war at no distant date. At first he may have thought of wintering in Armenia, but presently he seems to have decided to make his second attack from the south, beginning the new campaign, therefore, in the following autumn; and with this purpose in view he seems to have deemed it better to march back into Syria, where he could obtain money from Egypt and elsewhere with which to reward his men, and could more conveniently rest and reorganize his army.

But ill-luck dogged him. No sooner was he well upon his way than a spell of particularly severe weather set in, and during his march through Armenia Minor and Cappadocia there were almost continuous snowstorms. Epidemics of sickness attacked the troops, and before they had reached the warmer climate of Syria, eight thousand of them had died. He did not halt, however, at Antioch, but passed on down the Syrian coast to a point just to the south of Berytus (Beirût). This city stood at the western end of the great caravan-route which crossed the Lebanon to Damascus and thence traversed the desert by way of Palmyra to Mesopotamia. It was the most direct route to Ctesiphon, the southern capital of the Parthians; and Antony's selection of the neighbourhood of Beirût for his headquarters seems to me to indicate that he intended to take this desert route in his next campaign, as did Roman armies of later times.

The army which he thus brought back into Syria in the early days of 35 B.C. was but the sorry wreck of that with which he had set out in the previous spring. The men were emaciated and in rags; and Antony himself, in spite of his indomitable determination to attack again, was physically exhausted. Yet he sent off a report to the Senate in Rome in which he stated that his campaign had been most successful, and that he had returned undefeated to Syria to prepare for a second campaign. Meanwhile, however, the news which he received from Italy must have greatly disconcerted him.

In the summer of 36 B.C. Octavian had made another onslaught upon Sextus Pompeius, and, working in conjunction with Lepidus, who had brought a powerful force over from North Africa, he had attacked him in Sicily. At first he had been badly defeated, being more than once nearly taken prisoner, and on one occasion narrowly escaping assassination, while Sextus had inflicted enormous losses upon him; but at last the roving son of Pompey the Great had been overwhelmed by sheer numbers, and had fled to Mytilene in the isle of Lesbos. The third Triumvir, Lepidus—"the vainest of human beings," as Velleius calls him, [2] "who had merited not by a single good quality so long an indulgence of fortune"— had then quarrelled with Octavian, and as a punishment for a foolish attempt at rebellion, had been forced by him to retire into private life; and thus the Triumvirate had come to an end, Octavian and Antony being left as the sole rulers respectively of the west and east.

In November Octavian had returned to Rome in triumph, and, having decided that the time had come to improve his personal reputation, had adopted a conciliatory attitude to all parties and had even announced that he was prepared to lay down his exceptional powers if his colleague, on his return from Parthia, would do likewise. So far as Antony could make out, in fact, he had definitely turned over a new leaf, and now, in the twenty-seventh year of his age, was at last attempting to consolidate his position and to consider the future, instead of acting simply as the needs of the moment required, without policy, prudence, or principle. For the first time since the division of the empire into an eastern and a western area, Octavian's position was as powerful as his own; and Antony now learnt, with a sinking of his heart, that the Senate had invited the young man to assume any distinctive honour he cared to suggest, [3] and meanwhile had decreed him the right to wear on all occasions a crown of laurel, and had bestowed all manner of other privileges upon him, such as that of feasting annually with his wife and family in the precincts of the Temple of Jupiter Capitolinus upon the anniversary of his victory over Sextus Pompeius. [4]

Another piece of news which Antony now received was that Cleopatra in the early autumn had given birth to a son, whom she had named Ptolemy, according to the custom of her house. These tidings were interesting, to say the least, and, indeed, may

[2] Velleius, ii, lxxx.
[4] Dion Cassius, xlix, 15.
[3] Appian: *Civil Wars,* v, 130.

well have touched his sentimental heart, though the emotional
tremor of becoming a father must by repetition have lost its
poignancy; but since he knew that the announcement of the event
must have already reached Rome, its probable effect upon Octavia
and her brother was for him a further cause of anxiety. He was
determined, however, never to return to his Roman wife; and as
though to defy the gossip at home, he sent a letter to Cleopatra,
telling her to come to him at once, and incidentally, to bring with
her as much money as she could lay her hands on, and also all the
clothes and comforts she could collect for his men.

He then gave himself up to the only relaxation his tired body
and mind desired after these months of toil and fatigue: he turned,
that is to say, to the gods of oblivion, and drank himself daily into a
condition of complete stupor. During the next weeks, in his moments
of sobriety, he asked for news only of the Queen's coming; and when
at last he heard that she was on her way, not even his wine could
long detain him in the house or keep him from starting up every
now and then to scan the sea in the hope that the far line of the
southern horizon might be etched with the masts and sails of her
approaching fleet.

When at length Cleopatra arrived, bringing with her many
shiploads of clothing and supplies for the army, Antony's relationship towards her seems to have passed into that new phase to
which his impatience for her coming had been the prelude. It
would be perhaps a little too bold to say that now for the first
time he fell in love with her—the woman who in Tarsus, in Alexandria, and in Antioch had lived in such tender intimacy with
him, and as a consequence had borne him three children; and yet it
is not an uncommon experience in the life of errant men that at
middle age—and Antony was now about forty-eight—a pleasantly
amorous relationship widens and deepens into the proportions of a
lifelong devotion and dependence. Antony was at this time a tired
and disappointed man; and the comfort of Cleopatra's tactful sympathy, the brightness and charm of her society which not even her
worst enemies have denied, the encouragement of her unconquerable
optimism, and, above all, her masterfully feminine handling of his
masculine difficulties, combined to make her companionship for the
first time essential to him. From this date onwards his life was in-

separably linked to hers; and the reader will have seen that this was not the case before the present year, 35 B.C.

Having learnt from him that he intended to march upon Parthia from the south in the following autumn, she made him come back to spend the spring and summer with her in Alexandria, not only that she might revive his energies and restore his confidence in himself, but also that she might present him to her people as her husband and their sovereign lord. Antony, of course, was ready enough to be persuaded that he could make his military plans as well from Alexandria as from Beirût; and the luxury of Cleopatra's palace, the pleasures of her beautiful capital, and the well-remembered perfection of the banquets of the Inimitable Livers, were temptations which he could not resist. It is even possible, too, that he wanted to see the new baby and the twins.

Just as he was about to leave for Egypt he received news that Sextus Pompeius, in a desperate attempt to restore his fortunes, was attempting to stir up trouble in Asia Minor. He had sailed with the remnant of his fleet through the Dardanelles, had tried to capture Cyzicus (Kyzik) on the Sea of Marmara, had passed through the Bosporus into the Black Sea, and was attacking the coast of Bithynia prior to a movement towards Pontus and Armenia, which is said to have had as its object an alliance with the Parthians. Antony therefore despatched one of his generals, Marcus Titius by name, to suppress the marauder; and in anticipation it may be said that the unfortunate Sextus was at length captured in Phrygia and was put to death by Titius who had failed to receive Antony's instructions that his life should be spared. [5] It was an inglorious end to a romantic career; and with his death the line of Pompey the Great became extinct upon the male side. Sextus Pompeius may be described as the last of the militant republicans; but now, indeed, the democratic party, to which both Antony and Octavian belonged, was itself losing its identity and was, moreover, becoming divided by its allegiance to one or other of these leaders.

Antony's holiday in Alexandria was interrupted in the spring by the wholly unexpected arrival of an embassy from the King of Media, headed by King Polemo of Pontus, who, it will be recalled,

[5] Dion Cassius, xlix, 18.

had been captured by the enemy on the occasion of the disaster to Antony's siege-train, and who had now been released as an earnest of the Median monarch's good will. The King of Parthia, it appeared, had not behaved himself with proper regard to the terms of his alliance with Media; and the friction between them—which was perhaps the cause of the sudden abandonment of their attacks upon Antony's retreating army—had developed at last into open hostility. The Median King therefore proposed now that Antony should return at once into his country, and that they should together invade Parthia.

Antony was dumbfounded. As Plutarch puts it, "he was being asked, as a favour, to accept that very thing, the want of which had hindered his conquest of the Parthians before, namely a force of mounted bowmen." These Median horsemen, indistinguishable in skill and training from the dreaded light cavalry of Parthia, would make a Roman victory almost certain; and Antony, aflame with excitement, instantly agreed to march his men back into Armenia at once, so as to move into Media in the summer and thence to invade Parthia in the autumn. Now was his chance to recover the ascendancy of his position over that of Octavian, and by a spectacular conquest of the Orient to impose his dominant personality upon the mind of every man in the Roman world.

Cleopatra insisted upon coming with him, at any rate as far as Syria; but when he was once more back at his military headquarters, insurmountable obstacles to an immediate campaign presented themselves. What these were is not recorded, but we may conjecture that the depleted numbers of his soldiers, their reluctance to risk treachery on the part of the Median King, and certain rumours which were current in regard to the untrustworthiness of the King of Armenia, were amongst the objections advanced. It was not long, in fact, before Antony realized that protracted negotiations with both these monarchs would have to be undertaken before the campaign could be initiated; and at the same time a great deal of recruiting would have to be accomplished before his army could be brought to the necessary size. He had recently extended a pardon and a promise of employment to all the men in his area of governance previously in the service of Sextus Pompeius, and he had also used his right to send his recruiting officers into Italy; but the re-

sults of these efforts would now have to be awaited. Very reluctantly, therefore, he postponed the campaign until the following
spring.

While he was here in Syria, and before this decision had finally
been taken, he received letters from his wife Octavia, telling him
that she was on her way to join him, carrying with her not only
money, supplies, and comforts for his men, of whose return in rags
from the Parthian war she had just heard, but also bringing him
two thousand picked soldiers, perfectly armed and accoutred,
these being a present to him from her brother Octavian, who wished
thereby to show his good will.

This news was immensely embarrassing, and he sent an immediate answer, telling her that he was about to set out for Parthia
again, and that she was to await his return at Athens. But when
Cleopatra learnt that he had thus prevaricated, and had not taken
the opportunity to give Octavia her final dismissal, she was beside
herself with anxiety and annoyance. It is to be remembered that
the Queen's fate and that of her country, her dynasty, and her
children depended almost entirely upon Antony. Cæsarion, her
son by Cæsar, was now nearly twelve years of age, and would soon
be old enough to be regarded as a serious rival by Octavian: if,
then, Octavian were ever to attain to sole power in the Roman
empire, Cæsarion's arrest and execution would be certain—in which
regard it may be said in anticipation that Octavian did in the end
put the boy to death on the grounds that there could not be *two*
Cæsars in the world.

So long as Antony retained his power and continued to be her
consort and her protector she and her family were safe, and there
was every hope that one day he would found a throne for himself
and her at the steps of which the nations of the whole earth would
do obeisance. But if he were to return to Octavia, he might be in-
veigled into a new accommodation with his brother-in-law Octavian, and one of the terms of the bargain forced upon him by the
upholders of the Roman Republic might well be his abandonment
of his connection with the Egyptian throne.

The ancient historians have always endeavoured to present
Cleopatra as a wicked siren, scheming to hold Antony to her by
means of her voluptuous charms in order to use him for the pur-

pose of her personal aggrandisement; but actually, as has already been said, there is no evidence that her character was evil.[6] She was a brave, tenacious, anxious woman, the "widow" of Cæsar and the mother of his son, persistently fighting for the realisation of those ambitions with which the Dictator had once filled her head, but struggling also to maintain that security for herself and her line which would at once be menaced by the supremacy of Octavian.

She was not yet sure of Antony's devotion; and although it is to be presumed, I think, that she now loved him—had gradually passed, in fact, into that same condition in which he also found himself—she was continuously worried about him, asking herself whether Octavia's gentleness and goodness could make an appeal to his pity stronger than her own bright appeal to his manhood and his intellect, and wondering, too, whether he might think that there was a quicker route to the autocracy of the world by way of those sedate mansions in Rome and Athens over which Octavia presided than through the pleasant halls of the Alexandrian palace. Octavia still had the guardianship of Antony's two sons by Fulvia, and of his two infant daughters of whom she, Octavia, herself was the mother: would these parental ties outpull those which she, Cleopatra, could put forward in the existence of her twins and her latest baby? Antony, in spite of his feverish manner of life, was one of those good-natured giants who, at heart, love their homes and their children; and it may be supposed that the Queen often asked herself whether he would give heed to the call of his Roman family. Indeed, it was probably at her suggestion that not long afterwards he sent for his eldest son, Antyllus, who was now about ten years of age, the boy being brought at length to Alexandria as a playmate for the young Cæsarion.

Cleopatra was not very skillful in intrigue. Many of her actions suggest, in fact, that she was not easily able to conceal her feelings, or to play a sustained part; and one gets the impression that on most occasions her behaviour must have corresponded in a somewhat startling degree with her actual thoughts and emotions. Thus, in regard to this letter from Octavia and Antony's reply to it, she

---

[6] In my *Life and Times of Cleopatra* I have defended her character at length, and have explained how the prejudice against her originated.

did not attempt to hide her distress. She told her immediate circle
that he was not behaving fairly to her: she, the sovereign lady of
many nations, she cried out, had been content to be called his
mistress, and had not spurned such a relationship so long as she
might thereby enjoy his love; and what was her reward?—he was
still allowing Octavia to call herself his wife, although the marriage had been one of mere political convenience, and he was even
undecided as to whether or not to go back to her, although he
knew quite well that she, Cleopatra, could not survive his loss. He
was unfeeling and hard-hearted, she declared, thus to play fast
and loose with one who loved him and whose whole life depended
upon him.

Plutarch has supposed that this behaviour was play-acting on
her part. "She pretended," he writes, "to be dying of love for him,
bringing her body down by slender diet. When he entered the room
she fixed her eyes upon him in rapture, and when he left, seemed to
collapse and half faint away. She took great care that he should
see her tears, and, as soon as he noticed them, hastily dried them
and turned away, as if it were her wish that he should know nothing
of her feelings." But this was no pretense. The possibility of losing
him had served both to make clear to her her dependence upon
him, and to arouse her love for him into a turmoil of jealous and
passionate emotion. She knew from past experience that it was
useless to employ mere feminine wiles in dealing with a man of his
wide experience of the arts of woman, or to act in front of one who
was a patron of actresses; and her behaviour appears to me to have
been entirely sincere.

But her fears were unwarranted: Antony had no intention of
returning to Octavia. Yet he must have been sorry for his patient
Roman wife, who possessed in a high degree the typical Roman
virtues, and was reported to be looking after his children and attending to his interests in the most gracious and estimable manner.
The faults so often attendant upon these virtues, however, were
evidently very conspicuous in Octavia: the spiritless docility of an
obedient spouse, the conventionally-minded care of a woman of
good repute to be correct in all her behaviour, the indifference of a
domesticated wife to the mental and physical elegances of fashionable life, the limited outlook of a mind directed along the narrow

path of duty, the very absence of those culpable frailties which
make the human sinner eternally beloved—these things may well
have rendered a comparison between the good Octavia and the
unconscionable and hot-tempered Cleopatra wholly favourable to
the latter. The Queen of Egypt was not a bad woman; but it is
evident that she reflected just that little sparkle of the everlasting
fires which, in the eyes of a Cæsar or an Antony, is an indispensable
attraction in the female.

The Parthian campaign being postponed, Antony gladly went
back with Cleopatra to Alexandria; and here during the summer of
35 B.C. he received another letter from Octavia saying that she
would do as he bade her, and await his coming, asking him to
what place it was his pleasure that she should send the supplies
and troops which she had brought with her to Athens. Antony's
reply indicates the development of his relationship to Cleopatra.
There was now no prevarication in regard to his ultimate return:
he simply thanked her for the gifts, asked her to forward them
to Syria under the care of the troops, and bluntly told her to go
back to Rome.[7] He did not yet institute divorce-proceedings, for
he knew that such a step would cause an immediate rupture of his
relations with Octavian; and he was not prepared to come to grips
with him until his now hopeful Parthian schemes had been brought
to a successful issue, and his prestige raised to the consequent
heights.

Octavian, so his despatches from Rome informed him, was
equally anxious to maintain peace between them for the moment,
deeming it necessary to consolidate his own position in the west
before tackling the great problem of his rivalry with Antony. Moreover, he was now conducting a difficult campaign against certain
rebels in Illyria and Pannonia, his two most eastern provinces, at
the north-east corner of the Adriatic; and he had no wish to be
involved in a dispute with Antony while his attention was thus
distracted.

Thus, the summer passed into autumn, and the autumn into
winter, while Antony remained at Alexandria busy with the organisation of his coming campaign against Parthia, with the negotiations between himself and the Kings of Armenia and Media,

[7] Dion Cassius, xlix, 33.

and with the administration of his great empire. During this time his tendencies towards monarchy developed—indeed, it would hardly have been possible for him to live in the palace at Alexandria, as husband and consort of a Queen, without himself assuming the general aspect of royalty. At the state functions of the Egyptian capital, and in its many religious ceremonials, he was obliged, I suppose, to play his part as actual King, or Pharaoh, of Egypt, and to perform those immemorial rites wherein the sovereign acted as the representative and the incarnation of the sun-god.

It is of course an exaggeration to say, as does Florus,[8] that "he so openly aspired to sovereignty that, forgetting his country, his name, his toga, and the Roman magisterial insignia, he degenerated wholly, in thought, sentiment, and dress, into that monstrosity—a King, in his hand there being a golden sceptre, at his side a scimitar, his robe being of purple clasped with enormous jewels, and his head being adorned with a royal crown, to the end that as a King he might dally with the Queen." Yet it is probably true that neither his official manner nor his private outlook were any longer those of a chief magistrate of the Roman Republic, save to those of his own countrymen who were with him in Egypt, and to the Roman soldiers who were in his service. To these latter he was always a democratic general, a soldier like themselves, although, according to Dion Cassius,[9] he now termed his military headquarters "the Palace." The same writer says that "he sometimes dressed in a manner not in accord with the customs of his native land, wore an oriental dagger at his belt, and let himself be seen even in public upon a gilded couch or a chair of similar appearance"—a more modest statement than that of Florus, and one which we may accept.

As the spring of 34 B.C. approached, both he and Cleopatra became increasingly uneasy in regard to the Parthian adventure. It seemed so hazardous to stake their entire fortune upon a difficult campaign which might possibly end in disaster. If he were victorious, of course, his prestige would be enormously enhanced, and Rome would welcome him as a conquering hero; but if he were defeated not even his present eastern empire would maintain its

[8] Florus, iv, xi.   [9] Dion Cassius, l, 5.

allegiance, and Octavian might find himself in a position to force him to retire from public life, as he had forced the third Triumvir, Lepidus. This was not the time to go adventuring into the Orient; and, in fact, the dream of emulating the exploits of Alexander the Great and of carrying the Roman eagles to the confines of India had already faded from his mind. The farthest extent of his hope was now the infliction of a single, resounding defeat upon Parthia, and the recovery of those standards and those prisoners captured from Crassus.

At any rate he was set upon a military parade through Armenia, the fidelity of whose monarch, Artavasdes, was ever in doubt, and also upon the clinching of his alliance with Media, whose King was already impatient at his delay. In about April, 34 B.C., therefore he left Cleopatra and sailed across to Syria, where he placed himself at the head of his army—not the great army with which he had previously marched northwards, but a powerful force, nevertheless. He sent his friend Dellius ahead to the Armenian court with the proposal that a contract of betrothal should be made between his eldest son by Cleopatra—the young Alexander Helios, who was now in his sixth year—and one of the daughters of Artavasdes; and when he reached the city of Nicopolis on the borders of Pontus and Armenia Minor, he sent a further message to the King, inviting him to come there to discuss the general situation. Artavasdes, however, declined the invitation, making some specious excuse, and thereupon Antony marched upon Artaxata (Ardesh), the Armenian capital, which stood a few miles to the north-east of Mount Ararat.

Further negotiations, however, persuaded Artavasdes to come into the Roman camp to make his peace with Antony; but, upon doing so, he was at once put under restraint, and was compelled to accompany the army upon its tour through the country and to issue orders for the payment of a heavy tribute to the Romans, as compensation for his having deserted them in the last campaign in Media. Thereupon, the Armenians raised his eldest son, Artaxes, to the throne, and attempted to put up a fight; but they were quickly overcome, and the new King fled to Parthia. Antony then caused Artavasdes to be put in fetters, but, out of consideration for his rank, directed that the chains should be made of silver;

and presently he sent him as a prisoner back to Alexandria, permitting him to take his wife and children with him. His kingdom was afterwards freely looted, and it is said [10] that in the temple of Anaitis—the local Aphrodite—in Acilisene, a district in the south-west of Armenia, the soldiers found a statue of that goddess made of pure gold, which they melted down and divided among themselves.

Antony then got into touch with the King of Media, his former enemy; and a very satisfactory alliance was made with him, by the terms of which it was agreed that, in preparation for a campaign in the following year, a number of Roman legions should be left for the present in Armenia, which country should henceforth be regarded as a dependency of Media, both Armenia and Media, however, becoming an integral part of the Roman empire. It was further agreed that the son of Antony and Cleopatra, the little Alexander Helios, should at once be married by proxy to Iotapa, the infant daughter of the Median King, and that the King should make the boy his heir, so that one day he should be ruler of Armenia, Media, and of all Parthia, as far as the borders of India, when it should be conquered. Thus, by the arts of diplomacy, and without any actual campaign, Antony added an enormous area to the Roman dominions over which he ruled as Autocrat; and at the same time he so distributed his forces in Armenia and Syria that a double invasion of Parthia from the north and south—through Media, that is to say, on the one hand, and through Mesopotamia on the other—would have every chance of success. The faded vision of a march to the frontiers of India became bright once more with vivid possibility.

It was a splendid summer's work, and when Antony returned to Alexandria in the early autumn of 34 b.c., he had reached the highest peak of his power yet attained in his entire career. Moreover, the loot of Armenia, much of which was in precious metal able to be turned into money, was sufficient for the payment of his soldiers, all of whom were in high spirits and were ready to follow their general withersoever he should lead them. Like Octavian, Antony seemed to bear a charmed life, and to be able to extricate himself from every difficulty, rising, after each relapse, to a higher

[10] Orosius, vi, xix, 3.

level of attainment. His confidence in himself was fully restored. He appears to have felt young again in spite of his forty-nine years; and Cleopatra, who was nearing her thirty-fourth birthday and was the mother of four children, was so infected by his high spirits that she, too, must have been radiant with happiness.

The consciousness of his power caused Antony to take a step which he knew would be resented by Rome: he decided to celebrate a Triumph in Alexandria. Now a Triumph was a ceremony which had never yet been performed outside Rome; it was an honour accorded to a victorious commander only by the mother-city; it was the particular privilege and prerogative of the ancient capital; and that this Triumph should be held in Alexandria was tantamount to a declaration that Rome had ceased in his opinion to be the official center of the empire. Antony was quite aware of the fact, and in breaking thus with tradition he was definitely pursuing that policy to which attention has already been called, the policy of transferring the seat of supreme government from Octavian's western sphere to his own eastern dominions, so that in the end Italy should become what its geographical situation showed it to be—a western appendage to the world-empire of the Romans.

The great temple of Serapis was to Alexandria what the Capitol was to Rome, and, one bright, autumnal day, the triumphal procession made its way thither from the palace, through the Forum and along the famous Street of Canopus and Street of Serapis,[11] passing many of the celebrated buildings which made Alexandria so much more magnificent a city than the Rome of that date. Antony drove through the crowded streets in his triumphal chariot; and in the procession walked the captive King Artavasdes of Armenia with his wife and children, having chains of gold attached to their wrists, while behind them followed the wagons heaped high with the spoils of their country. Triumphal processions were always occasions for a striking display of wealth and might; and it may be supposed that amongst the military forces which took part in the spectacle were detachments of Roman legionaries and Roman and Gallic cavalry, Macedonian Household-troops which formed the permanent bodyguard of the sovereign, Egyptian sol-

---

[11] For a description of ancient Alexandria, see my *Life and Times of Cleopatra*, Chap. ii.

diers, mounted bowmen from Media, light cavalry from Pontus, and various units from Greece, Asia Minor, Syria, Arabia, Libya, the upper Valley of the Nile, and so forth.

In a certain open space, perhaps in front of the Temple of Serapis, Cleopatra sat upon a golden throne raised upon a platform plated with silver; and here the captive Armenian King was led forward to do obeisance.[12] He, however, while willing to pay homage to Antony, refused to bow to the Queen or to address her in any other manner than by her name, Cleopatra, without titulary embellishments; and though he was in consequence subjected to a good deal of rough handling, he maintained his proud dignity, standing upright before her until at last he was dragged away. It was the Roman custom, as we have seen, to put an important prisoner of this kind to death at the end of a Triumph; but the good-natured Antony had decided to break with tradition in this respect also, and he did him and his family no hurt, but kept them afterwards as honourable prisoners in Alexandria, where, no doubt, Artavasdes amused himself by continuing to write his historical books and his dramas.

On the following day, or at any rate shortly afterwards, a great public ceremony was held in the Gymnasium, a kind of stadium having a stone-built grandstand the columned frontage of which, facing the Street of Canopus, was more than two hundred yards in length. Here in the open air, upon a platform of silver, were two golden thrones whereon Antony and Cleopatra were seated side by side, while near them were four other thrones occupied by the four children—Cæsarion, now some months over thirteen years of age, the twins Alexandria Helios and Cleopatra Selene, six years old, and the little Ptolemy, two years old. (Antyllus, Antony's son by Fulvia, had not yet arrived from Rome.) Antony, speaking in Greek, then made a speech to the assembled crowds, announcing the honours and dignities which he had obtained for, or conferred upon, their royal family; and so splendid were these that the Alexandrians who heard his words must have been left almost breathless.[13]

---

[12] Dion Cassius, xlix, 40.
[13] The lands assigned to each are given differently by Plutarch and Dion Cassius, but I have tried to adjust the two accounts.

Cleopatra, he announced, was the true wife and widow of the divine Cæsar,[14] and as such, besides her kingdom of Egypt, he named her Queen of all Libya—the territory west of Egypt—except for the promontory of Cyrene, Queen of Syria north and east of Palestine, and Queen of Cyprus, and declared that her title henceforth would be Queen of Kings. Cæsarion, he said, was the only son of Cæsar, and in honour of that great name, he was to be entitled King of Kings, and was to rule jointly with his mother as Pharaoh of Egypt and King of Libya, Syria, and Cyprus.[15] Alexander Helios, he declared, was Prince, and future King, of Armenia and Media, and also of the Parthian realms as far east as the Indus when they should be conquered. Cleopatra Selene was to be Queen of Cyrene, that part of the Libyan seacoast just east of Tripoli, with which, so it seems, went the island of Crete, for Crete and Cyrene, since 95 B.C., had been regarded as a single Roman Province, though separated by a hundred and thirty miles of open sea. And finally the infant Ptolemy was declared King of the northernmost corner of Syria west of the Euphrates and north of Antioch, and of the adjoining Cilicia.

There followed a kind of coronation ceremony, in which Cleopatra was robed in the ancient Egyptian manner as the goddess Isis-Venus, assuming the famous vulture-headdress surmounted by the horns and disk; while upon the head of Cæsarion, it is to be supposed, was placed the old Pharaonic double-crown of Upper and Lower Egypt encircled by the golden diadem of his Macedonian line. Alexander Helios was presented to the people wearing Median costume and having upon his head the tall tiara of the ancient Persians, while a bodyguard of Armenians waited upon him; and the little Ptolemy, guarded by Macedonian troops, and dressed in Macedonian robes, was crowned with a cap and diadem such as had once been worn by Alexander the Great.

Two points must be noticed. Firstly, in declaring Cæsarion King of Egypt, Antony abandoned his own right to that title as consort of Cleopatra; and we may suppose that this was a gesture which was intended to contradict the common report that he had

---

[14] Dion Cassius, xlix, 41.
[15] So Dion Cassius, but Plutarch says that the title King of Kings was also conferred on the two younger boys.

ceased to regard himself as a magistrate of the Roman Republic. His title of Autocrator, however, was higher than that of any King, and he was satisfied with it, knowing that it would serve him even if he were to establish a throne for himself. Secondly, his insistence upon the fact that Cleopatra was the widow, and Cæsarion the son, of the great Cæsar, was clearly an attempt to show the world that he was acting as Cæsar's executor, so to speak, in thus honouring them. "It was his purpose," says Dion Cassius,[16] "in this way to cast reproach upon Octavian as being only an adopted, and not a real, son of the Dictator"; and in becoming openly the boy's patron and guardian he must have deliberately thrown down a gauntlet which his rival could not fail to see.

He then sent a report of the proceedings to Rome; and although, before leaving Italy, he had obliged the Senate to agree to an anticipatory ratification of all his acts, as has already been recorded, he now demanded that they should pass a special decree to ratify these latest dispositions. He declared also that he was quite willing to place himself at the disposal of the Senate and to abide by its wishes, being ready even to resign his command if he were required to do so.[17] He said this, however, knowing that his offer would not be acted upon. His letter would reach Rome at about the beginning of the new year, 33 B.C. when, by his general arrangements made with Octavian before he left Italy, the two Consuls-elect for the following year, 32 B.C., would be his friends and supporters, Domitius Ahenobarbus, and Sossius, his former governor of Syria.[18] Consuls-elect had the right of addressing the Senate before the other members [19]; and this fact, coupled with his belief that at least half of the Senators favoured him rather than Octavian, made him pretty sure that he would not be too greatly censured. Rome was thoroughly used to creating vassal kingdoms, if not quite on this vast scale. In any case he wished to show some outward deference to the Senate; for even if he were in the end to transfer the seat of government from Rome to the East, it was to be presumed that this ancient assembly would also be transferred, and not disbanded.

[16] Dion Cassius, xlix, 41.   [17] Ibid.
[18] Dion Cassius (xlix, 41) has made an error in calling these two the Consuls, and not the Consuls-elect, in this year.
[19] Sallust: Catiline, 1; etc.

Antony was at this time in a condition of great exhilaration; and his sense of the limitless power wielded by him throughout his eastern empire was a stimulant which projected him into his daily affairs with overwhelming zest. It is true that from time to time he drank heavily, and behaved riotously; but life itself was usually intoxication enough for him. The longer he lived with Cleopatra the more devoted he became to her; and though, obviously, there were quarrels between them, these had the nature of lovers' tiffs, and were soon followed by happy reconciliations. He was hardly willing to let her out of his sight; and it is said that sometimes when he was engaged in official business, or was acting as judge in the courts of law, he would start to his feet on seeing her passing in her litter, and, leaving his work, would hasten out to her, and walk through the streets at her side, laughing and talking with her.

He gave her a bodyguard of Roman soldiers, and caused their shields to be inscribed with the letter C, the initial of her name. He and she used frequently to sit together for the Alexandrian painters and sculptors, he being sometimes represented in the guise of Dionysus, or of the Egyptian god Osiris who was in certain aspects identified with that deity, and she being portrayed as Isis or Venus. He allowed the Alexandrians to begin the erection of a temple in honour of his divinity, corresponding to the temple of Isis-Venus which was dedicated to her. It pleased him to be hailed as the New Dionysus, and at certain festivals, he would appear in public in that guise, garlanded with ivy, wearing the Dionysian buskins on his feet, and holding the thyrsus in his hand; while Cleopatra played the part of the New Isis. In the great games held in the Gymnasium, however, he threw off his celestial character, and, to the huge delight of the crowds, assumed the office of Gymnasiarch, or Chief Steward of the Proceedings, conducting himself in the arena like a burly ring-master.

In the palace, meanwhile, magnificent banquets were held, at which he and his Greek and Roman friends became thoroughly inebriated, though Cleopatra herself drank little and was so habitually sober that people supposed her to wear a magic ring which had the faculty of preventing intoxication. At these parties Antony played the fool with carefree indifference to scandal: and it is related that on one occasion he made his friend Plancus dance before the guests in the guise of the Bœotian sea-god Glaucus, naked and painted blue, a chaplet of seaweed on his head, and a fish-tail tied to his waist. So wildly was money spent in these revels, that even the newly-arrived young Antyllus, Antony's son, on one occasion is said to have made a gift to one of his friends of all the rich silver plate used at a palace banquet.

Yet in spite of these splendid frivolities, Antony was daily busy with his administrative work, and with his preparations for the Parthian campaign of his dreams; and these tasks must have been so exacting that one cannot suppose him to have wasted undue time over his amusements. Five or six months of this full Alexandrian life were all that he allowed himself; and in the early spring of 33 B.C. he bade farewell to Cleopatra and her gay capital, and set out to join his army in Syria, preparatory to a new march into Armenia.

CHAPTER XIX

The Final Quarrel Between Antony and Octavian, and Rome's Declaration of War Against Cleopatra.

33–32 B.C.

ANTONY, it will be recalled, had left a considerable Roman force in Armenia, and had concentrated a large army in Syria. Still enthralled by his vision of Oriental conquest, his plan, I think, was now to march several more of his legions into Armenia, and thence to move on into Media, where he and the Median King would together work out their plan of campaign and make the proper disposition of their united armies. He intended then, it would seem, to leave the invasion of Parthia from the north in the hands of his generals, and himself to return to the south with a powerful force of Median mounted archers, and to lead these and the legions left in Syria together across the desert to Parthia by the Mesopotamian route. The double invasion from the north and the south would probably overwhelm the Parthians; and, with the attendance of good fortune, the two invading armies might meet again on the far-off banks of the Indus.

He marched to Armenia and thence to Media without mishap; and there he and his generals perfected their plans with the Median monarch, who handed over to him the required force of cavalry, and at the same time delivered to him his little daughter, Iotapa, so that Antony might carry her back to Syria with him, and send her on to Alexandria to be educated in Cleopatra's palace with her boy-husband, Alexander Helios, to whom, it will be recalled, she had already been married by proxy. As a further token of goodwill he returned to Antony the military standards captured from the Romans in the disaster to the siege-train. The scope of the alliance was then extended by the promise of the

Median King that he would give what aid he could to Antony in the event of a struggle with Octavian—a contingency which seemed likely to happen at no very distant date.

Antony had already—on his arrival in Armenia—received letters from his friends in Rome reporting the capital's first reaction to his announcement of his donations of territory to Cleopatra's family, which had been decidedly unfavourable; and he was expecting that his relations with Octavian would soon become strained. But when he was about to set out on his long march back into Syria at the head of the Median cavalry which he was going to use in his southern campaign, he received further despatches from Rome of so ominous a character that all his plans were upset. It was now mid-summer of the year 33 B.C., and these despatches, which had left Rome in the late spring, gave him details of what had happened there since the digestion of the news of his high-handed actions.

In the first place there was the matter of his relationship to Octavia. When he had told that unfortunate lady to go back to Rome, Octavian had very naturally felt that she had been insulted, and had advised her, though in vain, to cease to reside in Antony's house—that great mansion on the Palatine which had once belonged to Pompey. But when it had become clear that Antony had contracted some sort of marriage with Cleopatra, the angry Octavian had again pressed her to leave her errant husband's house, declaring that the insult could only be wiped out in blood. Octavia, however, had implored him with many tears not to resort to arms on her account, saying that it was intolerable that a great civil war should be waged simply because her husband, on the one part, had left her for another woman, and her brother, on the other, resented this treatment of his sister. "And her behaviour," writes Plutarch, "proved her words to be sincere, for she remained in Antony's house, and took the noblest and most generous care of his children, receiving all his friends who came to Rome on any business, and even doing her best to recommend to Octavian those who were seeking government employment; but this honourable behaviour of hers did unintentional damage to Antony's reputation, for the wrong he had done to such a woman caused him to be disliked, and now this donation of kingdoms to his children by Cleopatra in Alexandria also made him unpopular, for it seemed a theatrical piece of insolence to her and of actual contempt of his native land."

Again, Antony's declaration that Cleopatra was to be regarded as Cæsar's widow, and that Cæsarion was Cæsar's true son and heir, had raised a storm of protest amongst Octavian's supporters. Antony had declared, quite truthfully, that Cæsar himself had acknowledged the boy as his own [1]; and at this, Caius Oppius, a former friend of Cæsar who had attached himself to Octavian, had issued a pamphlet which he had written to prove that Cæsarion was not Cæsar's child at all.

Antony had assigned to Domitius Ahenobarbus and Sossius the duty of reading his despatches to the Senate; but he was now informed that these two men, the Consuls-elect for the next year, had decided that the documents ought not to be read in full in the present state of senatorial opinion, and had only communicated to the House those relating to the disaffection and suppression of the King of Armenia. Thereupon, Octavian himself had told the Senate all that Antony had done, and had used his influence to arouse the public against him and also against Cleopatra whom he accused of having placed Antony under a kind of enchantment. He said it was clear that Antony intended to transfer the seat of government from Rome to Alexandria [2]; and, indeed, it seems that in this he was quite correct, for, obviously, in view of the expected extension of the Roman empire into the Orient, Alexandria would be a much more convenient centre than Rome, as the great Cæsar had already seen.

It would appear that in private letters to friends in Italy, Antony had some time ago complained that Octavian had not behaved fairly by the terms of the Triumvirate in discharging Lepidus and in seizing that deposed Triumvir's legions and sphere of governance, and also in taking possession of all the lands, ships, and men of Sextus Pompeius, without proposing any division of these with Antony. Antony had also protested that Octavian had given all the available lands in Italy to his own ex-soldiers, and had left nothing for Antony's men when they should be demobilised. And now came a personal answer from Octavian to these complaints, saying cynically that he was perfectly willing to divide with Antony the new possessions which had come into his hands, on condition that Antony would, on his part, give him a share of Armenia and its loot; and that, as to the gift of lands to the soldiers, it was better, surely, to settle them on the new territory acquired in Armenia and Media.

In this same letter another sore spot was touched upon. The execution of Sextus Pompeius had been much regretted by the old republican party in Rome, and now Octavian, wishing to gain the approval of this section of opinion, accused Antony of having unkindly put him to death when he, Octavian, would have spared him [8] (Antony, it will be recalled, had also wished to spare him, but the execution had taken place before his orders to this effect had been received). Moreover, Octavian further accused Antony of having taken the King of Armenia prisoner by treachery when he had visited the Roman camp under a truce, which, apparently, was not true. Octavian also took the opportunity to make some rude remarks about Cleopatra, describing Antony's relations with her as immoral in view of the fact that he was married to Octavia.

These despatches made it clear that Octavian felt strong enough to press his quarrel with his rival to an issue, now that the five years of the renewed Triumvirate were drawing to a close. With the end of the present year the agreement made between the two rivals at Tarentum in 37 B.C. would terminate; and Octavian's truculence, which meant that he had no wish to renew the arrangement, came as a shock to Antony who, just now, was regarding himself as supreme in the world and was not prepared to brook defiance from any source whatsoever. He was beside himself with fury, and his anger was increased, no doubt, by the fact that he knew in his heart that, in regard to Octavia at any rate, these censures had good cause. He saw immediately that the Parthian adventure would have to be postponed, and that he would have to fight it out with his rival before venturing to lose himself in the Orient. Impulsively he wrote a reply to Octavian in which he hotly defended his relationship to Cleopatra, and asked how his colleague could dare to criticise him in that regard when he himself was notorious for his loose morals.

[8] Dion Cassius, l, i.

He spoke of the scandal of Octavian's divorce from Scribonia, which, he said, was due to that lady's resentment at her husband's misbehaviour with other women; and he declared that the circumstances of his hasty marriage to Livia had been disgraceful. He reminded him of an occasion when Octavian had, at a banquet, taken the wife of an ex-Consul from the table to his bedroom, and had brought her back to her outraged husband, who was also his guest, with her hair and clothes disordered and her ears very pink.[4] He stated, further, that Octavian's friends were in the habit of procuring women for him, and of making an inspection of them as though they were slaves in the market.

He then mentioned several of the young man's mistresses by name, referring in particular to a certain Drusilla who was his last fancy. "And you do not make free with Drusilla only," he wrote. "When you read this letter, if you still have your health and strength, you will probably be dallying with Tertulla, or Terentilla, or Rufilla, or Salvia Titiscenia, or all of them together, for what do you care where, or upon whom you spend your manly vigour? But why are you changed towards me? Is it because *I* live with a Queen? She is my wife. Is this a new thing with me? Have I not done so during these last nine years?"—that is to say from 41 B.C., in which year Cleopatra came to Tarsus.

He sent this angry and vulgar letter off, and therewith proceeded on his way to the south, despatching messengers back to the King of Media telling him that the invasion of Parthia must be postponed, and others ahead to Cleopatra notifying her of his change of plans and asking her to meet him.

History has nothing trustworthy to tell us of the meeting or the meeting-place.[5] and it is a question whether Antony crossed the Mediterranean to Alexandria, or made a rendez-vous with the Queen in Syria or Asia Minor. It was now his purpose to collect his forces at Ephesus, and presently to proceed to the western coast of Greece whence he could hurl his defiance at Octavian across the Adriatic and force him to fight; but, in the innumerable calls upon his time and in the urgency of the business of gather-

---

[4] Suetonius: Augustus, lxix.

[5] Bouché Leclercq (*Historic des Lagides*, ii, 286) thinks that Antony went to Alexandria.

ing men, ships, money, and munitions, it is a question whether he found it necessary to give his personal attention to the mobilisation of Egypt's contribution to the cause, or was content to leave the matter to Cleopatra. He knew, at any rate, that she would be glad to hear that he had decided to tackle Octavian at once; and he could be certain that she would strip her country to the bone to provide the sinews of war.

In the late winter of 33 B.C., or in the early weeks of 32 B.C., he and Cleopatra arrived together at Ephesus where the great gathering of his forces had already begun. Both of them must have been in a state of great excitement, though in the case of Antony there was an anger, an exasperation, in his heart which must have flashed its flames across the ferment of his hopes and plans. From Cleopatra's point of view the coming war was greatly to be desired, because the ending of the Triumvirate and the expected eclipse of Octavian would not only place her consort and lover, Antony, in a position to establish a world-throne for himself and her, but would raise her son Cæsarion—now nearly fifteen years of age—to the status of sole heir of the divine Cæsar. It was customary for a youth of Roman blood to assume the *toga virilis*, the dress of a grown man, on his fifteenth birthday; and thus Cæsarion would soon be able to be presented to the Roman world as something more than a child, and when she and Antony should enter Rome in triumph the boy would ride through the streets like a young soldier at the head of the adoring veterans of his father, the deified Cæsar. The crushing of Octavian had been delayed too long already; and the removal of that further cause of delay, the Parthian campaign, with its terrible risks of disaster, was a matter of extreme relief to the anxious Queen.

Antony himself viewed the situation somewhat differently. He had been so eager to have his revenge on the Parthians, to emulate the exploits of Alexander the Great, and to add the vast Orient to his Roman dominions; and this necessity of dealing first with Octavian must have come as a great shock to him. But now that he was committed to it, he had thrown himself into the enterprise with confident hopes of success. He knew that there was a large body of opinion in Rome which was warmly attached to him and hostile to Octavian. The two Consuls for the new year, 32 B.C.,

Domitius Ahenobarbus and Sossius, were his firm supporters; and
he could reckon on about half the members of the Senate as his
friends. Thus, his rival would be beset by enemies in his own camp.

Moreover Antony could undoubtedly put a larger army into
the field than Octavian; and Cleopatra's fleet, combined with his
own, would give him a superiority on the sea also. Again, Italy
was on the verge of financial ruin, whereas Antony could command
not only the wealth of Egypt but that of a hundred states and
cities in his Eastern empire.

The overthrow of Octavian, therefore, seemed almost a certainty; but when it should become an accomplished fact what,
then, would he do? For some time he would have to remain the
first magistrate of the Republic, having the title *Autocrator* in
the eastern empire, and its equivalent, *Imperator*, in the western
dominions; but at length, with Cleopatra as his consort, he would
convert his position into an actual sovereignty, and, in the end,
would hand on his throne to Cæsar's son, Cæsarion. His capital
would be Alexandria, or perhaps one of the great cities of Asia
Minor or Syria; and Rome would become this world-empire's
second city.

There was one all-important question, however, which must
have exercised his thoughts, and have overshadowed all else: during the coming war with Octavian, what would Rome's attitude
be towards Cleopatra? Gradually she had become a very part of
his existence. Not by a violent onrush of romantic passion, but by
the slow results of intimacy, interdependence, and familiarity,
she had taken possession of him little by little, until today he
could not think of a life that was separate from her. Octavian's
insulting remarks about her had aroused in him a fury of resentment, and had made him eager to secure her acknowledgment in
Rome as his legal wife; yet he knew well enough that her presence
at his side would displease all those who supported the old institutions of the Republic and still nursed that ancient hatred of
kingship which was the traditional mania of conservative Romans.

Already he had received a letter from Domitius Ahenobarbus
urging him to send Cleopatra back to Egypt to await there the
outcome of the struggle,[6] in order that public opinion in Rome

---

[6] Plutarch: *Antony*.

might not be outraged by his intimate relationship with a queen. But, apart from all other considerations, he could not in fairness dismiss her when he was spending her money—for she had brought with her a huge sum drawn from her Treasury—and was relying on her supplies and armaments, which included a quarter of the ships at his disposal. After all, as one of his generals, quoted by Plutarch, put it, "it would not be just that she who was bearing so great a part of the cost of the war should be robbed of her share of glory in carrying it on, nor would it be polite to offend the Egyptians who were supplying so considerable a part of his naval forces, especially as the Queen was not inferior in wisdom to any one of the kings who were serving with him, she having for years governed a great kingdom by herself alone, and having long lived with him and gained experience in public affairs."

Antony could argue, too, that his position was surely strengthened in its Cæsarian aspect by the fact that he had with him, under his protection, Cæsar's "widow" and the mother of his only son. Yet such arguments were superfluous for the reason that his determination to keep her with him was based upon a now genuine love for her and dependence upon her, and that this determination was rendered all the stronger by the opposition of his supporters in Rome. Opposition always stirred him to defiant, hostile action.

With the ending of the Triumvirate on January 1st, 32 B.C., and the beginning of Antony's great mobilisation at Ephesus, the situation became startlingly clear to the people of Rome, and the city was seething with excitement. On that date the Senate met, and the new Consul, Sossius, greatly daring, delivered a speech in praise of Antony and in denunciation of Octavian—who had gone out of town to mark by so doing the termination of his tenure of office as Triumvir. The speech has not been preserved, but it is to be supposed that he enumerated Antony's causes of complaint, and asked the senators to invite him to return so that he might be given special powers to reorganise the whole empire; and he told them, no doubt, that if by blind adherence to Octavian they were to give Antony cause for fear for his own position, a sanguinary war would result.

When this speech was reported to Octavian he at once convened the Senate again, and, on the appointed day, entered the assembly guarded by soldiers and by a large company of his supporters, all of whom carried daggers concealed beneath their robes.[7] Seating himself upon his chair of state between the two Consuls, he addressed the anxious senators, accusing Antony and Sossius of being engaged in a plot to overthrow the Republic; but when his words were received in nervous silence, nobody daring to take sides, he declared in anger that he would bring documentary proof before the House at its next meeting in a few days' time. This speech was regarded as tantamount to a declaration of war in defence of Rome, and within a day or so Ahenobarbus and Sossius, the two Consuls, together with several of the leading supporters of Antony, secretly left the city and made their way to Brindisi where they took ship for Greece to join their chief.

Octavian, now thirty-one years of age, was no longer the rash and hesitating opportunist of earlier days. The turmoil and racket of his strangely fated career had accustomed him to life's alarms, and he was able to think clearly in a situation fraught with dangers. The silent reception of his speech in the Senate revealed to him, perhaps for the first time, the extent of Antony's following in Rome; and with admirable cunning he decided to direct his attack not against his popular rival but against Cleopatra. Rapidly he spread the story that this unholy Queen of Egypt had set her dark heart upon the conquest of Rome, and with this object in view had bewitched the easy-going Antony by her voluptuous charms, assisted by magic, so that he was no more than her slave. He said that her common form of asseveration was "As surely as I shall one day reign in the Capitol in Rome"; and he told of her skill in enchantment, and how, for instance, she wore that magic ring which enabled her to remain sober while Antony, drinking with her, passed into oblivion.

He then issued an edict which had as its object the removal from the city of all those who would be likely to work against him: he announced that every senator who wished to leave Rome and go over to Antony might do so without hindrance. He was not prepared, however, for the great exodus which immediately took place; and when some four hundred senators promptly left Rome in a body to follow the two Consuls across the Adriatic, he

[7] Dion Cassius, l, 2.

must have received an unpleasant shock. The numbers of the Senate, however, had been greatly increased since the days of Sulla, who had raised them to six hundred; and the departing four hundred represented considerably less than half the assembly. It speaks highly for Antony's prestige, nevertheless, that so large a company of Rome's legislators should thus have placed their trust in him and their fortunes in his hands, and should have left their homes and their families in order to associate themselves with him. Allowing for the numbers of like-minded senators who yet did not dare to take the step, it may be supposed that more than half the Senate was really on Antony's side, in spite of his long absences from the capital, and in spite of the stories spread against him particularly in regard to his relations with Cleopatra and his desire to found a Roman throne for himself and her.

But if Octavian were disturbed by this debacle, Antony must also have been dealt a serious blow by the sudden flight of two of his most trusted friends, who slipped away from him and went over to Octavian. These two were Plancus and Titius. Plancus was last seen by us, it will be recalled, dancing about at one of the Alexandrian parties, painted blue in an impersonation of a sea-god: he had been the foremost of Antony's boon-companions, and having apparently fallen foul of the Queen, he carried to Rome an exaggerated tale of her influence over her lover which may well have almost raised the hair on the heads of conservative Romans. Titius was the man who had put Sextus Pompeius to death, and it may be that he had quarrelled with Antony in regard to the assigning of blame for that unpopular act. But whatever may have been their personal reasons for their departure, their change of sides must have been the cause of misgiving to Antony. Could it be possible, he may well have asked himself, that these two men supposed Octavian to have a chance of victory? He could hardly believe it, surrounded as he was by Roman legionaries and foreign soldiers in number like the sands of the sea.

From all directions fighting forces were trooping into Ephesus in response to his general call to arms. From Asia Minor came King Tarcondemus (or Tarcondimotus) of Upper Cilicia, and the young King Archelaus of Cappadocia whom Antony had raised to the throne in 36 B.C. as a tribute to the charms of his mother,

Glaphyra. The Cilicians and Cappadocians, with the Carians, were known as "the three bad C's"; and the troops which these kings brought with them must have been little better than brigands. Philadelphus, King of Paphlagonia, Amyntas, King of a part of Galatia and Lycaonia, and Deiotarus, King of the other part of Galatia, and son of the monarch of the same name who had been restored to his throne by Antony shortly after Cæsar's death, were three other sovereigns of Asia Minor who arrived with their contingents of troops; while King Polemo of Pontus and Armenia Minor, though unable to come in person, sent strong bodies of his celebrated javelin-throwers and light cavalry. The rulers of Bithynia, Phrygia, Pamphylia, Lydia, Lycia, Mysia, and other districts of Asia Minor, also provided their contingents of fighting men. Sadalas and Rhœmetalces, joint Kings of Thrace, arrived at the head of their world-renowned slingers; and the Athenians, Bœotians, Spartans, Macedonians, Thessalians, Rhodians, and other Greek nations, sent their still famous soldiery; while from Crete came a body of the unequalled bowmen of that island.

Mithradates, King of Commagene, the successor of that monarch whom Antony had besieged in Samosata, rode in with his contribution of men. King Herod of Judæa sent a contingent of Jewish troops; the soldiers of Syria were led in by their Roman officers; King Iamblicus of Emesa (Homs) and other kings of the Syrian desert and Sabæa (Sheba)[8] each provided a picturesque quota. King Artavasdes of Media had already supplied a force of mounted archers, and from his new realm of Armenia he now sent further detachments of light cavalry. Even from the shores of the far-off Sea of Azov, north of the Black Sea, came an unruly band of soldiers.[9]

From North Africa arrived King Bogud of Mauretania, son of that Bocchus who betrayed Jugurtha, bringing with him the flower of his army; Libyan troops and the warriors of Cyrene made the long voyage across the sea at Cleopatra's command; and from the Queen's own country came troops of Greeks, Egyptians, Ethiopians, and Bedouins. The Roman legions included men recruited in Italy, Gaul, Spain, and Illyria; and there were divisions of Gallic and German cavalry.

[8] Florus, iv, xi.   [9] Plutarch: *Antony*.

The total land-forces at his disposal—not counting four legions left in Egypt, four in Cyrene, three in Syria, and many others at different strategic points—amounted to between a hundred and a hundred and fifty thousand men; and against this Octavian could muster no more than eighty thousand, drawn from Italy, Sicily, Gaul, Spain, Sardinia, and parts of North Africa. Antony's ships numbered at least eight hundred, of which five hundred were men-o'-war [10]; but Octavian, according to Plutarch, had only two hundred and fifty first class fighting ships and a collection of other vessels, which brought his total fighting-force up to about four hundred.

It is not surprising, therefore, that Antony was confident of victory; and he must have felt himself already to be the sovereign lord of the world as he reviewed these troops who had come to him from the corners of the earth, watched the legions of Rome march before him in their tens of thousands, received the respectful salutations of the vassal kings, presided over the meetings of the four hundred senators who had now arrived at Ephesus, gave his orders to the two Consuls, the highest magistrates of Rome, and all the while enjoyed the loving attentions of Cleopatra, Queen of Kings, who, with admiration in her eyes, saw him thus transforming her dreams into reality. There can be no doubt that she loved him now to the depth of her capacity; for glory, magnificence, majesty, and power were the gods of her woman's heart, and Antony was ringed about with these in such a blaze of splendour that his hours of simple and intimate relaxation at her side or in her arms were a source of boundless pride to her—and pride in the loved-one is a very root of love.

When Octavian's defiant actions, and his libels upon Cleopatra, were reported to Antony he responded by sending a bill of divorcement to Octavia, at the same time ordering her to leave his house in Rome, which she did, taking with her her own three children by Marcellus, Julus, Antony's second son by Fulvia, and his two daughters, Antonia the Elder and Antonia the Younger. She wept bitterly as she took her departure; but, in view of the stories which had been spread of Antony's bewitchment by Cleopatra, "the Romans pitied her not so much as they pitied him, and more

[10] Plutarch: *Antony*.

particularly those who had seen Cleopatra, whom they reported to
have no sort of advantage over Octavia, either in youth or in
beauty." [11] Cleopatra, indeed, was not remarkably beautiful, though
it seems that she carried well her thirty-seven years: her attractions,
as I have already said, lay in her beautiful voice, her grace, her
elegance, her brilliance, her brains, her wit, and her general charm;
and with these the unfashionable Octavia's good looks and docile
nature could not compete.

It must be mentioned in passing that history tells us nothing
more of Antony's mother, Julia, after her visit to her son at Athens
in 40 B.C., eight years ago. If she were still alive she would now
have been nearly seventy years of age; but being herself a Cæsar
and a kinswoman of the great Dictator, she would have been in
no danger of molestation in Rome or anywhere else. It is not unlikely that she was spending the evening of her life in Athens.

Towards the end of April of this year 32 B.C. Antony transferred his headquarters to Samos, the historic city on the island of
the same name, lying off the western coast of Asia Minor not more
than twelve miles, as the crow flies, from Ephesus; and here he celebrated a great festival of some kind. The city was famous for its
beautiful buildings, amongst which was the Temple of Hera, the
goddess of marriage, which was supposed to mark the site where
she was wedded to Zeus. We are not told the nature of Antony's
festival, although Plutarch states that "the island resounded for
some days with the music of pipes and harps," and that "every
city sent an ox as its contribution to the sacrifices"; but I venture
to suggest that the celebrations were those of the marriage of Antony and Cleopatra according to Greek or Roman law now that
their union had been made legal by the divorce of Octavia, for it is
surely more than a coincidence that they should have thus held
high festival at a renowned nuptial shrine just at the time when this
divorce enabled them to be joined in recognized matrimony. Antony, of course, had regarded Cleopatra as his wife for several years,
but their marriage had not been legal outside the sphere of Egyptian
law until now.

For these festivities Antony gathered all the stage players
from round about to entertain the company, and rewarded them af-

[11] Plutarch: *Antony*.

terwards by assigning them lands near the city of Priene, a few miles south of Ephesus, thus founding a kind of theatrical colony. Magnificent banquets were given during these days at Samos, and the vassal kings are said to have vied with one another in the sumptuousness of their entertainments.

In May Antony sailed with Cleopatra across the Ægæan Sea to Athens, giving orders to the army to follow him into Greece so that a new concentration might be made on the coast opposite Italy. Now Octavia had made herself very popular with the Athenians during her residence there while waiting for Antony's return; and Cleopatra therefore felt it incumbent upon her to court public favour so that Antony's change of partners might be understood. So successful was she in this that the Athenians presently decreed her all sorts of civic honours; and Antony came under a good deal of criticism because, on the occasion of the sending of the humble deputation to her to confer upon her these honours, he insisted upon being its leader and making a speech to her. It was considered very droll of him by some, and very undignified of him by others, in view of the fact that he was the prospective lord of creation; but he caused an even greater sensation shortly afterwards by going over to her at a public banquet and affectionately patting her feet. People commented, too, on the way he followed her about; and it was said that when they were away from one another, even for a few hours, they were always exchanging tender little notes and messages.

Here at Athens, in fact, they were enjoying a belated honeymoon; and Antony, at the age of fifty-one, was at last in love to distraction. She was now his wife in the eyes of the entire world, and he was immensely proud of her. Her success in winning the affection of the Athenians seemed to prove to him that nobody could resist her; and he felt sure that she would one day have the heart of the good citizens of Rome at her feet as now she had that of the people of Athens. Ephesus, too, during their short stay there, had gone mad about her, and in the streets had shouted at her that they wanted her for their queen. He felt that he could not do enough for her; and he looked forward with eagerness to the day when he would be able to enthrone her at his side as sovereign lady of the whole earth.

Meanwhile in Rome Octavian was suffering from the fears which had followed his bold movement towards warfare, and was collecting his forces at the highest possible speed, believing that Antony would attack before the summer was gone. There is some indication [12] that he attempted to exact from all the cities of Italy an oath of fidelity to him; and he certainly imposed a heavy tax all round, demanding an eighth of the total property of the rich, and a quarter of the income of the small landowners. This, of course, led to riots and bloodshed which he suppressed with a heavy hand, his pitilessness serving him now in good stead, for he soon inspired the refractory elements with a blanched and open-mouthed dread of him little short of petrifaction.

At the same time, however, he made himself as condescending and gracious to his supporters as his callous nature would permit, and he went out of his way to win those whose friendship was doubtful. To Asinius Pollio, Antony's former governor of Macedonia, for instance, he offered a command in his army; but this old general, who had been in retirement for some years, made a reply which is worthy of notice. [13] "No," he said, "my services to Antony are too great; his kindnesses to me are too notorious: I must keep aloof from this war—and be the prey of the conqueror."

The renegades Plancus and Titius had both been witnesses of the will which Antony had made in the previous year before setting out for Armenia; and they now told Octavian of the contents of the document and revealed that it had been secretly deposited with the Vestal Virgins in Rome, it being customary to place important legal papers of this kind in the keeping of these sacrosanct nuns. Octavian at once caused the will to be seized by force, although an act of this kind was sacrilege; and, taking it to the Senate, he read to that assembly the clauses which in his opinion were likely to tell against his rival. The document, however, bore the impress of a sincerity by which only Octavian himself was too obtuse to be touched; and Plutarch tells us that many of the senators expressed the opinion that Octavian's action was scandalous, and "they deemed it unfair, in any case, to call a man to account for what was not to be until after his death." In this will Antony had

---

[12] *Monumentum Ancyranum,* v, 3 and 4. It was Ferrero who noticed the point.
[13] Velleius, ii, lxxxvi.

stated that his children by Cleopatra were to be his co-heirs with Cæsarion, whom he declared to be the rightful son and heir of Cæsar [14]; and he asked that his body should be carried to Alexandria and laid to rest in the tomb wherein Cleopatra was also to lie.

Few thought the less of Antony for the terms of this testament, but many saw in it a confirmation of the Queen's mysterious power over the great general, and they were ready enough to believe the tales which Octavian was assiduously spreading. He declared that Antony had allowed the people of Ephesus to hail Cleopatra as their queen, thereby indicating that he was going to add this part of Asia Minor to her dominions; he said—which was quite true—that Antony had made her a present of the great library of Pergamus, consisting of nearly a quarter of a million books, which ought to have been sent to Rome; and he repeated with awful gravity the story that the Queen had given love-potions to Antony to drink, which had bereft the poor fellow of his senses, so that nowadays her very ladies-in-waiting, Iras and Charmion, were amongst his chief councillors, and were the generals whom they would have to fight.

Antony's friends in Rome—and they were still many—at length decided that they must warn him of the great danger of this propagation of hatred against Cleopatra and contemptuous pity for Antony for his subservience to her: they felt that the Queen's presence at his side was likely to ruin his cause, and that he ought to be urged to send her back to Egypt at once to await the issue of the war. They therefore deputed one of themselves, an important personage named Geminius, to go over to Athens to try to persuade Antony to separate himself from her for the time being; but when this well-meaning envoy arrived there and made it known that he had something of a secret nature to say to Antony, all the staff regarded him as a spy, and treated him with studied rudeness at those daily banquets in the house of Antony and Cleopatra to which his high standing gave him entrance.

One day, however, when most of the company were slightly intoxicated, somebody brought the matter into the open by drunkenly demanding to know what was the business on which Geminius had

[14] Dion Cassius, l, 3. There is no mention of Antyllus, but doubtless he figured in the will amongst the co-heirs, and probably Julus too.

come; and to this, having lost his patience, he blurted out a truthful reply. "I will keep most of what I have to say for a soberer hour," he declared, "but this much I will say here and now, drunk or sober—all will be well if Queen Cleopatra will go back to Egypt!"

Antony turned upon him in anger and surprise; but Cleopatra, her voice icy with resentment, said: "You are wise to have told your secret, Geminius, without having to be put to torture." The unfortunate man, no doubt, was given an opportunity next day of explaining his mission to Antony; but the advice from Rome fell on deaf ears; and, in fear of his life, Geminius fled from Athens.[15]

With that began a struggle, partly hidden, partly open, which caused Antony's headquarters to become a hotbed of intrigue, and introduced a dark element of suspicion into all future discussions of plans and policy. From that hour there was no peace for Antony: Geminius, he discovered to his astonishment, had expressed the views not only of his friends in Rome but of the majority of the Roman senators and officers who were here with him. These men saw clearly that Octavian's cunning in arousing the resentment of the people at home against Cleopatra was a master-stroke which could only be countered by the Queen's retirement from active participation in the war. They knew that if the struggle were to be kept as a direct issue between the two great Roman commanders, each desiring simply the political leadership in the Republic, victory was pretty well assured to Antony, and, indeed, bloodshed on a large scale might be wholly avoided. He was far more popular than Octavian; and if he were to present himself to the yearning gaze of distracted Rome as democracy's hero coming to restore peace and prosperity to the Republic, there might well be a landslide in his favour. But the presence of royal Cleopatra at Antony's side gave Octavian the opportunity to pose as the defender of Rome against foreign monarchistic aggression, and placed in his hands a deadly weapon.

Octavian could say, and, in fact, was saying, that Cleopatra was bent upon establishing herself and Antony as actual sovereigns of the eastern empire over which they already ruled, and that she

[15] Plutarch: *Antony*.

intended to conquer Italy and the western empire so that it should become a vast appendage to the east, to the end that she might rule the whole world from her throne in Alexandria. Antony could be, and was being, presented as a tool in her hands, a man bewitched by her to serve her enormous ambition, and afterwards likely to be cast aside when Rome was under Egypt's heel. Everybody here in Antony's headquarters knew, of course, that Cleopatra's plans were not dictated by mere ambition: they knew that she was defending herself and her son, Cæsarion, the divine Cæsar's only real heir, from the murderous rivalry of Octavian; and they were prepared to accompany her so far as that obvious motive could carry her, namely, to the extinction of Octavian. But beyond that point lay difficulties which they knew not how to face.

The Queen was now Antony's wife: would she consent to play a dual rôle—to be a reigning sovereign over the limited area already in her power, and the untitled first lady of the Roman democracy outside that area? Would Antony aspire to monarchy? Most of them hoped devoutly that he would not; some were indifferent, so long as Rome were given peace and were to maintain its undisputed position as the ruling power in the world; and some were willing that he should establish that throne at which Cæsar had aimed—a Roman, not an eastern or Egyptian, throne. But although Cleopatra was thus no enemy to their hopes and desires, and was, in fact, a useful ally for whom there was some sort of a place in their future scheme of things, the majority fully realized that her presence at this moment was a disaster, because her motives were so capable of misinterpretation in the light placed upon them by the crafty Octavian. The minority, however, trusted the common sense of the Roman People to realise that Antony was not her tool, nor yet was under her magic spell; and they saw no reason why she should not remain at her husband's side, Queen or no Queen.

The difference of opinion, however, was widened into an absolute cleavage by the news which now arrived from Rome. Pursuing his deadly policy, Octavian had rejected the proposal of his supporters in the Senate to name Antony a public enemy, and, instead, had solemnly declared war on Cleopatra alone, performing all the ancient rites in the Temple of Bellona customary at the commencement of Roman hostilities against a foreign enemy,

and officially cursing the Queen of Egypt and all her works. [16]
"He had made no declaration of war against Antony himself,"
writes Dion Cassius, "knowing that he would be made an enemy in
any case, since he was certainly not going to betray Cleopatra
and take up Octavian's cause; and, indeed, it was desired that
this additional reproach should be placed upon him, that he had
of his own free will gone to war against his country in behalf
of this Egyptian woman, although no provocation had been offered
him, personally, by his countrymen." Nevertheless, he, Octavian,
deprived him officially of his authority, on the grounds that he had
allowed a foreign queen to exercise it in his stead [17]; but this action
meant little to Antony, of course, who had the two Consuls and a
great part of the Senate with him at Athens and could snap his
fingers at the assembly in Rome.

The leader of the party in Athens which advocated the retirement of the Queen to Egypt so that the issue between Antony
and Octavian might be clarified, was the Consul Domitius Ahenobarbus whose sympathies had always been stoutly republican and
who had been concerned, it will be recalled, in the conspiracy
against Cæsar. He was a Roman aristocrat of the old school, and
his training had imbued him with so proud a republican disdain
for all foreign royalty that he would never address Cleopatra
by her title, but only by her name, [18] as though to emphasise the
fact that she was now simply the wife of a plain Roman magistrate. The news from Rome made him all the more eager to be
rid of the Queen, so that Antony might give the lie to Octavian
and might, indeed, make a fool of the young man by telling him
that Cleopatra, against whom alone war had been declared, had
returned to far-off Egypt to await the threatened attack—an attack which could not be delivered without exposing Italy, almost
defenceless, to Antony's invasion. Ahenobarbus, therefore, implored his chief to send her away; but his appeal was received with
a distracted but absolute refusal.

Antony, indeed, was in a terrible dilemma. He saw the
force of these arguments, but against them he could advance the
plea that Cleopatra, as his wife, as the "widow" of Cæsar, and

[16] Dion Cassius, l, 4 and 6.   [17] Plutarch: *Antony.*
[18] Velleius, ii, lxxxiv.

as the mother of Cæsar's child, was too deeply involved in this business to withdraw from it, even if he could do without her aid in ships, supplies, and money. Supposing he were to tell her to go, what would she think? She would think that he was a traitor, abandoning her cause in the interests of his own ambitions; and his love for her did not permit him to tolerate the thought of hurting her thus. She would suppose that he had in mind an accommodation with Octavian, another patching up of their quarrel which, in the event of Antony's death or loss of power, would leave her and her boy at the mercy of this cold and heartless ruler of Rome. Her life, Cæsarion's life, and all their hopes of safety and happiness, depended upon Antony and upon the removal of Octavian from their path.

But, apart from these considerations, he wanted her to be with him because he loved her, and he believed that she loved him. His destiny had gradually become so linked with hers that he could not so much as consider an existence bereft of her presence. He needed her beside him; and all else in life, even his vast ambitions, had become secondary to this overwhelming necessity. The mere suggestion that she should leave him, moreover, had aroused, one may suppose, such a passion of anger and dismay in her that he could not discuss the matter with her nor face the rebuke in her eyes and the heart-breaking lash of her tongue.

I think she must have said to him that, so far as she was concerned, the matter of the creation of a Roman throne for herself and him could be relegated to the far future, since all she wanted was to be relieved of this gnawing dread of Octavian which haunted her thoughts by day and night. Octavian had let it be known that there could not be two Cæsars in the world, there could not be, that is to say, an Octavian and a Cæsarion now that the latter was about to come of age; and her one supreme desire was that Antony should rid her life of this menace, even though in doing so he would have to abandon all immediate thought of the dreamed-of throne of the world.

Be this as it may, Antony now told his Roman supporters that it was his chief purpose to re-establish the Republic, and he gave them the promise that immediately after victory had been assured he would place himself entirely in the hands of the Senate, so that the Roman People might decide in what future capacity he should act. He was able to say this with confidence—and I think he must have had Cleopatra's approval in saying it—because there was no real doubt in his mind that the extinction of Octavian, followed by the long deferred conquest of Parthia, would throw up a wave of enthusiasm for him which would carry him of itself to the desired throne. [19]

These protestations, however, did not mend the rift; and Ahenobarbus and his party continued with such vehemence to urge him to send Cleopatra away that the enemy's spies seem to have reported to Rome the likelihood of her immediate departure, and to have set Octavian thinking of the possibility of attacking her in her own country. Antony was harassed by these angry differences of opinion which were causing the Queen often to show towards him a mistrust and a defiant contempt most devasting to their loving companionship; and it seems that on many an occasion he turned for comfort to the wine-cup, and drank himself into a condition of quiescence. Cleopatra, as has been said, was a woman of great tenacity of purpose, and she was determined to prevent Antony from passing under the influence either of those who even now saw the possibility of a compromise between him and Octavian, or of those who desired him to assert his democratic standing by severing his connection with her. With this purpose in view she refused to consider the matter of her departure, but at the same time gave Antony no peace: she wounded him by withdrawing her love from him; she maddened him by her tearful mistrust; she alternately froze him by quarrels and melted him by passionate reconciliations.

In her anxious state of mind her own disposition became soured, and, suspecting enmity in all around her, she made enemies right and left. Ahenobarbus withdrew himself, insulted, from her society; Marcus Silanus, half-brother of Brutus, but a firm Cæsarian and friend of Antony, took his departure from Athens; and Dellius was so estranged that he, too, contemplated a return to Rome—the first cause of the quarrel being in his case no more than a remark of his that Cleopatra offered him wine of a poorer quality than that given by Octavian to his servants.

Antony ought to have struck at his rival in the early summer

[19] Octavian in the end obtained the throne, a fact which indicates that Rome was ready for it.

while he was yet unprepared and while Italy was seething with discontent at the taxes just imposed; but these troubles in his own camp dislocated his plans. Moreover, he had sent his agents over to Rome, well provided with money, to stir up rebellion there and to win adherents to his cause; and the reports of their activities were so promising that he believed delay to be in his favour. It was a serious mistake; for the disaffection around him in regard to Cleopatra was increasing more rapidly than were Rome's mutinous sentiments in regard to Octavian. At length, however, at midsummer, he sent his transports and a fleet of two hundred of his largest battleships, including the Egyptian squadron, to the Gulf of Ambracia (Arta), just to the south of Epirus on the western coast of Greece, opposite the toe of Italy, there to prepare for the attack [20]; and early in the autumn he transferred his headquarters to Patræ (Patras) on the west coast of Achaia, just south of the narrow entrance of the Gulf of Corinth, this town being a port much used in passenger-traffic between Italy and Greece.

At the same time, however, he placed ships and men at Corcyra (Corfu) and Leucadia (Santa Maura)—islands to the north and south of the Gulf of Ambracia; at Methone (Modon) on the southwest coast of Greece; at Cape Tænarium (Matapan) in southern Greece, below Sparta; and he increased the force in Cyrene on the opposite coast of North Africa, and presumably, sent men and ships to the western ports of Crete. These dispositions, which can only have been intended to defend the east-end of the Mediterranean from attack, indicate that he had reason to believe that Octavian, thinking Cleopatra would be forced to return to her own country, was seriously contemplating the expedition to Egypt, or a feint in that direction made plausible by the fact that he was nominally at war only with that country. It is possible, indeed, that while both commanders really expected the final clash to take place in the Adriatic, Octavian was anxious to distract Antony's attention from that area by appearing to wish to strike at Alexandria itself, and Antony was anxious to give the impression that he had been hoodwinked by this maneuver and was moving south to meet it.

At all events winter here intervened, and the war had to be

---

[20] Florus, iv, xi, gives 200 as the number, and this seems a probable figure for the big fighting ships.

postponed until the spring. It was a winter overshadowed for Antony by a cloud of misunderstandings and quarrels with Cleopatra which reduced him to a condition of such misery that he seems to have been as often drunk as sober. He knew that her presence was ruining his cause; he saw that in her state of nervous irritation she was becoming more and more unpopular with his Roman supporters, if not with the vassal Kings and princes; he heard continuously of the growing hatred of her in Rome, nurtured by those ridiculous tales of her vices, her cruelty, her arrogance, and so forth, which Octavian was gathering about her and which have survived to this day to blacken her memory. Yet he could not bring himself to capitulate to the force of public opinion and bid her go, since her retirement to Egypt would mean that he might not see her for a year or more, and would perhaps end for ever their mutual love and trust.

He was haunted, moreover, during this winter by an increasing dread of the uncanny Octavian who again was emerging, triumphant, from his difficulties, and whose mysteriously growing strength was being heralded or followed by strange portents and omens which were reported to him from time to time, or which he saw with his own eyes. The Temple of Hercules, his divine ancestor, in this town of Patræ where he was staying, was struck by lightning, and a cyclone at Athens threw down a figure of Dionysus, the god with whom he was identified, and damaged two statues inscribed with his name. Some swallows which frequented the rigging of Cleopatra's flagship, the Antonias, were attacked by other birds and driven off. At Pisaurum (Pesaro), on the east coast of Italy, a settlement of ex-soldiers founded by Antony was destroyed by an earthquake; and at Alba a statue of him oozed moisture like a bloody sweat.

A wolf entered the Temple of Fortune in Rome and was caught and killed, and a strange dog which had invaded the Roman racecourse was killed by a local dog—both of which occurrences indicated the coming destruction of the enemy. Somebody's pet monkey entered the Temple of Ceres, and tumbled the sacred furniture about before it was caught; and a large snake frightened many people in Etruria, but was killed by a flash of lightning. Some Roman boys, playing a game in which they called themselves Antonians, were defeated by their opponents who had named themselves after Octavian—an incident which indicates, by the way, that Antony was still a hero amongst the youth of the capital.

These and many other ominous occurrences spread an intangible feeling of depression throughout Antony's headquarters; but it would be a mistake to suppose that there was any real alarm or any serious doubts of ultimate victory. Antony, though drinking heavily and obviously worried almost to the point of frenzy by Cleopatra's doubts and fears, was still the greatest and most beloved figure in the world, and the expectation was still general that his progress to the dizzy summit of mortal ambition could not now be checked.

CHAPTER XX

The Battle of Actium and the Return of Antony and Cleopatra to Egypt.

31–30 B.C.

THE Gulf of Ambracia, or Arta as it is now called, is more than a natural harbour: it is a lake-like inlet of the sea, twenty-five miles long and ten wide, entered from the open water through a narrow mouth varying from seven hundred yards to half a mile in width. The south side of this mouth is formed by the promontory of Actium, the north side by a tongue of land of which the ancient name has been forgotten. The Gulf provided excellent winter-quarters for Antony's transports and the main battle-fleet of two hundred ships, and by placing strong garrisons on the two sides of the entrance he was able to feel that these vessels were safe from attack, although, as a matter of fact, Octavian did consider such an enterprise, and was only deterred by bad weather.

During the winter, however, the fleet suffered serious losses by an epidemic of some kind [1] which took a heavy toll of lives, its ravages having been the more widespread because of the under-feeding of the men, food being difficult to obtain in the country round about. Many of the galley-slaves had deserted; and although the officers had seized upon farm-labourers, herdsmen, and even unsuspecting wayfarers, and had pressed them into service at the oars, the crews of the big battleships were incomplete and all were out of training.

Meanwhile, the beginning of the new year, 31 B.C., found Antony still at Patræ, which place, though on the south side of the Gulf of Corinth, was close to the narrow straits between the promontories of Rhium and Anti-Rhium, whence a three or four days' march north-westwards would take him to the Gulf of Ambracia. It seems that he was now not sure whether Octavian would divide his

[1] Dion Cassius, I, 11.

428

forces and send a strong expedition to Egypt, or whether he would bring his main army over to southern Greece, south of Patræ, or to Epirus, north of the Gulf of Ambracia, or, again, whether he would retain his ships and men on the east-coast of Italy, in the neighbourhood of Brindisi, and wait to be attacked.

Antony's dispositions provided against all these contingencies; and towards the beginning of spring he must have watched anxiously and impatiently, endeavouring to discover his enemy's plans. He knew, at any rate, that if the attack on Egypt were launched, Octavian would assuredly attempt to occupy points in southern Greece, Crete, and Cyrene to protect his expeditionary fleet; and it was for this reason that strong forces of ships and men had been left to defend these areas. He must have hoped that Octavian would undertake this adventure, for then he, Antony, would be able to launch an attack on Italy from the Gulf of Ambracia or Epirus.

Early in March messengers suddenly arrived in Patræ with the news that an enemy fleet, under the command of Octavian's lieutenant, Agrippa, had appeared before Methone in southern Greece; and soon the tidings came that that port had been captured, and that King Bogud of Mauretania, whose troops were garrisoned there, had been killed. Antony, though disturbed by this defeat, was probably relieved by what he supposed to be the partial disclosing of the enemy's plans, and at once prepared to send troops to the south to recapture Methone, and he made ready to march in that direction himself with his main army if it should prove that Octavian intended to make southern Greece the scene of a decisive battle.

The enemy, however, had outwitted him; and while Antony's attention was thus directed upon the south, news arrived from the north that Octavian had descended in full force upon Corcyra (Corfu), which had surrendered to him. He had then disembarked his army on the coast of the mainland, and was marching at full speed to the Gulf of Ambracia. The attack on southern Greece had been a feint. Antony at once crossed the Gulf of Corinth, and, giving orders to his main army to come north with all speed, hurried ahead to the point of danger; but when he arrived at the mouth of the Gulf of Ambracia, on both sides of which his garrisons were stationed, he found that Octavian had taken up his position on the northern side of the mouth, upon high ground now called Mikalitzi, and then known as "The Ladle," just to the north of Antony's own lines. This high ground, where afterwards stood the city of Nicopolis, commanded a view, eastwards, of the waters of the Gulf of Ambracia, and, westwards, of the open sea; and between it and the latter, Octavian had thrown up defences so as to retain touch with his fleet.

Here Antony at once besieged him, increasing his forces on the northern tongue of land at the mouth of the Gulf, opposite Actium, and sending his cavalry round the Gulf to hem him in on the Ambracian side; but as the main army had not yet come up from Patræ, and as the fleet in the Gulf was in such poor condition, a full attack on the invaders could not be developed. Octavian then sent his fleet a few miles southwards to the island of Leucadia, which, following the example of Corfu, surrendered to him; and thus he obtained possession of the open sea in this area, and more or less bottled up Antony's ill-conditioned fleet and transports within the Gulf of Ambracia, although the Antonian land forces had possession of the two sides of the mouth of the Gulf. The position which therefore developed was curious: Octavian's army was besieged in the narrow strip of land at the northern end of the promontory which formed the north side of the mouth of the Gulf; but Antony's fleet was trapped inside the Gulf itself, for the two hundred battleships were in no shape to fight Octavian's fleet which now numbered, all told, some four hundred keels,[2] and lay for the most part anchored across the outside of the Gulf's mouth.

Antony's poor generalship, of course, cannot be excused. He ought to have invaded Italy in the previous autumn; or, having failed to do so, he ought to have given his closest attention during the winter to his fleet and its disposition, instead of leaving a great part of it to deteriorate at its moorings in the Gulf, and the rest to waste its time in guarding Egypt from a highly improbable attack. There can be no question, in fact, that he had frittered away his winter at Patræ; and the only explanation I have to offer is that his violent disputes with his Roman officers in regard to Cleopatra, and his personal quarrels with her and consequent drinking-bouts,

[2] Florus, iv, xi.

had played havoc with his abilities as a commander, and that he had allowed himself to underestimate his enemy and to drift along in the confused belief that everything would be all right.

The situation, however, was not desperate; and when Cleopatra arrived with the main army at Actium, and heard the news, she said with a laugh, "Dear me, we may well be frightened if Octavian has got hold of a ladle!" The invaders' position was precarious, and the troops which Antony sent round the Gulf to attack The Ladle on the far side nearly succeeded in cutting off their water supply which was obtained from the Charadrus, a river flowing down from the north. Moreover, Octavian's fleet was always open to attack by Antony's other squadrons when they could be recalled from the Mediterranean, and he failed to interfere with the corn-ships which brought their supplies safely to Antony from the east.

But a deadlock could not be avoided, since Octavian's defences repelled all assaults; and though the thought of a renewed period of waiting must have been very trying to Antony's nerves, he was obliged to make the best of it. He was forced to form a great encampment on the promontory of Actium, where around him and Cleopatra the vassal kings and princes, the Consuls and Senators, the military and naval commanders, and the soldiers, camp-followers and slaves of scores of different nations, were herded together, treading on one-another's toes, arguing with each other over the distribution of food, squabbling about precedence and privilege, and hotly debating the right thing to do. Octavian appeared to have no intention of bestirring himself save to make his defences more and more secure; and at length when he felt that his position was absolutely impregnable, he sent back to Rome for the entire body of senators who had remained faithful to him, obliging them to come across the sea to him in their hundreds. His object, one may suppose, was to have them here under his eye, for fear lest in the distant capital they might intrigue against him, or, weary of waiting for something to happen, might attempt to restore peace by a compromise.

Thus, the months of spring and summer went by, and small engagements by sea or land, of no great importance, alone served to break the monotony. Profound discontent developed in An-

tony's camp; but in his own mind there was more than discontent—
there was confusion of thought and consequent misery. Cleopatra
no longer gave him her confidence or her respect; yet her disdain-
ful attitude seems only to have induced in him a greater dependence upon her, a sort of dog-like devotion almost pitiful to behold. He continued to be frequently drunk, and when sober, was
overwrought and quarrelsome.

The question as to whether she should go back to Egypt or not
had for the moment been shelved, because her fleet was imprisoned in the Gulf of Ambracia, and could not force its way to
the open sea without a naval engagement of the first magnitude,
while her return overland would be a dangerous undertaking in
view of possible revolts inspired by Octavian's ubiquitous agents
in the countries through which she would have to pass, and, in any
case, would give a very widespread impression that she was in
flight. She herself was now willing to go,[3] and to take her Egyptian
fleet with her, for she was worn out by her domestic quarrels, and
was beginning, moreover, to doubt Antony's ability to defeat Octavian in battle, her confidence in him having been disturbed by
numerous ill-omens and by the more trustworthy portent of the
state of his nerves. She knew that she was unpopular in the camp,
for Antony, in his outbursts of temper, had doubtless told her
some home truths; and she must have realized by now that his cause,
which was hers also, would really be strengthened by her departure.
Moreover, in the event of disaster, she would be safer and of more
use in Egypt than here where she might be taken captive. Yet,
under the circumstances, she was obliged to stay on at Actium, and
to tolerate as best she could the nerve-racking quarrels and brief
reconciliations with the distracted Antony, life with whom was
at this time a tempestuous round of emotional crises. He loved her
passionately; and yet, so close is love to hate, their relationship
was like a skyscape of sun and thunderclouds shot through with
murderous flashes.

On a certain occasion he accused her of wishing to kill him,
and thereupon she resorted to a method of giving him the lie which
reveals the ferocious state of mind in which they were both passing
their days. One night at supper she handed him a cup containing

[3] Dion Cassius, l, 15.

wine of which she herself had just drunk half; and as he was raising it to his lips, happy at this gesture of reconciliation, she took a flower from her hair and dipped it into the wine. Antony was about to drink when she snatched the cup from his hand, and told him that the contents were poisoned. In fear and astonishment he asked her how this could be so, since she herself had just drunk some of the wine; and for a moment he must have supposed that she had intended to kill herself and him together. She thereupon explained that the flower which she had dipped into the cup was poisoned, and that she had chosen this method of proving to him how easy it would be to murder him did she desire to do so. "I could have killed you at any time," she smiled, "if I could have done without you." [4]

The great contention which now exercised the camp was as to whether it would be better to bring Octavian to battle by taking the fleet out of the Gulf and engaging him in a naval action, or by retiring inland, as Pompey had done in his war with Cæsar, so that a second Pharsalia might be fought out on a selected battle-field. Cleopatra favoured a sortie from the Gulf and a fight at sea, combined with an assault by land on The Ladle; for her Egyptian ships-of-war would thus gain the open water, and even if the battle should go against them, she would probably be able to make good her escape, whereas a defeat on an inland battlefield would mean her speedy capture. The fight she had in mind, in fact, was one which was about to be fought so that her Egyptian ships might break out of their prison and take her home, away from an intolerable situation. [5] She had no great hopes of victory, but if Antony should win she would still leave him for a while, her general unpopularity being now apparent to her, and her desire being intense to punish him by showing him her independence and her real need of rest away from him.

Antony and his generals, however, were set upon a land-battle, and with this object in view he sent Dellius and King Amyntas of Galatia into Thrace to raise more cavalry, for he had received word from Dicomes, King of the Getæ (or Daci), whose realms extended about the Danube, north of Thrace, offering to help him—a mes-

[4] Pliny, xxi, i, 12.
[5] Both Plutarch and Dion Cassius think this was her object.

sage which had greatly heartened him. The Consul Domitius Ahenobarbus, whose personal dislike of Cleopatra led him always to oppose her advice, was in full agreement with Antony in regard to
the desirability of an inland battle, in spite of the fact that he
would be rid of her more surely by means of a naval engagement;
and the fact that he and Antony were now making their plans together for a retreat into the interior, with the object of drawing
Octavian after them, led to renewed quarrels between the Queen
and her husband.

Antony was completely distracted by the furious scenes which
ensued around the private council-table—the impassioned demands
of Cleopatra that the blockade should be broken and her Egyptian
fleet released to sail away with her to her own country, and the
equally urgent insistence of Ahenobarbus and other generals that
the army should move inland, and, if necessary, let the ships in
the Gulf be destroyed. "It would not be any kind of disparage-
ment to Antony," these generals contended, "to yield the sea to
Octavian who, in the wars with Sextus Pompeius, had had such
long practice in naval warfare; but, on the contrary, it would be
simply ridiculous for Antony, who was by land the most experienced
commander living, to make no use of his well-disciplined and
numerous legions, but to scatter and waste his forces by parcelling
them out in the battleships."[6]

There must have been in the end some violent rupture and
patched up peace between Antony and Cleopatra in this regard;
for suddenly Antony agreed to postpone the plans for a land-
battle until after he had tried his luck at sea. What happened we
do not know: Plutarch states laconically that "Cleopatra prevailed," and we are left to picture Antony, urged by his wife's
tears and appeals, at last giving way to her, though he knew in his
heart that he was bringing about their separation in doing so. He
was too deeply in love with her, too heartbroken by their estrangement, too weary of their quarrels, to stand up to her any longer:
he would have to let her go. At the same time, however, he seems
to have insisted that Cleopatra should take with her only a few
of her ships, and that most of her powerful men-o'-war should be
used by him in the naval battle.

[6] Plutarch: *Antony*

It was in the month of August that he came to this decision and communicated it to Ahenobarbus, explaining to him, no doubt, that he did not feel it to be an honourable course after all the help in money and arms which Cleopatra had contributed, to leave her Egyptian fleet shut up in the Gulf, where it faced the risk of destruction by Octavian's ships as soon as the supporting army had been withdrawn into the interior. Ahenobarbus was suffering from a slight fever at the time, and, upon hearing that his advice had been overruled, he told Antony that he would go for a short sea-journey in the Gulf to recover his health and his equanimity. He boarded a small sailing-ship that same day, and never returned. He went straight across the water to the mouth of the river Charadrus, presented himself before the enemy's lines, and so was conducted to Octavian with whom he made his peace.

When it became known in Antony's camp that the Consul had deserted there must have been something like a panic. It was a crushing blow, and it struck fear into every heart, for it was felt that if a man of the importance of Ahenobarbus had elected to go over to the enemy, Octavian's chances must have appeared to him, with his inside knowledge, to be much better than those of Antony. Rumour said, too, that the Consul had been driven to this step by Cleopatra's insolence; and the general dislike of the Queen was thereby increased. Antony was staggered by the desertion, but he behaved with great magnanimity towards the traitor, and sent after him a ship containing all his baggage and effects and all his suite and slaves. The example of Ahenobarbus was speedily followed by other important personages. Philadelphus, King of Paphlagonia, and King Deiotarus of Galatia, both deserted, and went over to Octavian; and shortly afterwards King Iamblicus of Emesa and a senator named Quintus Postumius were caught in the act of making their escape to the enemy. To these latter Antony, in his anxiety, showed no mercy: both were put to death by torture.

The desertion of Deiotarus caused him to fear that the other royal Galatian, King Amyntas, might prove also to be untrustworthy, more especially since he now heard that Dellius, who was accompanying Amyntas on the above-mentioned mission to Thrace to raise reinforcements, was nursing a grievance against Cleopatra, as already recorded; and Antony was so distracted that

he actually set out, himself, to overtake the mission,[7] but presently
abandoned the pursuit and sent messengers after them, instead,
to recall them. When he arrived back in Actium he was greeted
with the news that a squadron of his ships, sailing to his aid from the
Mediterranean, had been routed by the enemy with great loss; and,
enraged by this reverse, he himself led out a strong force of cavalry
to attack Octavian's cavalry which were reported to be daily recon-
noitring outside their defences. But in the engagement which ensued he was defeated, and shortly afterwards he was almost captured near his own lines, being ambushed by Octavian's men and
having to take to his heels.[8]

These reverses, the increasing audacity of the enemy, and the
panicky condition in which he and his officers found themselves,
induced him hurriedly to decide upon an immediate naval battle,
and he gave orders to the captains of his ships to prepare to pass
out of the Gulf on August 29th, a few days hence. His plans seem
to me to have been these: he would send a small body of infantry
round the Gulf to attack Octavian's position on land, and at
the same time some twenty thousand Roman legionaries, and two
thousand archers, carried upon his best ships-of-war, would pass
out of the Gulf and attack the enemy's fleet at sea. If the sea-
battle should go in Antony's favour all his vast land-forces, not yet
engaged, would join in the assault upon The Ladle with the exception of the cavalry, which would be concentrated to the north
to cut off the enemy's retreat into Epirus; and Antony himself
would immediately lead his victorious fleet across the Adriatic
before the opposing ships could recover and reassemble, and, disembarking a small army on the Italian coast, he would march on
Rome, while Cleopatra would sail for Egypt with a small squadron
of her own ships, there to wait until he could send for her and
Cæsarion. If, on the contrary, the naval fight should go against
him, Cleopatra would seize her opportunity to sail away, touching
at some port of southern Greece to obtain news of the subsequent
movements; while Antony would retire to the Gulf, and, burning

---

[7] Dion Cassius, l, 13.

[8] Dion Cassius (l, 13) mistakenly says that Sossius was killed in this fight, a
statement which he himself contradicts in li, 2.

those of his ships which were unsunk, would lead his yet unused main army inland, in the expectation that Octavian would follow and that a land-battle would be fought with him on ground chosen by Antony.[9]

In order to put these arrangements into effect certain measures were taken, the references to which have much puzzled historians; but it seems to me that the explanation in each case is clear, if the above plan of action be correct.[10] Firstly, in the event of victory at sea and a consequent invasion of Italy, the Roman and Egyptian ships which were to take part in this enterprise would need to have their large sails aboard, as also would those of the Egyptian squadron which were to accompany Cleopatra to Egypt; and therefore orders were given to this effect, much to the surprise of the ship's captains who were accustomed to leave the sails behind when clearing for action. Secondly, since Cleopatra proposed to sail for Egypt whatever might be the outcome of the fight, her personal belongings were carried onto the vessels detailed to go with her—a fact which again caused much surprise. Thirdly, the smaller ships and those which were not to be used in the engagement were now burnt or scuttled, this drastic measure being taken so that, in the event of a defeat at sea and the retirement of the army inland, they should not fall into Octavian's hands, and also that the galley-slaves thus released might fill the vacancies at the oars of the larger men-o'-war. Fourthly—and this gives the chief clue to Antony's plan—the bulk of the troops stationed on the northern side of the mouth of the Gulf were withdrawn to Actium on the southern side, the obvious explanation being that Antony wished to concentrate his main army at a point from which, in the event of defeat at sea, he could march it inland, and he saw that any troops left on the opposite side of the mouth would have to surrender if Octavian should obtain the mastery on the water, whereas if Antony were successful in the naval battle his ships could quickly transport the

[9] This interpretation of his plans differs from that which I put forward in my *Life of Cleopatra*. It is a theory which has not before been advanced, so far as I know; but I think it meets all the known facts, and explains them more satisfactorily than any other.

[10] These seemingly mysterious arrangements are recorded by Plutarch and Dion Cassius.

army across the narrow straits to attack Octavian's position. Finally a large force of cavalry was sent round the Gulf to the north of The Ladle, to cut off Octavian's retreat if Antony were successful, cavalry rather than infantry being chosen partly because, in the event of defeat at sea, they could the more rapidly rejoin the main army retiring inland.

These arrangements reveal Antony's misgivings as to the result of the engagement at sea, and indicate that he was taking all the necessary steps to secure a successful march into the interior, there to renew the war on land if the naval project should fail. The battle at sea had really been forced upon him by tempestuous Cleopatra's decision to go back to Egypt, and by her determination to prevent her Egyptian fleet from being sacrificed by the retirement inland; but Antony, torn this way and that, at last had cleverly adjusted his plans to hers by preparing at the same time for an invasion of Italy, or, alternatively, for a march into the interior to a chosen battlefield, after the Queen had gone. He was going to use no more than a fifth part of his army in the sea-fight, and the remainder was ample to assure him the probability of victory on land if the naval battle should fail.

Those of his Roman troops who were to fight at sea much disliked the prospect, and Plutarch relates that he was accosted by one of the officers, who pleaded with him to abandon the project. "What have our wounds and our swords done to displease you," this man asked him, "that you should give your confidence to rotten timbers? Let Egyptians and Phœnicians fight at sea, but give us the land, where we know how to win or to die where we stand." To this, it is said, Antony made no answer, but by his looks and gestures gave the officer to understand that there was no cause for dismay.

On the eve of the battle Antony addressed his men, pointing out to them that he himself was at the height of his powers and was in no way the victim either of years or of dissolute habits, as some of them, perhaps, had begun to think, but that Octavian on the contrary, was a physical weakling who had never been the victor in an important battle in his life. Yet this Octavian, he declared, desired to make himself King of the Roman world, whereas he, Antony, had sworn to restore the Republic; and he bade them fight to the death for their just cause and for freedom.[11] A strong wind, however, arose in the night, and next day the sea was so rough that the battle had to be postponed. Everything was in readiness; everybody was keyed up; but for four days the gale blew, and nothing could be done. The cavalry had already gone round to the north of Octavian's position, and with them Antony had sent Dellius and King Amyntas, who had just arrived back at Actium, after being recalled from their mission to Thrace, as already mentioned. Antony's trust in them had been restored by an interview with them on their return; and as Amyntas had at his command two thousand of his own Galatian cavalry, it was felt that he and his men could best be put to use in this way. But the howling wind and the long delay played havoc with the King's nerves, already frayed by his sudden recall; and on the second or third day of the storm [12] he went over to Octavian with all his men, whereupon Dellius did the same.

The news of these latest desertions reached Antony, it would seem, on the first day of September, and struck him a blow which completely upset his equilibrium. He did not dare to delay the battle another day, and gave immediate orders that the fight was to take place on the morrow. Then, in a frenzy of dismay, he appears to have turned upon Cleopatra, and to have vented his wrath upon her; for subsequent events indicate clearly, I think, that a very serious quarrel took place between them a few hours before the battle. It may be that he accused her of having estranged his friends from him by what is spoken of as her "insolent usage" of them; and since Dellius is quoted by Plutarch as having declared that the Queen intended to murder him, we may suppose that this reason for his desertion had now come to Antony's knowledge, and that he charged Cleopatra with it.

The Queen, on her part, may well have retorted that he himself was alone to blame for the loss of confidence in him; and it seems likely that she indignantly accused him of being about to place her Egyptian battleships—except those which were to ac-

[11] The long speech given by Dion Cassius (l, 16) seems to be a composition written up by that historian from the data at his disposal, for it presents no new facts, and is not worth quoting, fine and imposing though it is.

[12] Dion Cassius (l, 23) says that Dellius was able to give Octavian details of Antony's final plans, which suggests that the desertion was not earlier than this.

company her to Egypt—in such a position that they would have to endure the brunt of the fighting, for such was certainly his intention,[13] the Egyptian vessels being the most powerful in his fleet. She may have reminded him, too, that her object in going to Egypt was not merely to strengthen his cause by ridding it of the only person—herself—against whom Octavian had been able to arouse popular resentment, but also to seek rest from these continuous domestic disputes which had made their relationship a misery to her.

Be this as it may, we may imagine that the quarrel was continued far into the night, and that both husband and wife were exhausted by it when at last they separated in ungovernable anger and sought the needed sleep which would not come to them. On the morrow Antony was to risk his life in battle, and, if he should survive, victorious or defeated, he was to see the last of Cleopatra for many a month, perhaps for ever. She was departing for her own country, and he was going either to death or to a lonely victory; and here they were, loving one another in the secret depths of their hearts, dependent upon one another, and yet, in spite of this bitter love, wholly estranged, silenced by mutual abuse into dumb separation, on this night of nights when they should have been so tenderly bidding each other farewell.

On the following morning there was no reconciliation; and Antony, exhausted by want of sleep, and probably befuddled as a consequence of having sought consolation from the wine-cup, went out to do battle with Octavian for the mastery of the world, not caring whether he should win or lose this prize which had once seemed to him to represent the summit of his ambition. Nothing mattered to him except that his wife should not leave him with this weight of anger crushing deeper the already buried sweetness of their love; and he was determined that, if the close of the day should find him still alive, he would see her again before her departure and make his peace with her. We are so apt to overlook the personal element in high affairs of worldwide importance; but the Battle of Actium which was fought on this day,

[13] Plutarch (*Antony*) says that the Roman legionaries were crowded onto the sixty best Egyptian battleships. Plutarch, in fact, indicates that the entire Roman force of 22,000 men was placed on the Egyptian vessels; but this, of course, is a mistake.

September 2nd, 31 B.C., cannot be understood unless we presuppose that condition of mind in Antony which I have attempted to indicate.

The sea was now calm; and Octavian, knowing from what Dellius had told him that the battle would not be delayed after the abating of the storm, prepared to draw up his fleet in three squadrons and to place them less than a mile away from the mouth of the Gulf. The left wing was commanded by Agrippa, the right by Octavian, and the middle by a certain Lucius Arruntius. Antony had also divided his fleet into three commands: the left, opposing Octavian, was in charge of Sossius, the right, opposing Agrippa, was under Antony's personal direction, and the middle was commanded by an officer named Marcus Insteius.

While Antony, during the early morning, went with aching head from ship to ship encouraging his men, Octavian addressed his troops which were about to embark; and though the words put into his mouth by Dion Cassius [14] are not to be regarded as those actually spoken, some sentences may be based upon genuine reports of the speech, and deserve to be quoted. "It is unworthy of our fathers," he is supposed to have said, "that we who are Romans and lords of the greatest and best part of the world should be despised and trodden under foot by an Egyptian woman: it is unworthy of ourselves, who have subjugated Gauls and other peoples, have crossed the Rhine, and have gone over into Britain. How could we fail to grieve bitterly if these conquered nations should hear that we had succumbed to an accursed woman, and were humbly bearing the insults of a crowd of Alexandrians and Egyptians?"

"Who can help lamenting to see Roman soldiers acting as the bodyguard of this queen? Who can help weeping when he both hears and sees that Antony himself has abandoned all his ancestors' habits of life, has emulated foreign and barbaric customs, and worships that woman as though she were the goddess Isis or Selene, calling her children 'Sun' and 'Moon,' and himself taking the title of Osiris or Dionysus, and bestowing kingdoms as though he were master of the whole earth? Fellow-soldiers, at first I was so devoted to him that I gave him a share of my leadership,

[14] Dion Cassius, l, 24.

married my sister to him, and granted him legions. Even after this I felt so affectionately disposed towards him that I was unwilling to wage war on him because of his insulting my sister, or because he neglected the children she had borne him, or because he preferred the Egyptian woman to her and bestowed upon *her* children your possessions. I deemed Cleopatra by the very fact of her foreign birth to be fundamentally hostile to his career, but I believed that he, as a Roman, could be corrected. Later I entertained the hope that, if not voluntarily, at least reluctantly, he might change his mind as the result of the declaration of war against *her;* and consequently I did not declare war upon *him*."

"He, however, has treated my efforts with haughtiness and disdain, and will neither be released though we would fain release him, nor be pitied though we try to pity him. He is either a fool or mad; and this which I have heard I do believe—that he has been bewitched by that accursed female, and is in slavery to her. What else, then, can be our duty but to fight him together with Cleopatra? Henceforth let no one call him a Roman, but rather an Egyptian, nor Antony but rather Serapio." [15]

In such scathing words as these the cunning Octavian aroused the contempt of his men for the great Antony who, even as he spoke, was preparing for battle with no thought in his bursting head save that of his quarrel with the woman he loved to distraction. Antony's plan of action, however, had been fully discussed, and now was automatically carried out, despite his abstraction. Before noon his ships passed through the narrows, and drew up in close formation in the open water outside the mouth of the Gulf, where Octavian, from no great distance, gazed at them in admiration, so it is said, the Antonian vessels being for the most part much larger and more powerful, though less numerous, than his own.

For some time no movement was made on either side, but at last Antony advanced, whereupon Octavian retired a little so as to entice him out to sea, and then maneuvered with the object of surrounding Antony's heavy and cumbersome men-o'-war with his own fleeter and more manageable vessels. Soon the fight had developed along these lines, and Antony's great battleships were

[15] A common Egyptian name.

being attacked as though they were besieged fortresses. For two hours or so the struggle continued, without advantage to either party; and soon after two o'clock, when a strong wind from the north had sprung up and had made the sea rough, the difficulties of maneuvering and getting to close quarters were so great that the casualties were few, and there was probably a good deal more shouting and swearing than actual exchange of blows.

Cleopatra, meanwhile, was on her flagship, the Antonias, riding at anchor near the shore, protected by those Egyptian vessels which were to go with her to Egypt. It had been arranged, as has already been explained, that in the event of obvious defeat, she was to sail away and make good her escape down the wind, which, in these parts, could be relied upon to blow from the north during each afternoon, and would thus speed her on her journey to the south. This wind, which was now whistling through her rigging, had pushed the contending fleets some distance southwards; and Antony, who was wearily directing the fight from behind his right, or north, wing was now at no great distance from her. If he were victorious, it was understood that he would board her ship at the close of the battle, and bid her farewell; but this, in her great anger, she did not wish him to do: she wanted to hurt him by leaving him without a word, and she began now to ask herself whether it would not be more dignified in her, and more painful to him, if she were to sail away at once.

The north wind usually sank at sunset, and if she were to delay her departure, she would perhaps be unable to sail until the next day. In the event of victory this would mean another distressing interview with Antony; in the event of defeat, it might mean that she would fail to escape. Moreover, she was finding it hard, as Dion Cassius says, "to endure the long uncertainty, and was harassed by womanly fears and terrible anxiety in regard to the outcome of the long-continued and doubtful struggle;"[16] and since Antony, in the madness of their violent quarrel on the previous night, had doubtless told her that he never wished to speak to her again, she felt that it would but serve him right if she were to slip away now while he was too busy to notice her departure, and thus have her revenge.

[16] Dion Cassius, l, 33.

These reckless thoughts led her at length to a reckless decision, and suddenly she gave orders to her little squadron [17] to hoist sail and run with the wind southwards. Both Plutarch and Dion Cassius state emphatically that the battle was still undecided when she sailed away; but it seems that she intended to touch at some port of southern Greece to obtain news of its result before crossing the Mediterranean, and she evidently preferred to endure the longer period of uncertainty than allow him the consolation of her forgiveness. History has regarded her as a cruel woman; but in this impulsive action the cruelty was of that feminine kind which is born of love—it was a case of cutting off her nose to spite her face.

Antony, at the height of the battle, saw her making off, and the insanity of his warring emotions overwhelmed his tired brain. She was going out of his life without a word of reconciliation; mortally wounded by his insults she was leaving him for ever. He was a man who, as Plutarch said of him in another connection, was given to sudden and extreme repentance, and was ready to ask pardon of those he had injured; and he could not now bear the thought of parting from his wife in this manner, unforgiven and unforgiving. His passionate desire to be reconciled to her in a last loving farewell was irresistible; and at the same time his anger and his dismay at her ability to leave him at a time when he was facing death, demanded a final explosion of fury and an adequate vent to his anguish.

Acting upon an impulse no less insensate than hers, he summoned the swiftest ship in his fleet—a galley of five banks of oars—and boarding it, told the captain to overtake the Antonias. The battle could be continued in his absence: indeed his departure would probably be unnoticed in the confusion of the fight, and it is to be supposed that he intended to be back at his post before long. The stubbornness of the conflict, and the roughness of the sea, already indicated that the day would end in a victory for neither side, and on the morrow the fight could be renewed. His one thought was that Cleopatra must not leave him until a reconciliation had been effected. "What was once said as a jest," writes

[17] Plutarch says that her sixty ships sailed away with her, but as he also says that the Roman soldiers were aboard these ships, it is evident that they were not with her; and Florus (iv, xi) is nearer the mark when he states that she went off alone.

Plutarch, "that the soul of a lover lives in the body of the beloved, he proved to be a serious truth; for, as if he had been born
part of her and must move with her wherever she went, he abandoned all those who were fighting and giving their lives for him,
and went after her." Both Plutarch and Dion Cassius, our two
main authorities for these events, suppose that, despairing of victory, he intended flight; but since they are agreed that the battle
was as yet wholly undecided, it seems far more probable that his
intentions carried him no farther than the present hour. He hardly
knew what he was doing or going to do. He knew only that he
must see his wife.

When he had overtaken the Antonias, Cleopatra gave a reluctant order that he was to be taken aboard, but she would not see
him nor speak to him; and he, refusing to be the first to make
the necessary overtures, went without a word to the prow of the
ship, and, sitting down, held his head in his hands like one who
was dazed. Very well then, if she would not be reconciled, he would
not go back to the battle: their cause could suffer complete disaster
for all he cared. He did not wish to live. He was mentally and physically tired out.

He was still sitting there, dumb and heartbroken, when night
fell. Now Octavian had seen him go in pursuit of Cleopatra, and,
supposing that he would presently come back, had at once despatched two or three fast Liburnian galleys [18] to attempt his capture while he was thus alone; and with them went a certain vessel
which had been provided and fitted out by a man named Eurycles,
a Spartan, who had placed himself and his ship at Octavian's
service in order to be revenged upon Antony for having condemned
his father, Lachares, to death for robbery. In the darkness these
vessels came up with the Antonias and the escorting ships which,
laden with Cleopatra's treasure and baggage, were sailing by her
side; and at this Antony rose to his feet, and called out: "Who is
this that wants Antony?" Across the water came the reply: "I am
Eurycles, son of Lachares, armed with the warrant of Cæsar Octavian's fortune to revenge my father's death."

Antony gave the order to turn about and face the danger, and
at this the Liburnian ships drew off in fear, only the vessel of

[18] The ships of Liburnia (Dalmatia) were famous for their speed.

Eurycles keeping to its course. For a moment this man was seen standing at the prow, holding aloft a spear which he was about to hurl at Antony, who faced him; but suddenly the ship collided with one of the Egyptian vessels, and both drifted away into the darkness, locked together. The Antonias then continued on her way, and Antony resumed his seat in the prow.

All through the summer night he sat there, waiting doggedly for Cleopatra to make some sign, but this she refused to do, and, in bitter retaliation, he refused to consider any means of returning to Actium to resume the direction of the war which was their one hope of life. They were sailing close to the coast, and at any time he could have gone ashore: he had with him two of his faithful servants, and with their help he could have obtained horses and ridden back to Actium. But he refused to take any action whatsoever. It was suicide, and he knew it; but the hopes and life of Cleopatra were as surely being destroyed by their mutual stubbornness as his own. Every mile that the Antonias carried him made the disaster more inevitable; and already their dreams of dominion had vanished, and their chances, even, of life were fading. The spectre of the cold and calculating Octavian, the man who had always beaten him, towered before his drooping eyes; but now no more did his heart sink at the menacing vision. He cared no longer what should become of him: he wanted to disappear from the face of the earth.

The sun rose and found him haggard and unkempt. His two servants brought him food, but if he ate at all he did not know what he ate. There was no message from Cleopatra's cabin, and he refused to move from the prow to go to her uninvited. The ship was now crossing the open sea at the mouth of the Gulf of Corinth, and his immediate return to Actium was out of the question. If the naval battle had ended in a victory for his ships, he could no longer hope to be present at the final assault upon The Ladle; if the victory had been Octavian's he could not be present to lead his army inland. He did not care.

The day passed, and night returned. Morning came, and now the Antonias was sailing down the coast of southern Greece; but still Cleopatra refused to be reconciled. Her ladies, Iras and Charmion, came to see him, yet could effect no accommodation; but whether, as Plutarch asks, it was because of his continued anger or because he did not wish to upbraid her, he would not go to her, and she would not ask him to come. The third night ensued, and during the next day they sailed across the Gulf of Messeniacus (Kalamata), and that evening reached Cape Tænarium, the southernmost point of Greece. Here a halt had to be made in order to obtain supplies and fresh water; and at last Iras and Charmion persuaded the Queen to send for her husband.[19]

We know nothing of the meeting beyond the statement of Plutarch that they were persuaded "first to speak to one another, and afterwards to eat and sleep together." Antony's condition, however, can hardly have failed to disinter their love from its grave and to prove it yet alive; and a night of exhausted slumber no doubt improved the spirits of both of them. During the day two or three ships came in, bringing refugees from Actium and news of the results of the battle. Octavian had been victorious, they said; and at four o'clock [20] in the afternoon, about two hours after Antony had left, the fleet had given up the fight and had surrendered, although not more than five thousand men had lost their lives, and few ships had been sunk. Including the transports and other shipping in the Gulf, about three hundred vessels had passed into Octavian's hands, of which the best part of two hundred were powerful men-o'-war by no means seriously damaged.[21] Antony's informants told him that only a few of the officers knew that he had deserted them and many of those to whom these had given the news had refused to believe it, supposing, rather, that he had been killed or had gone away on important business and would presently return. The army, it seemed, was standing firm, and was preparing to march inland.

At this Antony dispatched messengers to his generals, telling them to lead the troops eastwards through Macedonia and Thrace into Asia Minor; but he had no hope that these orders would be

---

[19] The long continuance of this quarrel disproves the suggestion of Dion Cassius (l, 15) that Antony had all along intended to accompany Cleopatra to Egypt; and indeed such a plan is of itself incredible, since their only hope lay in Antony's victory, if not by sea, then on land.

[20] Plutarch: *Antony*.

[21] Plutarch implies that the damage was not great, and the description of burning ships and terrible slaughter given by Dion Cassius (l, 33–35) may be discounted.

carried out. Long before they could reach the army, his desertion would have been apparent to all, and there would have been a general capitulation. It was too late for him to go back himself: he would almost certainly be captured and put to death. Nor had he any desire to continue the war or to sacrifice any more lives in the cause of a leader so worthless as himself. The Queen's mind, it is true, was already full of plans for defending herself in Egypt, whither, she supposed, Octavian would presently come to seek her out; but he himself could not think so far ahead as this. He wanted, for very shame, to die; and no one who has studied his face in the Vatican bust, and has observed the sensitiveness of his mouth, will fail to appreciate the agony of his humiliation.

Amongst the refugees there were several senators and officers whose plight was pitiful, and to these he offered a large sum of money and numerous plates and dishes of gold which Cleopatra had told him he might use for this purpose; but "they refused his kindness with tears in their eyes, and he, on his part, comforted them with all the goodness and consideration imaginable, begging them to leave him, and writing letters on their behalf to his steward at Corinth that he would provide for their safety and keep them concealed till such time as they could make their peace with Octavian." [22] There were two men, however, who elected to go with him across the sea: one was a Greek professor of oratory, named Aristocrates, and the other was that Roman officer, Lucilius, who, after the battle of Philippi, had pretended to be Brutus to save his defeated general's life, as already recorded, and who had been forgiven for his deception and spared by Antony.

Next morning the Antonias and her escorting ships set out to cross the Mediterranean; and the party arrived some days later at Parætonium (El Baratûn), a little port on the western frontier of Egypt, about two to three days sail west of Alexandria. Here water and provisions were to be taken aboard, after which the journey to the capital was to be resumed; but now Antony came to a surprising decision: he made up his mind to go ashore there, and to remain in seclusion while his wife went on to Alexandria. It is possible that some hope of renewing the war had revived in him, and that he wished to get into touch with his forces in Cyrene, [23]

[22] Plutarch: *Antony*.   [23] Dion Cassius, li, 5.

Parætonium being on the desert highroad between that place and Alexandria; but it seems to me to be more probable that he had no other wish than to hide here, and perhaps to put an end to himself.

During the voyage his mind, I think, had undergone a great revolution. He knew now that his love for Cleopatra, and all the tempestuous emotions which it had involved, had been his ruin; and he wanted to put her out of his thoughts, and to compose himself for death or for the only kind of life which still seemed possible, namely, that of an obscure personage living in complete retirement from the turmoil of the world. As often happens in the case of one who has passed through a great emotional crisis, the thought of peace and rest presented itself as a heavenly vision towards which his broken heart yearned with intense longing: had he lived in the Middle Ages he would, I dare say, have sought sanctuary from his cares in a monastery. His passionate devotion to the Queen, it seems to me, had shattered itself in the mental convulsions of those first three days during which he sat in solitude at the prow of the Antonias; and when at Tænarium he had returned to Cleopatra's arms he had become aware that their love, though still alive, was maimed out of all recognition. No longer did he feel that life was unthinkable without her: he wanted now to be alone. Thus, at least, I interpret the condition of his mind.

Cleopatra's attitude is not difficult to understand. Antony, as ruler of the eastern empire, and potential sovereign of the world, had been her one hope, her one protection against Octavian who was bent upon her destruction and the removal of her son, Cæsarion, from his path. But Antony—whether the fault were hers or his—had made her life with him intolerable during those last months at Actium, and she had determined to leave him: she had not dreamed, however, that when she made her hurried exit from the scene of his struggle against their common enemy, he would abandon all and follow her. By so doing he had consigned her and himself to their almost inevitable doom. Within a few brief hours he had wrecked their mutual hopes, and had converted a still radiant outlook into the darkness of impending death. Yet she was not prepared to accept her destiny in the limp condition of collapse in which he had accepted it: she was going to make a last bid for life and freedom if only by flight, and in her schemes he had no place. He was now an encumbrance; he was like a corpse attached to her by chains which she could not break. Her love for him was not dead, but he himself was dead, and she could but mourn for him as for one who was about to be buried. As she sailed away from Parætonium she did not expect to see him again, and she must have waved him her sorrowful farewell in this belief; while he, standing on the water-front of this desolate little settlement, could hardly have failed to impart a sense of finality into the drama of their leave-taking.

Aristocrates and the faithful Lucilius remained with him; and for several weeks they passed their days in wandering about the desert behind the sun-baked cluster of mud-brick houses which, with the small frontier-fort, constituted the township, or in walking along the interminable seashore. It may be supposed that a ship or two put in at the port to obtain water on the journey from Greece to Egypt; and Antony may thus have received news of what had happened to his army. "At first," says Plutarch, "nobody could believe a thing so incredible as that a general, who had a great army of infantry and cavalry upon land, could have abandoned everything and fled away—he, above all, who had so often experienced both good and ill fortune, and had in a thousand fights and battles been inured to such changes." At last, however, when a week had passed, and their commanding officers had all surrendered or fled, they made their submission to the bewildered victor, who could no more understand than they what had happened.

Then came news from Cyrene that the Antonian forces in that province had renounced their allegiance and had declared for Octavian; and at this Antony told his two friends that he saw no further reason to prolong his life, and that he was going to kill himself. They persuaded him, however, to wait yet awhile, and to die, if die he must, in Alexandria, where at least he might be buried with honour, beside the tomb of his hero, Alexander the Great. Thus, when the next ship came into port on its way to the Egyptian capital, Antony was persuaded to board it; and at about the end of October he presented himself once more at Cleopatra's palace.[24]

[24] Plutarch (*Antony*) thinks that Antony did not hear any news of his army until he had returned to Alexandria; but as Cyrene had had the news, and as the report of the consequent events at Cyrene had come to him, he must surely have heard of the surrender of the army at Actium.

He found the Queen busily engaged in preparations for the evacuation of Alexandria, and for the removal of the seat of her government to some far-distant point on the Red Sea such as the port of Berenice (Saket el-Kubli), near the headland now known as Râs Benâs, her design being, in the last extreme, to sail for India, with which country the Egyptian merchants for the past century or two had been in trade. She was already attempting to transfer some of her ships-of-war from the Mediterranean to the Red Sea by way of the disused channels which occupied, more or less, the site of the present Suez Canal; and, where these were blocked up with sand, the vessels were being dragged across the desert.

It may be that she felt some encouragement at first in the return of Antony, for her subjects had not yet accustomed themselves to the thought that he was bereft of all power, and his was still a great and inspiring name to them. But if this be so, Antony soon disillusioned her and them; for, refusing to resume his conjugal life and asserting that he was done with affairs of state, he betook himself to a little house which had once been used, it is to be supposed, by some port-official, and which stood at the end of a breakwater in the harbour. Here he said that he was going to live the life of a hermit, and that he would never again appear at court. He hated all men, he declared, and, like Timon of Athens, the famous misanthrope, he would pass his days in solitude, cursing all mankind. He called the house the Timoneum; and for the next few months he lived there alone, food being brought to him, presumably, from the palace. People passing in boats could see him sitting there in the sun, staring out across the harbour, or, perhaps, fishing, or, again, reading a book; and at nights the light in his window would sometimes indicate that he was not asleep.

I have said repeatedly in this biography that there was something of the actor in his character; and had he not been at this time a man practically under sentence of death, one would be inclined to smile at his impersonation of sour old Timon, deeming it a theatrical pose. But he had fallen headlong from too great a height, his wounds were too real, his situation was too hopeless, for such a criticism of his behaviour to be made with entire justice. This desire for solitude may well have been his nature's necessary reaction to the shock of his fall; and his hatred of his fellow-men was, very likely, an unconscious defence put up by his harassed mind to protect him against the battery of his shame. At any rate it is to be said in his favour that he maintained this character of a hermit for many weeks—that is to say during the remainder of the year 31 B.C., and well on into 30 B.C.; and during all this time he must have been fighting down the still smouldering fires of his love for Cleopatra, enduring the anguish of his memories, conquering his starved emotions, and struggling to overcome his jealousy and his chagrin when, across the water, there came to his ears the sounds of music in the palace, or when, at night, he saw the lights in the windows and knew that she was entertaining her friends.

One day in the spring, however, news was brought to him that the crisis was approaching. Octavian, who had gone back to Rome for a brief visit after his victory, had, in February, crossed into Asia Minor, and was now marching with a great army towards Syria, which province had declared for him, as had King Herod of Judæa. On the west of Egypt, one of Octavian's generals was preparing another large army in Cyrene for the attack upon Alexandria. Most of the vassal kings who had been with Antony at Actium had been killed or dethroned; and many of his friends had been put to death, while others had given their allegiance to the conqueror. Of all the countries in the Roman world Egypt alone remained hostile to Octavian; and from north, east, and west, the enemy was closing in on doomed Alexandria. Close on the heels of these tidings came the news that the ships which had been transferred by Cleopatra with such labour to the Red Sea, had been attacked and burnt by Bedouin Arabs, apparently incited by Octavian's agents.

At this a sudden revulsion of feeling overwhelmed Antony's misanthropy. Plutarch says that he received these evil tidings with a kind of quiet exultation, as though he were glad that the end was nigh. He was sick to death of melancholy and despair: he would make the most of these last months, and round his life off with music, feasting, love and laughter. He sent a message to Cleopatra, asking her if she were prepared to receive him back as her husband; and to this the lonely and anxious Queen seems to have replied in a nervous affirmative. And thus in the spring of 30 B.C., Antony turned his back upon his hermitage, and, abandoning his efforts to overcome that turmoil of his emotions which alone was left of his love, resumed his place at Cleopatra's side.

CHAPTER XXI

Octavian's Invasion of Egypt and the Death of Antony.

30 B.C.

I THINK it must have been in the month of March, 30 B.C., that Antony came back to the palace. During the whole winter he had refused to concern himself with public affairs; but now he found that Cleopatra had busily engaged herself in the attempt to renew her friendships with foreign kings. The Orient was her liveliest hope, and it seems that, immediately on her return from Actium, she had sent her ambassadors to Media to ask for help, and that an answer had lately been received. It will be remembered that the ex-king Artavasdes of Armenia had been a prisoner in Alexandria since 34 B.C.; and it appears that the Median monarch, fearing that Octavian would restore this sovereign to his throne, had asked Cleopatra to put him to death as an earnest of her good will. This she had done, and had sent the head of the unfortunate Artavasdes to Media. At the same time it seems probable that she had arranged that her and Antony's son, Alexander Helios, now nearly ten years of age, with his child-wife, the Median princess, Iotapa, should be sent presently to that country, so that they should be out of danger's way; but for the time being these two children remained at the palace.[1]

As to Cæsarion, she had another scheme. She proposed to send him to Berenice, on the Red Sea coast, so that he might sail for India [2] with the Egyptian merchants who each summer made the long journey to that country: she saw no other way of saving the

---

[1] After the death of Antony and Cleopatra Alexander and Iotapa fell into Octavian's hands. He sent the girl back to her father, and the boy was carried off to Rome.

[2] Plutarch: *Antony.*

boy's life. She did not suppose that any harm would come to her other two children, Cleopatra Selene, the twin-sister of Alexander, and the little Ptolemy who was but in his sixth year; and she had taken no steps for their safety. Antyllus, Antony's son by Fulvia, was also at the palace; but in his case, also, she had not made any plans: he would have to take his chance.

But when Antony abandoned his hermit's life, his mood was reckless and defiant, and he made short work of Cleopatra's arrangements, which, indeed, had been to a great extent upset by the destruction of her ships by the Arabs. He appears to have told her that the only thing to do was to let Octavian understand that they would defend Egypt against him; and then, when the time came, they could offer to surrender on terms. If those terms were rejected, they ought, he said, to fight him to the death, here in Alexandria, and, in the last extreme, die by their own hand. He found no attraction in the thought of a perilous flight into far-off Oriental lands; and the only tolerable alternative to suicide, so far as he was concerned at any rate, was that of being allowed to retire into unmolested private life—a fate which had proved not at all unpleasant to his late colleague in the Triumvirate, Lepidus, who, after his defeat by Octavian, was now enjoying a comfortable rustication at Circeii (Circello), on the coast not far south of Rome. Either that or a last fight and suicide.[3]

Orders were therefore given to put Alexandria into a state of defence, and to strengthen the eastern and western frontiers of Egypt; but in view of the possibility of making terms with Octavian, Antony advised his wife to hand over to her son, Cæsarion, a fuller share of the sovereignty of the country, so that she herself might be free to retire into private life. Now it so happened that Cæsarion's seventeenth birthday, which, according to Egyptian custom, was his coming of age,[4] was soon to occur[5]; and Antony therefore suggested that this event should be celebrated with grand

[3] In my *Life of Cleopatra* I indicated that the Queen, not Antony, had suggested this line of action; but in view of her subsequent actions I think we must credit Antony with this policy.

[4] I am not quite sure of this, but the evidence from earlier times in Egypt points to it.

[5] Cæsarion was born in the first days of July, 47 B. C., but the calendar had since been adjusted by Cæsar, and that date now corresponded to the middle of April.

festivities and that instead of the boy being sent away into hiding, he should be displayed to the Egyptians as their full-grown King. The fifteenth birthday of Antyllus, his son by Fulvia, would fall at about the same time; and as this was the date at which a Roman youth assumed the *toga virilis*, he proposed that the two events should be celebrated together.

He then called to him his former friends in Alexandria who had been members of his *Amimetobioi*, or Society of "Inimitable Livers," and invited them to form with him another club, the *Synapothanoumenoi*, or Society of "Die-Togethers," the idea being that they should entertain one another in a round of wild parties, thus putting into operation the old formula "Eat, drink, and be merry, for tomorrow we die." The proposal was promptly taken up, and soon Antony had flung himself headlong into such dissipations as even he had not before indulged in. He must have been drunk nearly every night, but it is a question whether Cleopatra accompanied him into these smiling and reeling realms of oblivion. She still hoped that she would be able to make her peace with Octavian, and she desired to keep her wits about her for this purpose. At the same time, however, she experimented with various poisons, trying their effect upon animals and condemned criminals; and it is evident that she was preparing to die, though it is not clear in what manner this dark cloud which hung over her days affected her ability to throw herself into these macabre festivities.

Certainly her relations with her husband were not happy, save in those brief periods when their old love, which never died, broke out from the chaos of conflicting plans and interests to shine for a while like the sun on a stormy day. She was now in her fortieth year, and Antony's fifty-third birthday was approaching: the resilience of youth had left them both, and, in the case of Antony, the fires of passion had perhaps given place to that kind of love which, in happier circumstances, would have carried their conjugal life through quarrels and flaring disputes to the comparative calm of a pleasant, if somewhat exhausted, autumnal devotion. They had been fated always to fight and to forgive, to hate and to love; and their relationship was still tumultuous, though now there was this difference, that, whereas before the catastrophe of Actium they were fighting each other chiefly over the means of obtaining world-dominion, they were today tragically bickering as to how best to ring down the curtain on the drama of their lives.

The birthday celebrations in honour of Cæsarion and Antyllus kept the whole city in a state of festal uproar for many days; and Antony was once more hailed as the jovial and bibulous Dionysus, the lord of good-will, enthroned above the carnival, or trundled through the streets in his Bacchic chariot to the sound of clashing cymbals. His winter's quiescence in his sea-girt hermitage was forgotten, or, maybe, was regarded, almost religiously, as a period of hibernal retirement ended by the return of spring; and few of the Alexandrians outside the circle of the court seem to have realized that these renewed antics were the dance of Death. But when the fun was over his troubles with Cleopatra broke out afresh, and during May and June the domestic situation was very strained.

King Herod, before making his peace with Octavian, had sent a confidential message to Antony strongly advising him to kill Cleopatra in order to save his own skin [6]; but Antony rejected this suggestion with abhorrence, and impulsively sent a letter to Octavian offering, magnificently, to kill himself if by this sacrifice the Queen's life would be spared.[7] There was a certain Roman senator, Publius Turullius, then seeking sanctuary in Alexandria, who had been one of the assassins of Cæsar, and was, in fact, the last of the Dictator's murderers still alive; and with a second letter Antony now sent the unfortunate man to Octavian for trial. It has generally been assumed that this action was a craven attempt to curry favour; but actually Antony, who had abandoned all claim to authority outside Egypt and was seriously offering to commit suicide, seems only to have wished to show that he no longer regarded himself or his stepson, Cæsarion, as Cæsar's representative and avenger—the right was now conceded to Octavian. The latter put the assassin to death, but made no reply to Antony's accompanying letter, in which he had stated that he was willing to go into retirement in Egypt or Athens.

Meanwhile, however, Cleopatra had notified Octavian that she had handed over her sovereign authority to a great extent to her son, and was likewise prepared to retire into private life; and with-

[6] Josephus: *Antiquities*, xv, vi, 6.　　[7] Dion Cassius, li, 8.

out telling Antony, she had sent her crown and sceptre to Octavian as a token of submission.[8] To this Octavian replied in secret
to her, saying "that there was no reasonable favour which she
might not expect if she would put Antony to death" [9]; but just as
Antony had spurned the suggestion that he should murder *her*, so
now she refused to entertain the thought of killing *him*. Nevertheless, rumours of these secret proposals got about, and, as a consequence, husband and wife regarded one another with cruel suspicion; and, indeed, no more pitiable situation can be imagined
than this, that these two harassed lovers found themselves forced
into mutual mistrust when in their hearts they each knew that the
other was incapable of such treachery.

Presently Octavian sent a certain freedman of his, named Thyrus, to Alexandria to discuss terms with the Queen; and this man,
ignoring Antony, held long and private conversations with Cleopatra, telling her that his master was really very sympathetically
disposed towards her as the lady whom his uncle and adoptive
father, Cæsar, had loved, and hinting that he, Octavian, had been
much attracted to her as a youth in Rome, when she was there
with the Dictator, and might again come under the spell of her
charms. Antony, of course, was infuriated by these lengthy inter-
views from which he was debarred, and, suddenly losing his temper,
pounced upon Thyrus as he was leaving the Queen's room, and
gave him a horse-whipping, thereafter sending him back, black
and blue, to Octavian with a droll message of apology for the beating. "The man's busy impertinent ways provoked me," he wrote,
"and in my circumstances I cannot be expected to be very patient.
However, if my action offend you, you have got my freedman,
Hipparchus, with you: hang him up and beat him to make us
quits."

Cleopatra, being a woman, was stirred and delighted by her
husband's violent action, which must have revealed again to her,
as it does to us, that unconquerable spontaneity of thought and
deed, that devil-may-care humour, and that audacious courage
which had once made him the hero of so many hearts; and thereafter their troubled relationship passed into a phase of mutual at-
tachment wherein they appear to have behaved once more like

---

[8] Dion Cassius, li, 6.   [9] Plutarch: *Antony;* Dion Cassius, li, 6.

young lovers. His fifty-third birthday was now due; and Cleopatra "observed it with the utmost prodigality of splendour and magnificence," [10] making him feel again that he was indeed her chosen consort and the sharer of her destiny. Much of her former pride in him was aroused, moreover, by the news which now came to them of a very curious enterprise which was being undertaken on his behalf.

At Cyzicus (Kyzik) in Asia Minor, on the Sea of Marmara, there was a great school of gladiators who, at the time of the battle of Actium, were practicing for the triumphal games which they expected to be held to celebrate Antony's anticipated victory over Octavian; but when, in September, they heard of their patron's flight to Egypt, they were at first dumbfounded, but at length decided to set out on the long march to Alexandria, to place themselves at Antony's disposal, their love for him, as a leader after their own hearts, being steadfast even in the face of his astonishing behaviour. They were several thousand strong, but when, in midwinter, they reached Galatia their progress was obstructed by King Amyntas who had been restored to his kingdom by Octavian, and who now fought them in numerous battles. At last, however, they burst their way through that country, and so came into Cilicia, where, again, they were obliged to fight their way towards the east.

In the spring they reached Syria, whence they sent messengers to Antony begging him to come to them, and to let them be his bodyguard; but Octavian's new Syrian governor intercepted these messengers, and it was, seemingly, not until the summer that Antony heard of their devoted offer. [11] He could get no communication through to them, however, and in the end, thinking he had perished, they abandoned their march and wearily made their peace with Octavian, who gave them lands at Daphne, near Antioch, on which to settle; and it may be added that some time later their new patron, with his habitual cynicism, broke his pact with them, and either dispersed or killed them all. Their steadfast loyalty to Antony, however, was a proof of the high esteem in which he was held by men of brawn; and its effect was not lost upon Cleopatra.

[10] Plutarch: *Antony.*
[11] Dion Cassius gives an account of this affair (li, 7) and indicates that the gladiators' offer reached him at about this time.

Antony might be in eclipse, but his stature was still that of a mighty warrior, and he was still the hero of a hundred tales.

At about the end of June news suddenly arrived that the enemy approaching from Cyrene and the west had seized the frontier fortress of Parætonium; and thereupon Antony put a sudden end to the already declining frivolities of the palace, and threw himself whole-heartedly into what he knew to be the last phase of the war. Embarking such troops as he could spare upon a squadron of Egyptian battleships, he sailed for the frontier and landed his men in the harbour of Parætonium, thence marching through the little town up to the mud-brick fort which was held by the enemy. He had hoped that the Roman legionaries behind its walls, who were all old comrades of his, would listen to him if he spoke to them; and he therefore went forward alone, and, though exposed to their arrows, shouted out his greeting to them. The commanding-officer, however, gave orders to the trumpeters to sound a continuous fanfare, and thus his words went unheard.

Disappointed in this stratagem, he then led an assault upon the walls, but he was beaten back to his ships after a stiff fight, and many of these were burnt or captured. Escaping with the remainder, he sailed again for Alexandria; but here he was received by the news that Pelusium, the powerful fortress guarding the eastern Egyptian frontier, had fallen to the advancing army commanded by Octavian. Soon a report came to his ears that this place had been surrendered at Cleopatra's orders, and that she was playing into Octavian's hands by secret arrangement. Antony could hardly believe it, but he furiously accused her of treachery, at which the distracted woman, who, apparently, was innocent of this baseness,[12] ordered the arrest of the wife and children of the commander of the fortress, and handed them over to her husband to wreak his vengeance upon them if he so decided. He did not harm them, of course, and the domestic incident closed with yet another passionate reconciliation.

During July Octavian advanced to the outskirts of Alexandria; and at length, in the last days of that month sacred to the memory of Cæsar, he pitched his camp outside the eastern walls of the

---

[12] Dion Cassius (li, 9) thinks she was guilty; but Antony did not afterwards think so himself.

capital. Antony at once led out a desperate sortie, drove in Octavian's advance-guard, and pursued them back to their main entrenchments. He was so elated by this little victory that, hastening back to the palace, he ran to Cleopatra, dressed as he was in his military armour, took her in his arms, and kissed her. He particularly recommended to her a certain officer who had distinguished himself in the fight, whereupon she presented the man with a helmet and breastplate of gold; but that very night the rewarded hero, fearing to lose tomorrow what he had gained today, deserted to the enemy.

Next morning Antony caused his archers to shoot into Octavian's camp a number of arrows to which letters were attached, offering a large sum of money to all those who would come over to his side; but when these documents had failed to elicit any response, he made up his mind to risk all in a last battle by water and land. It is said that, in the event of defeat, he intended now to sail for Spain with Cleopatra, if there yet remained to him a ship and an open passageway out to sea; but it is more probable that both he and she exchanged a promise to die together, although, in the case of the Queen, this tragic resolve must have been wrung from her by a sense of loyalty rather than by the conviction that there would then be no other escape. Octavian's lying messages to her had even given her hope that her throne would not be taken from her.

There was, of course, very little chance of victory in battle against Octavian, and it was now arranged that Cæsarion should slip out of the city and make his way to Upper Egypt, thence to sail for India if this throne were taken from him, or, alternatively, to return to Alexandria if Octavian should confirm to him the Egyptian sovereignty. The west side of the city, whence there was a desert highroad to the south, was still free of the enemy, as also was the south side, where Lake Mareotis provided a waterway to the Nile; and by one of these routes Cæsar's only son, so lately heir to the potential empire of the world, was packed off by night. It was too late now, however, to send Alexander Helios to Media, and he and Antyllus remained with the other children in the palace.

On the following day, the last of the month of July, Antony sent a challenge to Octavian to fight a duel with him and thus to settle their quarrel without causing the loss of so many lives; but Octavian replied coldly that Antony might find many other ways of ending his life. Thereupon Antony decided to give battle on the following morning. He had at his disposal, it would seem, the Roman force which had been left in Alexandria while he and Cleopatra were in Greece; and there were also the Macedonian household-troops, the native Egyptian army, and certain mercenaries. There was, too, a small Egyptian and Roman fleet; and Antony proposed to divide his men, placing some upon the ships so that they could sail along the coast to disembark and attack Octavian in the rear, while the main force would make a sortie from the city and fall upon the enemy's front. The invading army was not overwhelmingly large, and there was just a possibility that it would be defeated, while there was always the chance that the uncanny Octavian, whose menacing personality seemed to have spread itself over the whole earth, might be ignominiously killed in the fight and his power dissipated like a dream.

The prospects, however, were hardly cheerful, and that night at supper with the "Die-Togethers" Antony drank heavily, telling the servants to fill his cup liberally, since on the following day they might have a new master, while he himself might be lying dead upon the ground. "Tomorrow I may be a corpse, a *nothing*," he said [13]; and, the wine having loosened his tongue, he talked to his friends in a vein of such tragic and eloquent sorrow that soon nearly the whole company was in tears. At this, however, he pulled himself together, and remarked that they need not grieve, since they might be sure that he would not be about to lead his men into battle at all if he were hoping for nothing more than an honourable death.

Unfortunately, history makes no mention of Cleopatra at this last banquet, and we only read that "he pitied her more than himself" [14]—pregnant words, however, which indicate that his attitude towards her was now one of tender solicitude. He could not be sure that she would wish to die with him if the battle were to go against them, or even to escape with him if so events should shape themselves. He must have been haunted by the dread lest her woman's courage should fail her, and lest she should make terms with Octavian, leaving him to end his life in solitude; and it may be

[13] Plutarch: *Antony*.   [14] Dion Cassius, li, 10.

supposed that his last hours with her were clouded by the suspicion that her endearments were false. Yet he could not blame her if in secret she were clinging to the hope of life; and he must have known that whereas he could say of her that she had been the ruin of his career, she could reply that he had proved himself a broken reed. Their high hopes, their vaunting ambitions, their career of splendour, had been brought to this sorry pass by their personal quarrels and ungovernable tempers: the fault was mutual, and recriminations were useless.

At about midnight, when the whole city was hushed and silent, and the sea wind had dropped, leaving the menaced capital breathless in the summer heat, there came to the palace the far-off sound of pipes and cymbals, of voices singing a Bacchanalian chant, and of dancing feet, moving along the Street of Canopus towards the gate which overlooked the enemy's camp. Several persons heard the wild music, and listened in awe as at length it swelled out loudly from the direction of this gate, and then faded into the distance, as though the ghostly procession had passed out of the city. It may be that the noise came from some quarter where a drunken throng of soldiers or townspeople was passing the anxious night with music and song; but those who listened in the palace deemed it to be the unearthly clamour of the departure of Dionysus out of Antony's life. The god whose incarnation he had been had gone from him, they said, and had betaken himself to Octavian.

At sunrise next morning, August 1st, B.C. 30, Antony led his men out to do battle with the enemy; and, standing on the high ground outside the city, he watched his fleet move out from the harbour to attack Octavian's ships and to disembark the forces which were to menace the enemy's rear. But as he watched, he saw the sailors of each fleet salute those of the other and come to rest side by side, evidently by a secret arrangement made between them. While he was still staring in dismay at this spectacle, his cavalry suddenly galloped forward before his eyes, and were received into Octavian's lines. The enemy then advanced upon him, whereat his remaining troops fled back into the city, carrying him with them in their confused retreat, cursing them, as he went, for their refusal to obey his orders, and shouting at them his accusations of treachery. It was clear that the collapse was the result of a prearrangement with the enemy, and Antony made his way back to the palace, crying out that Cleopatra had betrayed him, and calling her every foul name he could lay his tongue to.

As he stormed into the building, she ran for her life to her unfinished mausoleum which stood on the far side of a courtyard, overlooking the sea. It was a stone structure of two storeys, there being, I suppose, a pillared hall on the ground level, wherein was her sarcophagus, and on the upper floor a series of rooms now furnished, perhaps, for the habitation of the superintendent of the builders whose work was not yet completed. Her two ladies, Iras and Charmion, and one eunuch,[15] accompanied her; and, dashing into the mausoleum, they closed and bolted the great doors and heaped against them whatever heavy objects they could lay their hands on, thereafter mounting the stairs to the upper floor, from the windows of which they could observe something of what was going on in the courtyard and palace.

It seems probable that the Queen was not responsible for the desertions, but she knew quite well that Antony would hardly be persuaded to think her innocent, and her flight was from his wrath, not from the enemy. Looking out of the window, one of her ladies called hysterically down to some servant or soldier below, telling him to go to Antony and to say that the Queen was about to kill herself[16]; but the man in his excitement misunderstood the message, I suppose, for the news that she was dead was presently brought to Antony as, with two or three faithful officers, he paced about, sword in hand, waiting distractedly for events to shape themselves. At this he cried out: "Well, then, why wait longer? Fate has taken away the only thing for which I could say I still wanted to live"; and with these words he rushed to his own room, tearing off his armour as he went, and calling to his personal servant, Eros, to come to him.

He was heard then to speak aloud to Cleopatra, whose spirit he thought to be hovering near to him. "I am not unhappy to have lost you for a moment, Cleopatra my beloved," he said, "for I

[15] So Dion Cassius, li, 10.
[16] Dion Cassius (li, 10), who assumes throughout his account that Cleopatra had betrayed Antony, says that she sent out a false message that she was dead in order to induce him to kill himself; but Plutarch does not seem to think that she had any wish to deceive.

shall soon be with you; but what so shames me is that a famous soldier should be found to have had slower courage than a woman." He then turned to Eros, and, handing him his sword, ordered him to be his executioner; but the man snatched the weapon and stabbed himself to the heart with it, falling dead at his feet. "Well done, Eros!" Antony exclaimed, looking down at him in admiration, and picking up the dripping sword. "You have shown your master how to do what you had not the heart to do yourself." Thereupon he plunged the blade into his own body, and fell back upon his bed, where he fainted away.

The wound, however, was not immediately mortal, and presently, coming to his senses, he entreated those who had gathered around him, to put him out of his pain; but at this they all fled from the room, leaving him groaning and struggling. Some of them ran to the mausoleum and called up to Cleopatra that Antony had stabbed himself, but was still alive, and thereat, flinging up her arms and tearing her hair, she screamed to them to bring him to her. They hastened back, therefore, and told him that the Queen was not dead, but that she was calling for him; whereupon he immediately struggled to his feet, but, falling back, gave orders to them to carry him to her, although every movement was agony to him.

In their arms they brought him, in the great heat of this summer's morning, to the door of the mausoleum, but this could not be opened, for the bolts had been shot too deep to be moved; and he was therefore laid upon the ground beneath the window of the upper room so that Cleopatra might speak to him. The mausoleum, however, as has been said, was still unfinished, and as some ropes were hanging down from the roof where the builders had been working, it was suggested by somebody that he should be placed upon a stretcher and hauled up to the window. A few minutes later the Queen and her three attendants were frantically tugging and pulling at these ropes, while the dying man, lying half-conscious upon the lurching and bumping stretcher, scorched by the sun, tormented by the flies, and agonized by every jolt, ascended inch by inch towards them.

As he came near to the window he regained full consciousness, and, holding out his red-stained hands towards his wife, tried to raise himself up. Somehow, at last, they managed to drag him through the window and to lay him upon a couch, all covered with blood and dripping with sweat as he was, and writhing in agony. Cleopatra then flung her arms about him in a frenzy of grief, calling him her beloved husband, her lord, and her emperor; and it is said that in that last frightful re-union all their misfortunes, all their bitter misunderstandings, were forgotten: for these short minutes of life which remained to him only their deathless love was remembered, and he was at peace at last in the knowledge that they two, in spite of the cleavages of their many quarrels, were indeed one flesh. She brought a cup of wine, presently, for him to drink; and when he had drunk he gasped out some words of advice to her, telling her not to trust Octavian, but saying that he thought she had a chance to save her life.

"You must not pity me in this last turn of Fate," he whispered, as her hands mercilessly beat her breast and tore her hair, and she was shaken by the convulsions of her weeping. "You should rather be happy in the remembrance of our love, and in the recollection that of all men I was once the most famous and the most powerful, and, now, at the end, have fallen not dishonourably, a Roman by a Roman vanquished." A moment later he breathed his last.

The remainder of the pitiful tale may be told briefly. Octavian's officers quickly arrived, and, climbing into the mausoleum through that same window, captured the Queen as she was about to stab herself with her dagger. Octavian presently entered the city, pardoned the inhabitants, and took possession of the palace; but he kept Cleopatra a close prisoner in the mausoleum, where for some days after she had attended, under a guard, her husband's burial, she lay in a high fever brought on in part by the inflammation of her breasts caused by the blows she had rained upon herself in the paroxysms of her grief. He was very anxious to save her life so that he might exhibit her in his Triumph, and he fortified her with promises of leniency; but at last it became clear to her that his intentions were neither kindly nor merciful, and thereupon she resolved to die.

She asked permission, therefore, to be allowed to visit the tomb where Antony was buried; and this being granted, she went there on August 29th with her ladies, and, it would seem, with her private physician, Olympus, upon whose diary Plutarch has drawn in his account of her last days. "O, dearest Antony," she said, when, in passionate tears, she had kissed his gravestone, "it is not long since with these hands I buried you; yet now I pay these last duties to you with a guard upon me, for fear that my natural griefs and sorrows should impair my servile body and make it less fit to be exhibited in their Triumph over me. Expect no further offerings or libations from me, Antony: these are the last honours that Cleopatra will be able to pay to your memory, for she is to be hurried far away from you. Nothing could part us while we lived, but death seems to threaten to divide us. You, a Roman born, have found a grave in Egypt. I, an Egyptian born, am to seek that favour, and none but that, in your country. But if the gods below, with whom you now are dwelling, can or will do anything for me, since those above have betrayed us, do not allow your living wife to be abandoned; let me not be led in this Triumph to your shame; but hide me, hide me; bury me here with you. For amongst all my bitter misfortunes, nothing has been so terrible as this brief time that I have lived without you."

That night she killed herself.

Octavian had no mercy either upon Cæsarion, whom he quickly caught, or upon Antyllus: both youths were put to death. The other children were spared, however, and eventually the little Cleopatra Selene was married by him to King Juba of Numidia and Mauretania, by whom she had a daughter, who married [17] Felix, the governor of Judæa in the reign of Nero—a personage who figures in the Biblical account of the life of St. Paul. Antony's other children in Rome were brought up by the good Octavia, who lived on until B.C. 11. His son Julus rose to high favour, but was executed in B.C. 2 for his adultery with Octavian's daughter, Julia. Antony's daughter, Antonia the Elder, was married to Domitius Ahenobarbus, the son of that general of the same name who deserted Antony before Actium; and she became the grandmother both of the Empress Messalina and of the Emperor Nero. His other daughter, Antonia the Younger, married Drusus, the son of Octavian's wife Livia, and

[17] Tacitus: *History,* v, 9.

was the mother of the Emperor Claudius and his brother Germanicus who was the father of the Emperor Caligula and of the Empress Agrippina, mother of Nero. Thus Antony's aspirations toward a throne were realized in his descendants; and we see that he was fully justified in deeming the Roman empire, in the last years of his life, ripe for monarchy. This throne was established by Octavian, who raised the title of *Imperator*, or Emperor, to sovereign standing, and reigned under the name of Cæsar Augustus until A.D. 14, when he died, full of years and honours, having successfully lived down the many disgraces of his youth.

Egypt, it may be added, became the personal estate of Octavian and, after him, of each succeeding Roman Emperor, who was in every case crowned by proxy as King or Pharaoh of that country.

Throughout the empire Antony's statues were everywhere overthrown, and the inscriptions bearing his name were destroyed. His birthday was marked in the calendar as a day of ill-omen, and it was decreed that no member of his family henceforth should bear the name of Marcus. His memory was grossly maligned by contemporary writers, but even so we find in the words of Plutarch and other authors a little-concealed admiration for him: it is as though they were conscious that had he not been upset by a lovers' quarrel at the time of the battle of Actium, he would in all probability have become the sole sovereign lord of the earth.

INDEX

Achaia, 352 *n.*

Actium, the battle of, 441 ff.; its result, 447

Afranius, Pompey's general, 153, 155, 187

Agricultural conditions in country around Rome at about the time of Antony's birth, 5; efforts of the Gracchi to ameliorate, 5 ff.

Agrippa, Octavian's lieutenant, 429, 441

Ahenobarbus, Cnæus Domitius, 309, 314, 345, 349, 401, 406, 410, 412, 422, 424, 434, 435

Ahenobarbus, Lucius Domitius, 121, 151, 159, 169, 170

Albinus, Decimus Brutus, 216, 217, 225, 229, 240, 243, 252, 258, 266, 267, 274, 275, 277, 279, 281–2, 284, 287–8

Alexander the Great, 330, 373, 379

Alexandria, 111, 202, 329–31

Ambracia (Arta), the Gulf of, 428

Amyntas, King of Galatia, 433, 435, 439, 459

Antigonus, 364, 374

Antioch, 374, 376

Antistius, the orator, 49

Antonia, wife of Antony, 158, 178, 179, 180

Antonii, the, 33–4

Antonius, Caius, uncle of Antony, 58, 65, 72, 73, 75, 76, 80, 84, 89, 98, 99, 164, 233

Antonius, Caius, brother of Antony, 233, 236, 257, 268, 273, 301

Antonius, Lucius, brother of Antony, 233, 234, 236, 239, 257, 279, 281, 327, 328, 335, 336, 340, 344

Antonius, Marcus, the orator, grand-father of Antony, 33, 34

Antonius, Marcus, father of Antony, 33, 34, 35, 59–61

Antony, Marc, birth of, 35; extrava-gances as a youth, 90–2; entrance into politics as a democrat, 98, 101, 102, 104; goes to Greece to study oratory, 104–5, 106; his personal appearance and character, 107–8, 127, 136–7, 177, 298–9; military experience in Palestine and Egypt, 108–13; joins Cæsar in

Gaul, 125; service in Gaul, 126 ff.; returns to Rome and election as Quæstor, 131; support of Cæsar in Rome by, 142, 145–6; as Cæsar's chief lieutenant in the Civil War with Pompey, 148 ff.; his life in Rome at this period, 157–9; in battle of Pharsa-lia, 170, 171; as vice-Dictator in Rome, 175 ff.; temporary estrangement from Cæsar, 184–6; marriage to Fulvia, 190–1; reconciliation with Cæsar, 193–5; as Consul in 44 B.C., 197 ff.; opposition to the ideas of kingship in the mind of Cæsar, 201 ff.; his act of offering Cæsar the royal diadem at the feast of the Lupercalia in 44 B.C., 209–11; loyalty to Cæsar, 211; the assassination of Cæsar and Antony's subsequent action, 215 ff.; his struggle to prevent civil war and his difficulties with Octavian, 224 ff.; Cicero's Philippics against him, 247–9, 259 ff.; his quarrel with Octavian comes to a crisis, 251 ff.; sets out for Cisal-pine Gaul to take over governorship, 257; his letter to Hirtius and Octavian as quoted in Cicero's Thirteenth Philip-pic, 271–3; failure to wrest Cisalpine Gaul from Albinus, 273–5; his retreat from Modena, 279 ff.; the alliance with Lepidus, 282 ff., and later with Octa-vian, 288 ff.; terms of the agreement between the resulting Triumvirate, 290–2; war against Brutus and Cassius, 301 ff.; the two battles of Philippi and the deaths of Cassius and Brutus, 305 ff.; decision to eliminate Lepidus from the government, 315; Antony's position at this time as the only ruler of the Roman world, 315–16; his tour of the East, 317 ff.; meeting with Cleo-patra in Tarsus and his winter with her in Alexandria, 320 ff.; his reasons for not wishing to return to Rome at this time and for visiting Egypt, 327–9; dis-quieting news from Rome and Syria brings his stay in Alexandria to a close, 336–8; affairs in Syria and Octa-

469